Antony and Cleopatra

Shakespeare Criticism
Philip C. Kolin, *General Editor*

Antony and Cleopatra

New Critical Essays

Edited by

Sara Munson Deats

ROUTLEDGE
NEW YORK AND LONDON

Published in 2005 by
Routledge
270 Madison Avenue
New York, New York 10016
www.routledge-ny.com

Published in Great Britain by
Routledge
2 Park Square
Milton Park, Abingdon
Oxon OX14 4RN
www.routledgefalmer.com

Printed in the United States of America on acid-free paper.
Typesetting: BookType

10 9 8 7 6 5 4 3 2 1

Shakespeare Criticism, Volume 30

Library of Congress Cataloguing-in-Publication Data is available from the Library
of Congress.

To Gordon
My peerless "man of men"

Contents

Acknowledgments

This book is the result of many years of reading about and teaching *Antony and Cleopatra*. Many individuals and institutions have contributed to the completion of this study and I would like to acknowledge at least some of them at this time.

First and foremost, my gratitude to my thirteen contributors for their innovative and inspirational essays o'erflows the measure. I am confident that these original essays, written especially for this anthology, through the variety of their subject matter and the diversity of their critical approaches, will significantly expand the critical contexts within which this vast and wonderful drama can be read, viewed, and analyzed.

I would also like to express my appreciation to the Chairperson of my Department, Phillip Sipiora, who offered continual support, both psychological and financial, for this project. In addition, I would like to thank the Sabbatical Committee at the University of South Florida, which granted me the research time absolutely necessary for the completion of this endeavor, and the USF Publications Council, which contributed funds to support this project. David Fuller also would like to acknowledge substantial financial support from the British Academy in carrying out the archival research for his essay.

I also am grateful to all of the librarians, curators, and theater personnel who graciously and tirelessly assisted me in finding necessary research material and illustrations for this collection. These include the library staff of the University of South Florida; Kathleen Coleman of the Harvard Theatre Collection; Janet Birkett of the London Theatre Museum; Audrey Hall of the National Museums of Liverpool; Stacy Bemento of the Philadelphia Museum of Art; Sylvia Morris, Marian Pringle, Susan Brock, and Helen Hargest of the Shakespeare Centre Library in Stratford-upon-Avon; Martin Durrant of the

V&A Picture Library in London; Emily Schulze of the Alley Theatre in Houston, Texas; Jo Phillips of the Globe Theatre in London; Amy Richard of the Oregon Shakespeare Festival in Ashland, Oregon; Abigail Jones of the Royal National Theatre in London; David Howells and Jane Ellis of the Royal Shakespeare Theatre in Stratford-upon-Avon; Catherine Taylor-Williams of Shakespeare & Company in Lenox, Massachusetts; Jo-Anne Jordan of the Shakespeare Festival of Canada in Stratford, Ontario; and Liza Holtmeier of the Shakespeare Theatre, Washington, DC. Particular thanks go to Giles Block, director of the 1999 production of *Antony and Cleopatra* for the Globe Theatre, London, who found time from his taxing schedule to grant Georgia E. Brown the interview that concludes this volume.

My deepest appreciation also goes to my editors at Routledge, Matthew Byrnie and Prudy Taylor Board, for their beneficial aid and advice throughout this endeavor, and to my superconscientious and organized research assistant, Robin Rogers, who indefatigably searched libraries and the Web for necessary materials, checked my multitudinous citations, and scrupulously proofread and formatted this manuscript.

I also am deeply indebted to my friends and colleagues, Shelia Diecidue, Robert A. Logan, and Merry Perry, who labored over the introduction to this collection and offered many valuable and perceptive comments, and also to Philip C. Kolin, general editor of this series, who first enlisted me as the editor of this collection and whose consistent support sustained me throughout the long hours of reading and editing.

Finally, most of all, I wish to thank my husband, Gordon Deats, my own paragon of husbands, whose encouragement throughout my scholarly career, like Antony's bounty, has no winter in it, but grows the more with reaping.

1.
Shakespeare's Anamorphic Drama
A Survey of *Antony and Cleopatra* in Criticism,
on Stage, and on Screen

SARA MUNSON DEATS

MARS OR GORGON

Of all Shakespeare's problematic plays, I find *Antony and Cleopatra* to be his
most anamorphic drama, a judgment validated by 350 years of vehemently
conflicting interpretations. For the almost four centuries since its composition,
critical controversy has seethed around every aspect of the tragedy—its value,
its ethos, its genre, its structure, and its characters.[1]

First, few of Shakespeare's tragedies have been both so admired and so
disparaged. Samuel Taylor Coleridge (1813–34) extols *Antony and Cleopatra*
as the most wonderful of Shakespeare's plays and includes it—along with
Hamlet, Othello, King Lear, and *Macbeth*—in Shakespeare's pantheon of
sublime masterpieces. Conversely, A. C. Bradley (1906), who faults the catastrophe as failing to evoke the requisite pity and terror, excludes the tragedy
from his big four. Bernard Shaw (1900) dismisses the play as a study in infatuation, a theme he deems more appropriate to comedy than tragedy, whereas
T. S. Eliot (1920) lauds the tragedy as "Shakespeare's most assured success"
(99), seconded by Bertolt Brecht (1920), who relishes it as a splendid, grip-
ping drama, and G. Wilson Knight (1931), who acclaims it as probably Shakespeare's subtlest and greatest play, perhaps "paragoned only by *The Tempest*"
(199).

Furthermore, throughout the centuries, the ethos of the play has been
fervently debated. Is *Antony and Cleopatra* a condemnation of irresponsible
lust, as moralistic critics from E. K. Chambers (1907) to Franklin Dickey
(1957) and Daniel Stempel (1956) insist? Or is it a celebration of a magnificent passion transcending traditional moral laws, as romantic critics from
Horace Howard Furness (1907) to Knight (1931) to Charles Wells (1992)
assert? Or is the play, as complementarians like John F. Danby (1949),
Maynard Mack (1960), and Norman Rabkin (1967) contend, both and neither,
a deliberately ambiguous drama that defies any permanent allegiance to either

Rome or Egypt, honor or love? Or does the play, as others like Derek Traversi (1963) and Julian Markels (1968) avow, ultimately reject both sets of values as incomplete, affirming instead a golden mean, or *via media*, between conflicting polarities?

And what of the play's genre? Responding to *Antony and Cleopatra*'s departure from standard tragic formulas and its pervasive potpourri of comedy and tragedy, critics have vied to classify this hybrid drama properly. Following Bradley (1906), many commentators have viewed it as a deliberate experiment in genre. For Arthur Symons (1889), the play introduces Shakespeare's tragic-comedy; for E. M. W. Tillyard (1938), it anticipates his late romances; for Stempel (1956), it epitomizes Shakespeare's tragical satire; for Ernest Schanzer (1963), it represents the quintessential problem play; for Katherine Eggert (2000), it heralds a new kind of Shakespearean drama, a feminine tragedy. In one of the definitive treatments of the genre of this dramatic polyglot, Barbara Vincent (1982) identifies Rome with the tragic muse, Egypt with the comic mode, arguing that the play never achieves a golden mean between generic opposites but rather a "heavenly mingle" (74).

And what of the play's structure? For centuries, some commentators have wrestled with the tragedy's total disregard of the unities (Johnson, 1765), its multiplicity of incidents (Gervinus, 1849–50), and what they perceive as its shapeless, episodic configuration (Whitaker, 1965), while others have defended the integrity of the play's form as reflective of its theme, variously identified as world catastrophe (Brandes, 1898), mobility and change (Van Doren, 1939), morality play *psychomachia* (Stoup, 1964), oscillation (French, 1981), and mutability (Wolf, 1982). To those who censure the play's sprawling, panoramic shape, Anne Barton (1973), in her brilliant structural apologia, juxtaposes a well-made play that separates neatly into five acts, demonstrating a recognizable dramatic mode—the tragedy with a divided catastrophe.

Finally, the play's central characters have aroused passionate and antithetical responses. Cleopatra, in particular, has excited both censure and celebration, in true anamorphic fashion painted sometimes as a dazzling Venus and often as a menacing Medusa. The hyperbolic reactions to this charismatic character range from "a tinsel pattern of vanity and female cunning" (Gentleman, 1774, p. 261), a coquettish, deceitful, calculating "paragon of female weakness" (Gervinus, 1849–50, p. 730), and "the spotted and slimy 'serpent of old Nile' " (Ulrici, 1839, p. 358) to "the perfect and everlasting woman" (Swinburne, 1879, p. 191), "not only the greatest of his [Shakespeare's] heroines but the culmination of feminine characterisation in all literature" (Simpson, 1928, p. 332). Levin L. Schucking (1922), unable to reconcile these contrasting portraits, posits a disjunctive character, the immoral courtesan of the first three acts versus the majestic queen of the final two. Antony, like Cleopatra, has evoked both critical cheers and boos. Moralistic critics denigrate Antony as "a flighty, infatuated slave to an excess of love and luxury" (Gentleman, 1774, p. 261), an ironic inversion of Christ (Battenhouse, 1969), and the prototype of the effeminized male (Little, 2000). Conversely, romantic critics exalt him as a true type of Christ, magnificent in his magnanimity and royal in his loyalty (Murry, 1936), "the most comprehensive character that Shakespeare set his hand to" (Stauffer, 1949, p. 240). Unable to resolve these contradictory portraits, Tillyard (1938), following Schucking, judges the character of Antony, as well as that of Cleopatra, to be disjunctive, insisting that "[the] vacillations of Antony and his neglect of duty, the cunning of Cleopatra, find no part in the creatures who are transfigured in death; they remain unassimilated, held in tension against the pair's expiring nobilities" (22). Finally, even Octavius, generally dismissed as cold, Machiavellian, mean-spirited, and a little priggish (Warburton, 1747, qtd. Spevack 714; Gentleman, 1774; Griffith, 1775; Schlegel, 1809–11; Quiller-Couch, 1922; Barroll, "Characterization of Octavius," 1970) has also attracted a surprising number of advocates, who present him as the ideal ruler (Phillips, 1940), "the agent of political order renewing itself" (Markels, 1968, p. 126), and the emblem of temperance (Wortham, 1995).

Thus, Shakespeare's great anamorphic drama cannot hold its visible shape as its images shift and change in the kaleidoscope of critical opinion, presenting sometimes a Mars, sometimes a Gorgon, depending upon the perspective of the individual commentator and the critical climate. Although almost every aspect of this dramatic oxymoron has provoked controversy, because of limitations of time and space, I will focus only on the play's most frequently debated aspects: its ethos, its genre, and its characters.

ETHOS

In an influential essay, Harley Granville-Barker (1930) argues that in *Antony and Cleopatra* "Roman and Egyptian are set against each other; and this operation braces the whole body of the play" (117), and this dialectic between dichotomous moral systems has dominated the criticism of the play for the last 350 years, although, like almost everything else in this oxymoronic drama, the exact lineaments of these mighty opposites have generated heated debate. One of the first commentators to discern this contrast, William Hazlitt (1817) defines these polarities as Roman pride versus Egyptian magnificence. Throughout the years, critics have expanded these antitheses to include the busy historical world versus the calm sensual life of enjoyment (Gervinus, 1849–50); the simple hardihood of the West versus the luxury of the East (Brandes, 1898); the world versus the flesh (Danby, 1949); war and business versus love and pleasure (Lloyd, 1959); and, more comprehensively, the love-pleasure principle, intuition, and spontaneous affection versus duty, practical and worldly reason, and a restrictive morality (Bethell, 1944). Adopting a mythic perspective, Northrop Frye (1967) characterizes the rival constructs as the Roman "day world of history"—an Apollonian realm of order, rule, and measure—and the Egyptian "night world of passion"—a Dionysian domain of gigantic feasting, drunkenness, and love-making (70–71). Assuming a psychoanalytical approach, Kenneth Tucker (1984) delineates these competing systems in terms of thinking types and feeling types. Susan Snyder (1980) further relates the binary opposites to patterns of motion, associating Rome with fixity and Egypt with fluidity. Summing up this traditional dialectic, Rosalie L. Colie (1974) states, "Rome is duty, obligation, austerity, politics, warfare, and honor. Rome is public life. Egypt is comfort, pleasure, softness, seduction, sensuousness (if not sensuality also), variety, and sport" (58). However, Colie, like many commentators, also suggests that these binary systems are not discrete but continually interpenetrate each other.

One of the first metadramatic critics of the play, Sidney Homan (1970) enlarges the value conflict to include a tension between affirmative (Egyptian) and negative (Roman) attitudes toward art and the imagination, a stance developed by both Phyllis Rackin (1972), who equates Rome with Platonic rationalism and Cleopatra and Egypt with the dramatic arts, and Janet Adelman (*Common Liar*, 1973), who pits Roman emphasis on logic and empirical evidence against the play's poetry, represented by Egypt. Expanding this metadramatic slant, Howard Felperin (1977) refocuses the competing polarities to include a contrast between two literary modes, the morality play and the heroic epic. Turning the traditional moralistic reading of the play on its head, Felperin asserts that the perspective of the morality play equates Rome with the temptations of the world and Cleopatra with the saving power of love, whereas the viewpoint of the Renaissance epic casts Cleopatra in her more traditional role as emasculating femme fatale with Antony as her enfeebled male victim. Vincent (1982) extends this metadramatic outlook to label Rome as the world of tragedy, Egypt as the realm of comedy. Taking a slightly different tack, Linda Charnes ("Spies and Whispers," 1995) also presents the conflict of the play as a struggle between representation modes, aligning Octavius and Rome with the authorized representational institutions of epic and narrative history, Cleopatra and Egypt with the less authorized but still influential place of the stage, the theater. Finally, playing a variation on this self-reflexive approach, Colie (1974) views the rival dichotomies of the play as reflecting not only different ethical systems but also different linguistic styles, which she terms Attic (Rome)—classical, economical, severe—and Asiatic (Egypt)—rich, abundant, hyperbolic. Two essays in this collection further expand these binaries: Garrett A. Sullivan, Jr. identifies Rome with the epic, Egypt with the romance mode, while Robert A. Logan associates Rome with the sociomoral and Egypt with the aesthetic perception of reality.

In the 1970s, feminist criticism discovered *Antony and Cleopatra*, and the antitheses of Rome and Egypt became associated not only with duty and love, the public and the private, and various literary modes, but also with masculine and feminine values, a connection anticipated by Homan's (1970) linking of Cleopatra and the theater with the feminine. One of the first commentators to discuss the play from this viewpoint, Michael Payne (1973) further amplifies the traditional binaries as follows: Rome/Egypt, masculinity/femininity, space-time boundary/space-time transcendence, death/love. Marilyn French (1981) enlarges this feminist perspective, identifying Roman values with the masculine ethos, valorizing power, hierarchy, ownership, war, and rivalry; Egyptian values with the feminine principle, atypically (for Shakespeare) uniting both the outlaw and inlaw feminine qualities. Thus, the Egyptian society, although linked with nature, procreation, beauty, and compassion (feminine in-law attributes), can also be cruel and variable (feminine outlaw attributes). Relating this feminist approach to linguistic styles, Russ McDonald (1994) augments the binary opposites to include a contest between Senecan (masculine) and Ciceronian (feminine) styles, and, passing feminist criticism through the prism of psychoanalytical theory, Adelman (1992) presents the conflict between Rome and Egypt, Caesar and Cleopatra, as a "contest between male scarcity and female bounty as the defining site of Antony's heroic masculinity" (*Suffocating Mothers* 177). Finally, postcolonial critic Carol Chillington Rutter (2001) adds race to the equation, expanding the familiar oppositions to include "Orient and Occident, duty and desire, bastard children and 'lawful' issue, space and empire, magnanimity and calculation, extravagance and measure, black and white," Cleopatra and Octavia (67).

However, a number of contemporary commentators—feminist, cultural materialist, new historicist, postcolonial—challenge the system of binary opposition venerated in established criticism. Jonathan Dollimore (1984), in his cultural materialist reading, interprets the play as skeptically interrogating both the celebration of honor and the affirmation of love in its relentless examination of political *realpolitik*, honor and policy, sexuality and power. Terence Hawkes (1973) further denies the venerated distinction between Rome and Egypt. And Carol Neely (1985), in her feminist reevaluation, contends that at the midpoint of the tragedy, the antitheses of love and honor merge: "Passion becomes for Antony a source of heroism, and heroism becomes for Cleopatra a source of passion. As love is merged with and expressed through war, heroic activity becomes personal, erotic, de-Romanized" (146). Postcolonial critics further reformulate the traditional Rome/Egypt dialectic as a type of cross-cultural encounter with topical resonance for the Jacobean period in which the play was written. Developing this postcolonial approach, John Michael Archer (1997) focuses on the relationship between racial and sexual constructions of Egypt during the period of the play's composition, tracing in particular two competing discourses informing the tragedy: one that connects Egypt with dignity and antiquity, and another that links it with cultural and racial degeneration. He concludes that Rome and Egypt are not the antithesis that they are often judged to be but instead share the qualities of mobility and lability. Geraldo U. de Sousa (1999) further defines the venerated Rome/Egypt polarities in terms of cross-cultural encounters that subvert the accepted image of Rome (and, he suggests, also of Jacobean England). Like Archer, de Sousa concludes that cross-cultural encounters in the play lead to an intermingling and exchange of identities and gender roles that dissolve the accepted dichotomies, a view supported by many more traditional critics. Thus, contemporary criticism has largely destabilized the conventional pattern of rigid polarities, presenting instead apposite systems of value that interpenetrate, shift, and merge in the "discandying" world of the play.

As noted earlier, most critics have traditionally identified a dialectical structure controlling the play, yet the vexing question still remains: What is the appropriate audience response to these rival systems? Although the reactions to this question are as varied as the play's many commentators, amid the welter of conflicting replies, central patterns of interpretation do emerge. Margot Heinemann (1994) succinctly summarizes the three dominant readings of the play:

> critics and readers have notoriously responded to the play in sharply opposed ways—G. B. Shaw and Croce, for example, condemning the lovers for voluptuousness and neglect of their plain duty; others (from G. Wilson Knight to Terry Eagleton and the Bremer Shakespeare Company) treating their reckless transgressive passion as the one meaningful, self-validating experience in a meaningless world; others again (like John Danby) sensing a deliberate dialectical ambiguity in the play itself as to whether one should opt for duty or love. (172)

Marvin Spevack (1990) further suggests that "[b]ecause it flouts conventions, *Antony [and Cleopatra]* tends to reflect changes in critical fashion" (611), and I would agree that with its notorious openness, the text often serves as a barometer of society's attitudes toward sex and gender, or, as David Bevington (1990) suggests, "a kind of Rorschach test for us and for those who have written about the play" (16).

In the seventeenth and eighteenth centuries, therefore, most critics viewed the play though their own moral prism. Focusing on Shakespeare's characters as emblems of the play's value systems, most expositors of that period accepted the immorality of the captivating Cleopatra and the irresponsibility of the emasculated Antony as données of the drama. The comments of Francis Gentleman (1774) epitomize the homiletic interpretation governing neoclassical criticism: "A double moral may be inferred [from the play], namely, that indolence and dissipation may undo the greatest of men; and that beauty, under the direction of vanity, will not only ruin the possessor, but the admirer also" (261). Yet, as early as the eighteenth century, ambivalence diluted the moral censure of the two monumental lovers. Thus, Thomas Davies (1783–84) demurs that amid all of Antony's "folly, profligacy, and mad flight," "some beams of great and generous soul break forth with inimitable luster," further declaring that "Cleopatra's preparation for death is animated to a degree of sublimity, which greatly raises the character of the Egyptian princess, and makes us lament her in death whom living we could not praise, though it was impossible not to admire her" (380). Even more approving, Elizabeth Griffith (1775) praises the "heroic liberality of soul" expressed in Antony's generosity to the perfidious Enobarbus" (472–73). Thus, Antony and Cleopatra recruited admirers even within the moralistic *zeitgeist* of the neoclassical period.

The debate concerning the morality of the lovers continued to dominate nineteenth-century criticism, with the emphasis remaining on character portrayal. At one extreme, moralists like G. G. Gervinus (1849–50) exemplify a continuation of the sexist, didactic criticism characteristic of the neoclassical period. Gervinus finds no ambivalence in the play: pleasure is bad, activity and duty good; Cleopatra represents the embodiment of female weakness; Antony is a "splendid nothingness" with only "seeming greatness" and "seeming nobility" (741). At the other extreme, critics and poets, like Victor Hugo (1859–66), J. A. Heraud (1865), and Algernon Charles Swinburne (1879), viewing the play from a romantic perspective, celebrate the lovers as superhuman figures, "exempt from all laws except their own wills" (Heraud 480), whose intensity of passion legitimates their actions (Hugo 498) in what is surely "the greatest love-poem of all times" (Swinburne, qtd. in Spevack 612). However, the mainstream critical tradition of the nineteenth century, like that of the twentieth, remains an ambivalent mixture of disapproval and admiration. Hartley Coleridge (1851) expresses this attraction/repulsion toward the two protagonists, whom he finds "too heroic to be pitied for weakness, and too viciously foolish to be admired for their heroism" (183–84).

With a few salient variations, the first seventy years of the twentieth century followed the critical trends of the preceding century, with romantic critics apotheosizing transcendent love and moralistic commentators censuring excessive passion, while the majority of the interpreters express ambivalence toward the lovers and the value system that they represent.

Typical of the moralistic school of criticism, Dickey (1957) surveys the treatment of lovers in classical and medieval literature and history, concluding that, with the exception of Chaucer in *The Legend of Good Women*, all the writers examined treat the famous paramours as negative exempla of the destructive effects of immoderate lust. Although admitting that Shakespeare's lovers are much more complex than those of his predecessors, Dickey still maintains that the superb love of Antony and Cleopatra is ultimately tarnished: "We are left feeling ... that the most magnificent love affair the world has ever known blazed like a fire in the night and like a great fire left sad ashes in the morning" (201–02). William Rosen (1960) differs from the majority of moralistic critics, locating the central conflict of the play not in the external clash between Roman and Egyptian values but in Antony's internal struggle between his heroic potential and the debilitating influence of Cleopatra, suggesting that Shakespeare's departures from Plutarch emphasize Antony's deterioration of willpower and judgment, rather than Cleopatra's overt influence, as responsible for his fall. More negative than either Dickey or Rosen, Virgil Whitaker (1965) stresses the unheroic nature of both Antony's life and death, contending that Antony dies a "strumpet's fool" and Cleopatra never achieves tragic stature. Roy Battenhouse (1969) supports this deflative reading, arguing that the glorification of passion in the play is consistently undercut by Christian symbolism. Adducing Antony's Last Supper with his followers, one of whom will betray him, Battenhouse limns Antony as an ironic inversion of Christ, even as Cleopatra, dying with her serpent "baby" at her breast, depicts a magnificent parody of maternal love. For Battenhouse, the triumph in death that the lovers imagine turns out to be both glamorous and hollow—"evidence of a nobility in phosphorescent decay" (173).

In the latter half of the twentieth century, a variation of the moralistic/ romantic debate evolved whereby commentators, instead of focusing so centrally on love versus lust, divided between those who privilege the theme of elevating love as the fulcrum of the drama and those who view the play as a study in statecraft. Whereas the first group almost always glorifies transcendent love, the second group tends to disparage the subversion of reason by passion, while stressing responsibility to the state (Spevack, 1990, p. 614). Typical of this second group, James Phillips (1940), long before the advent of new historicism, attempts to define the play in terms of its political impact on Shakespeare's audience. Evaluating Octavius, Lepidus, Pompey, and Antony against traditional standards of leadership, he appraises all except Octavius as flawed leaders. Stempel (1956) follows Phillips in seeing the play as centrally concerned with the problem of order. According to Stempel, the tragedy dramatizes an unnatural inversion of proper hierarchy: on the psychological level, the domination of reason by will; on the social level, the domination of man by woman; on the political level, the conflict between Antony and Cleopatra and the rational Octavius. Paul Lawrence Rose (1969) similarly attempts to embed the play in its political milieu, associating the monarchical styles of Antony, Octavius Caesar, and Cleopatra with archetypes of conflicting sixteenth-century attitudes toward kingship: Octavius views war as an instrument of policy; Antony, as a romantic, chivalric ideal; Cleopatra, as a vehicle for royal grandeur. Like the majority of the political exegetes, Rose rejects Antony and Cleopatra as flawed monarchs and identifies Octavius as the ideal ruler, even though Caesar's very political success entails rather unattractive characteristics, a view endorsed by Marilyn Williamson (1970) in her similar reading of the play as a kind of "mirror for magistrates." Taking a different tack, while still highlighting the topical political aspects of the tragedy, Dollimore (1984) posits *Antony and Cleopatra* as an interrogation of the military ideology valorized by Rome, relating this skepticism to the significant decline of martial honor as an ideal in the Jacobean period. Leonard Tennenhouse (1986) similarly situates the play within the ideology of Jacobean England, reading the play as Shakespeare's affirmation of male authority over the autochthonous female and thus as his "elegy for the signs and symbols which legitimized Elizabethan power" (146). More recently, Coppélia Kahn (1997) shifts the focus of the play from the heterosexual love of Antony and Cleopatra to the homosocial rivalry between Antony and Octavius, contending that Antony's suicide is not a *Liebestod* affirming his allegiance to Cleopatra, but an act of defiance against Octavius in defense of his male honor. In his poststructuralist reading, Jonathan Gil Harris (1994) advocates a similar reorientation, arguing that the play presents not "the serpent of the Nile," not the Ur-Woman, but the specular image of all the male Narcissuses in the play who have found themselves enthralled to their own seductive image. Thus, some contemporary political commentators tend to marginalize rather than demonize the extravagant passion of the two fabled lovers.

At the opposite end of the critical spectrum, the "transcendentalists" apotheosize Antony and Cleopatra and the Egyptian ethos that they represent. One of the most eloquent of the romantic apologists, Knight (1931) exalts the play as "not merely a story of a soldier's fall, but rather a spelled land of romance achieved and victorious: a paradisiacal vision expressed in terms of humanity's quest for love" (227), a tragedy in which the " protagonists change a crown of gold for the more sparkling and ethereal diadem of love" (248). Equally hyperbolic, John Dover Wilson (1950) reads the play as Shakespeare's Hymn to Man, "a symphony in five acts" (xxxvi), "no tragedy of hollow men in a wasteland but of a 'peerless pair' who 'stand up' against the widest and most splendid panorama Shakespeare … ever painted, and are magnified, not dwarfed, by it because it is represented as mere clay or dung in comparison to them" (xxv). Less grandiloquent but still firmly in the romantic camp, S. L. Bethell (1944) casts the drama as a morality play in which Cleopatra, the crystallization of Egyptian values, is Antony's "good, and not his evil genius, rescuing him from an undue preoccupation with the world, which is a snare and a delusion," while admitting that Egyptian values need a Roman purgatory to cleanse them of all selfishness and help them to achieve grace (131). Donald Stauffer (1949) continues this celebration, arguing that Shakespeare "takes the classical tragic theme—the conflict between love and duty—and treats it romantically," reversing the traditional classical paradigm to "wager all for love" (233, 234). Although in the latter half of the twentieth century the responses of both moralistic and romantic camps become somewhat tempered—perhaps in reaction to the extreme partisanship of much mid-century criticism—unreconstructed romantics still remain. French (1981) concludes that in *Antony and Cleopatra*, Shakespeare presents illegitimate sexuality as glorious: at the end of the play, "Caesar has the world; Antony and Cleopatra had the living" (267). Moreover, a contemporary analyst like Charles Wells (1992) can still declare unequivocally that Roman firmness seems "tedious and sterile against the lovers' quicksilver world of imagination," and that "[b]y comparison with Egyptian *brio* Rome seems staid and dull" (157–58).

Less rapturous than the transcendentalists and less censorious than the moralistic/political expositors, a third group of critics, often referred to as the complementarians, adopt a stance of ambivalence toward the two lovers and the two competing value systems from which Antony must choose. Although *Antony and Cleopatra*'s complex characters have traditionally elicited ambivalent reactions from both commentators and audiences, as far as I am aware, David Cecil (1949) ranks as the first critic to identify ambiguity as a deliberate dramatic strategy operating throughout the play. According to Cecil, whether dramatizing the desire for worldly success or the passion of love, Shakespeare remains completely impartial. From one perspective, Shakespeare depicts the world of public life negatively, as a "seething whirlpool of competition and intrigue"; however, at the same time, Shakespeare's attitude toward worldly ambition is not totally unsympathetic: "The love story is presented in an equally impartial way. Neither Antony nor Cleopatra is an ideal figure.... Antony's love is a self-indulgent passion that weakens his will and blinds his judgment. While Cleopatra is, by a strict moral standard, a vain, worthless, capricious coquette." However, despite all their faults, Cecil asserts, Shakespeare portrays the lovers as "resplendent with romance" (21–22). Danby (1949) follows Cecil in stressing the alternative perspectives pervading the tragedy, maintaining, "Not enough weight has been given in recent assessments of the play to the ambiguity which invests everything in Egypt equally with all things in Rome. Yet this ambiguity is central to Shakespeare's experience of the play. If it is wrong to see the 'mutual pair' as a strumpet and a fool, it is also wrong to see them as a Phoenix and a Turtle" (197). Centering on the conflicting evaluations of the protagonists offered by the other characters in the drama, Danby concludes that the play skeptically exposes the difficulty of making judgments about anything: "*Antony and Cleopatra* is Shakespeare's critique of judgment" (201). One of the most eloquent spokespersons for the ambiguous reading, Mack (1960) follows Cecil and Danby in his contention that the play deliberately educes ambivalent responses toward its two lovers—as our laughter *at* them conflicts with sympathy and admiration *for* them. According to Mack, "Tawdry though he [Shakespeare] has made these seasoned old campaigners in love and war, he also magnified and idealized them, to the point that their mutual passion becomes glorious as well as cheap" (15). Moreover, Shakespeare's duality of attitude extends beyond the lovers, pervading everything in the world of the play, in which nothing is stable, fixed, or sure. Finally, Rabkin (1967) gives definitive expression to the dualistic vision of the play endorsed by Brents Stirling (1956), Maurice Charney (1961), Stephen Shapiro (1966), and Duncan Harris (1977), as well as Cecil, Danby, and Mack. In developing this dual perspective, Rabkin stresses not only the double vision of the lovers but also the dual aspect of Rome and Egypt depicted in the play. He suggests that if one focuses on the image of Rome as "a world in which honor is the watchword, military men are giants," and "fame is a spur to noble men's ambitions," one might well deplore Antony's waste of a magnificent life in futile Alexandrian revelry. However, if one considers the other picture of Rome as a vicious political arena, treacherous and trivial, one might assume that "Antony alone among the men of Rome has found a way to escape its pointless way of life and to fulfill himself" (Rabkin 186). In Rabkin's vision, not only Roman honor but also Egyptian love is paradoxical. Ultimately, for Rabkin, *Antony and Cleopatra* is "a simultaneously exultant and despairing dramatization of the unresolvable dialectic between opposed values that claim us equally" (188). In one of the most comprehensive and influential studies of *Antony and Cleopatra*, *The Common Liar* (1973), Adelman expands Rabkin's skepticism to posit the play not only as a study in ambivalence, but—in an anticipation of both Derrida and deconstruction—as a study in indecidibility.

Other commentators play variations on the theme of ambivalence by interpreting the polarities of Rome and Egypt as complementary rather than contradictory. One of the first commentators to suggest this complementary reading, Norman Holmes Pearson (1954) follows Cecil and Danby in stressing the impartiality of the play and anticipates Sterling, Mack, and Rabkin in accentuating its ambivalence, while departing from their interpretations by positing the value systems inscribed in the tragedy as complementary rather than mutually exclusive. Thus, Pearson reads the tragedy as elevating the unity of complementary value systems—heart and head, love and honor—a harmonizing union of contraries that he sees as symbolized by the mystic marriage of Antony and Cleopatra in their mutual deaths. Benjamin T. Spencer (1958) reaches a similar conclusion, maintaining that the play utilizes the metaphor of paradox to dramatize "the contradictions and unpredictability and irrationality of human affection and passion," while modifying this contradictory reading to suggest that although the play fails to side with either Rome or Egypt, it ultimately presents an "as yet undefined synthesis lying beyond both Rome and Egypt but partaking of the values of each" (373, 378–79). Traversi (1963), like Mack and Rabkin, carefully delineates two antithetical interpretations of the lovers embedded in the play, both of which can be ably defended by reference to the text; however, ultimately he sees both readings as partial and incomplete—one, too romantic, the other, too moralistic—and, like Pearson and Spencer, maintains that these very different approaches must be seen "less as contradictory than as complementary aspects of a unified artistic creation which neither, taken in isolation, can exhaust" (79). Payne (1973) brings these readings to their logical conclusion, demonstrating how the play consistently undercuts the antithesis of Rome and Egypt as it strives to find a golden mean between polarities.

Thus, throughout the 1950s, 1960s, and 1970s, scholars continued to debate the claims of Rome versus those of Egypt, the heroic versus the erotic, with romantic critics transforming transgressive passion into transcendent love and moralistic critics reducing it to sexual infatuation, while others sought a mean or balance between competing polarities and the majority of commentators opted for an ambiguous liaison deliberately orchestrated to evoke ambivalent responses. Thus, the long debate over the ethos of the play—honor versus love, public versus private, masculine versus feminine— has been neglected in contemporary criticism with most expositors feeling that the dichotomous reading of the play has been resolved in one of two ways: either the play is deliberately ambiguous on these issues or both systems are presented as partial with the desired solution found in the balance of extremes. Nevertheless, even in the 1990s, the controversy continues to roil with Charles Wells's (1992) eloquent defense of transcendent passion as the fulcrum of the play and Charnes's ("What's Love Got to Do with It?," 1992) debunking of transhistorical love as a liberal humanist fiction. James Hirsh's essay in this volume reexamines this much-debated issue, exposing the difficulty of achieving the impartiality toward the play's conflicting values that so many critics endorse.

GENRE

The genre of *Antony and Cleopatra* has always bemused scholars. In many ways, the play is clearly a tragedy, dramatizing as it does the fatal errors in judgment leading to the catastrophic falls of two colossal figures. However, in other respects the play fails to conform to traditional tragic rubrics.

First, many commentators feel that the triumphant suicide of Cleopatra, with its lyrical affirmation of a love transcending death and its celebration of life transformed by art, fails to evoke the excruciating pain and devastating sense of loss that we normally associate with tragedy. As Bradley (1906) paradoxically observes, "it pains us that we should feel so much triumph and pleasure" (350); "the fact that we mourn so little saddens us" (351). Moreover, critics, like Antony Caputi (1965), see both Cleopatra's suicide and Antony's choice of Egyptian over Roman values as exonerated in the play, an affirmation of a more vital, abundant, joyful experience, if not perhaps the wisest decision from a pragmatic perspective. Others, like Markels (1968), propose that the depiction of death as apotheosis rather than catastrophe lifts the denouement beyond tragedy to anticipate Shakespeare's late romances, a view shared by Stauffer (1949), who insists, "In the sense that its protagonists finally create their own glowing worlds, the play is not the next-to-the-last of the tragedies, but the first and greatest of the dramatic romances" (247). From this perspective, the denouement of the play is too triumphant to be tragic.

Still other critics comment on the generic chiaroscuro achieved by the play's mixture of comic and tragic elements. As early as 1631, Richard Brathwait discusses the comic elements adulterating the play's tragic tone. Expanding these observations, Knight (1931) detects a delicate and boisterous humor pervading the play, a blending of the romantic comedies and the tragedies, whereas J. L. Simmons (1973) discovers in the play the familiar pattern of Shakespearean comedy (and also of some histories, especially *Henry IV*), with the worlds of Egypt and Rome analogous to Frye's (1967) "green world of comedy" and "red and white world of history." Vincent (1982) defines the ubiquitous Roman/Egyptian dichotomy in different generic terms. Masculine Rome, the realm of the individual in pursuit of power within history, combines the heroic and the ironic, recurrent elements in Shakespearean tragedy. Feminine Egypt, presided over by a dominant woman, embodies the conventions of Shakespearean comedy and romance. Thus, the struggle in the play becomes a combat between comedy and tragedy, and, according to Vincent, this contest of genres explains the conflicting interpretations that the drama has evoked, because, viewed from tragic or comic perspectives, Antony's actions would be judged very differently: what may be "dotage" from a tragic viewpoint becomes "nobleness of life" from a comic one (60). In one of the fullest treatments of the play's generic multiplicity, Martha Tuck Rozett (1985) details the numerous comic devices employed in the denouement of *Antony and Cleopatra*. These include: (1) the falsely reported death of the heroine (a strategy used in five Shakespearean comedies as well as *Romeo and Juliet* and *Antony and Cleopatra*); (2) Antony's suicide, which has been seen by some commentators to diminish the general's tragic stature; (3) scenes of trickery, such as the Seleucus scene; (4) the clown, who like the gravedigger in *Hamlet*, offers an alternative, more comic perspective of death; and (5) Cleopatra's triumphant death. Expressing a darker vision, Adelman (1973) identifies *Antony and Cleopatra* as "a tragic experience embedded in a comic structure," "as treacherous and painful as life itself" (*Common Liar* 52).

At the other end of the spectrum, critics find affinities in the play not primarily with Shakespeare's buoyant festive comedies but with his more scathing satiric ones. Although Harold Goddard (1951) focuses on the play's comic deflation of worldly power, Stempel (1956) and Stirling (*Unity in Shakespeare's Tragedies*, 1956) see the ironic tone as encompassing the lovers as well as their Roman antagonists. Stempel judges the play primarily satirical, revealing the "degradation of a strong man enslaved by lust to a woman who is the embodiment of physical desire in its most attractive form" (72).

Stirling stresses the play's contrariety, maintaining that the action and tone oscillate between "grandeur and ignominy," triumph and defeat, tragedy and satire, astringent deflation and sympathetic identification, with neither factor dominating (75–76). Thus, for Stempel and Stirling, as for William Blissett (1967) and Richard Nochimson (1977), the play's "satiric insistence on delusion and folly" undercuts "tragic effect through detachment and irony," thereby impeding the pity and terror normally associated with tragedy (Bevington, 1990, p. 31).

Other commentators have deciphered the play's generic ambiguity differently. According to Schanzer (1963), *Antony and Cleopatra* presents us with an ambiguous moral universe that educes from the audience a divided response, thus making *Antony and Cleopatra* "by far the greatest, as well as the most quintessential, of Shakespeare's Problem Plays" (183). Conversely, Traversi (1963) and M. W. MacCallum (1967) categorize it as a Roman play and a tragedy, whereas Dorothea Krook (1967) classifies the play as a "heroic drama," which she defines as a species of drama glorifying a heroic view of life, characterized by magnanimity, a quality that includes pride, passion for honor, and courage, and is represented in the Shakespearean canon by only two plays, *Antony and Cleopatra* and *Coriolanus* (199–200; qtd. in Spevack 634).

However, despite its many anomalies and its failure to conform to Aristotelian rubrics, many critics still insist that *Antony and Cleopatra* should be considered a tragedy. As Bevington (1990) suggests, perhaps *Antony and Cleopatra* is "Shakespeare's experimental and non-Aristotelian solution to the theatrical demands of the dramatist's material" (32). This view is endorsed by Peter Erickson (1985), who contends that the play debuts a new, distinctly different type of tragedy, unique in the Shakespearean canon, and by Eggert (2000), who also maintains that the drama represents a new genre, feminine tragedy, which she defines as "not simply tragedy that happens to women, but tragedy that happens when the very femininity that produces theater comes to an end" (133).

In summary, generically as well as ethically, *Antony and Cleopatra* eludes neat classification. Critics have diversely proclaimed it a tragedy, a comedy, a romance, a satire, a Roman play, and a heroic drama. Perhaps Neely (1985) offers the best solution to this generic quandary when she pronounces *Antony and Cleopatra* "a play which, like Egypt's crocodile, is shaped only like 'itself'" (137).

CHARACTERS

Although Aristotle identified plot as the soul of tragedy, for the past 350 years, it is primarily Shakespeare's characters, not his plots or even his themes, that have enthralled readers and audiences alike. And although critical consensus has traditionally identified Antony as the eponymous protagonist of the tragedy, in terms of space allotted and passion aroused, criticism has awarded Cleopatra pride of place. I will follow critical practice and also grant her priority in my discussion of the central characters in the play.

Cleopatra

Cleopatra—the very name conjures a world of danger and delight; it also invokes a variegated image: sexy siren, treacherous temptress, resplendent goddess, royal queen, noble lover, and tragic hero. Although Dante doomed Cleopatra to the second circle of his *Inferno* and Edmund Spenser in *The Faerie Queene* confined both Antony and Cleopatra in the dungeons of the House of Pride (Hughes-Hallett, 1990), Geoffrey Chaucer in *Legend of Good Women* elevated Cleopatra to first place in his hagiography of the saints of love and "John Gower includes Antony and Cleopatra among a procession of faithful lovers in his *Confessio Amantis*" (Bevington, 1990, p. 7). Thus throughout history, Cleopatra has been both damned and praised; Shakespeare's queen—or quean—has received similar denunciation and admiration.

As previously discussed, the morality of the lovers dominated criticism of the play from the seventeenth century until the mid-twentieth century. Moreover, viewed through the patriarchal lens of the seventeenth, eighteenth, and nineteenth centuries, the moral turpitude of Cleopatra was often considered a donnée of the play. This assumption of criminality underlies John Anton's 1616 poem, *The Philosopher's Satyrs*, generally considered one of the first extant references to Shakespeare's tragedy, in which Anton excoriates the wicked stage for enacting such deadly sins as "Orestes' incest" and "Cleopatra's crimes" (qtd. in Spevack 687). Moreover, even Samuel Taylor Coleridge (1813–34), although a great admirer of the tragedy and far from impervious to Cleopatra's allure, damns the queen with faint praise: "But the art displayed in the character of Cleopatra is profound in this, especially, that the sense of *criminality* in her passion is lessened by our own insight into its depth and energy, at the very moment that we cannot but perceive that the passion itself springs out of the habitual craving of a licentious nature ..." (77; emphasis mine). Similarly, Samuel Johnson (1765), although judging Cleopatra the most well-delineated character in the play, cavils at her "feminine arts, some of which are too low" (873). Furthermore, moralistic critics tend to treat Cleopatra, not as a three-dimensional dramatic character—what J. Leeds Barroll (1984) calls an "artificial person" (*Shakespearean Tragedy* 77)—but as an emblem of deleterious female traits. Thus, she has been defamed as a temptress, luring the hero from the strait and narrow road of duty to the primrose path of dalliance, "not so much a tragic slave of passion in herself as a symbol of Antony's slavery to desire" (Stempel, 1956, p. 63). As temptress, she has been identified not only with "the spotted and slimy 'serpent of old Nile,' " (Ulrici, 1839, p. 358), with "Eve and the serpent in one" (Brandes, 1898, p. 142), but also with "Lilith who ensnared Adam before the making of Eve" (Dowden, 1875, p. 307), and with the " 'dark lady' of the Sonnets," Shakespeare's own "black enchantress" (Brandes 144–45). She has been pilloried as the emasculating female—Circe transforming men into swine, Venus disarming Mars (Frye, 1967, p. 72), and Omphale enslaving and crossdressing Hercules (Schlegel, 1809–11, p. 416; Frye 72). She has been reprimanded as the unruly woman who does not know her "place" and who "pays the penalty of her temerity which hurried her out of the nursery and boudoir into the council-chamber, and into the midst of wars and battles" (Ulrici 358). She has been excoriated as the quarrelsome shrew, part Fury, part fishwife (Frenzel, 1871, p. 495). She has been reduced to "a tinsel pattern of vanity and female cunning" (Gentleman, 1774, p. 261) and dismissed as a coquettish "paragon of female weakness" (Gervinus, 1849–50, p. 730). Finally, she has been denigrated not only as the embodiment of female immorality but also as the representative of a corrupt oriental culture (Ulrici 358). Although few twentieth-century critics endorse such overtly sexist and racist views, several modern expositors view the play through the misogynistic spectacles of the period and position Cleopatra within this tradition. Thus, Stempel, claiming to speak for Shakespeare's contemporaries and never questioning whether or not Shakespeare is affirming the Jacobean party line, insists that in order to understand the play, we must "divest ourselves of that admiration for Cleopatra which comes instinctively, it seems, to the modern mind," and totally reject her as both tempter and temptation (64). Tennenhouse (1986) further links Cleopatra with Bakhtin's grotesque body and thus with pollution, and, as recently as 1994, Peggy Simonds identifies the changeable Cleopatra as a symbol of the capricious goddess Fortuna, whereas Mary Nyquist (1994) derogates her as the embodiment of feminine irrationality and despotic barbarism as constructed by the early modern white patriarchal society.

But, of course, Cleopatra has had numerous and eloquent apologists. Hugo (1859–66) epitomizes the romantic reading of the play, even as Gervinus (1849–50), his contemporary, exemplifies the moralistic approach. For Hugo, and romantic commentators generally, the lovers are purified by the power and depth of their transcendent love, and Antony's emotional merger with Cleopatra, not his marriage of convenience with Octavia, becomes the sanctified union in the play, a mating legitimized by the intensity of its passion. Furness (1907), another of Cleopatra's most enthusiastic defenders, agrees that Cleopatra never wavers in her wild and passionate feelings for Antony, which should not, he insists, be reduced to appetite or sensuality but praised as the deepest affection of love and wifely devotion. Even more romantic than Hugo or Furness, Heraud (1865) celebrates both Antony and Cleopatra as superhuman figures, who "in a species of heroic madness, had conceived themselves to be in the position of Divine Powers, exempt from all laws except that of their own wills." Moreover, according to Heraud, Shakespeare identifies with and exonerates his heroes for "[n]o notion of guilt attaches to the conduct of Shakspere's [*sic*] *Antony and Cleopatra* either in the poet's opinion or their own" (480). Other apologists laud Cleopatra as the most remarkable of Shakespeare's female creations. Paul Heyse (1867) praises her as "the very greatest masterpiece of female characterisation, alongside of which there can be placed no more richly devised figure in the whole literature of modern romance," while raising a question that has haunted performance criticism of the play—the doubt that any actress will be able to incarnate Cleopatra's magnetism and thus justify Antony's indifference to the gain or loss of a hemisphere (492). Even more enthusiastic in their admiration are Symons (1889), who acclaims *Antony and Cleopatra* as the most wonderful of Shakespeare's plays primarily "because the figure of Cleopatra is the most wonderful of Shakespeare's women" (119), and Lucie Simpson (1928), who argues that Cleopatra combines the traits of all Shakespeare's women and indeed that Cleopatra "is not only the greatest of his [Shakespeare's] heroines but the culmination of feminine characterisation in all of literature" (332). In a more tempered analysis, Colie (1974) describes Cleopatra as possessing "a girlish, hoydenish companionability" (188), and, although not blind to Cleopatra's failings, praises the queen as possessing an imagination as bountiful as Antony's generosity and a language as rich as her habitat. Finally, a number of critics maintain that the entire fifth act, particularly Cleopatra's magnificent suicide, vindicates the queen's transcendent love for Antony, her demi-Atlas, her paragon of men (Furness, 1907). Reuben A. Brower (1971) eulogizes Cleopatra's suicide as a type of Ovidian metamorphosis, in which she becomes not a "flower, a tree, or a bird, but 'immortal,' all 'fire and air,' star-like divinity, mother goddess and serpentine genius of sleep," a "super-woman who dreamed Antony's apotheosis" (353).

However, as the quotation from Brower exemplifies, Cleopatra's admirers, like her detractors, often treat her as an archetype and emblem, rather than a complex, interiorized dramatic creation. Indeed, Cleopatra's most ardent devotees often adopt an essentialist's approach that makes feminist critics squirm. Swinburne (1879), one of the first commentators to identify Cleopatra with the eternal female, extols the Egyptian queen as "the perfect and everlasting woman" (191). In a similar essentializing mode, Harold Fisch (1970) limns Cleopatra, as not simply " 'Miss Egypt,' but the eternal feminine, Tiamat, Venus, Aphrodite … as old as the race of man, the source of passion, reproduction, and death" (60); Georg Brandes (1898) depicts Cleopatra as not only "the woman of women, quintessential Eve," but also the incarnation of the Orient, even as Antony is the embodiment of Rome (144), while Bethell (1944) interprets Cleopatra not as a naturalistic character but as a symbol of Egyptian values. Donna Hamilton (1973) elevates both Antony and Cleopatra as prototypes of the noble lover, whereas Anne Higgins (1990) and Laura Severt King (1992) place Cleopatra within the hagiographic tradition of penitent prostitute-saints. However, for King, in her death Cleopatra becomes not Mary Magdalene (the prostitute saint) but the untainted Virgin Mary, nursing the divine serpent Christ.

However, despite the strong attraction/repulsion that Cleopatra has evoked from her defenders and attackers, the majority of commentators have selected the *via media* between the often partisan extremes of the moralistic and romantic interpretations, approaching Cleopatra with an ambivalence similar, although perhaps more pronounced, to that aroused by many of Shakespeare's tragic protagonists. This ambivalent interpretation has dominated criticism from Anna Brownell Jameson (1897), who depicts the queen as a "brilliant antithesis, a compound of contradictions, of all that we most hate with what we most admire" (222), to Mack (1960), who labels Cleopatra the "absolute oxymoron" (17), to Adelman (1973), who observes that "paradox itself is embodied in the person of Cleopatra" (*Common Liar* 116), to contemporary poststructuralist expositors, such as Cynthia Marshall (1993).

One solution to the ambivalence aroused by Shakespeare's enigmatic queen is offered by Augustus William Schlegel (1809–11):

> The seductive arts of Cleopatra are in no respect veiled over; she is an ambiguous being made up of royal pride, female vanity, luxury, inconstancy, and true attachment. Although the mutual passion of herself and Antony is without moral dignity, it still excites our sympathy as an insurmountable fascination—they seem formed for each other, and Cleopatra is as remarkable for her seductive charms as Antony for the splendour of his deeds. As they die for each other, we forgive them for having lived for each other. (416–17)

In the above passage, Schlegel implies that Cleopatra is redeemed by her noble death for love, a view first proposed by Thomas Davies (1783–84), who defends Cleopatra against those who would deny her tragic greatness, arguing that her sublime suicide leads the audience to "lament her in death whom living we could not praise" (380). Furness (1907) expands this suggestion to insist that the entire fifth act is a vindication of Cleopatra and her love for Antony, and even Gentleman (1774), one of her most militant detractors, grudgingly admits that in act 5, Cleopatra "displays great and becoming magnanimity of spirit, finely opposed to the equivocal treacherous behavior of Octavius" (356). Although Cleopatra's ennoblement in death has been widely accepted, some analysts find this transition jarring and Cleopatra's character disjunctive. Thus, Schucking (1922) avers that Shakespeare delineates two basically irreconcilable portraits of Cleopatra, contending that the intelligent, passionate, astute, heartless, essentially vulgar and profoundly immoral courtesan of the first three acts bears virtually no resemblance to the regal, loving, tender queen of the final two acts, a view supported by Tillyard (1938) for whom the two Cleopatras remain unassimilated since the cunning Cleopatra of the early scenes is strikingly dissimilar from the woman transfigured in death. In response to Schucking, E. E. Stoll (1928) insists, "On the stage, as in life, a character has the right to change—in Cleopatra's case, to cease from changing" (152), a view supported by C. H. Herford (1923). Defending the consistency of Cleopatra's character, Stoll further asserts that the queen is never the harlot depicted by Schucking in the first three acts nor totally the sublime queen in the final ones; rather, from first to last she is a mixture of admirable and deplorable traits. Moreover, as L. T. Fitz (1977) sensibly argues, much like Shakespeare's other tragic protagonists, Cleopatra is a developing character who learns and grows in the final act of the tragedy.

Nevertheless, problems remain that have vexed critics throughout the decades. The most important of these concerns the impetus for Cleopatra's suicide. Does she kill herself to avoid the degradation of being carried in triumph to Rome, or does she commit suicide because she finds life without Antony to be meaningless? Because for many critics Cleopatra's tragic greatness derives solely from her willingness to martyr herself for love, her motivation for suicide becomes a crucial issue (Hughes-Hallett, 1990). From the moment of Antony's death, Cleopatra affirms her decision to die in the "high Roman fashion." Yet many commentators berate her for vacillating, adducing the scene in which her treasurer Seleucus accuses her of withholding money and other assets from Caesar as proof that she is not resolute for death and is keeping all options open. Thus, the Seleucus episode has become a central crux of the play and because of its manifest ambiguities is often cut in performance. In response to these skeptics, commentators since Adolf Stahr (1864) have asserted that in Shakespeare's play, as in Plutarch, the episode of the concealed treasure is a ruse, orchestrated by Cleopatra and rehearsed with Seleucus, devised to gull Caesar into believing that Cleopatra desires to live, thus making him less vigilant in his guard; moreover, the subterfuge works perfectly, and Caesar is "unpolicied" (qtd. in Harris and Scott 239). Many critics have endorsed Stahr's reading (Furness, 1907; Wilson, 1950; J. Shaw, 1966; Muir, 1969), whereas others remain unconvinced (Ridley, 1956; Whitaker, 1965; Proser, 1965). In one of the most influential essays on the topic, Stirling ("Cleopatra's Scene with Seleucus," 1964) insists that Shakespeare has adapted Plutarch in a manner that renders the scene deliberately ambiguous—as it is not in Plutarch—thus inducing a mood of wonder and suspenseful ambivalence in the audience. W. L. Godshalk (1977) and Richard Levin (1997) offer a contrary interpretation, asserting that it is not Caesar who ultimately becomes an "ass unpolicied" but, rather, Cleopatra who is tricked by Caesar into committing suicide, thus ensuring his triumph. In response to this debate, Fitz (1977) suggests that the obsession with Cleopatra's death for love reveals the double standard so often used to evaluate the actions of Antony and Cleopatra. Thus, according to Fitz, Cleopatra adduces five motives for suicide, Antony, six; among these, both list their mutual love and their unwillingness to live without the other; but both also include the desire to escape the humiliations that Caesar has planned for them. Yet, although critics continually debate Cleopatra's motivations, no one questions Antony's multiple reasons for suicide. In her essay in this collection, Dorothea Kehler examines this critical obsession with Cleopatra's death for love, relating it to the Indian practice of *sati*.

Whereas "realistic" critics probe the motivations of Cleopatra, emblematic expositors, sensitive to the mythic aureole surrounding Shakespeare's elusive queen, seek to decipher her with the Rosetta stone of myth. For some commentators, the mythic resonances of the play highlight the contradictions of Shakespeare's oxymoronic queen. Blissett (1967) links Cleopatra with multiple deities—Circe (an evil figure), Venus (a double figure), and Isis (a loving, maternal, beneficial figure). Frye (1967) also stresses Cleopatra's multiple mythic guises: she is a Venus rising from the Nile; she wears the regalia of Isis; she assumes the roles of Circe and Omphale; and she bears affinities to the Whore of Babylon. Conversely, Michael Lloyd (1959) finds the mythic associations overwhelmingly positive, positing that Shakespeare received his inspiration for Cleopatra, a mixture of militant sexual love and wifely, maternal fidelity, from the image of the goddess Isis. Barbara Bono (1984) further examines the myth of Isis and Osiris as a parallel to Cleopatra's relationship to Antony as she "transforms 'angling' for Antony into elevating him, transforms sexuality into immortality, and transforms the barge of Cydnus into a celestial boat of the moon-goddess, now sailing away from the earth, which has fallen dark" (212). Finally, Heather James (1996) compares Isis, who collected and unified the dismembered fragments of Osiris's body, to Cleopatra, who, in act 5, through her "cosmic blazon" to Antony, restores her lover, so that " in death he finally becomes the integrated, magnanimous hero who is spectrally present in the play ..." (231), a view also endorsed by Suzanne Wofford (1996). Shifting from Isis to Venus, Raymond Waddington (1966) examines the analogies between Cleopatra crossdressing with Antony and Venus disarming Mars, noting the ambiguities in this topos, which comments not only on the emasculation of the warrior by love but more centrally on the concept of *concordia discors*, whereby Venus mitigates the fury of Mars, producing the child Harmony. Waddington concludes: "As much modern criticism has suggested, the whole play is an exposition of *concordia discors*; neither extreme, Roman or Egyptian, is sufficient in itself" (223), and the play's final achievement of harmony and balance is revealed in the mystic marriage of Venus and Mars at the end of the play. Both Adelman (*Common Liar*, 1973) and Bono further explore the "Venereal doubleness" of the myth, whereby Venus in all her many guises, including *venus armata, venus celeste, venus genetrix, venus pandemos, venus veretrix*, and *venus vulgare,* becomes an image of divine androgyny as well as lasciviousness. The union of Mars and Venus thus signifies generative harmony as well as emasculation (Adelman, *Common Liar*), and desire becomes either "a lustful fall into the world of matter, or an aspiration back to divine unity" (Bono 182). Marguerite A. Tassi's contribution to this volume develops the association of Cleopatra with Venus, embedding this nexus within the pictorial tradition of the early modern period.

In the 1970s, feminist criticism discovered *Antony and Cleopatra.* Of course, critical trends never adhere rigidly to chronological timetables; however, certain periods do favor certain distinct approaches. Thus, although both essentialist readings and realistic questions of motivation continue until today, in the 1970s and 1980s, with the emergence of new critical method-ologies—feminist, Marxist, new historicist, postcolonial—analysts began to pose different questions. One of the most important issues to surface in the 1970s concerned Cleopatra's role as tragic protagonist of the play that bears her name. Despite the numerous encomiums to Egypt's fascinating queen, expositors have been reluctant to accept her as a tragic hero, much less *the* tragic protagonist of the drama. Although, in 1859, Hugo first pronounced Cleopatra, not Antony, the primary hero, "the sovereign figure" that gives the play its unity (498), he failed to develop his argument in detail. This task was left to Simpson, who in 1928 took on the critical establishment to defend Cleopatra as the protagonist of the tragedy, insisting that "[t]he play, in fact, might have been called *Cleopatra* as appropriately as that of Hamlet is called *Hamlet,* or Othello *Othello*," further asserting that, like Shakespeare's other tragic heroes, Cleopatra has an individual history separate from the men in her life, and is transformed by the action of the play (333). However, Simpson's bold initiative was largely ignored by the critical establishment. Although at least two other commentators—Wilson in 1950 and Laurens J. Mills in 1964—endorse the view, first offered by Bernhard ten Brink in 1895, that the play has two protagonists with two tragedies, one for Cleopatra and one for Antony, by far the most persuasive case for Cleopatra as a tragic hero is made by Fitz (1977) in her landmark essay, "Egyptian Queens and Male Reviewers." In this essay, Fitz indicts the sexist bias that has marred the crit-icism of the play, citing as the most egregious example the unwillingness of the critical establishment to accept Cleopatra as a tragic hero. Fitz then proceeds to offer a persuasive rationale for Cleopatra as the central tragic hero of the drama: a sympathetic but flawed character who experiences inner struggle, makes mistakes, falls, and (unlike Antony) grows and changes, while dying heroically. Five years after Fitz's stunning defense of Cleopatra as tragic protagonist, her view found support from Fredson Bowers (1982), who contends on structural grounds that Cleopatra must be the single protagonist of the drama. First, he defines the protagonist as the central character around whom the plot revolves, the moving agent in both the climax and catastrophe, who makes a crucial but ethically flawed decision that leads to punishment by death. Although both Antony and Cleopatra commit tragic errors in judgment, according to Bowers, only Cleopatra achieves a heroic, expiating death.

In the later decades of the twentieth century, although not prepared to remove Antony from his traditional position as a tragic hero, the majority of commentators on the play have accepted Antony and Cleopatra as coprotagonists. However, there are still holdouts. Linda Bamber (1982) argues against Fitz that despite her centrality, complexity, and position as coprotagonist of the play, Cleopatra is not the Shakespearean tragic hero. Insisting that the Shakespearean tragic hero must be a divided self, struggling against Nature and the Other to achieve wholeness, Bamber contends that Cleopatra's conflicts, unlike those of Antony, are primarily external rather than internal. Bamber's response to Fitz demonstrates the complexity of the character of Cleopatra, showing how two highly intelligent feminist critics can closely examine this complicated figure and yet reach different conclusions.

In the feminist rediscovery of *Antony and Cleopatra,* the antitheses of Rome and Egypt become associated not only with duty and love, the public and the private, but also with masculine and feminine values. In one of the first discussions of the play from this perspective, Barton (1973) examines the exchange and union between masculine and feminine qualities that takes place, however briefly, in the play, citing, among other examples, the desire of the quintessentially feminine queen to participate in Antony's macho, military world. This foray, although fleeting and not really successful, nevertheless demonstrates an attempt to reconcile the opposites of masculine and feminine within the play. (Barton's delineation of Antony's journey into androgyny will be discussed later.) Among feminist critics, one of the most heated debates concerning the lovers focuses on the degree to which they explode accepted gender categories to achieve a state of androgyny. The majority of contemporary commentators agree with Irene Dash (1981) that Cleopatra unites sexual and political roles as well as love and marriage, and with Thomas McAlindon (1973), Richard Wheeler (1981), French (1981), Erickson (1985), James Greene (1987), and Gayle Whittier (1989) that the lovers exchange masculine and feminine qualities rather than simply inverting them, thereby showing a capacity for cross-gender identification. Conversely, Neely (1985) asserts that in the play gender distinctions "are not dissolved but are explored, magnified, and ratified" (165). On this issue, as so often in this paradoxical drama, the play engenders antithetical responses.

Criticism in the 1960s, 1970s, and 1980s foregrounded Cleopatra in other significant ways, portraying her not only as a tragic hero but also as a type of the artist. As early as the 1960s, Matthew Proser (1965), Robert Ornstein (1966), and Ruth Nevo (1967) introduced the metadramatic reading of the play that would become so popular with literary analysts in the 1970s and

1980s. Proser dubs Cleopatra a genius in the creation and manipulation of scenes, the "Duse of the Shakespearean world" (189). Ornstein depicts her as the artist of language who, in the final act of the play, transcends reality, through the power of her art creating her own imaginative conception of Antony. Moreover, Nevo insists, by her apotheosis of her lover and her magnificent death, she stages her own theatrical coup as an antimasque to Caesar's proposed triumph. Thomas Van Laan (1978) further presents Cleopatra as Shakespeare's most successful interior director who succeeds in "creating her own imaginative drama to replace the unbearable action of reality" (220), and Ronald R. MacDonald (1985) interprets the play as centrally concerned with the construction of the self through art, with Antony and Cleopatra "free to create themselves, to refuse the cultural representations that would reduce them or rob them of their reality" (98). Anticipating later feminist readings, Homan (1970) develops this approach to explore the play's linking of Cleopatra, and the feminine generally, with both the imagination and the theater. In one of the most perceptive and persuasive metadramatic readings, Rackin (1972) interprets the Rome/Egypt dichotomy as dialectic between the Roman reliance on Platonic rationalism and the Egyptian cele-bration of the theatrical. Thus, for Rackin, "the entire play turns on the ques-tion of the proper response to a show. To the Romans, and to the critics who follow them in discounting the seductions of rhetoric and the delusions of the senses, the shows are false and their sublimity merely 'theatrical.' To the sympathetic among her audience, Cleopatra's wiles identify her with her creator as a fellow artist," who, in her final scene, transforms the brazen world of reality into the golden world of art (204). In addition to examining the metadramatic motif of the play, Rackin combines the theatrical focus of critics like Granville-Barker (1930) and Michael Goldman (1985) with a femi-nist perspective to situate Cleopatra within the early modern convention whereby all the female characters would be performed by boys, a practice that Madelon Spengnether (1989) contends both subverts and upholds patriarchal values. The significance of the boy actor to the creation of the character of Cleopatra, first discussed by Granville-Barker, has been further examined by both Michael Shapiro (1982) and James Hill (1986). In addition, Jyotsna Singh (1989) unites feminist and new historicist methodologies to locate Cleopatra's histrionic puissance within the antitheatrical and antifeminist debates of the period, which gendered the theatrical as feminine. Ultimately, she concludes that the very qualities that the Renaissance condemned as duplicitous enrich and empower Cleopatra. Singh thus reads the play as a defense of both the feminine and the theatrical. Finally, Carol Cook (1996) delineates Cleopatra as a synecdoche not only for the theater but also for the feminine in language.

In the 1970s and 1980s, another important critical methodology, psycho-analytical theory, offered new perspectives on Shakespeare's elusive queen.

Employing this approach, Constance Brown Kuriyama (1977) interprets the play as a richly elaborated rendering of a basic human illusion, the union with the incestuously loved, bisexual mother in a particular kind of Oedipal fantasy. Kuriyama expands the traditional reading of the Roman/Egyptian dichotomy to postulate an Oedipal choice between a type of anal adulthood and an overwhelmingly oral childhood. Although Antony's choice of infantile regression would appear negative, Kuriyama asserts that "[in] the closing scenes of *Antony and Cleopatra*, physical defeat is transmuted into psychological victory, partially through the fantasy of regaining the pre-Oedipal paradise of complete union with the mother" (344). Kay Stockholder (1987), also applying an Oedipal paradigm to the play, sees Antony's conflict as the tension between two needs—the desire to assert and the desire to lose his Roman self. Ultimately, Antony embraces his loss of self, but Cleopatra, the good mother, grants the dying Antony a magnificent rebirth through the power of her language.

In the 1980s, two related critical methodologies, new historicism and cultural materialism, gained dominance. These two methodologies, which seek to situate literary texts within their historical milieus and read them in light of topical events of the period, naturally embraced Cleopatra, seeing in the queen of Egypt a fictional re-creation of the queen of England. However, long before the ascendancy of new historicism embedded the play within its topical milieu, scholars recognized the many parallels between the two canny and calculating queens who employed feminine wiles to govern their countries successfully. Kenneth Muir (1969), Helen Morris (1968–69), Keith Rinehart (1972), Theodora Jankowski (1989), and Paul Yachnin (1991) have all adduced a number of similarities between the two shrewd, unpredictable, yet charismatic queens. These analogies include the following: the now-famous incident in which Elizabeth queried the emissary from Mary Queen of Scots concerning the hair, height, and other qualities of her rival, much as Cleopatra quizzes the unfortunate messenger concerning similar qualities in Octavia; Cleopatra's comparison of herself to a milkmaid, echoing Elizabeth's use of the same metaphor in a speech to Parliament (Muir; Morris); the practice of both queens of floating down broad rivers in magnificent barges; and the militancy of both queens—Elizabeth at Tilbury; Cleopatra at Actium (Morris). Moreover, according to these commentators, both queens possessed the following traits: beguiling charm, vast intelligence, and keen wit, combined with an imperious nature and a fiery temper (Morris); a tendency toward rough treatment of servants and maids of honor, while simultaneously arousing their devoted loyalty; facility in foreign languages; skill in government; desire for amusement and revelry; and love of gorgeous apparel (Rinehart; Elizabeth A. Brown, 1999). Finally, they both devised a strategy for successful rule in a patriarchal society by uniting their natural bodies with their bodies politic (Jankowski). Michael Payne (1973) also posits that Queen Elizabeth, who famously combined masculine and feminine qualities, may have inspired Shakespeare's androgynous Cleopatra, whereas Yachnin enlarges this analogue, juxtaposing the aristocratic, chivalric ethos of the Elizabethan past embodied in both Antony and Cleopatra, with the mercantile, political ethos of the Jacobean present incarnated in Octavius Caesar.

As early as 1973, Adelman, in her pioneering study, *The Common Liar*, noted the widespread critical neglect of Cleopatra's race. In the 1980s and 1990s and the early years of the new millennium, postcolonial critics took up her challenge. In one of its most salient contributions to *Antony and Cleopatra* criticism, postcolonialism constructs Cleopatra as the threatening and seductive black African queen and the play as a penetrating study of racial, as well as sexual and ethnic, alterity. John Henrik Clarke (1984), Ania Loomba ("Theatre and the Space of the Other," 1989; *Shakespeare, Race, and Colonialism*, 2002), Nyquist (1994), Joyce Green MacDonald (1996), Mary Floyd-Wilson (1999), de Sousa (1999), Arthur L. Little (2000), Archer (1997), and Rutter (2001) all argue persuasively that despite the historical Greek heritage of the historical Egyptian queen, Shakespeare's play portrays Cleopatra as undeniably black. According to these analysts, the play establishes this darkness by two explicit references to Cleopatra's swarthiness: Philo's allusion to her "tawny front"—mulattoes were frequently termed "tawny Moors" (Clark, 1984, p. 126)—and Cleopatra's own admission, "Think on me, / That am with Phoebus' amorous pinches black / and wrinkled deep in time (1.5.29–30). Also adduced as evidence is Cleopatra's association with gypsies, frequently linked with blackness at this time (Nyquist), and her depiction as the incarnation of Egypt and thus as the descendent of Cham, father of the Negroid race (Loomba, *Shakespeare, Race and Colonialism*, 2002). However, Joyce Green MacDonald adds that in her witty reference to Phoebus's amorous pinches, Cleopatra rewrites the origin of black skin to undermine patriarchal and imperial myths of the origin of blackness, presenting dark pigmentation as resulting not from the curse of the Hebrew God but from coupling with a classical deity. Further excavating the subversiveness of the play, both Little and Loomba see the black queen's romance with a white Roman general as inverting both racial and gender traditions. According to Little, Antony's death not only reverses gender roles, but also reverses one of the foundational myths of the Western world, whereby "the white man sacrifices himself at the feet of a black woman," rather than vice versa (116). Developing this concept, Loomba observes that "imperial conquest is routinely demonstrated through the sexual possession of conquered women"; however, in Shakespeare's play, the black Egyptian conquers the white Roman general (*Shakespeare, Race, and Colonialism* 116). Finally, Little, Archer, and Loomba all associate Cleopatra and Egypt with other, more domestic examples of alterity, including not only gypsies but also the Irish, who were frequently connected with metamorphic blackness. As Loomba explains, "Cleopatra as the 'enchanting queen'

brings together magic associated with non-Western cultures, the sorcery associated with witches and enchantresses, domestic and alien, as well as the
trickery associated with petty crimes at home" (*Shakespeare, Race, and Colonialism* 129). In her essay in this collection, Lisa Hopkins demonstrates the
mobility of these ethnic constructions in their relationship to both Rome and
Egypt in the play.

Thus, in the past three decades, criticism has created new and intriguing
personae for Cleopatra, not only the temptress, goddess, and noble lover of
tradition but also tragic hero, artist, androgynous queen, fictional prototype of
Elizabeth I, and racial as well as sexual Other.

In her contribution to this anthology, Linda Woodbridge (a.k.a. L. T. Fitz)
adds another profile to Cleopatra's multifaceted portrait, depicting her as a
bold international gambler, who with great finesse plays for high stakes and,
although losing big, in the moment of her death trumps the Roman Empire.
Productions of the play during the past three decades reflect the influence of
Cleopatra's many new personae, placing her center stage and portraying her
as both androgynous queen and passionate lover, while also stressing the political aspects of the tragedy. There have even been a few black Cleopatras.

Antony

Antony and Cleopatra are frequently linked in critical debate much as they are
presumably joined in death and, like his much–lauded and much–maligned
consort, Antony has aroused vehement and antithetical responses. Criticism
has traditionally viewed him as a kind of magnified Everyman caught in a
psychomachia between love and duty, or passion and politics (depending on
one's interpretation of the tragedy). Moralistic interpreters demean him as a
mighty general, degraded and emasculated by sexual infatuation into a
strumpet's fool; romantic readers elevate him as Cleopatra's "paragon of
men," transfigured and fulfilled by a love transcending paltry power politics.
Again, as with Cleopatra, the majority of expositors maneuver a middle way
between these polarities.

Critics from the seventeenth century until the present have commented on
Antony's famed magnanimity, his exuberance, his vitality, and his excess.
Almost all agree that his capacity for experience—for drinking life to the
lees—o'erflows the measure, but they disagree as to the expected audience
response to this excess. For most moralistic expositors, such as Gentleman
(1774), this lust for life renders Antony a "flighty, infatuated slave to an excess
of love and luxury" (261). Although somewhat less severe, Chambers (1907)
concurs that the exuberance of Antony's vitality overflows into sensuousness
as well as into resource and endurance and that this capacity is ultimately his
undoing. Tracing the linking of food imagery with episodes of lechery and
sloth, Barroll ("Antony and Pleasure," 1958) further identifies Antony's tragic

flaw as an overindulgence in these sins of the flesh, which Elizabethans united under the concept of "pleasure," whereas John Draper (1965), employing humoral theory, traces Antony's deterioration from the choleric Roman of act 1 to the phlegmatic sybarite of acts 3–5. In their essays in this volume, Peter A. Parolin reevaluates the thematic implications of the food imagery in the play, whereas Garrett A. Sullivan Jr. reappraises the motifs of sleep and sloth.

However, other moralistic commentators concentrate not on Antony's sybaritic zest but on his subservience to a dominant woman as his most egregious flaw (perhaps, for the patriarchal society of the past three centuries, the most damning *hamartia* that a man could possess). Speaking for this view, Hazlitt (1817) disparages Antony's "effeminate character," which results in "his headstrong presumption and infatuated determination to yield to Cleopatra's wishes to fight by sea instead of land," an irrational action that, according to Hazlitt, ultimately brings a merited punishment (63). More censorious, Gervinus (1849–50) reduces Antony to a "splendid nothingness" with only "seeming greatness and seeming nobleness" (741), a man who, in subordinating himself to a woman, "becomes a woman" (730). And although this particular reading has fallen into disrepute in the more liberated twentieth century, nevertheless, in a recent essay, Charnes ("What's Love Got to Do with It?," 1992) examines what has always been a problem, particularly for moralistic critics of the play: how to recuperate Antony's epic masculinity, his worth and dignity as a legendary warrior-lover, when in this play he occupies a subject position almost always culturally reserved for women. In her essay in this volume, Lisa S. Starks denies that Antony assumes the female position in his relationship to Cleopatra, instead situating his behavior toward his beloved within the traditional narrative of male masochism.

Politically oriented analysts have shifted the focus from Antony's lusty hedonism and his uxorious submissiveness to Cleopatra to his instability as one of the triple pillars of the world. Thus, Phillips (1940) insists that Antony's capitulation to passion renders him an ineffectual leader, a view supported by Rose (1969), who observes that Antony, with his romantic, chivalric ideal of war, is never an efficient politician. In an early essay, "Antony and Pleasure," Barroll (1958) posits gluttony and sloth, aspects of pleasure in early modern parlance, as Antony's tragic failing. In a later study, he engraves a more complex portrait, an Antony controlled by two ruling passions—reverence for physical courage as the core of honor and an exuberant desire for sensual pleasure. More the twelfth-century chevalier than the shrewd military strategist or skillful politician, this Antony fatally risks all for his ladylove and for a dare. Moreover, Antony needs Cleopatra as his reflecting mirror, since she incorporates those traits that he most admires in himself; she is the "objective correlative of his own being," "his conception of himself made Flesh" (Barroll, *Shakespearean Tragedy*, 1984, p. 102). Thus, Barroll presents Antony as a figure for whom we feel both sympathy and disapproval, "one of Shakespeare's most complexly imagined tragic heroes" (83). In his essay in this volume, Barroll examines the image clusters surrounding both Antony and Cleopatra to explore further the complexity of our response to these multifaceted characters.

But, of course, Antony, like Cleopatra, has also enlisted ardent champions. Throughout the centuries, Antony's famed magnanimity has provided a mantra for romantic apologists, who have waxed eloquent in praise of the generosity, bounty, and royalty of this mighty general. Even in the moralistic eighteenth century, Antony recruited defenders. One of his earliest recorded admirers, Griffith (1775), praises the heroic liberality that prompts generosity to the perfidious Enobarbus, and other romantic interpreters exalt Antony to godlike stature (Heraud, 1865; Winter, 1892). One of Antony's most eloquent allies, John Middleton Murry (1936), links magnanimity and royalty with loyalty, persuasively demonstrating how Shakespeare employs prodigious and magnificent imagery to convince us of Antony's royalty. In his exegesis, Murry also identifies the biblical analogies implicit in the play: Antony's farewell dinner with his friends in act 4 parallels Jesus's Last Supper; Enobarbus's desertion echoes Judas's betrayal of Jesus. Conversely, fully aware of the biblical nuances in the play, Battenhouse (1969) interprets Antony as an antitype rather than a type of Christ, exemplifying how so often in Shakespeare's great anamorphic drama the same episodes invoke antipodal reactions, depending on the perspective from which they are viewed.

Antony's breadth and scope have also invited enthusiastic approval. If Simpson (1928) acclaims Cleopatra as the greatest of Shakespeare's heroines, Stauffer (1949) extols Antony as "the most comprehensive character that Shakespeare ever set his hand to" (240). Markels (1968) further departs from critical consensus by arguing that instead of choosing between the conflicting value systems presented in the play, "Antony grows larger in manhood until he can encompass both Rome and Egypt, affirming the values that both have taught him until both are fulfilled" (9). This view is further elaborated by Simmons (1973), who asserts that the tragedy of Antony "grows out of his heroic insistence on achieving both ideals, on maintaining the honor that is the necessary condition for love's integrity and fulfillment," whereas his "destruction results from the limitations and exclusiveness that the imperfect realities impose" (Simmons 124; Stilling, 1976). Wilson (1950), one of Antony's most fervent admirers, amplifies Antony's magnanimity to include an entire catechism of virtues: "Majesty, affability, benevolence, liberality, placability, amity, justice, fortitude, patience in sustaining wrong; all and more are Antony's" (xxx). For Wilson, as for many romantic analysts, Antony is the paragon of men.

However, the majority of interpreters rejects apotheosis or denunciation and, like Willard Farnham (1950), accepts Antony, like Cleopatra, as a figure of paradoxical nobility and delinquency. Thus, Nahum Tate, in 1680, praises the verisimilitude of this complex character: "You find his Antony in all the defects and excellencies of his mind, a soldier, a reveler, amorous, sometimes rash, sometime considerate, with all the various emotions of his mind" (qtd. in John Russell Brown 26). Thomas Davies (1783–84) underscores this contrariety, asserting that "[a]dmidst [*sic*] all the folly, profligacy, and mad flights of Mark Antony, some bright beams of a great and generous soul break forth with inimitable luster" (379). Bradley (1906), seeking to reconcile the romantic and moralistic readings of the play, presents Antony as simultaneously a "strumpet's fool" and Cleopatra's "peerless lover," a man whom we admire for his magnanimity but one who was not born for rule (341–43). Robert Heilman (1964) stresses Antony's paradoxical qualities, his ability to captivate, his combination of amiability and strength, and his singular magnetism, linked with his egregious lack of self-knowledge. Barton (1973) summarizes this Janus-faced portrait, noting that Enobarbus cannot "separate Antony's extravagance, that culpable waste about which Caesar is so censorious, from Antony's bounty: the godlike generosity of spirit which makes Antony send Enobarbus's treasurer after him when he defects to Caesar, and breaks the soldier's heart" (16). For Barton, both Antony and Cleopatra are as mysterious and contradictory as people in real life. Finally, many commentators have argued that Antony, at the very least the coprotagonist of the tragedy, combines the greatness and flaws that we associate with a tragic hero. According to Larry Champion (1976), through suffering Antony learns to transcend his own egomania, accept responsibility for his actions, develop concern for others—a concern shown in his magnanimity toward Enobarbus and his total forgiveness of Cleopatra at his death—and, before his death, like Lear, learns to know himself and recognize the true meaning of human relationships. Similarly, Richard C. Trench (1872) judges Antony a monumentally tragic figure, concluding that "the whole range of poetry offers no more tragical figure than he is [and] few that arouse deeper pity" (55–56).

The degree to which Shakespeare has altered his sources to ameliorate or derogate his male tragic hero has also been disputed. Trench carefully details the manner in which Shakespeare enhances the stature of Antony by omitting reference to his cruelties and treacheries. Conversely, R. H. Case (1906), although admiring Antony's magnanimity, criticizes Antony's treacherous and cold-blooded treatment of Octavia, calling into question the commonplace that Shakespeare changed his sources to civilize the portrait of Antony inherited from Plutarch.

Mythic exegetes have had a heyday with Antony, identifying in this colossal figure an avatar of Hercules, Mars, Bacchus/Dionysus, and even Osiris. Moreover, the multiple, often contradictory associations of these mythic deities enhance the contrariety of Antony's paradoxical image. Thus, viewing the play through the lens of the medieval moralistic tradition, Barroll ("Enobarbus' Description of Cleopatra," 1958) reads Antony's preference for

Cleopatra over Octavius as a reenactment of Hercules's famous choice at the crossroads between duty and pleasure. Equally negative in his exegesis, Schlegel (1809–11) associates Antony with Hercules in the chains of Omphale, a time-honored parallel also discussed by Blissett (1967), among others. However, other scholars decipher the Hercules analogue more favorably. Rejecting the homiletic reading of Antony's Herculean options as a choice between Roman duty (virtue) and Egyptian sensuality (vice), John Coates (1978) depicts Antony as the complete man who reconciles pleasure and virtue. In Plutarch, the departure of Antony's tutelary deity functions as a harbinger of defeat and disgrace. Conversely, both Coates and Richard Hillman (1987) read the exit of Hercules in Shakespeare's play as a prelude to Antony's spiritual ascent, asserting that in the interlude between the god's desertion and Antony's final loss of his fleet and army, Antony develops until he acquires courage, generosity, and a noble capacity to enjoy pleasure without being possessed by it, all traits traditionally attributed to Hercules. Finally, Eugene Waith (*The Herculean Hero,* 1962), in what is probably the definitive treatment of Antony as the Herculean hero, chronicles Antony's affinities to this mythological icon: like Hercules, he is unmanned by a powerful woman; like Hercules, he is bigger than life, subject to violent rages, extravagant feasting, remarkable generosity; like Hercules, he loses and recovers his honor. Waith concludes that, like Hercules, Antony is a paradoxical figure, an oxymoronic reading supported by Bono (1984).

Commentators have also debated the significance of the Mars/Venus association, querying: Does this parallel debase or elevate Antony? Those who see the parallel as debasing stress the emasculation of Mars by Venus, who in dozens of Renaissance paintings disarms the militant god, even as Cleopatra in the famous crossdressing scene—recounted rather than enacted in the play—robs Antony of his sword and attires him in her robes and mantles (2.5.21–23). Conversely, those who see the parallel as elevating portray the mating of Antony and Cleopatra as reflecting the creative union of Mars and Venus in which love conquers strife and produces Harmony (Waddington, 1966; Adelman, *Common Liar,* 1973; Bono, 1984). These commentators further contend that this crossdressing scene presents both Antony and Cleopatra as uniting masculine and feminine qualities, thereby attempting to regain the "wholeness, that primal sexual unity, about which Aristophanes is half joking, half deadly serious, in Plato's *Symposium*" (Barton, 1973, p. 6; Bono, 1984; Hillman, 1987). Coates (1978) further relates Cleopatra's arming of Antony in act 4 to the many Renaissance paintings in which Venus arms Mars, symbolizing that love not only conquers strife but also inspires the warrior to courage.

Therefore, the exchange of clothing referred to above constitutes one of the central cruxes of the play, interpreted variously as symbolizing "a violation of the proper hierarchical relationship between man and woman," or as the salubrious exchange of gender attributes culminating in a fuller, more comprehensive humanity (Adelman, *Common Liar*, 1973, pp. 94–96). The problematic scene in which Antony feels himself deliquescing (4.14) has prompted similar contrary readings. As Marshall (1993) observes, those in the Roman camp construe Antony's essential instability as a sign of his emasculation, his loss of his heroic masculine identity. Conversely, critics aligned with Cleopatra and with Egypt find positive value in his dissolution, explaining this blending or melting as an acceptance of his own femininity and as a union with the maternal (Adelman, *Suffocating Mothers*, 1992). Erickson (1985) summarizes this controversy: "Antony's relationship to Cleopatra can be read in two ways simultaneously. The negative version sees gender-role reversal: Cleopatra plays controlling woman to Antony's vitiated masculinity. In the positive version, Antony and Cleopatra engage in gender-role exchange that enlarges but does not erase the original and primary sexual identity of each" (133). Although traditional expositors adopt the negative reading of the lovers' relationship, during the past few decades commentators have tended to support the view that the love of Antony and Cleopatra "involves a collaboration to which Antony contributes a new male identity, the counterpart of Cleopatra's exceptional female identity," whereby both achieve a cross-gender identification that Erickson terms "heterosexual androgyny" (129, 133; Barton, 1973; Wheeler, 1981; Greene, 1987; Whittier, 1989; Adelman, *Suffocating Mothers*). McDonald (1994) expands this discussion to suggest that "[t]his imaginative union of the masculine and feminine helps to account for Shakespeare's reconceived attitude towards words, verse style, and 'dramatic mode,' and the theatrical enterprise itself" (103).

Finally, Antony's wrenching inner turmoil and sense of dissolving self have attracted sympathetic interest from psychoanalytical critics, who marshal various psychological theories to explain these conflicts. Freudian interpreters, like Kuriyama (1977), detail Antony's dilemma as a classical Oedipal choice between an anal adulthood and an oral childhood, or, as Stockholder (1987) phrases it, between his allegiance to parental power (Caesar) or maternal desire (Cleopatra). According to both Kuriyama and Stockholder, Antony ultimately resolves this conflict through his fulfillment of the infantile fantasy of reunion with the powerful pre-Oedipal mother. Adelman (*Suffocating Mothers*, 1992) appropriates object-relations theory to reach a similar conclusion, contending that the final *Liebestod* represents satisfaction of the desire to be merged with the mother. Adopting a different psychological paradigm, Lisa S. Starks (1999) employs the model of Giles Deleuze to establish Cleopatra as the triple mother of masochistic fantasy (the sadistic woman/Oedipal mother; the pagan goddess/uterine mother, and the ideal woman/oral mother) and to situate Antony within the scenario of male masochism. Finally, Marshall (1993) deploys the psychoanalytical theories of Freud, Lacan, Kristeva, and Butler to examine Antony's melancholic sense of discandying in the play, contending that Antony's dissolution of identity results from Cleopatra's own fluid identity that does not provide Antony with a stable Other against which to solidify a self. Thus, Cleopatra's insufficient Othering requires Antony to confront his own originary Otherness. As Marshall demonstrates, everyone in the play views Antony differently and he cannot incorporate these conflicting images into a stable self, with the result that he feels fragmented and psychologically dissolving.

A survey of performance criticism reveals that the actor who plays the role of Antony faces a similar dilemma: how to incorporate into one performance the many personae he is expected to portray—delinquent leader, besotted suitor, magnanimous general, peerless lover, androgynous male—while still maintaining his visible shape.

Octavius Caesar

In the oxymoronic world of *Antony and Cleopatra*, even Octavius Caesar has aroused radically different responses from commentators. Although certainly never a Mars, and perhaps not a Gorgon either, Octavius has been interpreted diversely as Shakespeare's ideal prince and as a scheming Machiavel.

Griffith (1775), one of Octavius's earliest detractors, establishes the foil relationship that has dominated criticism of the play, presenting Antony as not only a braver but a better man than his competitor for empire, whom she demeans as worthless, mean, jealous, and vengeful. Schelgel (1809–11) develops this comparison, asserting that "the open and lavish character of Antony is admirably contrasted with the heartless littleness of Octavius" (417), while Waith ("Manhood and Valor," 1950) rejects Octavius as a Machiavellian schemer, who compares unfavorably to the passionate, magnanimous Antony, and whose clever egotism alienates the sympathies of the audience. Even moralistic critics have found much to dispraise in Octavius. Gentleman (1774) grudgingly concedes that the magnanimity of spirit shown in the death of Cleopatra contrasts sharply with the equivocal, treacherous behavior of Octavius, and Arthur Quiller-Couch (1922), although often disapproving of the two lovers, prefers them to the cool and priggish Octavius. In one of the most comprehensive analyses of the passionless foe of the passionate Antony, Barroll ("The Characterization of Octavius," 1970) anatomizes Octavius, revealing him as the unmitigated pragmatist, who never performs a single act of gratuitous kindness, and who lives by a code of literalism and legalism. Barroll also notes the degree to which Shakespeare presents Octavius as a public figure, who speaks no soliloquies or asides and never appears on stage alone. Thus, censors of Octavius have stigmatized him as cold and calculating, at best a thoroughgoing pragmatist, at worse, a hypocritical Machiavel.

However, Octavius has found advocates, sometimes in surprising places. Furness (1907), one of the few romantic apologists for Octavius, argues that many interpreters have imposed the traditional cunning visage of the historical

Octavius on Shakespeare's more neutral portrait. Seeking to rebut the "cold, crafty, self-seeking" image projected by criticism, Furness maintains that Shakespeare expects us to accept Octavius's love for both Antony and his sister as "perfectly sincere and deep-seated" (x). More predictably, political exegetes have also defended Octavius, reformulating the contrast between the two competitors to present Caesar as possessing the traits of leadership that Antony so woefully lacks. Denton Snider (1876) was one of the first critics to identify Octavius as the "true Roman" and ideal ruler, a view espoused by Phillips (1940) who analyzes Octavius, Lepidus, Pompey, and Antony against traditional standards of leadership, concluding that only Octavius displays the capabilities of the successful leader, which he defines as reason ruling passion, sobriety, temperance, consistency, and, surprisingly—Antony's legendary virtue—magnanimity. Battenhouse (1969) expands the contrast between the temperate Octavius and the intemperate Antony, a critical position supported more recently by Christopher Wortham (1995), who presents Octavius as displaying "a kind of temperance that wins him the field and prepares him for empire" (27). A. P. Riemer (1968) concurs with these laudatory readings, denying that Octavius is a "ruthless megalomaniac"; instead, he depicts Caesar as "a noble, well-intentioned and generally just ruler," contending that he does virtually nothing treacherous nor underhanded, that he does not abuse his powers, and that he is much more than the Machiavellian opportunist that many critics brand him (38). Finally, Rose (1969) agrees that viewed from a political perspective, Octavius emerges as the ideal ruler, while granting, in contrast to Phillips, Battenhouse, Reimer, and Wortham, that his very political success entails rather unattractive characteristics, such as coldness and calculation.

Despite considerable controversy, majority critical opinion follows Rose in picturing Octavius as a disagreeable human being yet an effective ruler, an evaluation first offered by Hermann Ulrici (1839), who grants Octavius "moderation, prudence, and forethought," the virtues necessary to preserve Rome from disintegration, asserting that because he possesses these virtues, Octavius, although without "vigour or depth of mind," will prevail, whereas the "straight-forward and noble Antony" will be overcome by the course of history (357). Somewhat more disparaging, Blissett (1967) synthesizes the paradox of Octavius: "a great ruler, a great dissembler, a cold comedian, 'one of the most odious of the world's successful men' " (153). Similarly, although Markels (1968) judges Octavius "the most repellent Roman of them all" (43), the embodiment of political opportunism and human mediocrity, he also acknowledges that the timeserving Caesar "is 'predestined' to preserve the order of the state" (129). Bradley (1906), like so many interpreters, both admires and dislikes Octavius: "To Shakespeare he [Octavius] is one of those men, like Bolingbroke and Ulysses, who have plenty of 'judgment' and not much 'blood.' Victory in the world, according to the poet, almost always goes to such men; and he makes us respect, fear, and dislike them" (336). Charney (1961) responds similarly, portraying Octavius as a cold rather menacing individual, who nevertheless possesses the qualities that fit him for rule, qualities that Antony lacks, observing, "As in the case of Henry V, admirable sovereigns need not also be admirable and sympathetic persons" (91). In one of the most valuable studies of Octavius's dual persona, Robert Kalmey (1978) traces this diversity of response to the contradictory image of Octavius inherited by Shakespeare from Elizabethan histories of Rome, in which Octavius was simultaneously honored as an ideal prince and disparaged as a vicious tyrant fomenting rebellion.

Just as new historicist critics have traditionally linked Cleopatra with Elizabeth, so they have also drawn provocative analogies between King James, who explicitly associated himself with Augustus Caesar, and Octavius. In his *roman à clef* reading of the play, H. Neville Davies (1985) finds analogues not only between Octavius and James but also between James's brother, King Christian of Denmark and Norway, and Mark Antony. Like Antony, Christian was extravagant, physically strong, a womanizer, and a prodigious eater and drinker. Explaining the play as a response to the fiascos occurring during a royal visit of King Christian in 1606, Davies interprets the tragedy as a kind of morality play containing a personal warning to James to be politically astute and survive (like Octavius), rather than follow the path of self-indulgence and perish (like Antony). Following Davies, Wortham (1995) sees Octavius as an implicit analogue to James and the play as a veiled tribute to the monarch who, like Octavius Caesar, will usher in a time of universal peace. Similarly, in a classic new historicist essay, Yachnin (1991) locates the play within the political situation of its own period, equating Antony and Cleopatra with the aristocratic, chivalric ethos of the Elizabethan past and Octavius with the mercantile, pragmatic value system of the Jacobean present. In such terms, the play becomes both a contribution to and a critique of the emerging Jacobean culture.

As the above survey has attempted to demonstrate, in the characters, ethos, and genre of *Antony and Cleopatra,* Shakespeare has etched an intriguing anamorphic drama, whose contours have changed throughout the decades with shifts in critical perspectives. The performance survey below further examines the various metamorphoses that the play has assumed in its 250 years of stage history.

ANTONY AND CLEOPATRA IN PERFORMANCE

A total disregard of the unities of time and place; forty-two scenes ranging over the entire known world; a cast of thirty-four named characters; the most daunting female role in the history of the drama; a demanding male role; precarious tonal balance between heroic transcendence and ironic deflation—these are a few of the challenges that confront any director of *Antony and Cleopatra.* A performance history of the play thus becomes a narrative of attempts to surmount these formidable obstacles. These monumental problems may be one reason that the play, alone among Shakespeare's great tragedies, was not staged for over 150 years after its presumed premiere in 1607—and even then in a truncated form. Even today, it is performed much less frequently than Shakespeare's more popular tragedies, *Hamlet*, *Othello*, *King Lear*, and *Macbeth*.

The primary reasons for the play's initial neglect appear to be the following: first, the difficulty of staging the drama's forty-two scenes in the proscenium mode of the Restoration and eighteenth-century theaters, which privileged spectacle and scenery; second, the candid treatment of illicit sexual passion and emotional turmoil; and third, the almost insuperable challenge of finding actors to play the roles of the legendary eponymous heroes. In particular, the role of Cleopatra has become the Mount Everest for female actors. Herbert Farjeon delineates the obstacles facing the actor attempting to scale this peak:

> Playgoers will swallow a Desdemona, or an Ophelia, or even a Juliet who is merely sweet, as they will swallow a Lady Macbeth who is merely stark. But they will boggle at a Shakespearean Cleopatra who is merely any one thing, because the Shakespearean Cleopatra is obviously infinite in her variety.
>
> She is royal. She is riggish. She is vain. She is vulgar. She is cruel. She is cowardly. She is a born commander. She is a born slave. She is innately faithful. She is innately deceitful—deceitful even to the man she worships so passionately that she would rather die than live without him. (171)

Whether an actor playing Cleopatra need be all of these things is debatable, but audiences have traditionally expected Cleopatra to display abundant, if not perhaps infinite variety. Similarly, the actor performing Antony must capture both the titan's greatness and the lover's vulnerability; he must join in Cleopatra's sportive seduction, indulge in debilitating sexual infatuation, explode into jealous rages, and survive his blotched suicide and his hoisting onto Cleopatra's monument, all without diminishing his heroic stature and without forfeiting the sympathy and respect of the audience. No wonder, as David Bevington and David Scott Kastan observe, future generations neglected Shakespeare's heretical play and turned to "more classically regular and decorous treatments of the same story" (xxv). In his essay in this anthology, Bevington will examine some of the staging choices confronting any director of the play, focusing particularly on the significance and possible staging of the much-debated "monument scene."

The Jacobean Debut

Although there remains no written record of a performance of *Antony and Cleopatra* until after the Restoration, critical consensus agrees that it was first performed in 1607. The 1608 listing of the play in the Stationers Register establishes "the absolute *terminus ad quem*" for the play's presentation (Barroll, "Chronology of Shakesepeare's Jacobean Plays," 136); however, two dramas published in 1607 contain echoes of the tragedy, thus suggesting that it must have been staged at least a year earlier than 1608. The first of these, Samuel Daniel's revised version of his closet drama *Cleopatra*, published in 1607, includes stage directions graphically describing the hefting of Antony to Cleopatra in her monument, which scholars surmise that he saw performed, most probably in Shakespeare's play, earlier the same year. The second, Barnabe Barne's *The Devil's Charter*, acted by the King's Men at Candlemas (February 2, 1607) and printed in October of the same year, features a scene in which Pope Alexander Borgia dubs the asps that he uses to poison two sleeping boys "Cleopatraes [*sic*] birds" (Barroll, "Chronology of Shakespeare's Jacobean Plays," 138–149). These salient echoes have convinced scholars that *Antony and Cleopatra* debuted early in 1607, either at the Globe, the Blackfriars, or the court.

Scholars also conjecture that early modern stage managers probably ignored the challenges that have stymied so many directors from the eighteenth century to the present. Presenting forty-two scenes in a brisk, fluid manner would pose little problem on the Jacobean stage with its unlocalized settings, its bare, open playing space, and its minimal props designating Rome, Egypt, and Athens. Moreover, casting was most likely a *fait accompli*, since Richard Burbage doubtless assumed the role of Antony while some talented young male actor in Shakespeare's company "boyed" his Cleopatra (Lamb).

But these are, of course, only speculations, albeit educated ones. No theatrical record survives before 1669, when the Lord Chamberlain's office assigned performance rights of the play to Thomas Killigrew and the King's Men at the Theatre Royal, Drury Lane, observing that the play had been "formerly acted at the Blackfriars." However, there is "no record of Killigrew's company having played it during the Restoration" (Bevington and Kastan xxv). Thus, it appears that for almost one hundred years after the Restoration, *Antony and Cleopatra* was not staged at all, even in an abbreviated or hybrid form. As Margaret Lamb comments, "This bleak record is significant because it is unique: *Antony and Cleopatra* was the only Shakespearean tragedy not performed in some version in a hundred-year period of very free Shakespearean adaptation" (37).

Another probable reason for the almost universal neglect of the play, in addition to the theatrical challenges mentioned earlier, was the existence of several other dramatic treatments on the subject more compatible to both the Jacobean and the neoclassical *zeitgeist*. These included John Fletcher's *The False One* (1620), which focused on the intrigue between Cleopatra and Julius Caesar, Thomas May's *Cleopatra* (1626), and another *Cleopatra* by Charles Sedley (1677), all of which simplified the story line and observed classical dramatic rubrics, thus representing a "return to [the] normalcy" that Shakespeare had defied (Bevington and Kastan xxv). However, by far the most popular of these dramatic treatments was John Dryden's *All for Love, or The World Well Lost*, published in 1677 and staged seven times during the eighteenth century. The popularity of Dryden's play often led eighteenth- and nineteenth-century playwrights to conflate Shakespeare's and Dryden's plays into one script.

The Post-Renaissance Premiere

In 1759, a historic theatrical event occurred when David Garrick presented the first production of *Antony and Cleopatra* since Shakespeare's day and the first performance ever featuring a female actor, in this case the daring Mary Ann Yates, in the title role. However, in an effort to accommodate Shakespeare's wide-ranging epic to the tastes of the day, including a preference for pageantry over poetry and love stories over historical chronicles, Edward Capell radically altered the script, excising eight minor characters, cutting and transposing speeches, and honing the play's forty-two scenes to twenty-seven. In his amputation, "[p]ageantry and spectacle replaced political parleys and military skirmishes" (Lamb 46). However, despite lavish costumes—Romans in the obligatory armor, women in modified contemporary dress—and elaborate scenery—including an ornate two-tiered monument onto which Garrick was hauled to die in Yates's arms—the production did not please and closed after six performances. Apparently, even the truncated text offered too many scenic changes for classically indoctrinated audiences, and neither of the principal actors—not even the great Garrick and certainly not the relatively inexperienced Yates—was deemed adequate for the roles of the legendary lovers. Thus, in its very first post-Jacobean performance, *Antony and Cleopatra* encountered the formidable obstacles that would haunt future revivals: the difficulty of staging the play and the even more arduous challenge of finding the appropriate actors to inhabit the roles of the protagonists.

Hybrid Productions

William Garrett failed in his valiant attempt to stage Shakespeare's play, albeit in an abridged version, and for the next ninety years, actor-managers mounting productions of the drama took even greater liberties with Shakespeare's text. A draconian solution to staging the play's forty-two scenes was to excise half of them. J. M. Kemble's revival at Covent Garden in 1813, starring Charles Young and Helen Faucit, radically cut Shakespeare's text, interpolating not only passages from Dryden's *All for Love*, but two wholly original scenes— the sea fight at Actium and a funeral-procession finale with full chorus— producing what Lord Byron despairingly termed "[a] salad of Shakespeare and Dryden" (qtd. in Madelaine 34). In its mutilation of Shakespeare's text,

Kemble's production carefully bowdlerized all ribald banter and omitted all problematic episodes—banishing the bawdy clown and eliminating the monument scene, long considered the most vexing staging crux in the play. In the production, spectacle totally upstaged character. Although Hazlitt judged Young "just and impressive" in the role of Antony (*Morning Chronicle*; qtd. in Madelaine 36), other reviewers caviled that he lacked Kemble's "faculty of sometime electrifying the audience with enthusiasm" (*The Examiner*; qtd. in Madelaine 36). It appears that Kemble had originally intended to take the role of Antony himself and had urged his sister Sarah Siddons to play opposite him as Cleopatra. However, Victorian prudery overcame histrionic ambition and Siddons famously refused, declaring, "If I should play the part as it should be played I should ever after hate myself" (Wingate 10), whereupon Kemble apparently abandoned all desire to play Antony. What Siddons might have done with the role of Cleopatra had she "played the part as it should be played," one can only surmise, but Faucit generated little enthusiasm, with Hazlitt criticizing her for displaying "the affected levity of the modern fine lady" (*Morning Chronicle*; qtd. in Madelaine 36). Unremarkable in its performances, Kemble's pastiche is remembered primarily for its antiquarian focus and Egyptian motifs, which led to a vogue for Egyptian as well as Greek and Roman accoutrement in the neoclassical stagings of the play. At any rate, Kemble's attempts to cater to the taste of the time were no more successful than Garrett's and the production closed after nine performances.

William Macready's 1833 revival followed the formula of Kemble: cut and rearrange scenes from the play, adulterate Shakespeare's text with material from Dryden, and submerge everything in splendor and pageantry. Neither Macready nor his costar Louisa Anne Phillips achieved memorable performances as the doomed lovers: reviewers found Macready more impressive as the fallen soldier than the ardent lover and criticized Phillips's Cleopatra for her "boisterous nervousness" and her "ludicrous overplaying of passion" (Lamb 65). Like Kemble's earlier production, Macready's revival was not a success and ran for only three performances. The failure of the three productions mounted by Garrett, Kemble, and Macready—a trio of the greatest actor-managers of the time—led literary critics, like Charles Lamb, to speculate that Shakespeare's plays "should be read, rather than seen" (4: 188–213; qtd. in Lamb 60). The tragedy fared no better in America in similar elaborate, amalgamated versions, presented first in New Orleans (1839) and later in New York (1846), in which lavish costumes and opulent sets failed to salvage the show (Madelaine 45).

Victorian Extravaganzas

Samuel Phelps's revival at Sadler's Wells in 1849 marks the first recorded popular success of the play, running an impressive twenty-two nights. This production also introduced Isabella Glyn, the first actor to become famous in the role of Cleopatra, a part that she would reprise twice more to the hyperbolic applause of critics and audiences alike. Phelps's production thus demonstrated the "actability (and financial viability) of an all-Shakespeare text," however abbreviated and sanitized, thus assuring that the script would never again be "Drydenized, as a matter of course" (Madelaine 45). How did Phelps do it? His winning formula combined scenic embellishment with virtuoso acting. Although his lavish revival eliminated twelve of the play's scenes, there were no interpolations from Dryden or any other author and the remaining thirty scenes created a captivating *mise en scene,* universally praised by critics for its magnificence and historical accuracy. Even more important, the production assembled a strong cast featuring leading actors capable of capturing the magnetism and stature of the two protagonists. However, although generally lauded for his passion, vigor, and declamatory skills—and particularly for his portrayal of the Bacchanalian reveler aboard Pompey's barge—Phelps was clearly upstaged by his enchanting costar. Critics captured in her strong toil of grace extolled Glyn's infinite variety and rapturous death, praising her as "[g]orgeous in person, in costume, and in her style of action," "the Egyptian Venus, Minerva, Juno—now pleased, now angry— now eloquent, now silent, capricious and resolved, according to the situation and sentiment to be rendered" (*The Illustrated London News*; qtd. John Russell Brown 51). Rather incongruously, although in all Glyn's appearances in the role (1849, 1855, 1867) reviewers commended her dark-skinned, dark-haired beauty, her "witchery," and "her Asiatic undulations" (Lamb 76), illustrations present her as gowned in an "elegant, white, floor-length Victorian gown with a lace-trimmed over-skirt and portrait neckline" (Adler 457; see fig. 1), looking more like a swarthy Queen Victoria than the Queen of the Nile.

Phelps's successful revival of *Antony and Cleopatra* ushered in a rash of productions, each more flamboyant than the previous. Charles Calvert's extravagant 1886 version of the play exaggerated the formula that had ensured Phelps's success, including magnificent scenery and an acting script that reduced the text from forty-two to twelve scenes, with no hoisting to the monument and Antony and Cleopatra dying in the same scene. Frederick Chatterton staged a similar extravaganza at Drury Lane in 1873, in which the scenery became fatter and the script thinner, and the emphasis shifted more sharply from poetry and performance to pictorial splendor, rendering the scene designer the star and the actors and the playwright almost supernumeraries. This staging omitted everything that detracted from the passion of the lovers, including the episodes with Pompey, the camp scenes with Antony and Octavius, the death of Enobarbus, Antony's second defeat, the hauling up of Antony to the monument, the Seleucus scene, and the final confrontation between Cleopatra and Caesar. At the same time, Chatterton added a number of spectacular sequences, including "a Roman festival procession of

Fig. 1.: Isabella Glyn as Cleopatra in the scene with Thidias (3.13), with Samuel Phelps as Antony in the background, in Samuel Phelps's 1849 production of *Antony and Cleopatra* at Sadler's Wells. Courtesy of Theatre Museum; Copyright © V & A Images.

Amazons, thirty choirboys, and a ballet called 'The Path of Flowers'" (Bevington and Kastan xxviii).

Richard Madelaine and Doris Adler, between them, list nine non-British productions in the fifty years following Phelps's revival; Madelaine relates this flurry of interest to the "Egyptomaniacal appropriation" sweeping the world at the time (59). These non-British stagings, presented in New York, Sidney, Melbourne, and in Paris, all followed the established pictorial model that drastically abridged the text and foregrounded pageantry, including dissolving Sphinxes, magnificent barges, and panoramas of the Nile. Of special interest are an opulent version at Her Majesty's Opera House in Melbourne in 1889, which out-Kembled Kemble by adding a rocking stage for the galley episode and a wrestling scene to the now *de rigueur* dancing and singing, and Henry Abbey's sumptuous production at the Palmer Theatre, New York, also in 1889, which carried the textual honing to excess by lopping

Octavia from the cast of characters (Madelaine; Adler). In the last half of the Victorian age, *Antony and Cleopatra* suddenly became a hot property. But, as many critics queried, was it Shakespeare's play?

Adler argues that the revival at the Palmer Theatre is memorable for two reasons: first, it holds the distinction of being the most commercially successful production of *Antony and Cleopatra* in theatrical history; second, it introduced, in the person of Cora Urquardt Potter, an exciting, new model for Cleopatra. Adler credits this American actor with effecting the metamorphosis of Cleopatra from the statuesque, majestic Juno, embodied in Isabella Glyn, into the seductive, voluptuous Venus, incarnated in Potter. The first unlaced Cleopatra, Potter was, by all reports, a lovely queen, gorgeous in archeologically accurate Egyptian costumes, with long flowing, unbound red hair, clinging, revealing garments, and unstained cheeks. One reviewer describes her as "sensuous, purring, feline" (*New York Morning Journal*; qtd. in Adler 457–58), and critics saved their greatest accolades not for her death scene (as with Isabella Glyn) but for her dramatic debut on a glittering barge, for her erotic love scenes with her paramour, and for her tempestuous attack on the unfortunate messenger who brought the news of Antony's marriage. However, on opening night, her suicide reportedly provoked quite a scandal when "she became so rapt that she tore away the concealing [flesh colored] silks and literally laid bear her breast for the audience to see and the asp to bite" (Shattuck 123). According to Adler, this seductive actor succeeded in transforming Cleopatra from the royal queen to the royal wench, an interpretation that has dominated many modern productions, although the most acclaimed Cleopatras have encompassed both. Famous actors on both sides of the Atlantic imitated Potter's Egyptian queen: Sarah Bernhardt (Paris, October 1890), Lily Langtry (London, November 1890), and Fanny Davenport (New York, December 1890) copied her clinging Egyptian costumes as assiduously as they mimicked her entrance on the barge, her pale makeup, her flowing red hair, and (with the exception of Langtry) her use of live snakes in the suicide scene. Directors ignored Cleopatra's explicit reference to her corset—"Cut my lace, Charmian" (1.3.71–73)—and after Potter the laced Cleopatra became the exception rather than the norm. Moreover, despite the continued dominance of dark-haired Egyptian queens, the pale-skinned, red-haired Cleopatra has resurfaced periodically in British productions from Lily Langtry to Janet Achurch to Peggy Ashcroft to Vanessa Redgrave.

For pure opulence, the Lily Langtry extravaganza presented at the Princess Theatre in 1890 surpassed all previous stagings of the play. Reviews extolled "architectural scenes, purple galleys, Roman chariots, and milk white steeds," while magazine illustrations displayed lion chairs and lion sculptures, barges and chariots (Lamb 81). The sets dazzled, but the performances stultified. The *Times* reviewer chafed that the four-hour-plus production (as much the result of cumbersome scenery changes as interpolated spectacles) evoked only one emotion—"a sense of boredom"—further complaining that the spectacular scenery "dwarfed Shakespeare's poetry as well as the performances of Lily Langtry as Cleopatra and Charles Coghlen as Antony" (10; qtd. in Sandra L. Williamson 120). Although praising the "dazzling beauty" and archeological accuracy of the sets and costumes, one critic found Langtry, although lovely, cold as an icicle, grumbling that she played the fiery queen as "a mild eyed saint instead of a passionate animal" (*The Illustrated London News* 647; qtd. in Sandra L. Williamson 117). However, although the architectural glory of the sets overwhelmed the two protagonists, paradoxically, for the first time, the role of Octavius began to achieve prominence.

Action frequently evokes reaction and Louis Calvert's 1897 revival at the Olympic Theatre in London restored some of the balance between scenic splendor and histrionic skill lost in the elaborate Chatterton and Langtry productions. William Archer admired the presentation, proclaiming it "five times as vital and interesting" as Miss Langtry's "at about one-fifth the cost" (qtd. in Lamb 84). Given the relatively austere scenery, the critics focused not on the spectacular sets but on the provocative performances of Jane Achurch as Cleopatra and Calvert as Antony, although the drastic cuts in the script inhibited full character development by either actor. Achurch followed the model established by Potter and played Cleopatra as sensuous, passionate, and majestic, with "Rossettian [red] hair and beauty to match" (George Bernard Shaw 244; qtd. in Lamb 85), although she was also one of the first actors to accentuate the comic elements of the play. One reviewer proclaimed her the best Cleopatra he had ever seen with "looks which might have unpeopled a city, and tones which might have quelled provinces" (Agate 175). Critics pronounced Calvert's Antony vital, impressive, and an adept lover, although lacking in heroic stature—Shaw deemed him "inexcusably fat" (193; qtd. in Lamb 86). On the whole, commentators applauded Calvert's revival as a welcomed relief from the pageantry of the pictorial mode.

The elaborate productions of the Victorian period reached their apogee in Herbert Beerbohm Tree's pictorial masterpiece at His Majesty's Theatre in 1906 (Madelaine), which indeed "o're flowed the measure." Like the extravaganzas of the nineteenth century, Tree's revival honed the text and interpolated scenes—to the traditional choruses, marriages, funerals, and dance numbers adding a "*tableau vivant* of the 'serpent of Old Nile,' arrayed in the habiliments of Isis, walking in a procession through the streets of Alexandra among the screaming populace"—and framed all the action in magnificent scenery: a dissolving Sphinx, gold bedizened palaces, a gigantic Alexandrian marketplace, massive interiors, and a glorious barge for Cleopatra (Speaight, *Shakespeare on Stage* 126). Tree's pomp and circumstance received mixed reviews, and although some commentators applauded his ravishing decors, others lamented that scenic spectacle should so overshadow Shakespeare's verse and reduce the actors to "a mobile section of the scenery" (*Punch* 2–5; qtd. in

Sandra L. Williamson 119). Totally overwhelmed by the colossal sets, the actors struggled to hold their own. According to critics, Constance Collier, dressed like a Dionysiac priestess in her heraldic Egyptian helmet and mantle of tiger and leopard skins (see fig. 2), dominated all her scenes with Antony. Additionally, reviewers admired Basil Gil as Octavius Caesar and Lyn Harding as Enobarbus. Conversely, many commentators found Tree, like so many Antonys both before and after, to be more effective as the remorseful Roman soldier than the infatuated lover. However, given the monumental scenic competition and the butchered text, it would have been well-nigh impossible for any actor to capture the multiplicity of either of the two lovers.

Neo-Elizabethan Revivals

Spectacular productions of *Antony and Cleopatra* in the pictorial mode continued for several years after Tree's extravaganza, but clearly the handwriting was on the wall. Critical and financial disasters, like the 1909 ill-fated inaugural spectacle at the New Theatre in New York starring the famous American thespians E. H. Sothern and Julia Marlowe in the leading roles, clearly indicated that both monetary and aesthetic rationales demanded a change (Shattuck). The catalysts for this change were two practical men of the theater—William Poel, founder of the Elizabethan Stage Society (1894), and Harley Granville-Barker, playwright, director, and scholar. Both of these theatrical pioneers advocated Elizabethan-style performances of Shakespeare's plays, and Granville-Barker's highly acclaimed *Prefaces to Shakespeare* introduced these ideas to both the scholarly and theatrical world.

In his *Prefaces,* Granville-Barker complains that even after three centuries of commentary, we still have much to learn about Shakespeare the playwright and about the original production of his plays, lamenting that "the Procrustean methods of a changed theater deformed the plays, and put the art of them into confusion" (1). In his ambitious *Prefaces*, he attempts to rectify this confusion by constructing a blueprint showing how the plays were originally staged and acted and how they should be performed in later periods. His first pronouncement, heresy to the aficionados of the Victorian pictorial mode, insists that Shakespeare's theater conjured the sense of "place" through allusion and language rather than through scenic design, and that scenery should never detract from character and action, the focus of Shakespeare's drama. In terms of costume, Granville-Barker asserts that "[h]alf the plays can be quite appropriately dressed in the costume of Shakespeare's own time," although "[i]t is false logic which suggests that to match their first staging we should dress them in the costume of ours," because "with costume goes custom and manners—or the lack of them" (17). In addressing the costuming of *Antony and Cleopatra*, he offers a compromise that has influenced productions from William Bridges-Adams (1921) and Robert Atkins (1922) to Peter Hall (1987)

Fig. 2. Constance Collier as Cleopatra in Herbert Beerbohm Tree's 1906 production of *Antony and Cleopatra* at His Majesty's Theatre. Courtesy of Theatre Museum; Copyright © V&A Images.

and John Caird (1992): he suggests that if the sight of "the serpent of old Nile" in a farthingale offends us, then the apparel in Paolo Veronese's "Alexander and the Wife and Daughter of Darius" might not only provide the model for Shakespeare's Roman figures but perhaps for Cleopatra as well—for "though Cleopatra might be given some Egyptian stigmata, there would still be laces to be cut." Thus, he contends, although Veronese's garments might be grievously incorrect from an archeological perspective, they might be gloriously correct from a dramatic one (Granville-Barker 408–09). On addressing the quandary of casting the most taxing female role in theater history, Granville-Barker reminds his readers that Cleopatra had to be acted by a boy, speculating that this expediency determined not Shakespeare's view of the character but his presentation of it. Thus, rather than depicting Cleopatra's irresistible sensuality in action, Shakespeare creates her erotic aura through language, particularly her magnificent description by the misogynist Enobarbus, with her sexual magnetism developed not through her own actions and dialogue but through her effect on others. Finally, Granville-Barker addresses the integrity of the text, so blatantly violated in eighteenth- and nineteenth-century productions of the play. Although defending discreet bowdlerizing, observing that Shakespeare's characters often make obscene jokes of a kind no longer appropriate, he warns that the scalpel is a dangerous weapon and that "we cut and carve the body of a play to its peril" (21–22). His final advice, "Gain Shakespeare's effects by Shakespeare's means when you can; for, plainly, this will be the better way" (23), became the motto for the neo-Elizabethan directors during the next decades.

If Poel and Granville-Barker articulated the rubrics of neo-Elizabethan staging, two directors, William Bridges-Adams (Stratford 1921) and Robert Atkins (Old Vic 1922), represented these concepts in action. Both of these two watershed revivals departed from Victorian practice to present a comparatively uncut text—which won one of the directors the fond soubriquet "unaBridges-Adams"—employing the simple staging and rapid pace of the early modern stage. However, although rejecting the contemporary dress of the Victorian theater but not yet ready to embrace the Renaissance attire recommended by Granville-Barker, both directors compromised with Roman and Egyptian costumes. Despite a few Victorian vestiges—a cyclorama and a traverse curtain—the action of both productions remained brisk and effective. Significantly, the Bridges-Adams presentation reintroduced Dorothy Green as the Egyptian queen. Reviewers effused that not since Isabella Glyn had a Cleopatra so mesmerized audiences. Perhaps influenced by Potter, Green departed from tradition to accentuate Cleopatra's role as both vamp and queen; like Potter, she presented a "highly Anglicized" concept of wantonness with porcelain skin, long red hair, and scanty, revealing attire (Madelaine 82). The acceptance of this unabashedly erotic Cleopatra may reflect the rejection of the Victorian prudery that had shackled the play for over one hundred years;

paradoxically, one of the few dissenting voices found Green's Cleopatra not too sexy but "too English" and "too correct" to capture the exotic sensuality of the Egyptian queen (*Truth*; qtd. in Madelaine 77). Green reprised the role three more times (1924, 1925, 1930), always to enthusiastic reviews, although in her final performance, one critic censured the intelligence of her portrayal, complaining that her conception of the part "suggested qualities of brain which Antony's mistress certainly never possessed" (*Era*; qtd. in Madelaine 83). However, despite these minority naysayers, critical consensus agreed that in all her embodiments of the Egyptian queen Green fulfilled the role admirably, overshadowing her various Antonys who never seemed to encompass the complexity of the part. Conversely, commentators dismissed Atkins's Cleopatra, Esther Whitehouse, as "too slight" and his Antony, Wilfrid Walter, as all vigor and little poetry. Nevertheless, both productions played to crowded, enthusiastic audiences and were praised as successful revolutions in the production of *Antony and Cleopatra*.

Revolution was in the air, and during the next few decades experimental versions of *Antony and Cleopatra* abounded, many of which aroused the ire of critics. Frank Reicher's 1924 production at the Lyceum in New York, an odd conglomeration of tradition and innovation, used Tree's much-abbreviated text while, at the same time, updating the play through the use of twenties costumes. Andrew Leigh's 1925 revival at the Old Vic departed totally from both the Victorian search for archeological authenticity and the comparatively bare stage of the neo-Elizabethan mode to incorporate a contemporary setting and modern costumes accentuated with exotic accents. Edith Evans's Cleopatra, wearing a fringed costume, cobra circlet, and braided hair, looked more like a native American than an Egyptian, and Baliol Holloway's Antony sported a leopard skin that recalled Tarzan rather than a Roman soldier. As usual, critics faulted the two leading actors as incapable of capturing the multiplicity of the dual protagonists (Lamb, Madelaine). Finally, Henry Case's 1934 revival at the Old Vic departed from the partially bare stages of the neo-Elizabethan productions of the twenties, seeking to combine a controlled sumptuousness with a change of period and place. Mary Newcombe, who reminded one reviewer of Greta Garbo, played Cleopatra as a "brilliant, clever, highly complex, neurotic lady of our times" (Agate 179), but reviewers found her Cleopatra, like that of Green, too intelligent and the relationship of the lovers composed more of rage than love. As Farjeon groused, "I have never seen an Antony who appeared to be less in love with Cleopatra. I have never heard an Antony who made more noise" (174).

Harcourt Williams's production at the Old Vic in 1930 offered the first revival of the play in Renaissance dress since the Jacobean period. Victorian spectacles had favored the ruffles and bustles of contemporary attire; the neo-Elizabethan presentations of Bridges-Adams and Atkins preferred Roman and Egyptian regalia. However, under the influence of Poel and Granville-Barker,

Williams adapted costumes based on Veronese paintings to capture "the peacock strut of the Renaissance Orient with all the archaeology left out and all the romance left in" (Ivor Brown; qtd. in Madelaine 80). Some critics objected that the similarities in the wardrobe blurred the conflict between Rome and Egypt, but others commended the director's boldness in making the production not only lovely to look at but also unified. The revival was triply memorable: it not only pioneered the Renaissance costumes that would dominate twentieth-century versions of the play but also marked both the valedictory performance of Green as Cleopatra and the debut of a rising young star, John Gielgud, as Antony. In addition, it introduced Ralph Richardson as an excellent Enobarbus. However, although both Gielgud and Richardson received many accolades, Green stole the show as she had in all her incarnations as Cleopatra. Bridges-Adams, when producing his final *Antony and Cleopatra* the very next year, followed Williams in his use of Renaissance costumes, shocking London audiences by dressing his Cleopatra, Dorothy Massingham, in a pink farthingale.

The most notorious of these experiments, the first foreign production of the play to be performed in London, was staged by Theodore Komisarjevsky in 1936 to hoots of outrage by the critics. This highly iconoclastic revival featured a fixed set, bizarre costumes—"Veronese gone modern," according to Madelaine (85)—a rearranged script that harkened back to Victorian excesses, and a foreign Cleopatra, whose heavy Russian accent rendered the verse almost incomprehensible. Critics were choleric. One fumed, "Seldom has a play been so tormented and twisted and stifled or a work of genius been so casually scorned" (*The Times* 12; qtd. in Sandra L. Williamson 70). Interpolations abounded (the soothsayer wandered through the scenes speaking the lines of both major and minor characters) and "[c]uts bled the text" (Trewin 155). The result was a hodge podge of badly spoken verse with only one redeeming performance, Leon Quartermaine as Enobarbus (Farjeon). Scarcely more successful was Reginald Bach's 1937 production at the Mansfield Theatre in New York. The modern dress—Tallulah Bankhead swathed in lavender organdy with sequins—and Cleopatra's "hootchy-kootchy posturing" aroused the disdain of critics, as did Conway Tearle's rambunctious Antony (Madelaine 83). The production closed after five performances.

As far as I am aware, only two commercial revivals of *Antony and Cleopatra* were mounted during World War II. In 1945, the last year of the war, after a hiatus of eight years, the play was produced in both Stratford and Paris and the contrast between these two versions of Shakespeare's tragedy highlights the difference between modern and Victorian stagings of the play. Jean-Louis Barrault's extravaganza at the Comedie-Francaise in Paris, complete with sea fight, a spectacular galley scene, and twenty-three changes of scene, re-created the scenic glories of the Victorian pictorial mode (Fluchere), whereas Robert Atkins's neo-Elizabethan production at Stratford, recalling the method that he had pioneered twenty-three years earlier, featured a relatively uncut text, simple sets and colorful costumes, and continuous action, snappy pace, and brisk speech (Madelaine).

All-Star Theater

The first postwar commercial revival of *Antony and Cleopatra*, Glen Byam Shaw's 1946 production at London's Picadilly Theatre, established a trend that would typify Shakespearean productions in Britain until the 1960s, when the emergence of two subsidized companies—the Royal Shakespeare Company and the National Theatre—would popularize repertory Shakespeare. This practice included the temporary return of Shakespeare to the West End of London, spearheaded by eminent actors—whose star power helped to attract the audiences needed to finance these productions. These actors continued to work in films and contemporary productions as a way of financing their dedication to Shakespearean acting (Lamb). In the seven years following the end of the war (1946–53), four productions debuted featuring well-known stars of film and stage in the leading roles, three in London, one in New York. Although three of these four revivals received mixed reviews—alone among these four, the Ashcroft/Redgrave pairing garnered almost universal accolades—the appearance of star power helped to make Shakespeare's controversial play a financial as well as a critical success.

Shaw's 1946 production exemplified the prewar neo-Elizabethan style originally introduced by Bridges-Adams and Atkins: a permanent set, minimal scenery, continuous action, relatively uncut text, modified Veronese-style costumes with Roman and Egyptian accents, and occasional use of transverse curtains (Madelaine). The response to the production was hugely favorable, with most of the reviewers welcoming the permanent set as a means of facilitating entrances, increasing the pace of the action, and imposing continuity on the scattered action of the drama. In the roles of the aging lovers, Edith Evans and Godfrey Tearle, both established stars, excited admiration among critics, although Evans, fifty-seven and playing Cleopatra for the second time, received the mixed triumph that had greeted her first attempt: "she was generally believed to be technically brilliant, always interesting—and miscast" (Lamb 136). Conversely, Tearle's emotional sincerity, his resonant voice, impressive presence, and verse speaking ability won wide approbation from reviewers. The supporting cast also received praise, although some critics found Antony Quayle's Enobarbus unnecessarily deflative.

One year after his success in Shaw's version, Tearle starred again in the play, this time opposite film star Katharine Cornell in a revival directed by her husband Guthrie McClintic, at the Martin Beck Theatre in New York (1947). No neo-Elizabethan production, this mounting was lavishly appointed with gorgeous sets and color-coordinated costumes—red for Egyptians, blue for

Caesar (Leiter 23). This prophetic production, perhaps the first to adapt the play to a topical political agenda, commented negatively on imperialist expansion by presenting "Shakespeare's soldiers as Nazis, Pompey a Göring, Caesar a Baldur von Schirach, the rank and file a squad of heiling stormtroopers," a politicizing that Eric Bentley protested caused the poetry to dwindle into journalism (27). Despite these and other critical cavils—one critic complained that Cornell's elegant, "fastidious" Cleopatra lacked sensuality (Brooks Atkinson; qtd. in Leiter 23), another that Tearle's "lusty, vigorous" Antony captured the debauched warrior better than the passionate lover (Rosamond Gilder; qtd. in Leiter 23)—the revival was a smash success, running 127 performances before touring the country for another 73.

In 1951, Michael Benthall staged *Antony and Cleopatra,* in tandem with Shaw's *Caesar and Cleopatra,* first at the St. James Theatre in London and later at the Ziegfeld Theatre in New York. Featuring superstars Laurence Olivier and his wife, Vivien Leigh, both productions achieved financial and critical success. Benthall offered an innovative solution for the problem of the multitudinous scenes, a revolving stage that transported the audience easily from Rome to Egypt and back again, facilitating the scene changes that had always been a stumbling block for the play with dark marble pillars representing Rome and slender Corinthian ones indicating Egypt. Costume functioned symbolically (as in the McClintic version) with Romans in cobalt blue fighting scarlet-clad Egyptians. In keeping with the modern trend, the text was only minimally cut, with a few important scenes (the Ventidius and Seleucus episodes) omitted to romanticize the two lovers. Although reviewers almost universally acclaimed the overall production, the performances of Olivier and Leigh aroused vigorous debate. Some critics judged her superb Cleopatra one of the best performances of Leigh's career (Barker), insisting that she not only looked glorious but "captured the infinite variety of the ruler of the Nile" (Atkinson 22), while others demurred that she was neither riggish nor regal and lacked classical stature, wishing wistfully that her Cleopatra might have had more variety and intensity (Worsley, "The World Well Lost"; Rylands). Another commentator posed the familiar question of how Cleopatra should be portrayed, noting that Shakespeare's Cleopatra is "hot, bewrinkled, and black-complexioned," whereas Leigh's is "cold, smooth, pale, and dazzlingly beautiful" (see fig. 3). However, this critic ultimately concluded that Leigh's Cleopatra was also extremely intelligent and that this quality proved "an adequate substitute for heat, duskiness, and even wrinkles" (Harold Hobson; qtd. in John Russell Brown 55). Although more enthusiastic in their praise of Antony, critics still had reservations. For some, Olivier was "exactly right to the last hair" (Worsley, "The World Well Lost," 560), whereas others regretted Olivier's reduction of the military warrior to the domestic lover, uxoriously muting his own performance to match that of his wife (Rylands; Speaight, *Shakespeare on Stage*).

The last of the all-star revivals, Glen Byam Shaw's 1953 production at Stratford featuring Peggy Ashcroft and Michael Redgrave, has long been considered a splendid triumph, one of the most successful productions of this controversial play. Reviewers almost universally commended the uncut text with all forty-two scenes retained. They also approved the spare, uncluttered set in which changes of scene were accomplished swiftly and unobtrusively, the clash between Egypt and Rome being created as much by costumes and lighting as by scenery, with the vivid colors of Egypt contrasting sharply with the cool silver and grays of Rome. The focus remained where it should be, on the characters and their actions.

From all reports, the acting was magnificent. In Michael Redgrave, critics at last discovered an Antony who could achieve the multiple dimensions of the part. His striking physical appearance and superb poetic delivery invested Antony with the heroic stature of the great warrior—Cleopatra's "man of men"—whereas his depth and honesty of feeling endowed the role with the passion and inner suffering of the anguished lover. For many reviewers, Redgrave was the definitive Antony (Findlater). Similarly, critics acclaimed Peggy Ashcroft's Cleopatra, but with a difference. Just as reviewers agreed that Redgrave was perfectly suited for Antony, so they also concurred that Ashcroft, diminutive beside Redgrave's towering Antony, was miscast in the role, both in size and temperament (Hobson). Nevertheless, commentators almost unanimously conceded that she overcame these limitations and succeeded splendidly, achieving the infinite variety of the seductive queen, at once riggish, viperish, imperious, sensuous, and regal. A classically British Cleopatra, with pale skin and flaming red ponytail, although adding the innovation of a Greek costume, Ashcroft played the role "not as a wily oriental but as a highly intelligent Greek Ptolemaic queen" (*Picture Post*; qtd. in Madelaine 96), and, according to Madelaine, the widespread acceptance of Ashcroft's intellectual equality with Antony marked a cultural change toward male/female relationships. Michael Billington sums up the critical consensus: "The majority verdict was that Peggy had triumphed over her own temperament and physical limitations to become the Cleopatra of her generation" ("Infinite Variety" 150). Through their bravura performances, Ashcroft and Redgrave captured the play's paradoxical tension between heroic transcendence and ironic deflation and the two actors have long been held up as standards for the roles. As J. C. Trewin effused, "Glen Byam Shaw's production, in the fullest text, rolled forward like the flood waters of the Nile, and Michael Redgrave and Peggy Ashcroft took it at the flood" (233–34).

However, not everyone was convinced. Kenneth Tynan complained that both Ashcroft and Redgrave lacked sensuality, insisting, "There is only one role in *Antony and Cleopatra* ... , which English actresses are naturally equipped to play. This is Octavia, Caesar's docile sister." According to Tynan, "The great sluts of world drama, from Clytemnestra to Anna Christie, have always puzzled our girls; and an English Cleopatra is a contradiction in terms"

Fig. 3. Vivien Leigh as Cleopatra and Laurence Olivier as Antony in Michael Ben-thall's 1951 production of *Antony and Cleopatra* at the St. James Theatre. Angus McBean Photograph, Copyright © The Harvard Theatre Collection, The Houghton Library.

(*Evening Standard*). If Tynan revealed a sexist bias in equating all sexually liberated women with sluts, Richard Findlater projected another kind of patri-archal prejudice in his assessment of Ashcroft's Cleopatra as "too intelligent for such exotically feminine stupidity." Findlater summed up this alleged catch-22 as follows: "no English player, it seems, can act Cleopatra, and no actress of any other nation can speak it" (qtd. in Neill 62).

Repertory Reruns

In 1957, Robert Helpmann staged the last *Antony and Cleopatra* at the Old
Vic before it became the National Theatre, a production primarily remembered
for its Cecil B. De Mille cinematic style—with large sets, blasting fanfares,
and a shapely Cleopatra—and its innovative lighting, which transformed
Egyptian obelisks into Roman columns, thereby accomplishing the shift from
Egypt to Rome through light and shadow rather than through ponderous
scenery. Eschewing the prevailing star system, Helpmann cast young, relatively unknown actors in the leading roles, and the youth of the two leading
players—Margaret Whiting, twenty-three, and Keith Mitchell, thirty—
blurred the poignancy of the aging lovers. Although reviewers criticized both
principal actors for lacking sexual passion, the vivid contrast between the delicate "feminine" Cleopatra and the robust "masculine" Antony stressed the
polarity between "feminine" and "masculine" values that many literary critics
see as central to the play (Madelaine).

Lamb comments that the "establishment of the Royal Shakespeare
Company and the National Theatre, as well as the new prestige and prolifera-
tion of provincial repertory, radically changed the conditions of Shakespearean production in Britain," as the Bard's plays were more often produced
outside of London and Stratford—at Birmingham, Oxford, and Chichester
(155). A similar phenomenon occurred in the flourishing Stratford Festival in
Ontario, Canada, and in Shakespeare festivals throughout America, not only
in New York, but also in California, Colorado, Connecticut, Georgia, Maine,
Oregon, and Washington, D.C., among others.

During the period from 1950 to 1967, the Oregon Shakespeare Festival
(OSF) in Ashland, Oregon, produced an unprecedented three revivals of
Shakespeare's epic tragedy. The 1950 presentation introduced the neo-
Elizabethan mode to American audiences and all three of the productions
adopted this model. The open-air facility in Lithia Park in which the plays
were performed, although not a facsimile of the Globe, Fortune, or any other
Elizabethan playhouse, nevertheless approximates the conditions of Shakespeare's theater. The 1950 version of the play, directed by James Sandoe, also
adapted the minimal scenery and fast pace of the neo-Elizabethan style,
moving breathlessly along without an intermission (Hobart 10). Following the
recommendation of Granville-Barker, the costumes imitated the Renaissance
style in Veronese's paintings with the addition of ethnic accents: modified
togas, classical sandals, armor, and helmets for the Romans; turbans, gold, and
jewels for the Egyptians. The leading actors were universally acclaimed. Don
Gunderson's very young (twenty-three years old) Antony received plaudits for
his vigor, fine voice, remarkable diction, and ability to become "the absolute
soldier" (B. F., Marks, Hobart 10). Although admiration for Gunderson dominated the reviews, critics also commended Clare Daniels as a "stately," "rich-

voiced" Cleopatra, who alternated easily from sovereign queen to brawling hussy (B. F.), and approved Philia Hanson's smug, prissy, thoroughly distasteful Octavius (B. F., Marks, Larson). Nine years later (1959), the OSF reprised its runaway 1950 success, again directed by Sandoe in the neo-Elizabethan style, this time with an equally dynamic Cleopatra and a much older, more world-weary Antony. For one reviewer, Barbara Waide created a Cleopatra of infinite variety—coy, tempestuous, passionate, tricking, railing, always magnificent (Dawkins). "In splendid contrast to the strength and resourcefulness of Cleopatra," Ted Marcuse played Antony as "a middle-aged man who had enjoyed too many gaudy nights.... An ex-hero more sunken than fallen" (Dawkins). If the charismatic young Antony stole the show in the 1950 production, Waide's enchanting queen took center stage in 1959. Also, Nagle Jackson's uncertain, conflicted Octavius departed from tradition to prefigure future complex portrayals of the role (Dawkins). In 1967, the OSF again revived the play in the neo-Elizabethan mode to enthusiastic reviews, this time guided by the skillful hand of Jerry Turner. Generally, critics agreed that it would be difficult to "imagine two people more perfectly suited to these roles than Glen Mazen and Ann Kinsolving" (Bishoff). Although one commentator observed that the fair, slim Glen Mazen resembled a poet or a scholar rather than a powerful general (Mahar), all of the reviewers praised his emotional depth. However, at least one reviewer felt that "[t]he evening belonged to Miss Kinsolving," who, in an unforgettable performance, "skillfully slipped from empress to coquette to jealous lover" (Mahar). In addition, Jackson reprised his complex portrayal of Octavius Caesar. The success of these three productions indicates that in the 1950s and 1960s, Shakespeare was alive and well in American regional theater.

In 1960, perhaps inspired by Joseph Mankiewicz's cinematic extravaganza starring Elizabeth Taylor and Richard Burton, Hollywood came to the Stratford Festival in Connecticut, which revived *Antony and Cleopatra* with magnificent costumes, a spare, abstract set, director Jack Landau, and two Hollywood stars—Kathrarine Hepburn and Robert Ryan—in the leading roles. From all accounts, as one would expect, Hepburn fashioned an intelligent, passionate, regal Egyptian queen, who combined both monarch and strumpet; however, Ryan, whose verse-speaking allegedly left much to be desired, although soldierly and charming, was judged shallow and unaffecting as Antony (Louis Funke, Claire McGlinchee; qtd. in Leiter 28).

In 1963, Joseph Papp staged a decidedly unromantic production of the play for the New York Shakespeare Festival, in which, at least according to one reviewer, Colleen Dewhurst's Cleopatra appeared not to love Michael Higgins's Antony (*Saturday Review*; qtd. in Madelaine 102n187). Moreover, other critics censured her bourgeois portrait that failed to rise above "an ordinary suburban housewife," while also deploring Higgins' "prosaic, puzzled Antony" (Louis Funke, Alice Griffin; qtd. in Leiter 18).

The 1970s were dominated by antiromantic approaches to *Antony and Cleopatra*. On the one hand, these productions accentuated the political aspects of the drama, often at the expense of the romantic elements. On the other hand, many of these stagings deliberately presented small-scale versions of the play that minimized its tragic scope (Neill 57).

Anticipating these trends, Michael Langham's 1967 revival at the Stratford Festival, Ontario, starring Zoe Caldwell and Christopher Plummer, diminished the romantic elements of the tragedy, portraying the two protagonists not primarily as great lovers caught in the throes of irresistible sexual passion but, rather, as political schemers fascinated with the game playing of political intrigue. So highlighted were the political aspects of the play that romance almost got lost, and, as with Dewhurst, one reviewer expressed doubts that Caldwell's Cleopatra really loved Antony. According to this critic, the grand love became "a sophisticated affair pursued as a merry release from the world's sobriety," enjoyed between a hearty, large-souled Antony and a lusty, nymphomaniac Cleopatra (Hewes 22). Another reviewer commented on the metadramatic qualities of the production, which continually reminded the audience that Antony and Cleopatra were players in their own theatrical tour de force (Kerr). The production thus emphasized elements of this many-faceted play obfuscated in most previous presentations but beginning to be stressed in scholarly criticism: particularly, the centrality of both the play's political elements and the self-reflexive theatricality of the lovers. Also, it developed aspects of Helpmann's influential, cinematic staging, whereby scene shifts were achieved primarily by lighting rather than by set changes. However, in its sympathy for Antony, and its reduction of the centrality of Cleopatra, it harkened back to the moralistic criticism of an earlier period.

Peter Dews presented another innovative version of the play at the 1969 Shakespeare Festival in Chichester, England. Although the condensed text, cutting nearly forty minutes of playing time, and somber permanent set, lacking any of the exciting cinematic lighting effects of Langham's staging, recalled early-twentieth-century productions, the ages of the two leading actors—Margaret Leighton, forty-seven, and John Clement, fifty-nine—allowed the production to stress some of the poignant nuances of the play lost in earlier renditions: the disillusionment of middle age, the almost conjugal quarrels, a sense of long domesticity (Madelaine). Nevertheless, the familiar critical refrain emerged: the two principal actors failed to generate the sexual passion required by the roles (Leiter). However, one actor in the production received universal accolades: Keith Baxter as Octavius Caesar. Gone was the icy-cold, manipulative politician of earlier versions, and in his place appeared a young man, who began as a hero-worshipping boy and hardened into an enemy only after Antony's rejection of his beloved sister Octavia. A number of reviewers judged the performance "extraordinarily attractive," the kind of interpretation that permanently altered the conception of the role (Speaight; qtd. in Leiter 30).

The unromantic treatment of the lovers (characteristic of Papp's and Langham's productions) and the centrality of Octavius Caesar (introduced in Dews's presentation) perhaps influenced Ellis Rabb's 1971 revival at the Old Globe Theatre in San Diego, featuring Michael Learned and Ken Ruta. Learned's Cleopatra—as "beautiful, regal, and coolly aloof as Nefertiti's mask"—like Dewhurst and Caldwell, apparently lacked love for her colorless Antony (Horobetz 386). According to Lynn K. Horobetz, Rabb attempted to make "the play seem grand, Herculean, larger than life," but, instead, "the production remained a woodenly, overstaged pageant which never touched the heart" (386).

In 1972, Trevor Nunn presented *Antony and Cleopatra* as part of his saga of the Roman plays. Nunn's revival, the first production of the play to be performed by the newly organized Royal Shakespeare Company and the tragedy's first staging at Stratford since Shaw's much acclaimed triumph in 1953, departed from the tradition of minimal scenery and creative lighting that had dominated the British stage since the neo-Elizabethan productions of the 1920s. Some reviewers applauded the elaborate, hydraulically engineered sets as stunningly picturesque, whereas others criticized the cumbersome machinery as a step backward to the pictorial tradition of the Victorian theater. Nunn's version also followed tradition by using color symbolically to stress the polarities dominating the play, in this case, black, white, and purple for the Romans, pink, mauve, and orange for the Egyptians. Madelaine suggests a connection between the archeological authenticity of both sets and costumes and the worldwide "Egyptomania" accompanying the global tour of the international Tutankhamun exhibit the same year (105).

However, if the magnificent sets harkened back to the pictorial mode of the nineteenth century and Janet Suzman's swarthy, raven-haired Cleopatra recalled the pre-Potter models, in other respects the presentation was very "modern." The production followed Langham's Stratford revival by accentuating both the political elements of the tragedy and the metadramatic nuances, presenting the protagonists as both shrewd political schemers and "monumental actors, who need the presence of an audience" (Tierney 42). Moreover, Suzman accentuated the intelligence rather than the voluptuousness of the Egyptian queen. Reviewers approvingly noted the "touch of masculinity" distinguishing Suzman's Cleopatra, likening her to "an Egyptian Elizabeth I" (Young 3), the "Ptolemaic equivalent of your modern emancipated woman," whom you would expect to catch "reading the *Female Eunuch* rather than dallying with male ones" (Nightingale, "Decline and Growth" 265). On the whole, reviewers agreed that Suzman captured both Cleopatra's strength and her sensuality (compare figs. 4 and 12). Nevertheless, although critics universally praised the breadth and variety of Suzman's Cleopatra, some felt that she was so manipulative that only in act 5 did the audience believe that she truly loved Antony (Tierney). Moreover, some also expressed disappointment at the perceived failure of this South African actor to break from the "innate gentility,"

Fig. 4. Janet Suzman as Cleopatra with her Court (1.5) in Trevor Nunn's 1972 production of *Antony and Cleopatra* at the Memorial Theatre in Stratford-upon-Avon. Photographer Reg Wilson © Royal Shakespeare Company.

which, in their opinions, had hindered so many English actors from encompassing the essence of the role (Hurren 292). However, Suzman's emphasis on Cleopatra's wit and intelligence rather than her eroticism was clearly intentional, and Juliet Dusinberre posits a link between her formidable, even masculine, queen and the emergence in the 1970s of the Women's Liberation movement. Richard Johnson also received mixed reviews. Although some found his Antony very moving, others complained that he was "too much in decline" and that he missed "that residual greatness that might have carried them both to the heights of tragic greatness" (Hurren 292). Critics traced a contradictory progression whereby Antony declined and Cleopatra grew in stature, with many feeling that the play lost its equipoise when Cleopatra became too strong, Antony too weak (Nightingale, "Decline and Growth"). Although many reviewers thought Colin Redgrave's Caesar too cold-blooded and demented (Lewsen; Nightingale, "Decline and Growth"), almost all praised Patrick Stewart's warm and moving Enobarbus (Crick; Hurren; Nightingale, "Decline and Growth"; Tierney). In summary, Nunn's revival was very much an *Antony and Cleopatra* for the 1970s, with its foregrounding of the play's political issues and metadramatic resonance, its emphasis on the tragedy's ambivalence toward the two lovers, and its stress on Cleopatra's centrality, her androgyny, and her similarity to Elizabeth, all issues dominating the scholarship of the 1970s. Both David Fuller and Dorothea Kehler examines Nunn's production from these perspectives later in this volume.

In 1973, the year following Nunn's historically accurate spectacle, Tony Richardson mounted an antithetical version of the play at the Bankside Theater in London. Richardson's staging marked the first totally modern dress production of the play—a strategy employed, according to the director, to comment on "international party politics" (qtd. in Lamb 170)— for although late-nineteenth-century treatments of the tragedy tended to dress the female hero in Victorian attire, these versions always retained some vestiges of Roman armor and Egyptian paraphernalia. The dress code was eclectic. The costumes of Vanessa Redgrave's "decadent imperialist" Cleopatra ran the gauntlet from evening gowns, cocktails sheaths, and fringed robes to a white pantsuit with stiletto heels and a red wig (Lamb 170); Antony, a dandyish, "soldier playboy in khaki uniform," sported a white silk scarf and flashy ring; briefcases and dark glasses transformed the triumvirate into "a trio of back-stabbing businessmen"; and khaki fatigues morphed Pompey's band into Castro guerrillas (Madelaine 109). The production evoked heated debate; reviewers appear to have agreed only on descriptive details and the director's hatred of Cleopatra. However, different as they were, both Nunn's and Richardson's revivals minimized the romantic and maximized the political elements of the playtext.

In 1977, Robert Loper directed the fourth revival of *Antony and Cleopatra* for the Oregon Shakespeare Company. Departing from the neo-Elizabethan strategies of its earlier productions, this version employed spectacular, realistic sets—which some reviewers felt distracted from the action of the drama (Dessen)—and lavish costumes combining the Roman and the Egyptian. The political focus central to the Langham and Nunn productions also dominated Loper's interpretation. Although admiring aspects of the production, one reviewer regretted the lack of inner turmoil and irresistible passion in the portrayal of the lovers, Elizabeth Huddle and Ted D'Arms: "What 'Antony' becomes is a big-statement play about power politics, with— alas—little about the heedless and headstrong lovers who brought about the fall of kingdoms" (Kaufman B6). In keeping with this emphasis, Huddle (like Suzman) depicted a wily, resourceful queen rather than a passionate lover.

Nunn's and Richardson's revivals were followed by a number of productions that, however different in many respects, all attempted a return to the formula of the neo-Elizabethan stagings of the 1920s, which stressed fidelity to the text, minimal scenery, and brisk pace. These productions also sought to diminish the heroic scope of the tragedy and, to varying degrees, to minimize the romantic elements of the play.

In Robin Phillips's 1976 revival at the Stratford Festival in Ontario, the epic drama was enacted on an almost bare stage before a canopied set. However, deviating from tradition, Phillips established a contrast not between Rome and Egypt but between court and camp, with Cleopatra and her retinue clad in long, flowing robes and both armies uniformed in short, white, pleated skirts, which (at least to me, as I attended the play) suggested not so much Roman togas as majorette costumes. Following the trend established by Suzman, Maggie Smith played Cleopatra as highly intelligent rather than sensual, dominant yet vulnerable. She also portrayed the queen as an accomplished actress, a kind of interior director of her own heroic drama, always in control of Antony. Both Keith Baxter (who had scored such a success as Octavius in Dews's Chichester production of the play) and Smith received accolades from reviewers who felt that they captured the mutual fascination of the two egotistical lovers as well as both the comedy and tragedy of their love affair (Berners Jackson). Less successful was Frank Dunlop's revival at the Young Vic the same year, which, like Phillips's version, embraced neo-Elizabethan strategies: full text, brisk pace, and almost bare stage. However, although French actress Delphine Seyrig rendered an intelligent Cleopatra, she "could give only an alert sketch, never letting the great verse rise and shine" (Trewin; qtd. in Madelaine 110n202).

To the familiar neo-Elizabethan formula, Toby Robertson in his 1977 production, first at the Edinburgh Festival and later at the Old Vic, added lavish Elizabethan costumes that contrasted effectively with the simple stage décor. Critics found much to praise in the production but, in an all too familiar refrain, regretted the lack of sexual obsession between the two lovers. Dorothy Tutin, like Suzman and Smith, portrayed a politically adept queen rather than a voluptuous seducer, and Alex McCowen, like the majority of Antonys before him, was more credible as the military leader than as the lover. As so often, commentators agreed that Tutin and McCowen "lacked the requisite stature" and "failed to convey the heroism and passion" that the two roles require (Chaillet; qtd. in Sandra L. Williamson 116; Berkowitz; qtd. in Sandra L. Williamson 115).

The tendency toward downsizing and ironizing the play continued in Peter Brook's 1978 iconoclastic, Kott-influenced production for the Royal Shakespeare Company (RSC). Although some critics lauded Brook's expressive, elegant stage décor, composed of a semicircle of long translucent, plastic panels (Elsom), others found the set to be antiseptic (Wardle, "Antony and Cleopatra"). Moreover, many reviewers grumbled that Brook's antiromantic reading worked against the text (Wardle, "Antony and Cleopatra"; Knoll, "Oh, To Be in England"; Eder). In direct contrast to Nunn, Brook sought to domesticate the tragedy, to present it as a play of private emotion rather than public rhetoric. Glenda Jackson carried the androgynous, liberated Cleopatra of Suzman to an extreme. Mannish and commanding, with her cropped black hair and flowing kaftans, she displayed power and wit but little vulnerability, passion, or sensuality (Wardle, "Antony and Cleopatra"). Although some critics liked Alan Howard's athletic, "strong," and "eloquent" Antony (Blumenthal 112), others found his portrait "effete," "absurd," and "childish" (Watters 27; Kennedy 423). Like so many Antonys before him, Howard was judged more convincing as a warrior than a lover, and both of the protagonists were criticized as too egotistical and narcissistic (Elsom; Wardle, *Antony and Cleopatra*). Perversely, Brook reversed expectations to associate Rome with warm generous feeling and Egypt with coldness and manipulation. Developing the interpretation introduced by Baxter in 1969, Jonathan Pryce portrayed Octavius as a gentle and affectionate brother to Octavia and comrade to Antony, who develops from a hero-worshipping adolescent to a disillusioned enemy when his idol betrays him (Watters; Trewin, "Shakespeare in Britain"). Patrick Stewart also confounded expectation, playing Enobarbus not as a detached, cynical observer, but as a warm and feeling companion to Antony (Elsom).

The trend toward scaling down Shakespeare's grandest tragedy reached its zenith in Adrian Noble's 1982 revival for the RSC. This tendency may have been partially ideological—expressing the antiheroic *zeitgeist* of the 1970s and 1980s—and partially pragmatic—revealing the financial exigencies of theatre production. At any rate, Shakespeare's grandest tragedy was enacted on the miniscule stage of The Other Place at Stratford (and later at the equally tiny London Pit) with virtually no set, the changes in scene and the contrast between Rome and Egypt being essentially accomplished by lighting and costume, with the Romans dressed in austere, uniform-like outfits and a blond, bare-footed Cleopatra clad in extravagant gold with her women in multicolored silks (Madelaine). The performances of the principal actors, like the scaled down staging, drew mixed responses. Some reviewers praised Michael Gambon's aging roué (Russell Jackson 108–09; qtd. in Sandra L. Williamson 117)—although others found him an unusually cold and unconvincing lover (Warren, "Shakespeare in England, 1982–83" 337). And although critics responded more favorably to Helen Mirren's "willful, sexy, commanding" Cleopatra (Russell Jackson 108–09; qtd. in Sandra L. Williamson 117), particularly her death scene with its hints of dementia (Burrows; qtd. in Sandra L. Williamson 116), on the whole, they felt that Mirren captured Cleopatra's sensuality but not her majesty. Moreover, Mirren's stress on Cleopatra's insecurity reflected the tendency in literary criticism to see the Egyptian queen as vulnerable and sympathetic, trying desperately to hold on to her man in the face of age and political reversal. Jonathan Hyde's "impassioned Octavius" developed the trend introduced by Keith Baxter, with his affectionate treatment of Octavia offering a "huge contrast" to "Antony's perfunctory treatment of Cleopatra" (Warren, "Shakespeare in England, 1982–83" 337).

Like Noble's revival at The Other Place, the production at the Nottingham Playhouse the same year eschewed spectacle and pageantry in favor of

simplicity and austerity to present an equally antiheroic and ironic interpretation of the play. The action was presented before a huge screen on which was
projected an unchanging cloudscape and nothing else. Rome and Egypt were
indistinguishable, as a similar set was used for both locales and both factions
wore black, thus obliterating any possibility of contrast between the two. This
production carried the minimalist style to an extreme, obliterating even the
use of props (Warren, "Shakespeare in England, 1982–83" 336).

Maintaining the popular neo-Elizabethan pattern, Robin Phillips's 1985
revival in Chichester nevertheless deviated from the pervasive anti-heroic
mode in an attempt to reromanticize the lovers, excising episodes that might
detract from their heroic stature (the galley scene, the Seleucus scene, and the
false report of Cleopatra's death). Nevertheless, Phillips's surgery failed to
achieve its goal and most reviewers felt that the lovers—Diana Rigg and
Denis Quilley—continued to appear small-scale and unheroic, their affair
constituting not a world-shaking event but "a storm in a teapot" (Peters; qtd.
in Madelaine 120). Like so many Cleopatras before her, Rigg was considered
too British to capture the eroticism of the role. Some reviewers felt that in
keeping with the modern fashion, Octavius and Enobarbus were played with
greater complexity than the two protagonists, while one reviewer grumbled
that the flimsy white costumes worn by both Romans and Egyptians created
"a clinical, almost antiseptic feel to the Egyptian court, removing any hint of
hedonistic luxury, and failing to suggest any contrast with Rome" (Warren,
"Shakespeare in Britain, 1985," 119).

Perhaps reacting to the extreme minimalism of the Brook and Noble
revivals, a number of productions in the 1980s introduced large-scale images
to emphasize the decay of the heroic while simultaneously stressing the
middle-aged fantasies of the lovers (Madelaine 119). One of the first productions to reflect this approach, Keith Hack's 1983 presentation at the Old Vic,
employed a giant headless statue of a warrior in gold robes—Mars? Hercules?
Antony?—as a backdrop, with the change of scenes accomplished by creative
lighting. Keith Baxter, returning to the role after his teaming with Maggie
Smith in 1977, created a grizzled, swaggering, definitely middle-aged Antony.
Judy Parfitt, like Mirren, stressed Cleopatra's insecurity, portraying a very
English, middle-aged Cleopatra, whose "defiant pale make-up and blaze of
auburn curls" concealed "a frightened woman clutching on to the glories of
her own myth" (Jack Tinker; qtd. in Madelaine 119n217). Brian Deacon
followed Baxter and Hyde by making Octavius "most expressive and even
attractive" (Michael Coveney; qtd. in Madelaine 120).

Developing the template set by Hack at the Old Vic, Toby Robertson's
1986 production at the Haymarket employed a huge, dilapidated rotunda with
doorways and arches to symbolize the imperial decay of both Rome and its
renegade leader Antony. The most controversial aspect of the production,
Vanessa Redgrave's Cleopatra (her second opportunity), aroused both critical

ire and approval. Many reviewers found Redgrave's "middle-aged punk tomboy"—in some respects resembling the boy actor who originally played the role—too shrill and lacking majesty (Peters 49; qtd. in Sandra L. Williamson 118), while others praised her "vain, arrogant, androgynous" queen (Wardle, "Grandeur in a Mocking Grimace" 19). Most agreed that her "rampant, sexy, crewcut" Cleopatra totally overshadowed her rather weak, naive Antony (Morley; qtd. in Sandra L. Williamson 118).

Two productions in the 1980s and 1990s departed from the trend toward both down-sizing and ironizing the play—Peter Hall's for the National Theatre (1987) and John Caird's for the Royal Shakespeare Company (1992). Both plays were successful, critically and financially; fortunately, I had the privilege of seeing both of these memorable productions.

Hall's revival of *Antony and Cleopatra*, starring stage legends Judi Dench and Anthony Hopkins, aroused fervent enthusiasm from both critics and audiences. The components of designer Ailson Chitty's great, bronzed, crescent-shaped structure shifted and merged into different scenic configurations suggesting Renaissance paintings with the fluidity of the cinema, while never detracting from the action of the drama (Stanley Wells). Following tradition, the costumes, combining Renaissance and Roman in a style reminiscent of Veronese, were color-coded, with warm reds and browns for Egypt, cool blues and greens for Rome. Although most of the reviewers commended the stage design, as they praised all aspects of this remarkable production, a few felt that the unlocalized setting blurred the dominant clash between Rome and Egypt, substituting instead the contrast between the heroic ideal and the often less-than-heroic reality (Wardle, "Electrifying Detail" 14). The text, virtually uncut, ran four hours; however, the rapt audience that shared this riveting experience with me gave witness that, properly performed, Shakespeare need not be pared to cater to an attention-deficit audience.

Many reviewers concluded that this was the definitive *Antony and Cleopatra* for our time, at least since the Ashcroft/Redgrave pairing. Acclaiming Dench and Hopkins, one critic rejoiced, "for the first time in living memory, the English stage has two actors capable of doing full justice to the roles" (Wardle, "Electrifying Detail" 14), while another extolled their "two massive but golden performances from a golden age" (Peters, "Renaissance of the Golden Age" 55). Commentators agreed that one reason for the play's splendid poignancy—in addition to the brilliant speaking of the verse—was the disparity it presented between the ideal and the real, a discrepancy accentuated by the unconventional physical appearance of these two defiantly middle-aged actors; as one critic phrased it, the production "is about two 'middle-aged' people—carnal, deceitful, often sad—seeking in love a reality greater than themselves" (Billington; qtd. in Madelaine 123). Most reviewers granted that the drama achieved a brilliant balance between the heroic and the ironic, asserting the ideal in the very act of denying it (Warren, "Shakespeare in England, 1986–87"). Dench, in particular, inspired hyperbole as she laid to rest, hopefully forever, the hoary view that no British actor could play this incredibly difficult role. Reviewers, with only one exception that I have found, agreed that Dench's Cleopatra magnificently merged the "impossible" variety that Shakespeare had written into the role—the comic, the shrewish, the passionate, the majestic; that exception, Barbara Everett found both Dench and Hopkins "just too nice, too sympathetic" (439). However, the majority of critics assented that Dench achieved the full possibilities of the role, dying with matchless majesty as she, like Hamlet, was carried from the stage on the shoulders of the soldiers (Warren, "Shakespeare in England, 1986–87"). Although praising Hopkins's "affectionate, exhausted, and introspective old lion" (Ratcliffe 18), some critics judged him overshadowed by the superb Dench. This was perhaps inevitable, since from the opening tableau when Antony entered carried piggyback by Mardian, who was yanked along by Cleopatra at the end of a rope, until his death when he was again hefted to die in his beloved's arms, Cleopatra dominated the drama. Reviewers also praised the entire ensemble, particularly Tim Piggot-Smith's sympathetic Octavius and Michael Bryant's blunt but lyrical Enobarbus. On the whole, critics concurred that it was a play for all seasons. David Fuller discusses this production in detail in his essay in this collection.

John Caird's 1992 production for the Stratford Memorial Theatre, like Hall's revival, staged a drama of middle-aged love, and, like Hall's version, represented a reaction against the modern proclivity to minimize both the scope of the play and the stature of its protagonists. Using a large flexible set of sliding walls depicting crumbling masonry, massive stone monuments, and a pyramid that pulled apart to reveal the warm blue sky of Egypt and slid together to create the indoor claustrophobia of Rome, the staging established an effective contrast between the two locales, a contrast accentuated by the traditional costumes: Romans in crested helmets and leather skirts, Cleopatra and her ladies in clingy dresses accented with "Tutankamen gold and blue" (Smallwood 354). Caird's rendition revived the romantic transcendence that distinguished the Olivier version. Like Hall, Caird conceived of the play as primarily concerned with middle-aged passion, but whereas Hall accentuated the disparity between the lovers' transcendent dream and their more prosaic reality, Caird idealized the dream. He achieved this by omitting episodes that detracted from the romance of the play (e.g., the Ventidius and Seleucus scenes) while interpolating a final apotheosis in which after their deaths the walls parted and the lovers embraced in silhouette. Moreover, Caird staged the coronation of the lovers and their children recounted in act 3, scene 6 in a mode that harkened back to the pictorial tradition of the nineteenth century (Madelaine). The role of Antony marked Richard Johnson's return to the London stage after a twenty-year hiatus (his last performance being Antony in Nunn's 1972 production), and at least one reviewer felt that his efforts to "recapture his past" added a "touching poignancy" to his performance as the aging general engaged throughout the play in the same endeavor (Smallwood 354). Although some commentators lauded Clare Higgins's incisively intelligent, infinitely varied Cleopatra (Edmonds, "Infinite Variety Keeps This Affair Fresh"; Holland; Nightingale, "Infinite Variety"), others predictably found the lovers lacking sensuality and passion. Moreover, several reviewers complained about the omnipresent, spooky soothsayer who hovered over the production, even taking the role of the Clown who brings the asps in the last scene (Nightingale, "Infinite Variety"). In a gesture toward modernity, the play featured a black Iras and a sympathetic Octavius.

Experimental Stagings

Tony Richardson in his 1973 revival at the Bankside Theatre presented the first genuinely outrageous staging of the play. The genie was out of the bottle and, in the following three decades, experimental treatments of the play proliferated. Not all of these experiments were equally effective. One of the most bizarre, Robert Colonna's 1979 production for the Rhode Island Shakespeare Theatre, staged the play in a Berlin cabaret sometime between World War I and World War II. While the setting suggested *Cabaret*, the costumes recalled *Guys and Dolls*, complete with gangsters (Octavius and his cronies) and dancing flappers (Charmian and Iras). Despite—or perhaps because of— these novel effects, the lovers, like more traditional Antonys and Cleopatras, apparently failed to achieve requisite depth and passion (Leiter 186). Another very experimental version of the play, Rex Cramphorn's 1984 revival at the Playbox in Melbourne, Australia, configured the play's many scenes by reassembling three mobile steel platforms on wheels, which were used to represent battering rams in scenes of combat, draped with curtains to compose Cleopatra's monument, and festooned with paper ships to create a miniature sea battle. However, although the giant set dwarfed the actors, even the experimental décor was upstaged by real four-foot pythons substituting for asps. Reviewers applauded the "irresistible zest" of Linday Davis's volatile yet maternal Cleopatra, while regretting the intrusion of both set and live props on what might otherwise have been a rewarding production (Heales and Bartholomeusz 483–84; Leiter).

Less radical, perhaps, but still very much a contemporary *Antony and Cleopatra*—with its political emphasis and its androgynous, yet seductive tomboy Cleopatra—Charles Towers's 1993 version for the Oregon Shakespeare Company contrasted sharply with the company's earlier neo-Elizabethan revivals and also with its 1977 spectacle. Rejecting the opulent costumes of previous presentations, Towers had all his characters "dress down." One critic complained that "The Romans march[ed] about in designer Candice Cain's drab, dun-colored martial togs," whereas the allure of Megan

Cole's "tanned, sinewy Queen of the Nile," who clearly spent "more time at the gym than lolling in a milk bath," was hampered by her shag haircut and unisex togs (Berson F6). Another reviewer suggested that the costumes made a political statement, asserting that since the production is all about the piti-less exercise of power, "It's no wonder designer Candice Cain has cloaked the Roman triumvirate and their fellows in anonymous, corporate-look uniforms of undecorated brown" (Winn). According to commentators, Henry Woronicz played Antony, as "the eternal adolescent, superabundantly energetic and vastly moody" (Adcock) and Cole's Cleopatra was "almost campy in its show-boat grandeur" (Winn), a "leaping, prowling temptress," "a sexual explosion in a frightened and unforgiving world: a riot of corn rows for her hair, a flim-sily flowing white frock, bare thighs and outthrust breasts, bangles against dark-honey flesh" (Hicks; see fig. 5). However, despite the decidedly sexy Cleopatra, some critics regretted the lack of romantic electricity between the paramours, who, one commentator complained, seemed more like "competi-tive siblings than red-hot lovers" (Berson F6).

In this atmosphere of experimentation, even the venerated RSC got into the act. Steven Pimlott's 1999 revival at the RSC never allowed the audience to forget that they were attending a play and never let them accept the lovers' heroic dreams as a reality. The iconoclastic staging included piles of props, the kinds of paraphernalia normally associated with this play—standards, weapons, feathered fans, and cushions—stacked on either side of the stage as Brechtian reminders to the audience that they were watching a drama about Rome and Egypt. However, the play itself eschewed these traditional artifacts, instead setting the action in a contemporary Alexandria nightclub with cocktail glasses and cigarettes instead of fans and ankhs. The production developed the familiar theme of middle-aged lovers enjoying the last fling of their amorous careers, opening the action with Antony performing cunnilingus on Cleopatra amid a jaded nightclub crowd. According to one reviewer, Frances de la Tour's Cleopatra was not beautiful in any conventional sense but was commanding and powerful, "rawly passionate" and broadly comic, and certainly neither too British nor too nice to play the erotic queen (Russell Jackson, "Shakespeare at Stratford, 1999–2000" 222). Others caviled that both Alan Bates and de la Tour sidestepped grandeur (see fig. 13), portraying not great, mythic lovers but a middle-class, middle-aged couple confronting mid-life crises (Edmonds, "Fine Romance"; Taylor, "Misplaced Imagination"). Bates's Antony was generally conceded to be "amiable, ener-getic, but unheroic," whereas Malcolm Storry's warm and witty Enobarbus presented the more convincing warrior and, according to some, stole the show (Russell Jackson, "Shakespeare at Stratford, 1999–2000" 222; Billington). In one of the production's most controversial gestures, Cleopatra donned a magnificent robe for her suicide, then after her "death" discarded the garment and left the stage completely naked. Developing the association of clothes

Fig. 5. Megan Cole as Cleopatra and Henry Woronicz as Antony in Charles Towers's 1993 production of *Antony and Cleopatra* at the Oregon Shakespeare Festival. Photographer Christopher Briscoe; courtesy of the Oregon Shakespeare Festival.

with corporality, Enobarbus exited after his death, leaving his jacket behind. For a fuller discussion of this iconoclastic production and its relationship to the Indian practice of *sati*, see Dorothea Kehler's essay in this volume.

In the very same year, the Globe Theatre in London essayed another, very different kind of experiment. Carrying the dedication to neo-Elizabethan staging to its logical conclusion, director Giles Block's attempted to reproduce the circumstance of the play's original production even to the point of using an all-male cast to perform the play. In doing so, Block bucked the modern ironizing trend to present the drama as the triumph of a gloriously human couple. Commentators generally applauded Mark Rylance's Cleopatra, often played barefoot and dressed like a gypsy (see fig. 16); according to one, here was a queen who "really did look as if she might decide to hop forty paces through the public street" (Potter 514), while another argued that Rylance's sex became an asset, rather than a detriment, in the role, positing that a transvestite Cleopatra can enhance the audience's sense of the queen "as a fluid and compulsive actress who has enjoyed playing drunken gender-bending games with her lover and who always, even as she goes to her final, glorious apotheosis, keeps you guessing about the exact degree of seriousness behind the role-play" (Taylor, "Review of Globe *Antony and Cleopatra*" 9). Somewhat more qualified, another reviewer praised Rylance's performance as "animated" and "captivating," although almost "over the top" in its camp/comic exuberance, at least until Cleopatra's suicide scene (Gandrow 123). In an inversion of traditional interpretations, in this production Antony, rather than Cleopatra, became the love object of both Cleopatra and Enobarbus, and Cleopatra, not Antony, assumed the role of the deeply divided individual, who grew and developed throughout the play, as literary critics like L. T. Fitz insist that she should. Conversely, Paul Shelley's Antony was portrayed as a man of instinct, passion, and generosity. Among the all-male cast, John McEnery presented an admirable and complex Enobarbus and Danny Sapani a wonderfully comic black Charmian. Conversely, in a deviation from current precedents, Ben Walden's Octavius lacked complexity (Potter). Block discusses this highly successful experiment in his interview with Georgia E. Brown in this anthology.

Interracial Casting

One of the most daring of these early experiments was Estelle Parsons's Off-Off-Broadway mounting at the Interart Theatre in 1979, which employed unexpected alienation devices to highlight significant aspects of the tragedy. This revival employed both modern dress and bilingual dialogue, casting Hispanic actors speaking their lines in Spanish as the Romans, and fair-skinned actors delivering their lines in English as the Egyptians. The linguistic contrast foregrounded the issue of "cultural otherness," while the reversal of conventional expectations demystified cultural dominance. According to reviewers, Kathleen Gaffney portrayed a "gorgeous," sexy Cleopatra, bare-breasted in her suicide, and Francisco Prado presented a "super-macho" Antony, with the erotic sparks crackling in the scenes between the two lovers (Leiter 20), something rare in performances of the play.

Throughout the production history of Shakespeare's epic tragedy, directors have tended to ignore Cleopatra's wry description of herself, "I am with Pheobus' amorous pinches black and wrinkled deep in time," portraying the Egyptian queen with either porcelain skin and flaming hair or a "tawny front" and straight black wig. However, during the 1980s and 1990s, a number of revivals heeded Shakespeare's script and cast black actors in the role of Cleopatra. As far as I can discover, the 1986 production by Shakespeare & Company of Lenox, Massachusetts, was the first version of the play to respond to the growing critical awareness of the African nature of Cleopatra and her court, featuring "black, sensual, bewitching Michele Shay and pale, grizzled, eloquent Richard Oberlin" in the leading roles, flanked by an excellent acting ensemble (see fig. 6). Although reviewers lauded the spectacle of "trampling phalanxes of Roman soldiers, gory clashes of arms, the billowing sails in sea battles, and bloody, emotional death scenes," Shay's Cleopatra—sexual, "arrogant, arbitrary, duplicitous, but also bluntly honest"—clearly stole the show (Johnson D7).

Apparently less successful, the Los Angeles Center 1987 production also cast a black actor, Rosalind Cash, as Cleopatra. As so frequently, critics complained that the actors playing Antony and Cleopatra failed to portray the passion expected of the fabled lovers, protesting that the show "goes through the motions, but its life signs are nil," since the director "hasn't found a way to put his two stars in the same play" (Dan Sullivan; qtd. in Royster 111).

A year later in 1988, Michael Kahn's production for the Shakespeare Theatre, performed at the Folger Theatre in Washington, DC, not only cast black actor Francehelle Dorn as Cleopatra, but also peopled the entire Egyptian court with black actors, thus attempting to stress the cultural clash between Rome and Egypt in racial terms. The experiment received mixed reviews. Although Dorn's "sensuous, seductive" Cleopatra was generally much admired (Erstein E3), one reviewer complained that Dorn's naturalistic acting style differed so strikingly from the "Edwardian orotundity" of Kenneth Haigh's Antony that the Rome-Egypt cultural contrast was reduced to a clash of acting styles (Neill 65). Another critic, although agreeing that Haigh and Dorn were "out of kilter" and never seemed to generate an "explosive chemistry," placed the blame firmly on Haigh's Antony, arguing that while Dorn had "never looked quite so ravishing or exercised such exotic appeal," Haigh's Antony seemed "to be nurturing a hangover, rather than a grand passion" (Richards C13). The staging of the play also generated controversy. While one reviewer praised Michael Kahn's ability "to represent the

Fig. 6. Michele Shay as Cleopatra and Robert Oberlin as Antony in Tina Packer's 1986 production of *Antony and Cleopatra* for Shakespeare & Company. Courtesy of Shakespeare & Company, Lenox, Massachusetts, photo by Richard M. Feldman.

exotica of Alexandria and the formality of Rome with a vest-pocket grandeur" (Erstein), others faulted the director's solutions to the monumental staging challenges offered by the play. Critics were particularly chagrined at the director's attempt to stage the Battle of Actium through the use of miniature ships floating on a small pool of water, through which the lovers dejectedly waded after Antony's defeat, embracing amid the toy armada (Rousuck).

Pauline Black, the first black British actor to perform the role of

Cleopatra, appeared in a radically adapted version of Shakespeare's play entitled *Cleopatra and Antony* presented by the Actors Touring Company at the Lyric Studios in Hammersmith in 1989. Although panned by critics, this experiment reflected the modern tendency in literary criticism to place Cleopatra center stage and accept her as the protagonist of the tragedy. Also, Black's portrayal epitomized the trend in both scholarship and production (beginning with Suzman and continuing through Smith, Jackson, and Redgrave) to stress Cleopatra's androgyny and to present her not simply as the traditional siren but as a highly intelligent politician, perhaps inspired by Queen Elizabeth. In the most radically cut version since the days of "unaBridges-Adams," this production omitted most of the Roman episodes in order to concentrate on Cleopatra and Egypt, while interpolating scenes from Plutarch and Dryden. Critics generally praised Black as both majestic and erotic, while finding Patrick Wilde, who doubled as the Clown, a weak Antony, but then that was part of the conception. On the whole, reviewers dubbed the effort stimulating but "misjudged" (Madelaine 129–30).

Vanessa Redgrave's 1995 production at the Riverside Studio expanded the concept of interracial casting, including a Vietnamese Charmian, a Bosnian Iras, and an African American Antony. Except for Pompey and Lepidus (themselves victims of imperial Rome), all the Romans were played by black actors in a reversal of traditional associations of dominance and exploitation that recalled Parsons's revival for the Interart Theatre in 1979. Clearly, Redgrave wished to highlight the "contemporary resonance of this powerful political drama" with its portrayal of colonialism and invasion, a motif accentuated by the grim, vast set that reminded reviewers of Bosnia. However, Redgrave's multiracial version aroused negative critical responses primarily on the grounds that the mixture of accents distracted from the action of the drama and that the verse was not well delivered. Like so many other Antonys and Cleopatras, Redgrave and her Antony Paul Butler were censured for lack of passion, with the warmth and feeling rather incongruously transferred to Enobarbus (Madelaine 135).

Even more innovative was the 1996 collaboration between the Moving Theatre (directed by Colin and Vanessa Redgrave) and the Alley Theatre in Houston, Texas. Following neo-Elizabethan conventions, the production used a simple set and Elizabethan costumes, except that Redgrave's Cleopatra generally wore masculine attire, only deviating from this practice in two scenes—one of these the messenger scene (the episode that, scholars argue, closely correlates with events in the life of Elizabeth I), when her costume and hair style mimicked portraits of Queen Elizabeth (see fig. 7)—thereby "emphasizing Shakespeare's chutzpah as he drew parallels between Elizabeth I and his Caesars and Cleos" (Knoll, "Deep in the Heart of Texas" 82). Although Redgrave's pale-skinned, red-haired Cleopatra followed British tradition, the otherwise iconoclastic production, like the earlier staging at the

Riverside Studios, reversed expectations by casting the Romans (including Antony) with dark-skinned actors (African American or West Indian) and the Egyptians with fair ones. The mélange of different races, different accents, and different acting styles added to the internationalism of the production. Although some critics found this pastiche confusing, at least one lauded the production as fresh and illuminating (Greenwald) and others praised Redgrave's "epic volatility" and her "radiant combination of girlish breathlessness and ripe, all-consuming eroticism" (Knoll, "Deep in the Heart of Texas" 82; Brantley).

Downsized Shakespeare

The Talawa Theatre Company at the Bloomsbury Theatre in London staged the first all-black British production of the play in 1991, thus negating the cultural clash implied by a multiracial casting. As in neo-Elizabethan productions, the scenery was simple—a few cushions and rugs represented Egypt, metal furniture suggested Rome. Costumes also functioned symbolically: white shifts and ballet slippers for Cleopatra and her women and identical body warmers for both Antony and Octavius. The text was drastically cut and the characters were amalgamated to accommodate the small cast, which

Fig. 7. Shelley Williams as Charmian, Vanessa Redgrave as Cleopatra, Jeffrey Bean as Mardian, and Monica Koskey as Iras in the scene with the Messenger (2.5) in Vanessa Redgrave's 1995 production of *Antony and Cleopatra* at the Alley Theatre, Houston, Texas. Courtesy of Jim Caldwell, Photographer.

totaled fifteen. According to one critic, "the play has been pruned, characters amalgamated and even unsexed" (Martin Hoyle; qtd. in Royster 110).

Tony Hegarty's 1991 presentation for the Commonwealth Theatre Company, first at the Shaw Theatre in London and later on tour, further accentuated this downsizing trend, drastically abridging the text and doughtily doubling the cast. The production economically contrasted Rome and Egypt by means of "panels of Roman numerals and Egyptian hieroglyphics." One result of this minimizing was the miming of props, which many critics found distracting. Moreover, as so often, reviewers regretted both Antony and Cleopatra's lack of passion and heroic stature (Madelaine 131).

Wayne Harrison and Philip Parsons's 1992 revival at the Wharf Theatre in Sidney, Australia, carried the neo-Elizabethan movement to its logical conclusion: reproduce the working conditions of an Elizabethan repertory company. These conditions included "a small company" with much doubling, "a short rehearsal period," and "a raised stage in an equally lit auditorium in which the audience was encouraged to mix freely and take refreshments." This version also employed eclectic costumes—a mixture of the contemporary and the historical—an almost uncut text, a brisk pace, and competent actors (Madelaine 132).

Also developing the minimalist trend dominating late-twentieth-century productions, Barrie Rutter set his 1995 production for the Northern Broadsides Company in the basement of a transformed carpet factory, amid ancient flagstones, brick tunnel, and rust-red steel girders. "On a stage bare except for a draped rostrum and cushions, Egypt was indicated by attendants in orange and red and Rome by functionaries in blue suits" (Madelaine). Rutter's Antony sported orange and fawn to stress his allegiance to Egypt; Ishia Bennison's Cleopatra lounged in white lace bodice and orange slacks; and Octavia wore a prim blue suit. Reviewers enjoyed the energetic, sinewy acting of the entire cast, observing that the flinty atmosphere allowed the poetry of the play to soar (Madelaine; Holland). According to one reviewer, "*Antony and Cleopatra* is a frighteningly difficult play to stage well: by the simplest means and the utmost trusting of the text, Northern Broadsides achieved far more than most" (Holland 236).

Postmillennium Productions

Despite the many experiments proliferating throughout the past three decades, Poel and Granville-Barker continue to rule the new millennium. Returning to the neo-Elizabethan style that had dominated twentieth-century productions and departing from the opulence of Nunn's and Caird's revivals and the experiments of Pimlott, Michael Attenborough's 2002 production for the Royal Shakespeare Company used minimal props and set to present an ironic, antiheroic *Antony and Cleopatra*. Few reviewers liked the set, which consisted of a map of the world suspended above the action, featuring what one critic described as a "prude's version of a brothel" for Egypt (replete with hookahs and cushions) foiling a bleached and arid Rome (Clapp). Although several critics expressed reservations about Stuart Wilson's aging rock star Antony, sporting braided hair and beads, many applauded Sinead Cusuck's tough and tender Cleopatra, finding her glamorous, volatile, and queenly (Billington; Nightingale, "Volatile Cleopatra"). However, one reviewer judged the lovers—"a grizzled old salt" and a "lethal Lady Macbeth"—ill-equipped to convey the out-of-control passion that feeds the play (Clapp), while others reiterated the familiar complaint that the chemistry between the two lovers failed to ignite (Spencer; Taylor).

I attended another postmillennium neo-Elizabethan staging of the play at the Stratford Festival of Canada (2003). In this production, the action of the tragedy revolved around a steel monument in the shape of a pyramid and achieved its changes of place through the consistent reconfiguration of eight inverted pyramid-like stools, with the *de rigueur* contrast between Rome and Egypt created primarily though color-coded costumes authentic to the period of the play's setting. With a few exceptions, the cast was excellent. Diane D'Aquile and Peter Donaldson, like so many contemporary Cleopatras and Antonys, played the lovers as aging paramours engaged in their last great romance, fighting not only Caesar and his legions but that more indomitable enemy—age. D'Aquile—alternately riggish, raffish, shrewish, funny, regal, and tender, but first and foremost the actor—never dropped her histrionic mask until the death of Antony, when shedding both her wig and her thespian role, she became the feeling, caring woman that she had repressed throughout the earlier acts. Conversely, Donaldson played Antony with a fierce sincerity, capturing both the dignity and suffering of the tormented soldier/lover. However, despite their fine performances, D'Aquile and Donaldson, like so many of the doomed lovers before them, failed to generate the sexual magnetism associated with their roles, and, quite surprisingly, despite the many cues in the text, the lovers never kissed on the lips. Moreover, Paul Dunn failed to achieve the complexity associated with contemporary interpretations of Octavius; instead, he portrayed Antony's rival not as an icy, calculating Machiavel or as a disillusioned young ally turned enemy but simply as a bland bureaucrat.

Foreign Language Shakespeare

Even as Sarah Bernhardt mimicked Cora Potters's vampish Cleopatra, so more recent non-English productions of the play have followed the patterns and trends of their English counterparts. Thus, exaggerating the political aspects highlighted in so many British revivals of the 1970s, Evgenii Simonov's 1971 production at the Vanhtangoc Theatre in Moscow, translated by Boris

Pasternak and starring Luliana Borisova as Cleopatra and Mikhail Ul'ianov as Antony, transformed Shakespeare's epic tragedy into a cautionary Soviet fable. This adaptation presented Antony as the titan whose affiliation to Roman honor contrasted starkly with Caesar's shifting *Realpolitik,* and Cleopatra as the untamed, meddlesome woman who fractured male bonds. The climactic death of Antony served as catalyst to the *anagnorises* of both Cleopatra and Caesar: only after Antony's death did Cleopatra realize how much she loved the noble general and only then did the two sinners (Cleopatra and Caesar) accept and eulogize Antony's greatness (Makaryk).

Aft Sjöberg's 1975 staging of the play at the Royal Dramatic Theatre in Stockholm further developed both the antiromantic emphasis and the minimalist staging that dominated English productions in the 1970s. Employing the cinematic techniques popularized by Helpmann and Langham, Sjöberg's production employed a stark, almost bare stage and sophisticated lighting to transform Shakespeare's epic romance into an unheroic existential journey of self-discovery by two tormented Strindbergian pilgrims. Ulla Sjöblom as Cleopatra and Ånders Ek as Antony shared an existential soul sickness and an alienation from the "new, cold, and realistic" age of Caesar, the "archetypical Puritan." However, in the much-debated monument scene, the "elevated" Antony achieved redemption in Cleopatra's arms, and the death of both lovers became an existential affirmation of freedom (Leiter 32–33).

Senda Koreya's revival at the National Theatre in Tokyo in 1979, instead of following contemporaneous trends, returned to the practice of the eighteenth century by interpolating three new scenes into the text to explain Cleopatra's deliberately obscured motivation. However, this attempt to resolve Shakespeare's notorious ambiguity was not deemed a success (Leiter 20).

In the spring of 1984, China experienced its first production of *Antony and Cleopatra*, performed by the Shanghai Youth Theatre. East met West in Hu Wei Min's provocative staging, which combined the stylization of classic Chinese opera with the naturalism of the Stanislavsky method, and despite the incongruities resulting from this clash of cultures, at least one critic pronounced the production a success. According to Arthur Gerwirtz, Jiao Huang created a larger-than-life Antony, whose craggy face eloquently reflected his "pain and puzzlement," whereas Li Jia-yao's Octavius, "cool, sure, clear headed, served as a foil for the emotional, uncertain, baffled Antony." Li Yuan-yuan at twenty-three was apparently too young for the role, and although she invested her queen with ample energy, she failed to project Cleopatra's "queenliness, guile, or ripeness." Hu's interpretation stressed the contrast between Rome—with its search for power without humanity—and Egypt— with its "warmth, intimacy, and generosity," an opposition that Hu finds relevant to world politics today (Gerwirtz 237).

Equally radical but more successful, Peter Zadek's 1994 adaptation, first mounted at the Edinburgh Festival and later transferred to Berlin and Vienna, was presented in German (with English subtitles in Edinburgh). The action occurred in a colonial world with Romans dressed in frock coats, soldiers sporting pith helmets, Antony—"looking like Lawrence of Arabia"—wearing long flowing robes and turbans over a khaki uniform (Madelaine 144) and Cleopatra and her court scantily clad in flowing garments "straight out of some Hollywood epic" (Spencer; qtd. in Madelaine 134). Anachronisms abounded to stress the political topicality of the play, and the performances of the principal actors—Gert Voss's "reckless hedonist ready to satisfy a sexual itch" and Eva Mattes's "restless nympho" (Billington; qtd. in Madelaine 135)—although highly praised, further developed the modern tendency to debunk the great lovers.

Departing from the antiromantic trend of so many modern productions, Peter Stein's 1994 staging of the play for the Salzburg Festival reinforced the revival of romanticism epitomized by Caird's RSC 1992 production. Performed in a vast arena as part of the Roman cycle, the drama achieved both scope and size. Reviewers described Michael Rehberg as a "tough" and "soldierly" Antony and Edith Clever as "a self-consciously regal Cleopatra," but the two, like Caird's Johnson and Higgins, were found lacking in "erotic tension." Most commentators judged the play rather pedestrian until the death scene when a retractable roof plunged the stage into "flame illuminated darkness," investing the catastrophe with a "dream-like majesty" that stressed the transcendence of Cleopatra's death (Billington; qtd. in Madelaine 128).

Other Media

Despite its much-touted cinematic qualities, *Antony and Cleopatra* has been filmed only four times for television and once for the cinema. In 1963, the BBC presented *Antony and Cleopatra*, directed by Peter Dews and featuring Keith Mitchell and Mary Morris in the principal roles, as part of the nine-segment BBC series *The Spread of the Eagle*, which consisted of three of Shakespeare's Roman plays—*Coriolanus*, *Julius Caesar*, and *Antony and Cleopatra*, in that order. Unfortunately, this television version has not been preserved on video and I have not been able to discover any reviews of the production. Later, Trevor Nunn's highly touted 1972 RSC revival, starring Janet Suzman and Richard Johnson, was re-created for television by RSC/Audio-Visual Productions and aired on ABC January 1, 1975, receiving the same enthusiastic plaudits evoked by the 1972 stage production.

In 1981, Jonathan Miller made his directorial debut for the Time/Life BBC Shakespeare Series with his rendition of *Antony and Cleopatra*. This presentation reflected many of the trends so prevalent in modern theatrical revivals of the tragedy: the antiheroic, antiromantic perspective, the neo-Elizabethan staging, and the post–Granville-Barker preference for Veronese-style costumes and sets (Willis). To these strategies, Miller added his own signature style through his painterly *mise en scene*, thereby paradoxically reducing Shakespeare's most volatile and sweeping tragedy to a static Old Master's tableau and, according to Samuel Crowl, dissolving distinctions between Rome and Egypt (156). Moreover, to accentuate his anti-heroic stance, he cast a "tough" rather than "stereotypically noble" Colin Blakely as Antony and a strong rather than sensual Jane Lapotaire as Cleopatra (Willis 116), who presented a "belle dame sans merci," rather than a sensuous serpent of Old Nile (Crowl 156). His experiment evoked mixed reactions. Some critics endorsed Miller's approach, hailing the production as "gorgeous" and "handsomely, even superbly mounted" (Mitchell; qtd. in Bulman and Coursen 270), while commending Blakely's "warm-blooded, witty, and gentle" soldier and Lapotaire's radiant, high-spirited queen (Ratcliffe; qtd. in Bulman and Cousen 270). Others shared my own reservations and disappointment, in particular criticizing the production for its total lack of tragic dimension and its domestication of the two fabled lovers into a "bright, witty suburban housewife" and a pedestrian soldier (Cecil Smith; O'Connor; Lowen; qtd. in Bulman and Coursen 270). Even more censorious, H. R. Coursen panned the production as "static, passionless, undramatic, and frozen in time" (qtd. in Bulman and Coursen 273).

Finally, in 1985, the Bard series, which, as Crowl explains, "originated in Los Angeles as an American challenge to the BBC Shakespeares" (162n16), aired its TV version of the play featuring Lynn Redgrave as Cleopatra, Timothy Dalton as Antony, and Barrie Ingham as Octavius Caesar. Having seen the production, I concur with Crowl's judgment that Redgrave's Cleopatra was "too pleasant," lacking both "depth" and "allure," and that Dalton's too-young Antony was played as a "dashing buccaneer," rather than as a "grizzled military veteran" (157). On the whole, the production was not a critical success.

Although, as Charlton Heston proclaimed, Shakespeare's *Antony and Cleopatra* "cries out for a camera" (qtd. in Brode 196), the play has been filmed only once for the large screen. Douglas Brode chronicles the many attempts to film the tumultuous romance of the fabled lovers, beginning with George Melies's screening of Cleopatra's suicide (1899) and continuing through Ferdinand Zecca's Gallic version (1910), Charles Gaskill's American rendition (1912), and Erico Guazzoni's operatic treatment (1913). Hollywood also participated, presenting Theda Bara's vamp (1912), Claudette Colbert's kittenish coquette (1934), and Elizabeth Taylor's gorgeous feminist queen (1963). However, none of these cinematic efforts have much to do with Shakespeare. Thus, although the Cleopatra story and particularly Shakespeare's version "saturate Hollywood history" (Eggert, "Age Cannot Wither" 198), only Heston has had the courage to film Shakespeare's play. Unfortunately, his experiment was a disaster.

Shot on a low budget in Spain, using interpolated sea battles from the film *Ben-Hur* to pad out the action and a relatively inexperienced and unknown actor, Hildegard Neil, in the challenging role of Cleopatra, the severely pruned version enjoyed a world premier in London and a brief screening in Washington, DC, but was not distributed in the United States. Reviewers judged the film derivative and disappointing, complaining that Heston attempted to "domesticate" his Shakespearean material, creating a version of "Egypt as Hollywood" (Crowl 158), and that the two leading actors failed to convey the range and complexity of Shakespeare's monumental protagonists. Neil was labeled pedestrian, totally lacking the stature of a queen, and sadly deficient in Cleopatra's fabled variety. While some critics praised Heston for his rugged charm as the dissipated warrior (Brode 201), to others he fell far short of Cleopatra's "noblest of men" (Tatspaugh 154). Most serious of all, commentators reiterated the familiar refrain that the two lovers lacked the fire that one might expect from such passionate figures (Welsh, Vela, and Tibbetts 2–3).

Finally, like so many other Shakespeare plays, *Antony and Cleopatra* has been adapted to operatic form. In 1966, the Metropolitan Opera presented Samuel Barber's 1960 opera version with the libretto adapted from Shakespeare by Franco Zeffirelli. In his contribution to this collection, David Fuller compares the Barber/Zeffirelli version to the landmark Byam Shaw, Trevor Nunn, and Peter Hall productions.

Reincarnations in Modern Drama and Popular Culture

As noted earlier, there have been multiple film versions of the Antony and Cleopatra story. The legend of the two great lovers has also experienced numerous reincarnations in the modern drama. The most famous redux is George Bernard Shaw's *Caesar and Cleopatra*, which, as the title indicates, adopts a very different focus from Shakespeare's tragedy. In Shaw's play, Antony, although often discussed, never appears, even as in Shakespeare's drama Julius Caesar is present only by report. Moreover, Shaw's playful royal minx bears little resemblance to Shakespeare's tempestuous yet noble empress. More recently, in *A Branch of the Blue Nile* (1983), Derek Walcott dramatizes the attempts of a black theatrical company in Trinidad to stage *Antony and Cleopatra*, using Shakespeare's play as a springboard for his own ruminations on love, religion, race, and theater. Perhaps more intriguing than these explicit adaptations or revisions are the echoes of Shakespeare's play that resonate throughout much modern drama. In one of the most provocative of these examples, Philip C. Kolin identifies Blanche DuBois in Tennessee Williams's *A Streetcar Named Desire* as the Cleopatra of the French Quarter (27), enumerating the many similarities between these two earthly Venuses: both are associated with desire; both have reputations as "sirens of pleasure"; and both are "frequently vilified as whores" (25).Kolin finds the most prominent parallels between Cleopatra and Blanche surfacing during their respective death scenes, when both "women find themselves in similar tragic predicaments: awaiting the arrival of their executioners and, at the same time, readying themselves to meet their recently apotheosized lovers" (26). According to Kolin, "Williams uses Shakespeare as his palimpsest to ennoble Blanche's tragedy" (27).

The image of Cleopatra also saturates contemporary popular culture. Francesca T. Royster cites several examples of Cleopatra's emergence as an icon in black cinema, focusing particularly on Tamara Dobson's Cleopatra Jones as an avatar of Shakespeare's Egyptian queen. According to Royster, the 1973 film *Cleopatra Jones* recasts Shakespeare's temptress as a black crime fighter, whose multiple arrivals and departures via airplane, Corvette, or motorbike re-create Enobarbus's famous description of Cleopatra on her barge for the modern media, with the queen's "cloth-of-gold of tissue" replaced by "fur, kente cloth, or red leather" (Royster, *Becoming Cleopatra*, 146–49). Other contemporary permutations of the Antony and Cleopatra story include the 1996 film *Set It Off*, in which Queen Latifah's Cleo morphs into a black lesbian bank robber (Royster, *Becoming Cleopatra* 172), the 1970 wacky sex comedy *The Notorious Cleopatra*, the sexy 2004 French farce *Asterix and Obelix Meet Cleopatra*, and the futuristic 2004 TV show on the SciFi channel, *Cleopatra 2525*. This multicultural *femme fatale* has even inspired a 2002 Japanese animated movie entitled *Cleopatra D.C.*[2] Although most of these modern metamorphoses also feature an Antony persona, the Cleopatra figure remains dominant. Finally, Duke Ellington complements these cinematic portraits with his own musical tribute to Cleopatra in his jazz celebration of Shakespeare's characters, *Such Sweet Thunder*. None of these popular culture Cleopatras bears much resemblance to Shakespeare's queen except as celebrations of the glamorous, empowered female achieving agency in a male-dominated society. However, these multiple reincarnations do indicate that despite her death in Egypt in 30 BC and her repeated suicides on stages throughout the world for the past 250 years, Cleopatra remains alive and well in modern drama and contemporary popular culture.

CONCLUSION

In reviewing the stage and screen history of this challenging drama, we can trace a movement from the "salad days" of the Dryden-Shakespeare mélanges to a progressively fuller text, although, even today, problematic scenes are sometimes lopped away to create a simplified procrustean version of Shakespeare's complex play.

Concerning staging, we can delineate a progression from the pictorial extravagances of the eighteenth and nineteenth centuries to the minimal settings of the neo-Elizabethan postwar productions to the alternating spectacular and minimalist revivals of the twentieth and twenty-first centuries. The most successful productions seem to be those that capture the splendor and vast scope of the play without detracting from Shakespeare's central focus on poetry and character.

Perhaps the most problematic issue remains how to maintain the play's precarious equipoise between heroic transcendence and ironic deflation and between the play's romantic and political emphases—the issues most vigorously debated in the scholarship of the play. Nineteenth-century versions of the tragedy tended to omit political sequences that detracted from the romance (the Roman encounters, the barge bacchanal) and ironic scenes that deflated the lovers (the Ventidius and Seleucus episodes). Conversely, modern renditions alternate between those that stress the romantic elements through textual honing and direction, those that maintain the problematic scenes while interpreting them in a nonironic manner, and those that foreground the deflative material to ironize the lovers. Other productions have maintained Shakespeare's full text while employing costume, setting, or dramatic interpretation to highlight either the political or romantic elements of the play. Again, the revivals receiving the most universal accolades seem to be those that balance the transcendent and the ironic, the romantic and the political aspects of this oxymoronic drama.

Theatrically, the greatest debate has centered on how Cleopatra should be played. The list of actors who have attempted this role reads like a "Who's Who" of British and American stage aristocracy: Isabella Glyn, Cora Potter, Lillie Langtry, Sarah Bernhardt, Fanny Davenport, Janet Achurch, Constance Collier, Dorothy Green, Edith Evans, Tallulah Bankhead, Katharine Cornell, Vivien Leigh, Peggy Ashcroft, Katharine Hepburn, Janet Suzman, Vanessa Redgrave, Maggie Smith, Dorothy Tutin, Glenda Jackson, Helen Mirren, Diana Rigg, Judi Dench. Some, like Glyn, portrayed the Egyptian queen with dark hair, stained face, and Victorian crinoline. Others, like Potter, Langtry, Bernhardt, Achurch, and Ashcroft, combined flowing gowns with long red hair and pale skin, or, like Leigh and Suzman, dressed in magnificent, archeologically accurate Egyptian regalia and wigs. Still other Cleopatras, conforming to Granville-Barker's recommendations, were garbed in Renaissance costumes, such as Dorothy Massingham's pink farthingale, Green's and Dench's Veronese-styled gowns, or Vanessa Redgrave's Queen Elizabeth imitation. Some, like Collier, donned leopard robes; others, like Evans, added Native American touches to Egyptian garments, and some even sported modern dress, like Redgrave in a different guise.

Plutarch tells us that Cleopatra was not beautiful and a Roman coin displaying her visage confirms that judgment (Hughes-Hallett; see fig. 2). Moreover, historically, Cleopatra was thirty-nine at her death, quite young by contemporary standards but considerably more middle-aged in the early modern period, and Shakespeare's queen describes herself as both black and wrinkled. However, Cleopatra has frequently been played as pale-skinned, young, and exquisitely beautiful, although middle-aged actors have assayed the part with varying success: Green performed the part for the last time at sixty to enthusiastic ovations; Evans portrayed the role at fifty-nine with less success; the American actor Helena Modjeska attempted the part for the first time "at age fifty-eight" (Shattuck 135); and Vanessa Redgrave, a young fifty-nine, romped through the role in her most recent performance of the part. The late twentieth century, a time of increased longevity and interest in aging, has stressed the play as a drama of middle-age love. Moreover, twentieth-century presentations, perhaps responding to the increased liberation of women—and also to scholarly trends—have accentuated the androgyny of Cleopatra and her similarity to Queen Elizabeth I.

Ultimately, I would like to suggest that critical responses to Cleopatra provide a barometer for society's attitudes toward gender differences at a particular period. For example, prudish Victorian critics often criticized the actors playing Cleopatra as too sensual. Conversely, in the 1920s, a period that celebrated femininity and domesticity, many reviewers accepted the eroticism of Green's Cleopatra, while criticizing her shrewd intelligence. Thirty years later, realizing that one can be both sexy and smart, more enlightened critics extolled the same traits in Ashcroft's Cleopatra that earlier pundits had condemned in Green's. In the 1970s, in the wake of the Women's Liberation movement, reviewers accepted the androgynous Cleopatras of Suzman and Jackson, although some still had reservations concerning Redgrave's "punk tomboy." Moreover, in the last thirty years, productions have often fore-grounded Cleopatra as the protagonist of the play. Juliet Dusinberre suggests that because of the centrality of the Egyptian queen to the tragedy, British revivals of the play have been more frequent when a "woman ruler was on the throne" (61), or, I would add, occupying 10 Downing Street.

Although the theatrical annals contain hyperbolic plaudits to Cleopatra, reviewers have judged the majority of Antonys upstaged by their more charismatic paramours. Critics have found Antonys from William Macready to Alan Howard more effective in portraying the fierce despair of the fallen warrior than the doting amorousness of the passionate lover. Exceptions to this rule include Laurence Olivier, who was criticized as too romantic and domestic in the role, and Michael Redgrave and Anthony Hopkins, who were generally lauded by reviewers for achieving the proper balance between lover and soldier. More often than not, however, critics have faulted both lovers as deficient in the sexual magnetism that one expects these two famous lovers to project.

Perhaps in response to the increasing critical interest in Octavius Caesar and his relationship to King James, productions during the past thirty-five years have etched a more sympathetic portrait of Antony's antagonist than in earlier productions. Keith Baxter initiated this trend in Peter Dews's 1969 Chichester revival with his memorable portrayal of the sensitive young man who becomes disillusioned when his erstwhile hero betrays his beloved sister. Jonathan Pryce developed this depiction into a sensible, peace-loving man, whose genuine concern for his sister won the allegiance of the audiences of

Brook's 1978 RSC revival. Reviewers also applauded Jonathan Hyde's commanding and passionate Octavius in Noble's 1984 presentation. These approving interpretations of Octavius are almost always linked with a deflative treatment of the two lovers.

The performance history of *Antony and Cleopatra* reflects the dual aspects of all three of the play's central characters. Different periods have favored Cleopatra the siren, Cleopatra the shrew, or Cleopatra the androgynous queen. Similarly, different decades have stressed Antony the debauched roué, Antony the mighty soldier, or Antony the passionate lover, as well as Octavius the repellent Roman Machiavel or Octavius the effective statesman. Significantly, Octavius has fared better on the contemporary stage than in traditional productions. Similarly, different periods have accentuated the drama as Shakespeare's passion play, his study in kingship, or his metadramatic commentary on the transforming power of art. In the arena of performance, therefore, as in the area of literary criticism, attitudes toward the play's contradictory figures, its ethos, its structure, and its tone, like a vagabond flag upon a stream, have swayed back and forth, lackeying the varying critical tides, rotting themselves with motion.

NOTES

1. The critical canon of *Antony and Cleopatra*, like that of all of Shakespeare's tragedies, is vast and rather intimidating. For obvious reasons, this introduction cannot attempt a comprehensive survey of all the valuable exegeses on this intriguing drama but can only highlight the dominant trends in the criticism of the play. Those who wish to probe more deeply into this criticism should consult the expansive annotated bibliographies by Michael Steppat and Yashdip S. Bains, as well as Marvin Spevack's invaluable Variorum edition. The excerpts from criticism of the play compiled by Laurie Lanzen Harris and Mark W. Scott and Michael Magoulias also offer valuable scholarly aids, as do the anthologies of essays on *Antony and Cleopatra* edited by John Russell Brown and John Drakakis. The introductions by David Bevington and Michael Neill to their editions of the play also provide succinct and perceptive guides to the major critical issues evoked by this oxymoronic drama.

   In the area of performance criticism, I am deeply indebted to the reviews and commentaries collected by Sandra L. Williamson, to the pioneering work of Margaret Lamb and Samuel L. Leiter, to the insightful comments of David Bevington and David Scott Kastan, and, most of all, to Richard Madelaine's astute and perceptive theater history of *Antony and Cleopatra*.

   I am, of course, also indebted to many other critics and theater historians whom I have tried to acknowledge properly throughout this introduction.

2. I am indebted to Francesca's Royster's excellent book *Becoming Cleopatra* and to the media expertise of my colleagues Robert Logan and Merry G. Perry for the identification of these popular culture Cleopatras.

WORKS CITED

Adcock, Joe. "Bards of a Feather: Contemporary Playwrights Also Well-Represented." *Seattle-Post Intelligencer* 8 July 1993: N. pag.

Adelman, Janet. *The Common Liar: An Essay on* Antony and Cleopatra. New Haven, CT: Yale UP, 1973.

———. *Suffocating Mothers: Fantasies of Maternal Origin in Shakespeare's Plays,* Hamlet *to* The Tempest. New York: Routledge, 1992.

Adler, Doris. "The Unlacing of Cleopatra." *Theatre Journal* 34 (1982): 450–66.

Agate, James. *Brief Chronicles: A Survey of the Plays of Shakespeare and the Elizabethans in Actual Performance.* 1943. New York: Benjamin Blom, 1971.

Archer, John Michael. "Antiquity and Degeneration in *Antony and Cleopatra.*" *Race, Ethnicity, and Power in the Renaissance.* Ed. Joyce Green MacDonald. Madison, NJ: Farleigh Dickinson UP, 1997. 145–54.

Atkinson, Brooks. "First Night at the Theatre." *The New York Times* 21 Dec. 1951: 22.

Bains, Yashdip S. Antony and Cleopatra: *An Annotated Bibliography.* New York: Garland Publishing, 1998.

Bamber, Linda. *Comic Women, Tragic Men: A Study of Gender and Genre in Shakespeare.* Stanford, CA: Stanford UP, 1982.

Barker, Felix. "Tradition at the St. James's. 1948–1953." *The Oliviers: A Biography.* Philadelphia, PA: J. B. Lippincott, 1953. 334-60.

Barroll, J. Leeds. "Antony and Pleasure." *Journal of English and Germanic Philology* 57 (1958): 708–20.

———. "The Characterization of Octavius." *Shakespeare Studies* 6 (1970): 231–88.

———. "The Chronology of Shakespeare's Jacobean Plays and the Dating of *Antony and Cleopatra.*" *Essays on Shakespeare.* Ed. Gordon R. Smith. University Park, PA: Pennsylvania State UP, 1965. 115–62.

———. "Enobarbus' Description of Cleopatra." *Texas Studies in English* 37 (1958): 61–78.

———. *Shakespearean Tragedy: Genre, Tradition, and Change in* Antony and Cleopatra. Washington, DC: Folger Books, 1984.

Barton, Anne. *"Nature's piece 'gainst fancy": The Divided Catastrophe in* Antony and Cleopatra. An Inaugural Lecture. Bedford College: U of London, 1973.

Battenhouse, Roy W. *Shakespearean Tragedy: Its Art and Its Christian Premises.* Bloomington: Indiana UP, 1969.

Bentley, Eric. *In Search of Theater.* New York: Vintage Books, 1954.

Berkowitz, Gerald M. "Review of *Antony and Cleopatra.*" *Educational Theatre Journal* 30 (1978): 113–14. In Sandra L. Williamson.

Berson, Misha. "Shakespeare Summer." *Seattle Times* F1, 6.

Bethell, S. L. *Shakespeare and the Popular Dramatic Tradition.* Westminster: King and Staples, 1944. Introd. T. S. Eliot. Ann Arbor, MI: U Microfilms, 1968.

Bevington, David. Introduction. *Antony and Cleopatra.* The New Cambridge Shakespeare. Cambridge: Cambridge UP, 1990. 1–70.

Bevington, David, and David Scott Kastan. "*Antony and Cleopatra* in Performance." *Antony and Cleopatra.* Ed. David Bevington. Rev. Ed. Bantam Books, 1988. xv–xxiii.

B. F. " 'Antony' said finest performance in 10th Shakespeare Festival." *The Oregonian* 7 Aug. 1950: N. pag.

Billington, Michael. "Infinite Variety." *Peggy Ashcroft*. John Murray, 1988. 125–50.

Bishoff, Don. "Difficult 'Antony and Cleopatra.' " *Register-Guard* 25 July 1967: N. pag.

Blissett, William. "Dramatic Irony in *Antony and Cleopatra*." *Shakespeare Quarterly* 18 (1967): 151–66.

Blumenthal, Eileen. "Toils of Grace." *The Village Voice* 27 Nov. 1978: N. pag.

Bono, Barbara J. *Literary Transvaluation: From Vergilian Epic to Shakespearean Tragicomedy*. Berkeley: U of California P, 1984.

Bowers, Fredson. "The Concept of Single or Dual Protagonists in Shakespeare's Tragedies." *Renaissance Papers* (1982): 27–33.

Bradley, A. C. "Shakespeare's *Antony and Cleopatra*." *The Quarterly Review* 204: 407 (1906): 329–51.

Brandes, Georg. *William Shakespeare: A Critical Study*. Trans. William Archer, Mary Morison, and Diana White. 2 vols. 1898.

Brantley, Ben. "Redgraves Are Paired in 2 Plays in Houston." *The New York Times* 8 Feb. 1996: B1.

Brathwait, Richard. *The English Gentlewoman, drawne out to the full Body...* London: B. Alsop and T. Fauucet, 1631.

Brecht, Bertolt. *Bertolt Brecht Diaries, 1920-1922*. Ed. Herta Ramthun. Trans. and introd. John Willett. New York: St. Martin's P, 1979.

Brink, Bernhard ten. *Five Lectures on Shakespeare*. Trans. Julia Franklin. 1895.

Brode, Douglas. *Shakespeare in the Movies: From the Silent Era to* Shakespeare in Love. Oxford: Oxford UP, 2000.

Brower, Reuben A. *Hero & Saint: Shakespeare and the Graeco-Roman Heroic Tradition*. Oxford: Oxford UP, 1971.

Brown, Elizabeth A. " 'Companion Me with My Mistress': Cleopatra, Elizabeth I, and Their Waiting Women." *Maids and Mistresses, Cousins and Queens: Women's Alliances in Early Modern England*. Ed. Susan Frye, Karen Robertson, and Jean E. Howard. New York: Oxford UP, 1999. 131–45.

Brown, John Russell, ed. *Shakespeare:* Antony and Cleopatra: *A Casebook*. 1968. Rev. Ed. London: Macmillan, 1991.

Bulman, J. C., and H. R. Coursen, eds. *Shakespeare on Television: An Anthology of Essays and Reviews*. Hanover: UP of New England, 1988.

Caputi, Anthony. "Shakespeare's *Antony and Cleopatra*: Tragedy Without Terror." *Shakespeare Quarterly* 16 (1965): 183–91.

Case, R. H. Introduction. 1906. *Antony and Cleopatra*. By William Shakespeare. Ed. M. R. Ridley. Cambridge, MA: Harvard UP, 1956. xxv–xliv.

Cecil, David. "*Antony and Cleopatra*." *Poets and Story-Tellers: A Book of Critical Essays*. New York: Macmillan, 1949. 1–24.

Chambers, E. K. *Shakespeare: A Survey*. 1907. London: Sidgwick & Jackson, 1925.

Champion, Larry S. *Shakespeare's Tragic Perspective*. Athens, GA: U of Georgia P, 1976.

Charnes, Linda. "Spies and Whispers: Exceeding Reputation in *Antony and Cleopatra*." *Notorious Identity: Materializing the Subject in Shakespeare*. 1993. Cambridge, MA: Harvard UP, 1995.

———. "What's Love Got to Do with It? Reading the Liberal Humanist Romance in Shakespeare's *Antony and Cleopatra*." *Textual Practice* 6.1 (Spring 1992): 1–16.

Charney, Maurice. "The Imagery of *Antony and Cleopatra*." *Shakespeare's Roman Plays: The Function of Imagery in the Drama*. Cambridge, MA: Harvard UP, 1961. 79–141.

Clapp, Susannah. "Time for a Radical Shape-Up." *Observer* 28 Apr. 2002: N. pag.

Clarke, John Henrik. "African Warrior Queens." *Black Women in Antiquity*. Ed. Ivan Van Sertima. New Brunswick, NJ: Transaction Books, 1984. 123–34.

Coates, John. " 'The Choice of Hercules' in *Antony and Cleopatra*." *Shakespeare Studies* 31 (1978): 45–52.

Coleridge, Hartley. *Essays and Marginalia*. Ed. Derwent Coleridge. 2 vols. 1851.

Coleridge, Samuel Taylor. *Coleridge's Shakespeare Criticism*. 1813-34. Ed. Thomas Middleton Raysor. 2 vols. Rev. ed. London, 1960.

Colie, Rosalie L. *Shakespeare's Living Art*. Princeton, NJ: Princeton UP, 1974.

Cook, Carol. "The Fatal Cleopatra." *Shakespearean Tragedy and Gender*. Ed. Shirley Nelson Garner and Madelon Sprengnether. Bloomington, IN: Indiana UP, 1996. 241–67.

Crick, Bernard. "The Politics of Rome." *The Times Higher Educational Supplement* 21 Dec. 1973: 11.

Crowl, Samuel. "A World Elsewhere: The Roman Plays on Film and Television." *Shakespeare and the Moving Image: The Plays on Film and Television*. Ed. Anthony Davies and Stanley Wells. Cambridge: Cambridge UP, 1994. 146–62.

Danby, John F. "The Shakespearean Dialectic: An Aspect of *Antony and Cleopatra*." *Scrutiny* 16.3 (September 1949): 196–213.

Dash, Irene G. *Wooing, Wedding, and Power: Women in Shakespeare's Plays*. New York: Columbia UP, 1981.

Davies, H. Neville. "Jacobean *Antony and Cleopatra*." *Shakespeare Studies* 17 (1985): 123–58.

Davies, Thomas. *Dramatic Miscellanies: Consisting of Critical Observations on Several Plays of Shakespeare*. 3 vols. Dublin: S. Price, 1783–84.

Dawkins, William. "Cleopatra Captivating in Ashland Presentation as Shakespeare Festival Completes First Cycle." *The Oregonian* 2 Aug. 1959: N. pag.

de Sousa, Geraldo U. *Shakespeare's Cross-Cultural Encounters*. London: Macmillan P, 1999.

Dessen, Alan C. "Oregon Shakespearean Festival." *Shakespeare Quarterly* 28.2 (1977): 244–52.

Dickey, Franklin M. *Not Wisely But Too Well: Shakespeare's Love Tragedies*. San Marino, CA: Huntington Library, 1957.

Dollimore, Jonathan. *Radical Tragedy: Religion, Ideology, and Power in the Drama of Shakespeare and His Contemporaries*. Chicago, IL: U of Chicago P, 1984.

Dowden, Edward. *Shakspere: A Critical Study of His Mind and Art*. 1875. London: Routledge & Kegan Paul, 1957.

Drakakis, John, ed. *New Casebooks:* Antony and Cleopatra. New York: St. Martin's P, 1994.

Draper, John W. "Shattered Personality in Shakespeare's Antony." *Psychiatric Quarterly* 39 (1965): 448–56.

Dusinberre, Juliet. *Shakespeare and the Nature of Women.* 2nd ed. 1975. New York: St. Martin's P, 1996.

———. "Squeaking Cleopatras: Gender and Performance in *Antony and Cleopatra.*" *Shakespeare, Theory, and Performance.* Ed. James C. Bulman. New York: Routledge, 1996. 46–67.

Edmonds, Richard. "Fine Romance for Wash and Go World." *Birmingham Post Weekend.* 25 June 1999: N. pag.

———. "Infinite Variety Keeps This Affair Fresh." *Birmingham Post Weekend.* 7 Nov. 1992: N. pag.

Eggert, Katherine. "Age Cannot Wither Him: Warren Beatty's Bugsy as Hollywood Cleopatra." *Shakespeare: The Movie.* Ed. Lynda E. Boose and Richart Burt. New York: Routledge, 1997. 198–214.

———. *Showing Like a Queen: Female Authority and Literary Experiment in Spenser, Shakespeare, and Milton.* Philadelphia, PA: U of Pennsylvania P, 2000.

Eliot, T. S. "Hamlet and His Problems." *The Sacred Wood: Essays on Poetry and Criticism.* London: Methuen, 1920. 95–103.

Elsom, John. "An Indulgent Affair." *The Listener* 19 Oct. 1978: N. pag.

Erickson, Peter. *Patriarchal Structure in Shakespeare's Drama.* Berkeley: U of California P, 1985.

Erstein, Hap. "Powerful Tragedy of 'Antony and Cleopatra.' " *The Washington Times* 28 Sept. 1988: E3.

Everett, Barbara. "On a Sumptuous Scale." *The Times Literary Supplement* 24 Apr. 1987: N. pag.

Farjeon, Herbert. *The Shakespearean Scene: Dramatic Criticism.* London: Hutchinson, 1949.

Farnham, Willard. *Shakespeare's Tragic Frontier: The World of His Final Tragedies.* Berkeley, U of California P, 1950.

Felperin, Howard. *Shakespearean Representation: Mimesis and Modernity in Elizabethan Tragedy.* Princeton, NJ: Princeton UP, 1977.

Findlater, Richard. "Shylock, Lear, and Antony (1953)." *Michael Redgrave, Actor.* London: W. Heinemann, 1956. 118–32.

Fisch, Harold. "*Antony and Cleopatra*: The Limits of Mythology." *Shakespeare Studies* 23 (1970): 59–67.

Fitz, L. T. "Egyptian Queens and Male Reviewers: Sexist Attitudes in *Antony and Cleopatra* Criticism." *Shakespeare Quarterly* 28 (1977): 297–316.

Floyd-Wilson, Mary. "Transmigrations: Crossing Regional and Gender Boundaries in *Antony and Cleopatra.*" *Enacting Gender on the English Renaissance Stage.* Ed. Viviana Comensoli and Anne Russell. Urbana: U of Illinois P, 1999. 73–96.

Fluchere, Henri. "Shakespeare in France: 1900-1948." *Shakespeare Survey* 2 (1949): 115–25.

French, Marilyn. *Shakespeare's Division of Experience.* 1981. New York: Ballantine, 1983.

Frenzel, Karl. *Berliner Dramaturgie.* Vol 1. Hannover, 1877.

Frye, Northrop. *Fools of Time: Studies in Shakespearean Tragedy.* Toronto: U of Toronto P, 1967.

Furness, Horace Howard. Preface. *A New Variorum Edition of Shakespeare: The Tragedie of Anthonie, and Cleopatra.* Vol. 15. Ed. Horace Howard Furness. Philadelphia, PA: J. B. Lippincott Co., 1907. v–xx.

Gandrow, Kristen E. "Performance Reviews: *Antony and Cleopatra.*" *Theatre Journal* 52 (2000): 123–25.

Gentleman, Francis. *Bell's Edition of Shakespeare's Plays.* Vol. 6. 1774. London: Cornmarket P, 1969.

Gervinus, G. G. "Third Period of Shakespeare's Dramatic Poetry: *Antony and Cleopatra.*" *Shakespeare Commentaries.* 1849-50. Trans. F. E. Bunnett. Rev. Ed., 1877. Reprint, AMS Press, 1971. 722–45.

Gerwirtz, Arthur. "*Antony and Cleopatra* in Shanghai." *Shakespeare Quarterly* 36 (1985): 237–38.

Goddard, Harold C. *The Meaning of Shakespeare.* 2 vols. Chicago: U of Chicago P, 1951.

Godshalk, W[illiam] L. "Dolabella as Agent Provocateur." *Renaissance Papers* (1977): 69–74.

Goldman, Michael. *Acting and Action in Shakespearean Tragedy.* Princeton, NJ: Princeton UP, 1985.

Granville-Barker, Harley. *Prefaces to Shakespeare.* 1930. 2 vols. Princeton, NJ: Princeton UP, 1946.

Greene, James J. "*Antony and Cleopatra*: The Birth and Death of Androgyny." *Hartford Studies in Literature* 19.2-3 (1987): 24–44.

Greenwald, Michael. "An Enterprise of Great Pitch and Moment": *Julius Caesar* and *Antony and Cleopatra* at the Alley Theatre, 1996." *Shakespeare Quarterly* 48 (1997): 84–90.

Griffith, [Elizabeth]. *The Morality of Shakespeare's Drama Illustrated.* London: T. Cadell, 1775. New York: AMS P, 1971.

Hamilton, Donna B. "*Antony and Cleopatra* and the Tradition of Noble Lovers." *Shakespeare Quarterly* 24 (1973): 245–51.

Harris, Duncan C. "'Again for Cydnus': The Dramaturgical Resolution of *Antony and Cleopatra.*" *Studies in English Literature, 1500-1900* 17 (1977): 219–31.

Harris, Jonathan Gil. "'Narcissus in thy face': Roman Desire and the Difference It Fakes in *Antony and Cleopatra.*" *Shakespeare Quarterly* 45 (1994): 408–25.

Harris, Laurie Lanzen, and Mark W. Scott, eds. *Shakespeare Criticism: Excerpts from the Criticism of William Shakespeare's Plays and Poetry, from the First Published Appraisals to Current Evaluations.* Vol. 6. Detroit, MI: Gale Research, 1984-.

Hawkes, Terence. "*King Lear* and *Antony and Cleopatra*: The Language of Love." *Shakespeare's Talking Animals: Language and Drama in Society.* London: Edward Arnold, 1973. 166–93.

Hazlitt, William. "Characters of Shakepear's Plays: *Antony and Cleopatra.*" *Characters of Shakespear's Plays, & Lectures on English Poets.* 1817. London: Macmillan, 1903. 58–63.

Heales, Robyn, and Dennis Bartholomeusz. "Shakespeare in Sidney and Melbourne." *Shakespeare Quarterly* 35 (1984): 479–84.

Heilman, Robert B. "From Mine own Knowledge: A Theme in the Late Tragedies." *Centennial Review* 8 (1964): 17–38.

Heinemann, Margot. "'Let Rome in Tiber Melt': Order and Disorder in *Antony and Cleopatra.*" *New Casebooks:* Antony and Cleopatra. Ed. John Drakakis. New York: St. Martin's P, 1994. 166–81.

Heraud, John A. *Shakspere: His Inner Life as Intimated in His Works.* 1865.

Herford, C. H. *A Sketch of Recent Shakespearean Investigation 1893–1923.* 1923.

Hewes, Henry. "Rare Spirits." *Saturday Review* 50 (1967): 22.

Heyse, Paul. "An Essay." 1867. *A New Variorium Edition of Shakespeare: The Tragedie of Anthonie, and Cleopatra.* Vol. 15. Ed. and Trans. Horace Howard Furness. Philadelphia, PA: J. B. Lippincott Co., 1907. 494–93.

Hicks, Bob. "Cleopatra in a Man's World." *The Oregonian* 20 June 1993: N. pag.

Higgins, Anne. "Shakespeare's Saint Cleopatra." *Dalhousie Review* 70 (1990-91): 5–19.

Hill, James L. "Shakespeare's Tragic Women and the Boy Actors." *Studies in English Literature* 26 (1986): 235–58.

Hillman, Richard. "Antony, Hercules, and Cleopatra: 'The Bidding of the Gods' and 'the Subtlest Maze of All.' " *Shakespeare Quarterly* 38 (1987): 442–51.

Hobart, John. "Shakespeare in Oregon." *San Francisco Chronicle* 13 Aug. 1950: 10.

Hobson, Harold. " 'Richard III' and 'Antony' at Stratford." *The Christian Science Monitor* 16 May 1953: 10A.

Holland, Peter. *English Shakespeares: Shakespeare on the English Stage in the 1990s.* Cambridge: Cambridge UP, 1997.

Homan, Sidney R. "Divided Response and the Imagination in *Antony and Cleopatra.*" *Philological Quarterly* 49 (1970): 460–68.

Horobetz, Lynn K. "Shakespeare at the Old Globe, 1971." *Shakespeare Quarterly* 22 (1971): 385–87.

Hughes-Hallett, Lucy. *Cleopatra: Histories, Dreams and Distortions.* New York: Harper & Row, 1990.

Hugo, Victor. "An Essay." 1859-66. *A New Variorium Edition of Shakespeare: The Tragedie of Anthonie, and Cleopatra.* Vol. 15. Ed. and Trans. Horace Howard Furness. Philadelphia, PA: J. B. Lippincott Co., 1907.

Hurren, Kenneth. "Two on the Nile." *The Spectator* 9 Aug. 1972: N. pag.

Jackson, Berners. "Stratford Festival, Canada." *Shakespeare Quarterly* 28.2 (Spring 1977): 197–206.

Jackson, Russell. "Shakespeare at Stratford-upon-Avon: Summer and Winter 1999–2000." *Shakespeare Quarterly* 51 (2000): 217–29.

James, Heather. "The Politics of Display and the Anamorphic Subjects of *Antony and Cleopatra.*" *Shakespeare's Late Tragedies.* Ed. Susanne L. Wofford. Upper Saddle River, NJ: Prentice Hall, 1996. 208–34.

Jameson, Anna Brownell. *Shakespeare's Heroines.* 1897. London: George Bell & Sons, 1898.

Jankowski, Theodora A. " 'As I am Egypt's Queen': Cleopatra, Elizabeth I, and the Female Body Politic." *Assays: Critical Approaches to Medieval and Renaissance Texts* 5 (1989): 91–110.

Johnson, Malcolm L. "Brilliant Production in Lennox." *The Hartford Courant* 18 July 1986: D7.

Johnson, Samuel. "Preface to Shakespeare, 1765." *Johnson on Shakespeare.* Ed. Arthur Sherbo. New Haven, CT: Yale UP, 1968.

Kahn, Coppélia. *Roman Shakespeare: Warriors, Wounds, and Women.* London: Routledge, 1997.

Kalmey, Robert P. "Shakespeare's Octavius and Elizabethan Roman History." *Studies in English Literature, 1500-1900* 18 (1978): 275–87.

Kaufman, Edward. "OSF's Beautiful Combination." *Los Angeles Herald Examiner* 17 July 1977: B6.

Kennedy, Dennis. "Review of *Antony and Cleopatra*." *Theatre Journal* 3 (1979): 420–23.

Kerr, Walter. "Cleopatra: The Games She Plays." *The New York Times* 17 Sept. 1967, sec. 2: 1, 17.

King, Laura Severt. "Blessed When They Were Riggish: Shakespeare's Cleopatra and Christianity's Penitent Prostitutes." *Medieval and Renaissance Studies* 22 (1992): 429–49.

Knight, G. Wilson. *The Imperial Theme: Further Interpretations of Shakespeare's Tragedies Including the Roman Plays.* Oxford: Oxford UP, 1931. London: Methuen & Co, 1965.

Knoll, Jack. "Oh, To Be in England." *Newsweek* 27 Nov. 1978: N. pag.

———. "Deep in the Heart of Texas." *Newsweek* 12 Feb. 1996: 82.

Kolin, Philip C. "Cleopatra of the Nile and Blanche DuBois of the French Quarter: *Antony and Cleopatra* and *A Streetcar Named Desire*." *Shakespeare Bulletin* 25 (1993): 25–27.

Krook, Dorothea. "Tragic and Heroic: Shakespeare's *Antony and Cleopatra*." *Scripta Hierosolymitana* 19 (1967): 231–61. Rpt. in *Elements of Tragedy*. New Haven, CT: Yale UP, 1969. 184–229.

Kuriyama, Constance Brown. "The Mother of the World: A Psychoanalytic Interpretation of Shakespeare's *Antony and Cleopatra*." *English Literary Renaissance* 7 (1977): 324–51.

Lamb, Margaret. Antony and Cleopatra *on the English Stage*. Rutherford, NJ: Fairleigh Dickinson UP, 1980.

Larson, Herbert. "Anthony Role Well Filled." *The Oregonian* 6 Aug. 1950: N. pag.

Leiter, Samuel L., ed. *Shakespeare Around the Globe: A Guide to Notable Postwar Revivals*. Westport, CT: Greenwood P, 1986.

Levin, Richard A. "That I Might Hear Thee Call Great Caesar 'Ass Unpolicied.' " *Papers on Language and Literature* 33.3 (1997): 244–64.

Lewson, Charles. " 'Antony and Cleopatra': Stratford-upon-Avon." *The Times*, London 16 Aug. 1972: 13.

Little, Arthur L., Jr. *Shakespeare Jungle Fever: National-Imperial Re-Visions of Race, Rape, and Sacrifice*. Stanford, CA: Stanford UP, 2000.

Lloyd, Michael. "Cleopatra as Isis." *Shakespeare Studies* 12 (1959): 88–94.

Loomba, Ania. "Imperial Romance." *Shakespeare, Race, and Colonialism*. Oxford: Oxford UP, 2002.

———. " 'Traveling thoughts': Theatre and the Space of the Other." 1989. *New Casebooks:* Antony and Cleopatra. Ed. John Drakakis. New York: St. Martin's P, 1994. 279–307.

MacCallum, M[ungo]. W. *Shakespeare's Roman Plays and Their Background*. Fore. T. J. B. Spencer. New York: Russell & Russell, 1967.

MacDonald, Joyce Green. "Sex, Race, and Empire in Shakespeare's *Antony and Cleopatra*." *Literature and History* 5.1 (1996): 60–77.

MacDonald, Ronald R. "Playing Till Doomsday: Interpreting *Antony and Cleopatra*." *English Literary Renaissance* 15 (1985): 78–99.

Mack, Maynard. Introduction. *Antony and Cleopatra*. Ed. Maynard Mack. Rev. ed. 1960. New York: Penguin, 1976. 14–21.

———. "The Jacobean Shakespeare: Some Observations on the Construction of the Tragedies." *Jacobean Theatre*. Stratford-upon-Avon Studies 1. Ed. John Russell Brown and Bernard Harris. 1960. 10–41.

Madelaine, Richard. Introduction. *Antony and Cleopatra*. Ed. Richard Madelaine. Cambridge: Cambridge UP, 1998.

Magoulias, Michael, ed. *Shakespeare Criticism: Excerpts from the Criticism of William Shakespeare's Plays and Poetry, from the First Published Appraisals to Current Evaluations*. Vol. 27. Detroit, MI: Gale Research, 1995.

Mahar, Ted. "Cleopatra Triumphant in Shakespeare Festival." *The Oregonian* 25 July 1967: N. pag.

Makaryk, Irene R. "Woman Scorned: *Antony and Cleopatra* at Moscow's Vakhtangov Theatre." *Foreign Shakespeare: Contemporary Performance*. Ed. Dennis Kennedy. Cambridge: Cambridge UP, 1993. 178–94.

Markels, Julian. *The Pillar of the World:* Antony and Cleopatra *in Shakespeare's Development*. Columbus: Ohio State UP, 1968.

Marks, Arnold. "'Antony and Cleopatra' Reveals Roman Conflict." *Oregon Journal* 6 Aug. 1950: N. pag.

Marshall, Cynthia. "Man of Steel Done Got the Blues: Melancholic Subversion of Presence in *Antony and Cleopatra*." *Shakespeare Quarterly* 44 (1993): 385–408.

McAlindon, Thomas. *Shakespeare and Decorum*. London: Macmillan, 1973.

McDonald, Russ. "Late Shakespeare: Style and the Sexes." *Shakespeare Survey* 46 (1994): 91–106.

Mills, Laurens Joseph. *The Tragedies of Shakespeare's* Antony and Cleopatra." Bloomington: Indiana UP, 1964.

Morris, Helen. "Queen Elizabeth I 'Shadowed' in Cleopatra." *Huntington Library Quarterly* 32 (1968-9): 271–78.

Muir, Kenneth. "Elizabeth I, Jodelle, and Cleopatra." *Renaissance Drama* NS 2 (1969): 197–206.

Murry, John Middleton. "*Antony and Cleopatra*." *Shakespeare*. 1936. London: Jonathan Cape, 1961. 352–79.

Neely, Carol Thomas. *Broken Nuptials in Shakespeare's Plays*. New Haven, CT: Yale UP, 1985.

Neill, Michael, ed. *The Tragedy of Antony and Cleopatra*. Oxford: Clarendon P, 1994.

Nevo, Ruth. "The Masque of Greatness." *Shakespeare Studies* 3 (1967): 111–28.

Nightingale, Benedict. "A Cleopatra of Infinite Variety." *The Times*, London 7–8 Nov. 1992: N. pag.

———. "Decline and Growth." *New Statesman* 25 Aug. 1972: N. pag.

———. "Volatile Cleopatra Gets Tough and Tender." *The Times*, London 25 Apr. 2002: N. pag.

Nochimson, Richard. "The End Crowns All: Shakespeare's Deflation of Tragic Possibility in *Antony and Cleopatra*." *English* 26 (1977): 99–132.

Nyquist, Mary. "'Profuse, Proud Cleopatra': 'Barbarism' and Female Rule in Early Modern English Republicanism." *Women's Studies* 24.1-2 (1994): 85–130.

Ornstein, Robert. "The Ethic of the Imagination: Love and Art in *Antony and Cleopatra*." *Later Shakespeare*. Stratford-upon-Avon Studies 8. Ed. John Russell Brown and Bernard Harris. London: Edward Arnold, 1966. 31–46.

Payne, Michael. "Erotic Irony and Polarity in *Antony and Cleopatra.*" *Shakespeare Quarterly* 24 (1973): 265–79.

Pearson, Norman Holmes. "*Antony and Cleopatra.*" *Shakespeare: Of an Age and For All Time.* The Yale Festival Lectures. Ed. Charles Tyler Prouty. Hamden, CT: Shoe String P, 1954. 125–47.

Peters, John. "For Disservices Rendered." *The Sunday Times* 1 June 1986: 49.

———. "Renaissance of the Golden Age." *The Sunday Times* 12 Apr. 1987: 55.

Phillips, James Emerson, Jr. "The Monarchic Cycle in *Julius Caesar* and *Antony and Cleopatra.*" *The State of Shakespeare's Greek and Roman Plays.* New York: Columbia UP, 1940. New York: Octagon Books, 1972. 172–205.

Potter, Lois. "Roman Actors and Egyptian Transvestites." *Shakespeare Quarterly* 50.4 (1999): 508–17.

Proser, Matthew N. *The Heroic Image in Five Shakespearean Tragedies.* Princeton, NJ: Princeton UP, 1965.

Quiller-Couch, Arthur. "*Antony and Cleopatra.*" *Studies in Literature, Second Series.* Cambridge: UP, 1922. 169-206.

Rabkin, Norman. *Shakespeare and the Common Understanding.* New York: Free P, 1967.

Rackin, Phyllis. "Shakespeare's Boy Cleopatra, the Decorum of Nature, and the Golden World of Poetry." *PMLA* 87 (1972): 201–12.

Ratcliffe, Michael. "Triumph in Death on the Nile." *The Observer* 12 Apr. 1987: 18.

Richards, David. "*Antony and Cleopatra* Sans Lust." *Washington Post* 28 Sept. 1988: C1, C13.

Ridley, M. R., ed. *Antony and Cleopatra.* By William Shakespeare. Cambridge, MA: Harvard UP, 1956.

Riemer, A. P. *A Reading of Shakespeare's* Antony and Cleopatra. Sydney Studies in Literature. Sydney: Sydney UP, 1968.

Rinehart, Keith. "Shakespeare's Cleopatra and England's Elizabeth." *Shakespeare Quarterly* 23 (1972): 81–86.

Rose, Paul Lawrence. "The Politics of *Antony and Cleopatra.*" *Shakespeare Quarterly* 20 (1969): 379–89.

Rosen, William. *Shakespeare and the Craft of Tragedy.* Cambridge, MA: Harvard UP, 1960.

Rousuck, Wynn. "'Antony and Cleopatra' Fails to Achieve Potential." *The Baltimore Sun* 30 Sept. 1988: N. pag.

Royster, Francesca T. "Cleopatra as Diva: African-American Women and Shakespearean Tactics." *Transforming Shakespeare: Contemporary Women's Re-Visions in Literature and Performance.* Ed. Marianne Novy. New York: St. Martin's P, 1999. 103–27.

———. *Becoming Shakespeare: The Shifting Image of an Icon.* New York: Palgrave, 2003.

Rozett, Martha Tuck. "The Comic Structures of Tragic Endings: The Suicide Scenes in *Romeo and Juliet* and *Antony and Cleopatra.*" *Shakespeare Quarterly* 36 (1985): 152–64.

Rutter, Carol Chillington. *Enter the Body: Women and Representation on Shakespeare's Stage.* London: Routledge, 2001.

Rylands, George. "Festival Shakespeare in the West End." *Shakespeare Survey* 6 (1953): 140–46.

Schanzer, Ernest. *The Problem Plays of Shakespeare: A Study of* Julius Caesar, Measure for Measure, Antony and Cleopatra. London: Routledge & Kegan Paul, 1963.

Schlegel, Augustus William. *Course of Lectures on Dramatic Art and Literature.* Trans. John Black. London: Henry G. Bohn, 1846. New York: AMS P, 1965.

Schucking, Levin L. *Character Problems in Shakespeare's Plays: A Guide to the Better Understanding of the Dramatist.* 1922. Gloucester, MA: Peter Smith, 1959.

Shapiro, Michael. "Boying Her Greatness: Shakespeare's Use of Coterie Drama in *Antony and Cleopatra.*" *Modern Language Review* 77 (1982): 1–15.

Shapiro, Stephen A. "The Varying Shore of the World: Ambivalence in *Antony and Cleopatra.*" *Modern Language Quarterly* 27 (1966): 18–32.

Shattuck, Charles H. *Shakespeare and the American Stage: From Booth and Barrett to Sothern and Marlowe.* Vol. 2. Washington, DC: The Folger Shakespeare Library, 1987.

Shaw, Bernard. "Better than Shakespear?" *Three Plays for Puritans.* Vol. 3. New York: Herbert S. Stone, 1900. New York: Brentano's, 1906. xxviii–xxxvii.

Shaw, J. "Cleopatra and Seleucus." *A Review of English Literature* 7 (1966): 79–86.

Simmons, J. L. "*Antony and Cleopatra* and *Coriolanus*, Shakespeare's Heroic Tragedies: A Jacobean Adjustment." *Shakespeare Studies* 26 (1973): 95–101.

Simonds, Peggy Munoz. "'To the Very Heart of Loss': Renaissance Iconography in Shakespeare's *Antony and Cleopatra.*" *Shakespeare Studies* 22 (1994): 220–76.

Simpson, Lucie. "Shakespeare's Cleopatra." *Fortnightly Review* NS 129 (1928): 332–42.

Singh, Jyostna. "Renaissance Anti-theatricality, Anti-feminism, and Shakespeare's *Antony and Cleopatra.*" *Renaissance Drama* 20 (1989): 99–119.

Smallwood, Robert. "Shakespeare Performed: Shakespeare at Stratford-upon-Avon, 1992." *Shakespeare Quarterly* 44 (1993): 343–62.

Snider, Denton J. "*Antony and Cleopatra.*" *Journal of Speculative Philosophy* 10 (1876): 52-69. Rpt. in *Systems of Shakespeare's Dramas.* Vol. 2. St. Louis, MO: G. T. Jones, 1877. 260–84.

Snyder, Susan. "Patterns of Motion in *Antony and Cleopatra.*" *Shakespeare Studies* 33 (1980): 113-22.

Speaight, Robert. *Shakespeare on the Stage: An Illustrated History of Shakespearian Performance.* Boston: Little, Brown, 1973.

Spencer, Benjamin T. "*Antony and Cleopatra* and the Paradoxical Metaphor." *Shakespeare Quarterly* 9 (1958): 373–78.

Spencer, Charles. "Plenty of Smoke, Not Enough Fire." *Daily Telegraph* 25 Apr. 2002: N. pag.

Spengnether, Madelon. "The Boy Actor and Femininity in *Antony and Cleopatra.*" *Shakespeare's Personality.* Ed. Norman Holland, Sidney Homan, and Bernard J. Paris. Berkeley: U of California P, 1989. 191–224.

Spevack, Marvin, ed. *Antony and Cleopatra.* A New Variorum Edition of Shakespeare. MLA, 1990.

Stahr, Adolf. *Cleopatra.* Berlin, 1864.

Starks, Lisa S. "'Like the Lover's Pinch, Which Hurts and Is Desired': The Narrative of Male Masochism and Shakespeare's *Antony and Cleopatra.*" *Literature and Psychology* 45.4 (1999): 58–73.

Stauffer, Donald. *Shakespeare's World of Images: The Development of His Moral Ideas*. New York: Norton, 1949.

Stempel, Daniel. "The Transmigration of the Crocodile." *Shakespeare Quarterly* 7 (1956): 59–72.

Steppat, Michael. *The Critical Reception of Shakespeare's* Antony and Cleopatra *from 1607 to 1905*. Amsterdam: Grüner, 1980.

Stilling, Roger. *Love and Death in Renaissance Tragedy*. Baton Rouge: Louisiana State UP, 1976.

Stirling, Brents. "Cleopatra's Scene with Seleucus: Plutarch, Daniel, and Shakespeare." *Shakespeare Quarterly* 15.2 (1964): 299–311.

———. *Unity in Shakespearian Tragedy: The Interplay of Theme and Character*. New York: Columbia UP, 1956.

Stockholder, Kay. *Dream Works: Lovers and Families in Shakespeare's Plays*. Toronto: U of Toronto, 1987.

Stoll, E. E. "Cleopatra." *The Modern Language Review* 23 (1928): 145–63.

Stoup, Thomas. "The Structure of *Antony and Cleopatra*." *Shakespeare Quarterly* 15.2 (1964): 289–98.

Swinburne, Algernon Charles. *A Study of Shakespeare*. 1879. 4th ed. London: Chatto & Windus, 1902.

Symons, Arthur. "*Antony and Cleopatra*." *Studies in the Elizabethan Drama*. 1919. New York: AMS, 1972. 1-20. Rpt. of "*Antony and Cleopatra*." *The Works of William Shakespeare*. Vol. 6. Ed. Henry Irving and Frank A. Marshall. London: Blackie & Son, Ltd., 1889. 119–24.

Tate, N[ahum]. *The Loyal General: A Tragedy. Acted at the Duke's Theatre*. William Wolf, 1680.

Tatspaugh, Patricia. "The Tragedies of Love on Film." *The Cambridge Companion to Shakespeare on Film*. Ed. Russell Jackson. Cambridge: Cambridge UP, 2000. 135–62.

Taylor, Paul. "Misplaced Imagination." *The Independent* 26 June 1999: N. pag.

———. "Review of the Globe *Antony and Cleopatra*." *The Independent* 3 Aug. 1999: 9.

———. "A Slightly Stilted Seduction." *The Independent* 29 Apr. 2002: N. pag.

Tennenhouse, Leonard. *Power on Display: The Politics of Shakespeare's Genres*. New York: Metheun, 1986.

Tierney, Margaret. "Review of Antony and Cleopatra." *Plays and Players* 20 (1972): 42–43.

Tillyard, E. M. W. "The Tragic Passion." *Shakespeare's Last Plays*. London: Chatto and Windus, 1938. 15–25.

Traversi, Derek. *Shakespeare: The Roman Plays*. Stanford, CA: Stanford UP, 1963.

Trench, Richard C. *Plutarch—His Life, His Parallel Lives, and His Morals: Five Lectures*. 1872. 2nd ed. London: Macmillan, 1874.

Trewin, J. C. *Shakespeare on the English Stage, 1900-1964: A Survey of Productions Illustrated from the Raymond Mander and Joe Mitchenson Theatre Collection*. London: Barrie and Rockliff, 1964.

Trewin, J. C. "Shakespeare in Britain." *Shakespeare Quarterly* 30 (1979): 151–58.

Tucker, Kenneth. "Psychetypes and Shakespeare's *Antony and Cleopatra*." *Journal of Evolutionary Psychology* 5 (1984): 176–81.

Tynan, Kenneth. "Theatre." *Evening Standard* 1 May 1953: N. pag.

Ulrici, Hermann. *Shakespeare's Dramatic Art: And His Relationship to Calderon and Geothe*. Trans. A. J. W. Morrison. Chapman Brothers, 1839. 357–59.

Van Doren, Mark. "*Antony and Cleopatra*." *Shakespeare*. New York: H. Holt, 1939. 267–81.

Van Laan, Thomas F. *Role-playing in Shakespeare*. Toronto: U of Toronto P, 1978.

Vincent, Barbara C. "Shakespeare's *Antony and Cleopatra* and the Rise of Comedy." *English Literary Renaissance* 12 (1982): 53–86.

Waddington, Raymond. "*Antony and Cleopatra*: 'What Venus did with Mars.' " *Shakespeare Studies* 2 (1966): 210–27.

Waith, Eugene M. "Manhood and Valor in Two Shakespearean Tragedies." *ELH* 17.4 (Dec. 1950): 262–73.

———. "Shakespeare." *The Herculean Hero in Marlowe, Chapman, Shakespeare, and Dryden*. New York: Columbia UP, 1962. 112–43.

Wardle, Irving. " 'Antony and Cleopatra': Royal Shakespeare." *The Times*, London 11 Oct. 1978: 9.

———. "Electrifying Detail and Tragic Exhilaration." *The Times*, London 11 Apr. 1987: 14.

———. "Grandeur in Mocking Grimace." *The Times*, London 28 May 1986: 19.

Warren, Roger. "Shakespeare in Britain, 1985." *Shakespeare Quarterly* 37 (1986): 114–20.

———. "Shakespeare in Britain, 1982–83." *Shakespeare Quarterly* 34 (1983): 334–40.

———. "Shakespeare in Britain, 1986–87." *Shakespeare Quarterly* 38 (1987): 359–65.

Watters, Jamie. "Brook Continues His Shakespearean Surprises." *The Christian Science Monitor* 17 Nov. 1978: 27.

Wells, Charles. *The Wide Arch: Roman Values in Shakespeare*. New York: St. Martin's, 1992.

Wells, Stanley, ed. *Shakespeare: A Bibliographical Guide*. New Edition. Oxford: Clarendon P, 1990.

———. "Shakespeare Performances in London and Stratford-upon-Avon, 1986–7." *Shakespeare Survey* 41 (1989): 159–81.

Welsh, James M., Richard Vela, and John C. Tibbetts, et al. *Shakespeare into Film*. New York: Checkmark Books, 2002.

Wheeler, Richard. *Shakespeare's Development and the Problem of Comedies*. Berkeley: U of California P, 1981.

Whitaker, Virgil K. *The Mirror up to Nature: The Technique of Shakespeare's Tragedies*. San Marino, CA: Huntington Library, 1965.

Whittier, Gayle. "The Sublime Androgyne Motif in Three Shakespearean Works." *Journal of Medieval and Renaissance Studies* 19 (1989): 185–210.

Williamson, Marilyn. "The Political Context in *Antony and Cleopatra*." *Shakespeare Quarterly* 21 (1970): 241–51.

Williamson, Sandra L., ed. *Shakespeare Criticism: Excerpts from the Criticism of William Shakespeare's Plays and Poetry, from the First Published Appraisals to Current Evaluations*. Vol. 17. Detroit, MI: Gale Research, 1992.

Willis, Susan. *The BBC Shakespeare Plays: Making the Televised Canon*. Chapel Hill: U of North Carolina P, 1991.

Wilson, John Dover. Introduction. *Antony and Cleopatra*. By William Shakespeare. 1950. Cambridge: Cambridge UP, 1954. vii–xxxvi.

Wingate, Charles E. L. Review. *The Cosmopolitan* 60.1 (May 1891): 3–13.

Winn, Steven. "Ashland's Uneven Trio from the Bard." *San Francisco Chronicle* 26 June 1993: N. pag.

Winter, Walter. *Old Shrines and Ivy*. New York: Macmillan, 1892.

Wofford, Susanne Lindgren, ed. *Shakespeare's Late Tragedies: A Collection of Critical Essays*. Upper Saddle River, NJ: Prentice Hall, 1996.

Wolf, William D. " 'New Heaven, New Earth': The Escape from Mutability in *Antony and Cleopatra*." *Shakespeare Quarterly* 33 (1982): 328–35.

Worsley, T. C. "The World Well Lost." *The New Statesman & Nation* 19 May 1951: N. pag.

Wortham, Christopher. "Temperance and the End of Time: Emblematic *Antony and Cleopatra*." *Comparative Drama* 29.1 (1995): 1–37.

Yachnin, Paul. " 'Courtiers of Beauteous Freedom': *Antony and Cleopatra* in Its Time." *Renaissance and Reformation* 15 (1991): 1–20.

Young, B. A. "*Antony and Cleopatra*." *The Financial Times* 16 Aug. 1972: 3.

2.
"Above the element they lived in"
The Visual Language of *Antony and Cleopatra,* Acts 4 and 5

DAVID BEVINGTON

Much has been written about the staging of the monument scenes in *Antony and Cleopatra* by way of speculating on how they were physically managed on Shakespeare's stage, presumably at the Globe Theatre. Much, too, has happened in theater history by way of experimenting with numerous possibilities. Less has been done with what the staging can mean thematically to the rest of the play and to its triumphant and tragic conclusion. My hope is to draw these worlds—the world of criticism and the world of the theater—together by asking how various stage configurations seem suited to close readings of the script not only as implicit stage directions but also as thematic explorations of the rise and fall of reputations, the dreams and aspirations of humans caught in the crossfire of their contradictory hopes and needs, the undulating oscillations that underlie so much of history as one civilization or regime replaces its predecessor, and still more. Our context is the early modern stage, in particular the Globe, with its "heavens" above the main stage painted with zodiacal signs and its trap door leading downward to the unknowable world of death, and the main stage itself providing the locus for human action in the brief moment of time that comprises the present. This "idea of a theater," in Francis Ferguson's memorable phrase, seems ideally suited to plays like *Hamlet* and *Cymbeline* and *The Tempest*, in which characters appeal directly to the heavens and in which the gods, whether Christian or heathen, make their appearances in or from those heavens. What does this theatrical world portend in a play like *Antony and Cleopatra*, based on classical history and affording no certain presence of the gods other than in the verbal asseverations of various speakers?

Prior to the final action in Alexandria, *Antony and Cleopatra* occupies the main stage as the theater of this world, brilliantly peopled with physical juxtapositions and contrastive locations. Demetrius and Philo frame the opening scene from their separate vantage point, perhaps downstage and to one side:

through their disapproving eyes we see at once the opulence and the degeneracy of Antony's enslavement to Cleopatra. Rome and Egypt come before us in paired and contrasted scenes, inviting endless staging opportunities for visual contrasts: in Egypt, eunuchs bearing fans and dark-skinned waiting women jesting about male potency, in Rome, powerful statesmen and their efficient lieutenants jockeying for position. Verbal evocations of Cleopatra on the River of Cydnus among her Nereid-like gentlewomen and fan-carrying boys "like smiling Cupids" are all the more erotic and incantatory because they are heard and savored voyeuristically by dutiful Roman soldiers (Bevington, *Complete Works* 2.2.201–50). Banquets onstage contrast the relaxed hedonism of Egypt with the competitive drinking rituals of the Roman rivals.

Warfare is conducted not by the usual strategies in Shakespeare of siege warfare but by alternating brief appearances of the generals at Actium (3.8–9) and then by the land army of Canidius marching *"one way over the stage"* while simultaneously the army of Caesar, led by Taurus, marches *"the other way,"* whereupon *"After their going in is heard the noise of a sea fight"* (3.10.0.1–4). This dramaturgic method of staging military conflict affords Shakespeare several advantages in this play. It puts theatrical emphasis on the moods and whims of the participants as they make momentous decisions, react to unexpected news, and (in Antony's case) brood shamefully over defeat. It relies to an unusual degree on the audience's imagination, even more so than at Agincourt in *Henry V*; here, after all, Shakespeare is dramatizing a naval battle. Most of all, perhaps, and most relevant to the argument of this essay, Shakespeare avoids quite literally the upstaging of his finale. Siege warfare, in all the *Henry VI* plays (at Orleans, Bordeaux, the Cade rebellion, York, Coventry), in *King John* (at Angiers), in *Richard II* (at Flint Castle), and in *Henry V* (at Harfleur), makes elaborate use of appearances *"on the walls"* in an *"above"* location over the rear wall of the tiring house, where those appearing in this location are to be understood as defenders of a besieged fortification defying or negotiating with their attackers facing them on the main stage. *Antony and Cleopatra* does not do this; it follows instead a convention found earlier in the battles of Shrewsbury and Agincourt, for example, complete with alarums and excursion. The choice in *Antony and Cleopatra* is better suited to the tactics of a naval battle; it also delays the play's use of the upper acting location until the moment of Antony's defeat in Egypt.

Prior to that final sequence, Shakespeare makes use of the unseen location below the stage, in what Hamlet calls the "cellarage" (*Hamlet* 1.5.160). When a company of Antony's soldiers post the guard on the night before Antony is to face Octavius Caesar in the field, placing themselves *"in every corner of the stage"* as though on the perimeter of their assigned encampment, they hear *"Music of the hautboys"* *"under the stage"* (4.3.8.1–12.1). This they take as a sign, as do we, though whether for good or evil is less certain. One guardsman ventures that " 'Tis the god Hercules, whom Antony loved, / Now leaves him" (4.3.21–22). We cannot even be certain (despite the accusative "whom," since "whom" and "who" are often interchangeable in Shakespeare) if this means that Hercules loved Antony or that Antony loved Hercules; oracular utterances are often bafflingly ambiguous, as when it is predicted in *2 Henry VI* that "The duke yet lives that Henry shall depose" (1.4.31), meaning either that the Duke of York will depose Henry VI or that Henry will depose the Duke, or perhaps both. The wailing sounds of the oboes are ominous and portend the sad moment when the sentry soldiers will come across the dead body of the heartbroken Enobarbus (4.9).

The effect of otherworldly sounds emanating from beneath the stage is like that of Hamlet Senior's Ghost, who *"cries under the stage"* (*Hamlet* 1.5.158) and obliges the guardsmen accompanying Hamlet on the battlements to shift their ground *"Hic et ubique"* (1.5.165) as they swear themselves to silence. To be sure, the Ghost can appear later to Hamlet in his mother's chambers as though by a regular stage door, and there is no indication that his appearances onstage in 1.1 and 1.4–5 are by means of the trap, just as the ghost of Julius Caesar appears to enter to Brutus and exit by regular means in that play (*Julius Caesar* 4.3.276–88). The trap is of course needed for Ophelia's grave, in act 5 of *Hamlet*, when, according to the unauthorized first quarto of 1603, *"Hamlet leaps in after Laertes"*; similarly, the author of an elegy on Richard Burbage reports that "Oft did I see him leap into the grave." *"Hautboys"* sound in *Macbeth*, preceded by thunder, as three successive apparitions manifest themselves to Macbeth and then descend, presumably by means of the trap. The stage directions specify that each apparition *"descends"* in turn once it has spoken, until at last the cauldron around which the weird sisters have danced and fed ingredients itself disappears. "Why sinks that cauldron?" cries Macbeth. "And what noise is this?" (4.1.69–106). *Titus Andronicus* demands a trapdoor for the foul pit into which Martius and then Quintus fall through the machination of Aaron and Tamora's two sons (2.3.185–246); it is variously described as a "deep pit" and a "gaping hollow of the earth," a "fell devouring receptacle / As hateful as Cocytus' misty mouth" (2.3.235–49). *Timon of Athens* may use the trap when he finds and then buries hated gold (*Timon* 4.3.25ff.). The supernatural sounds issuing from the space beneath the main stage thus provide *Antony and Cleopatra* with an unsettling and prognosticatory prologue to the play's final action, even though otherworldly associations and appearances need not be restricted to that dramatic model.

In fashioning his dramatic representation of the final monument sequence, Shakespeare began with Plutarch's account of how Cleopatra "had long before made many sumptuous tombs and monuments, as well for excellency of workmanship as for height and greatness of building, joining hard to the temple of Isis" (North's translation, 1006D). Plutarch reports how Diomedes, secretary to Antony, "was commanded to bring him [Antony] into the tomb or monument where Cleopatra was," after Antony had received the (false) report of Cleopatra's suicide, had condemned himself for being "of less courage and noble mind than a woman," and had summoned Eros to assist him in his own suicide. (Antony's meditations on bodily dissolution and his touching response to the seeming news of Cleopatra's death, spoken to Eros as a naive audience, are Shakespearean additions.) Plutarch names "Dercetaeus" (variously represented in the Folio text of *Antony and Cleopatra* as "*Dercetus*" or "*Decretas*," abbreviated in the speech headings as "*Dec.*" and "*Decre.*") as one of the guard who stayed behind when the rest fled. Shakespeare learned further from Plutarch that Cleopatra had "locked the doors unto her and shut all the springs of the locks with great bolts." When informed that Antony had been brought to her, dying, Cleopatra "would not open the gates, but came to the high windows, and cast out certain chains and ropes in which Antonius was trussed; and Cleopatra her own self, with two women only, which she had suffered to come with her into these monuments, triced Antony up" (1006D). In their last moments together, Antony bade Cleopatra "that she should not lament nor sorrow for the miserable change of his fortune at the end of his days," called for wine, and advised her "that chiefly she should trust Proculeius above any man else about Caesar" (1006F, 1007A).

Proculeius, having been sent by Caesar "to do what he could possible to get Cleopatra alive," since "she would marvelously beautify and set out his [Caesar's] triumph," set up a ladder "against that high window by the which Antonius was triced up" (1007C); Gallus held Cleopatra in conversation at the barred gate of the "monument" in order to distract her attention while Proculeius gained access to her locked space. Having discovered the intrusion, Cleopatra "thought to have stabbed herself in with a short dagger she ware of purpose by her side" but was prevented from doing so by Proculeius's coming suddenly upon her and "taking her by both the hands" (1007D). Subsequently, after Caesar's one visit to Cleopatra in her "monument," Dollabella, "a young gentleman" and "one of Caesar's very great familiars," "sent her word secretly, as she had requested him, that Caesar determined to take his journey through Syria, and that within three days he would send her away before with her children" (1009A–B). (Shakespeare elaborates the way in which Dollabella is infatuated by Cleopatra's beauty and listens sympathetically to her evocation of Antony as a godlike hero.) In his report of Cleopatra's interview with Caesar, Plutarch characterizes Seleucus as "one of her treasurers who, to seem a good servant, came straight to Caesar to disprove Cleopatra, that she had not set in all but kept many things back of purpose" (1008E); in Plutarch's view, Cleopatra's motive was plainly that of tricking Caesar into thinking that she desired to live.

Plutarch describes the visit to Cleopatra of the countryman (as he is called in North's translation) with a basket of figs, having informed us earlier, at the time of the battle of Actium, that Cleopatra had conducted tests to see what poisons "made man die with least pain," concluding that the "aspic" was best of all, since its fatal bite induced only a "heaviness of the head" and "a great desire to sleep" (1004C–D). Of the death scene, Plutarch reports simply that Cleopatra was found dead with "one of her two women, which was called Iras, dead at her feet" (1009E). The asp bites were found, according to some authorities consulted by Plutarch, on her arm (1010B). Concerning Charmian's death, Plutarch's account is close to Shakespeare's: "One of the soldiers, seeing her, angrily said unto her, 'Is that well done, Charmian?' 'Very well,' said she again, 'and meet for a princess descended from the race of so many noble kings.' She said no more, but fell down dead hard by the bed" (1009F–1010A). "No mark was seen of her body," says Plutarch of Cleopatra, "or any sign discerned that she was poisoned" (1004C–D, 1010B).

What staging choices and tactics does Shakespeare employ in drama-tizing this account? An overall impression is that he has omitted very little and has found visual equivalents for almost every detail. The stage direction at the head of 4.15, "Enter Cleopatra with her maids aloft, with Charmian and Iras," may mean that she appears in her monument with her two maids only, as Plutarch insists. The stage direction at the head of the final scene is essentially the same: "Enter Cleopatra, Charmian, Iras, and Mardian," with Mardian as a mute throughout the scene. Mardian accompanies these same three in the brief scene (4.13; "Enter Cleopatra, Charmian, Iras, Mardian") when Cleopatra announces to her women her determination to take refuge in the monument. The staging choice stresses her isolation and loss of the appurte-nances of power as she prepares for her end. She is visited by others in turn, in a sequence that is essentially that of Plutarch: Antony and the guard, Proculeius, the soldiers (probably including Gallus) who take her prisoner, Dollabella, Caesar and his train (including Maecenas), Seleucus, and the Clown or countryman with figs. Throughout these events she is the domi-nating presence, the presiding figure receiving attentions and giving orders, even when Caesar, too, is present. Rhythmically, in the concluding action of the play, her entries alone with none but her women and Mardian (4.13, 4.15, 5.2) alternate with more "Roman" sequences of Antony's abortive suicide (4.14) and Caesar's planning of strategy "with his council of war" (5.1). Shakespeare centers the final action of his play on Cleopatra through staging devices such as these.

An equally important sequence in the play's final action focuses on suicide. All is designed to lead up to the concluding tableau of Cleopatra, enthroned and in her regalia, declaring great Caesar "ass / Unpolicied" by her brave defiance (5.2.307–08). First, Cleopatra sends a false report of her suicide to Antony; he blunders in his attempt to kill himself, but is fatally wounded; she resolves, after his death, to take her own life "after the high Roman fashion" (4.15.92); Caesar receives a report of Antony's suicide, and thereupon orders Proculeius to

capture the Egyptian queen lest she take her own life; Cleopatra, surprised by
Caesar's soldiers, attempts to kill herself with a knife but is disarmed, as
reported in Plutarch; she succeeds in learning of Caesar's plan for her from Dollabella, and thereupon orders her women to attire her "like a queen," "crown and
all," in order that she may join Antony in death (5.2.227–32); Cleopatra dies
from the poisoned bite of asps, having been preceded by Iras (the cause of
whose death is left unexplained) and followed by Charmian, who imitates her
royal mistress in applying an asp to herself. Shakespeare found these materials
in Plutarch; the staging pattern is his.

Shakespeare underscores the visual prominence of Cleopatra in this final
sequence by specifying her entrance "*aloft*" in 4.15. He anticipates this
striking entry first with Cleopatra's announcement to her women that they are
to take refuge in the "monument" in the brief scene 4.13, and then with
Antony's hearing the supposed news of Cleopatra's suicide from Mardian,
prompting him to attempt suicide himself. That distressing action, of Antony's
falling on his sword and then, in pain, calling for his guard only to be left
unaided by them and deserted especially by Dercetus, whose only craven
response is to pick up the sword that has fatally wounded Antony in hopes of
gaining reward from Caesar by its means, leads to the irony of Antony's
learning from Diomedes that Cleopatra has sent to him, fearful of what he
might have done on the supposed news of her suicide; she herself is "Locked
in her monument" (4.14.125). As in the case of that younger pair of unlucky
lovers, Romeo and Juliet, the man chooses to end his life on a mistaken
assumption, only moments too soon, though in this instance the couple is
doomed by more weighty political and military circumstances. The irony of
this timing is at any rate a stageworthy device of pointing scene 14 forward
to Cleopatra's entrance "*aloft*." Scene 14 ends as Antony's guards, having been
summoned back by Diomedes, are bidden by him to "Bear me, good friends,
where Cleopatra bides" (136). They exeunt, "*bearing Antony*" (and presumably the dead Eros) offstage.

The insistent immediacy of the guards' destination makes for an especially
close link between scenes 4.14 and 4.15. Cleopatra enters "*aloft, with Charmian
and Iras*"; Mardian is not mentioned, and evidently is not there—perhaps, in
the dramatist's view, because he had been sent to give the false report of Cleopatra's suicide to Antony. (The care with which Shakespeare calculates the need
of persons onstage is shown in the fact that he adds Mardian to Plutarch's list
of those accompanying Cleopatra when she first takes refuge in the "monument"; she needs a messenger.) Cleopatra is given only a few lines to insist that
"I will never go from hence" (line 1) before Diomedes enters with the news of
Antony's imminent arrival, whereupon "*Enter Antony, and the Guard*" (4.9.1).
They are carrying him, and are on the main stage.

Scholars have devoted much attention to Diomedes's sole speech in this
scene as the first clue we are given as to stage arrangement. Asked by

Cleopatra if Antony is dead, he answers:

> His death's upon him, but not dead.
> Look out o'th'other side your monument;
> His guard have brought him thither. (4.15.7–9)

What does "o'th'other side your monument" mean spatially, and how is Cleopatra to signal that meaning by her own bodily movement? Is the upper acting area, in the gallery above the main stage, of sufficient dimensions to contain a crucial scene involving at least four actors portraying Cleopatra, Charmian, Iras, and Antony? Are sightlines a problem? True it is that scenes *"above"* throughout the plays of Shakespeare and his contemporaries are careful not to overload the upper acting area with large casts and busy action. The sequence of Romeo's departure from Juliet to his banishment stages them together at first *"aloft"* (3.5.O.1), but then specifies (line 42) that he quickly descends to the main stage (presumably by rope ladder, in full view of the audience) and then departs, at which point Juliet herself descends backstage to greet her mother and act out the rest of this busy scene (involving also the Nurse and Capulet) on the main stage; the unauthorized first quarto of *Romeo and Juliet* provides the evidence that *"She goeth down from the window."* Siege sequences, like that at Harfleur in *Henry V* (3.3) or at Angiers in *King John* (2.1), regularly introduce the defenders of the besieged city *"upon the walls"* (*King John* 2.1.200.1) speaking from above to the attackers on the main stage; the arrangement requires little space in the gallery, and invariably emphasizes a meaningful vertical relationship between those *"above"* and those who are below (Bevington, *Action Is Eloquence*, 99–114). Richard II's parleying with the surrounding army of Bolingbroke at Flint Castle (*Richard II* 3.3) makes poignant thematic use of this spatial relationship, concluding as it does in Richard's coming down into "the base court" like "glistering Phaëthon" (lines 178–82). Richard appears aloft with several of his supporters (Carlisle, Aumerle, Scroop, and Salisbury), but he does most of the talking in a static tableau before descending. In Fletcher's *The Tamer Tamed*, the rebellious women gather *"above"* to hurl taunts at the fathers and would-be husbands below on the main stage, indicating again how the gallery space could have held several actors in plain view of the audience, so long as their speaking is directed in some measure to actors on the main stage and so long as the scene above does not in itself become unduly elaborate. If the gallery was sometimes used for spectators, as is seemingly indicated in the De Witt sketch of the Swan Theater in about 1596, that space could presumably have been reserved for acting in plays requiring appearances *"above"* or *"on the walls."*

Cleopatra's scene *"aloft"* seems in keeping with these and other instances in early modern staging. She and her women are above, Antony and his guard below, at first; the vertical relationship is particularly vivid and essential to the story (see fig. 8). The movement of Antony himself is vertical, as in the

Fig. 8. The monument scene (4.15) with Vivien Leigh as Cleopatra and Laurence
Olivier as Antony in Michael Benthall's 1951 production of *Antony and Cleopatra* at
the St. James' Theatre. Angus McBean Photograph, Copyright © The Harvard Theatre Collection, The Houghton Library.

instances of Romeo and Richard II. The speaking above is mostly between
Antony and Cleopatra. None of this would seem to require a special structure.
The consensus today, with which I am in agreement, is that theories of a stage
"monument" built forward from the tiring house wall are unnecessary even if
not impossible. Diomedes's bidding Cleopatra to "Look out o'th'other side
your monument" would appear to be adequately visualized if Diomedes enters

from one door, whereupon Antony and his guard enter at another door, moving the audience's gaze from left to right or right to left, with Cleopatra turning one way to speak to Diomedes and the other way to behold Antony's entrance.[1] How did Shakespeare envisage the lifting up of Antony to Cleopatra? Plutarch, cited above, described how she "would not open the gates, but came to the high windows, and cast out certain chains and ropes in which Antonius was trussed; and Cleopatra her own self, with two women only, which she had suffered to come with her into these 'monuments,' triced Antony up." The "high windows" for Shakespeare, as in *Romeo and Juliet*, where Juliet's appearances above are always at a "window," never a balcony, meant that Cleopatra would be in the gallery. How high above the main stage was this gallery? And was there a railing to contend with? Richard Hosley reckons the height at fourteen feet to the top of the railing or barrier, though perhaps it might have been somewhat less in an age when ceiling heights were lower than today. Then, too, if there was a railing it might have been opened or removed for performance.[2] At all events, the task of lifting Antony aloft was a daunting one. Shakespeare capitalizes on the difficulty by giving lines to Cleopatra that stress Antony's heavy weight and the women's weakness in managing the task:

> Here's sport indeed! How heavy weighs my lord!
> Our strength is all gone into heaviness,
> That makes the weight. Had I great Juno's power,
> The strong-winged Mercury should fetch thee up
> And set thee by Jove's side. Yet come a little;
> Wishers were ever fools. Oh, come, come, come!
>   *They heave Antony aloft to Cleopatra.* (4.15.33–38)

These are highly pragmatic lines in the theater. They give time for the completion of a complicated action, while at the same time thematizing it through the wordplay on "heaviness" as sadness as well as considerable physical weight. The lines emphasize the bodily substantiality and earthbound qualities of Antony even while the movement is upward. This chiasmic and paradoxical movement is characteristic of the play's concluding action.

Did Cleopatra and her women employ chains and ropes in their task? Plutarch invites some such staging arrangement. Shakespeare's text does not specify, and so we are left to speculate. David Garrick, in the eighteenth century, specified that *"Cleopatra and her women throw out certain tackle, into which the people below put Antony, and he is drawn up."*[3] Peter Brook, in his production for the Royal Shakespeare Company at Stratford-upon-Avon in 1978, chose to have Cleopatra (played by Glenda Jackson) and her women tug at Antony (Alan Howard) with long cloth banners wrapped around Antony's body, and onto a red carpet (representing the monument) without actual

lifting; the actors mimed the difficulty of their task with grimaces and exclamations, leaving it to the audience to imagine the rest.[4] Conversely, Laurence
Olivier and Vivien Leigh at the St. James Theatre in 1951 needed only to cope
with a sphinx monument of about six feet in height, set on a turntable that
could rotate and display its back for the play's final scene (Lamb 140–41).
Shakespeare's only stage direction, "*They heave Antony aloft to Cleopatra*,"
with its ambiguous "*They*," certainly invites the participation of Antony's
guard in lifting Antony as high as possible in order to put Antony within reach
of the women, and perhaps no more was required than that. At the opposite
end of the scale of options, Richard Hosley proposes a harness attached to a
chair in which Antony could have been carried onstage connected by a rope
line to a winch and pulley housed in the "heavens" above (Hosley 64–65).[5]

Once Antony is above, dying in Cleopatra's arms, the staging is
eloquently simple, focusing on the lovers and then on Cleopatra's pitiful plight
and her brave resolution. It all seems well suited to the gallery space. Staging
questions do nonetheless remain. Do the guard soldiers who brought Antony
on, and Diomedes, remain onstage in silence during Antony's death scene, or
do they unobtrusively exit? And how is Antony to be removed at the scene's
end? The stage direction is laconic: "*Exeunt, bearing off Antony's body*." Does
this mean that Cleopatra and her two women are to accomplish this removal
by themselves? Cleopatra's concluding words seem to stress the task at hand:
"Come, away. / This case of that huge spirit now is cold. / Ah, women, women!
Come" (4.15.93–95). Because it would be awkward and wholly implausible
to bring on guards above, this seems to be the only option. It is one that again
stresses painful difficulty and the insistent heaviness of the dead body. The
more awkward the removal, the more the point is made that Cleopatra and her
women are left alone under formidably difficult circumstances.[6]

Cleopatra reenters after a scene (5.1) devoted to Caesar's learning of
Antony's death and his planning how to take Cleopatra captive. Proculeius and
Gallus are dispatched on this assignment; Dolabella is to follow. They know,
from the report of an Egyptian who has served Cleopatra, that she is "Confined
in all she has, her monument" (5.1.53). Caesar is particularly concerned that
she be taken by surprise, "Lest, in her greatness, by some mortal stroke / She
do defeat us" through suicide (64–65). The instructions to Proculeius and
Gallus are thus specific and frame our immediate understanding of act 5, scene
2. Cleopatra is indeed in her monument, with Charmian and Iras. Mardian is
back, though silent throughout (5.2.0.1). They are almost certainly on the main
stage, since the requirements of this final scene are large and almost sumptuous. The words "*above*" or "*aloft*" are absent from the stage directions,
unlike 4.15, where the wording is exact.[7] Shakespeare invites his audience to
transfer the imagined location of the interior of the monument from the
gallery to the main stage, much as he did earlier with Juliet's scene of farewell
to Romeo and her subsequent encounter with her mother, father, and nurse.
The practicalities of the transfer are paramount in each instance.

Such a transfer of a single locale from one staging area to another seems to have been imaginatively easy for early modern audiences, as it also can be in today's presentational theater, but it does present a difficulty in reshaping Plutarch's "against that high window by the which Antonius was triced up," whereupon Gallus holds Cleopatra in conversation at the barred gate of the monument in order to distract her attention while Proculeius gains access to her locked space. Scholars have attempted to reconstruct this business by bringing on a ladder and having Proculeius and others ascend to the gallery while Gallus speaks to Cleopatra through a grill in a specially constructed monument jutting out from the tiring house wall, or in a similar space fashioned out of the supposed "inner stage" located between the main stage doors. Proculeius thereupon comes down behind the scene and catches Cleopatra by surprise. The long remainder of the scene could thus be conducted in the supposed "inner stage" or spilling out onto the main stage.[8] Such an interpretation capitalizes on the elaborate stage structure posited by those who find it easier to account for Antony's entrance and his being lifted up to Cleopatra (in 4.15) with something more than the usual tiring-house wall.

Shakespeare's text mentions no ladder, nor does it provide any dialogue that implies climbing. Still, the difficulty remains at the start of 5.2: when Proculeius enters to Cleopatra and her women at line 8 (the stage direction says simply "*Enter Proculeius*"), how are the actors spatially grouped and in what way are the gates of the monument visually presented or implied? The ensuing dialogue between Proculeius and Cleopatra clearly presupposes that he does not yet have access to her and that she still is relying on locked gates to provide her security. And what is Gallus to do meantime, presuming that he is in fact present, as Caesar ordered? Gallus has no lines, in 5.1 or 5.2, and no specified entry during the arrest of Cleopatra, though later he does silently enter with Caesar's train at 5.2.109. Editors have sometimes brought him on with Proculeius and have then given him the line "You see how easily she may be surprised" (5.2.35), although it makes good enough sense assigned to Proculeius as in the Folio text.[9] This editorial emendation has generally gone along with a stage arrangement reduplicating Plutarch's account, giving Gallus the active role of holding Cleopatra in conversation while Proculeius and other soldiers prepare to come at her from behind.

Given the sparsity of stage directions in the Folio text, we are free to speculate about a staging plan that involves the main stage only, relying on the audience's imagination and the actors' skill in conveying a sense of separation. A parallel situation might be found in *Romeo and Juliet*, 2.1. Nineteenth-century directors worried about this "scene," since its implied location is some space adjacent to the garden behind the Capulets' house; Benvolio is sure that Romeo, for whom he and Mercutio are looking, has "leapt this orchard wall" (2.1.6). Staging conventions of the nineteenth century required that such a space be provided with its own scenery, however briefly, and separated by a curtain from what follows, since in 2.2 Romeo is clearly in the garden or orchard itself. Yet directors and editors alike have acknowledged since then that scenes 1 and 2 are linked by a rhymed couplet ("found ... wound") and that the action must be continuous. Romeo conceals himself from his friends by hiding behind a pillar or in some similar fashion, and the action proceeds without interruption, relying on the audience's ability to comprehend the semiotic convention that allows such an easy transfer. Similarly then in *Antony and Cleopatra* the actors might make use of the stage doors and perhaps the pillars, along with their furtive gestures of self-concealment, to signal to the audience their being "in hiding" or behind some understood barrier while Proculeius negotiates with Cleopatra. The very fact that Gallus is deleted from the account lends plausibility to such an arrangement as theatrically simpler. (*The Comedy of Errors* may provide a precedent here, when Antipholus and Dromio of Ephesus approach their dwelling only to be confronted by Dromio of Syracuse speaking from the other side of some door, 3.1. And, of course, overhearing scenes abound in early modern drama.) Proculeius's conversation with Cleopatra is long enough to give his fellow soldiers time to maneuver into position for the arrest; he himself takes over the role assigned to Gallus in Plutarch, of distracting Cleopatra's attention from what is about to happen. Perhaps Proculeius speaks from one of the stage doors, leaving the audience to understand that it represents the gates of the monument. Thereupon the soldiers, having stealthily entered from the other door and having hidden behind a pillar, rush forward (Neill Appendix B). (The two doors, as Neill observes, have been put to good use in 4.15.) Proculeius himself disarms Cleopatra in her first attempt at suicide, and the action is complete. Only an insistence on nineteenth-century literalism of stage business presents any serious difficulty with this sort of solution.

The concluding action of the play presents few staging difficulties. Cleopatra presides, despite her evident loss of power. She holds court, conversing with Proculeius and then Dolabella, receiving Caesar and his train in a kind of state visit, interrogating the countryman and his folk wisdom about snakes and women, and staging the magnificence of her suicide. Editors and stage directors do need to decide whether Mardian is silently present throughout and whether Charmian goes with Iras at line 232 to fetch Cleopatra's royal attire, but any plan will work here; Cleopatra is always on display, so that quiet observers of her presiding actions would not be out of place. Her speeches and stage action alike underscore the ceremonial importance of her staging of her death. She will meet Mark Antony "like a queen," in her "best attires," with "crown and all" (5.2.227–32). Charmian's last act before she too dies is that of "trimming up the diadem / On her dead mistress" (342–43). A "bed" must be provided for Cleopatra in which she is ceremonially carried from the stage: "Take up her bed, / And bear her women from the monument" (356–57). Her departure from the stage is thus strikingly different from the way in which Antony is awkwardly borne off by Cleopatra and her women. Cleopatra's final exeunt is more like the ending of *Hamlet*, where Fortinbras orders that "four captains" are to "Bear Hamlet, like a soldier, to the stage," to the accompaniment of "The soldiers' music and the rite of war" (5.2.397–401). Cleopatra is theatrically the hero of the ending in *Antony and Cleopatra* and is to "be buried by her Antony"; "No grave upon the earth shall clip in it / A pair so famous" (5.2.358–60).

Concurrent with the play's spatial exploration of verticality and enthronement in its ending cadences, *Antony and Cleopatra* dwells lovingly on images and themes of upward and downward movement in patterns of chiastic mirroring (Ornstein 42 and Charney 133–35). The defeat of the lovers at Actium introduces a series of metaphors evoking the imminent fall and bodily dissolution of Antony and Cleopatra as measured against the continuing rise of "high-battled Caesar" (3.13.29). Cleopatra sends word to Caesar that she is prepared to "lay my crown at's feet, and there to kneel / Till from his all-obeying breath I hear / The doom of Egypt" (3.13.76–78). In his savage rage at Cleopatra's favorable reception of Thidias, Antony pictures himself "Upon the hill of Basan, to outroar / The hornèd herd" (3.13.129–30). "Our terrene moon is now eclipsed, / And it portends alone the fall of Antony," he laments (3.13.156–57). Cleopatra responds by calling down on herself a deluge of unhappiness if she is guilty of coldheartedness toward him: "if I be so, / From my cold heart let heaven engender hail, / And poison it in the source, and the first stone / Drop in my neck; as it determines, so / Dissolve my life!" "By the discandying of this pelleted storm," she and all Egypt are to "Lie graveless till the flies and gnats of Nile / Have buried them for prey!"(3.13.161–70). After his defeat at Alexandria, Antony pictures his disgrace as dissolution and fall: "The hearts / That spanieled me at heels, to whom I gave / Their wishes, do discandy, melt their sweets / On blossoming Caesar; and this pine is barked / That overtopped them all" (4.12.20–24).

The turning occurs at the very moment of Cleopatra's taking refuge in the monument. As he meditates on death in his conversation with Eros, Antony's mind fills with images that are directed upwards. He pictures "a cloud that's dragonish, / A vapor sometime like a bear or lion, / A towered citadel, a pendant rock, / A forkèd mountain, or blue promontory / With trees upon' t that nod unto the world / And mock our eyes with air" (4.14.1–7). The images are insubstantial, evanescent, dreamlike, but they ascend. Learning of Cleopatra's supposed death, he embraces a vision of their abode "Where souls do … make the ghosts gaze" (4.14.51–52). Cleopatra, as she labors to lift Antony up to her in the monument, contrasts his heaviness and weight with the wished-for power of Juno and "strong-winged Mercury" by means of which she longs to fetch Antony up and set him "by Jove's side" (4.15.33–37). In Antony's death, she perceives, "The crown o'th' earth doth melt" and "withered is the garland of the war; / The soldier's pole is fall'n" (4.15.65–67), and yet her desolation" does "begin to make / A better life" (5.2.1–2). Rather than be hoisted up to "the shouting varletry / Of censuring Rome," she would prefer to be hung in chains in her country's "high pyramides" (5.2.55–61). In her dream of "an emperor Antony," she insistently represents him in images that aspire upward, his legs bestriding the ocean, his reared arm cresting the world, and his delights "dolphinlike" in showing "his back above / The element they lived in" (5.2.75–89).

Such images are "past the size of dreaming" (5.2.96). They counter and negate the aspirations of Caesar to take Cleopatra in triumph to Rome, where "Mechanic slaves" will "Uplift" her and her women "to the view" of the populace and portray her Alexandrian revels with Antony on public stages (5.2.209–21). The theater itself becomes a contested space in the rival dreams of the play's great antagonists. In order to defeat Caesar's plan to display her to the Roman public as a debased sort of freak show featuring the monster woman of devouring sexual appetite, Cleopatra will produce her own finale. She will "call great Caesar ass / Unpolicied" (5.2.307–08) by ascending to her greatness as queen, in her "monument," fully attired and wearing her diadem. The stage picture of the concluding action of *Antony and Cleopatra* confirms this account of a royalty that triumphs in defeat.

NOTES

1. Many students of the play have proposed a special stage structure, beginning with Thomas Hanmer and Lewis Theobald in the eighteenth century. Theobald provides the following stage direction: "*Here Gallus, and Guard, ascend the Monument by a Ladder, and enter at a back-window.*" Edmund Malone follows suit. J. Dover Wilson proposes that a monument be erected on the main stage over the trap door, enabling Cleopatra and her women to enter it by this means. C. Walter Hodges (*The Globe Restored*) places a special structure in front of the tiring house façade, from which vantage Cleopatra can look to one side of her monument and then the other as Antony is carried in by his guard. John Cranford Adams addresses this staging requirement by providing a bay window in a casement six feet wide, with window openings in the sides looking to the left and the right (268). Ernest Rhodes's windowlike bay structure based on Robert Fludd's stage-illustration *Theatrum Orbi*, serves a similar purpose ("Cleopatra's 'Monument' and the Gallery in Fludd's *Theatrum Orbi*" 41–48). Leslie Hotson's proposed monument is free-standing and obligingly only six feet high to the platform on which Cleopatra and her women are placed, though it provides surrounding pillars around her to create the impression of a room (*Shakespeare's Wooden O*). See M. R. Ridley's Arden edition of 1954 and 1962, Appendix IV, for a summary and analysis, and a comprehensive survey of criticism regarding the staging of 4.15 and 5.2 in Marvin Spevack's New Variorum edition of the play, pp. 777–93. The theories of Adams et al. are now generally discounted, though Andrew Gurr (*The Shakespearean Stage* 137) clings to the idea that the

    gallery would have been too problematic and that the monument must have been one of the "special properties" in the Globe's inventory.

2. Granville-Barker (1.404–05) argues that "The balustrade must ... have been removed for the occasion or made to swing open, if the ordinary upper stage was used." The matter is discussed also by Beckerman.

3. Cited in Madelaine. This edition is richly informative on stage history.

4. Brook may have known of Frank Benson's 1898 production in which the women, placed in a large set representing the monument, lowered strips of linen which the guards wound around Antony and then assisted by hoisting Antony up with the butt ends of their halberds while the women hauled on the linen. Herbert Beer-bohm Tree also used linen in 1906. Glen Byam Shaw, with Michael Redgrave and Peggy Ashcroft in the leading roles at the Shakespeare Memorial Theatre, Strat-ford-upon-Avon, in 1953, had the women use their scarves. See Madelaine's edition (289–90) and Margaret Lamb (145 ff.). This tradition may owe something in turn to an odd passage in Samuel Daniel's *Cleopatra*, 1607 version, describing how Cleopatra "drawes him up in rowles of taffety / T'a window at the top, which did allow / A little light into her monumint" (quoted in Lamb 183, and discussed by Joan Rees [91–93]). Plutarch gives chains and ropes to the women, with no mention of taffeta or other cloth.

5. Lamb (182) plausibly objects that there is "only one other recorded contemporary theatrical hoisting, in which a boy was lifted only a few feet; and there is no conclusive evidence that the Globe had flying machinery in 1606."

6. Thompson (77–90) speculates that Antony might have been lifted up to Cleopatra in the gallery but not onto it, thereupon being lowered to the main stage to die and be carried offstage by his men at the end of the scene; but an awkward exit above might seem more in keeping with the main argument of Thompson's otherwise excellent article. The suggestion has not caught on with theater directors.

7. Benson, in 1598, staged act 5, scene 2 atop the monument, in accord with nine-teenth-century dictates of full-scale "realistic" theatrical locale; Hanmer, among other early editors, assumed that the scene should be staged "aloft." Benson has had few imitators since (Madelaine's edition, 301).

8. Jenkin (1–14) elaborately and implausibly stages the arrest of Cleopatra in the "inner stage" by having Gallus and two soldiers ascend to the gallery and come from behind. He follows Theobald, Hanmer, and others; see note 1.

9. Theobald was the first to reassign the line to Gallus, basing the emendation on Plutarch. Among more recent editors who have followed suit is Ridley in his Arden 2nd edition, p. 210. The repetition in the Folio of the speech heading "Pro." is not uncommon following a stage direction and need not indicate a new speaker.

WORKS CITED

Adams, John Cranford. *The Globe Playhouse: Its Design and Equipment*. Cambridge, MA: Harvard UP, 1942.

Beckerman, Bernard. *Shakespeare at the Globe, 1599–1609*. New York: Macmillan, 1962, 1967.

Bevington, David. *Action Is Eloquence: The Language of Stage Gesture in Shake-speare*. Cambridge, MA: Harvard UP, 1984.

————. *The Complete Works of Shakespeare*. 5th ed. New York: Longman, 2003.

Charney, Maurice. *Discussions of Shakespeare's Roman Plays*. Cambridge, MA: Harvard UP, 1964.

Ferguson, Francis. *The Idea of a Theater*. Princeton: Princeton UP, 1949.

Granville-Barker, Harley. *Prefaces to Shakespeare*. Princeton: Princeton UP, 1952.

Gurr, Andrew. *The Shakespearean Stage, 1574–1642*. Cambridge: Cambridge UP, 1970.

Hanmer, Thomas, Ed. *Works*. London: 1743–44.

Hodges, C. Walter. *The Globe Restored*. London: Benn, 1953, 1968.

Hosley, Richard. "The Staging of the Monument Scenes in *Antony and Cleopatra*." *Library Chronicle* 30 (1964): 62–71.

Hotson, Leslie. *Shakespeare's Wooden O*. London: Rupert Hart-Davis, 1959.

Jenkin, Bernard. "*Antony and Cleopatra*: Some Suggestions on the Monument Scenes." *Review of English Studies* 21 (1945): 1–14.

Lamb, Margaret. *"Antony and Cleopatra" on the English Stage*. Rutherford, NJ: Farleigh Dickinson UP, 1980.

Madelaine, Richard, Ed. *Antony and Cleopatra*. Shakespeare in Production. Cambridge: Cambridge UP, 1998.

Malone, Edmund, ed. *Works*. London, 1790.

Neill, Michael, Ed. *Anthony and Cleopatra*. Oxford: Oxford UP, 1994.

Ornstein, Robert. "The Ethic of the Imagination: Love and Art in *Antony and Cleopatra*." *Later Shakespeare*. Eds. John Russell Brown and Bernard Harris. *Stratford-upon-Avon Studies* 8 (1966).

Plutarch, *Lives of the Noble Grecians and Romans*. Trans. Thomas North from the French of Jacques Amyot. London, 1579. Citations are from Geoffrey Bullough, ed. *Narrartives and Dramatic Sources of Shakespeare*, 8 vols. London, 1957–1975.

Rees, Joan. "An Elizabethan Eyewitness of *Antony and Cleopatra*?" *Shakespeare Survey* 6 (1953), 91–93.

Rhodes, Ernest. "Cleopatra's 'Monument' and the Gallery in Fludd's Theatrum Orbi." *Renaissance Papers* (1971, 1972): 41–48.

Ridley, M. R., Ed. *Antony and Cleopatra*. The Arden Shakespeare. London, 1954, 1962.

Spevack, Marvin, Ed. *Antony and Cleopatra*. The New Variorum Shakespeare. New York: MLA, 1990.

Theobald, Lewis, Ed. *Works*. London, 1752.

Thompson, Leslie. "*Antony and Cleopatra*, Act 4 Scene 16: "'A heavy sight.'" *Shakespeare Survey* 41 (1989): 77–90.

Wilson, John Dover, Ed. *Antony and Cleopatra*. Cambridge: Cambridge UP, 1950.

3.
Passion and Politics

Antony and Cleopatra in Performance

DAVID FULLER

I

"Ein alter Mann," wrote Goethe, "ist stets ein König Lear" (*Zahme Xenien* I).
Shakespearean tragedy deals in characters and forces that can be seen as
embodying realities beyond the terms of their primary articulation. Iago and
Othello are individuals: but the play carries such a weight of feeling in part
because they also epitomize the will of cynicism to destroy idealism. Hamlet
is an individual whose mother marries his father's murderer: he is also the
embodiment of *Weltschmerz* and *Unheimlichkeit*. Similarly in *Antony and
Cleopatra*, representative value lies most obviously in the competing locations, Rome and Egypt. Any shorthand for what they represent will be partial:
politics and love, the material and the spiritual, male and female, even those
Blakean complementarities, Reason and Energy. And, as with Blake's angels
and devils, though the ultimate human need may be a marriage of heaven and
hell, any given situation is within, not above the contingencies of existence.
"This angel, who is now become a devil, is my particular friend": Blake's
devil-narrator rejoices in conversion and a soul saved. Where there is competition of values, choices are to be made. Alternative ways of valuing the
central characters and the attitudes to experience they personify are written
into *Antony and Cleopatra*. Cleopatra, from one perspective a "lass unparalleled" who, in her "infinite variety," "o'erpictur[es] Venus," is, from another, a
"gipsy," "strumpet," and "whore." Antony is "Mars," "Jove," "the crown
o'th'earth," "the solder's pole"; his love is also "dotage" and "lascivious
wassails." Although there is no simple scheme, these alternative ways of
valuing tend to be placed: they emerge, that is, from characteristic speakers
and positions that are themselves evaluated by the play as a whole. Any
production will present a view of this contest: the view a production finally
presents will be fundamental to the nature of the dramatic experience it offers
and to the sense in which the play emerges as the tragedy of its protagonists.

111

But, although a production should know from the outset what view of this contest it will elicit, it need not affirm one side or the other at every point; rather the reverse, as the worldviews in contest, although finally irreconcilable, are both profound. Shakespeare probes the virtues and the limitations of both. The play corresponds in part to Hegel's idea of tragedy as the clash of irreconcilable opposites: Creon and Antigone—both forms of the good in their different spheres, although incompatible, bound one to destroy another, when brought into opposition.

Any production puts its thumb in the scale, with implications about how these alternative ways of valuing are themselves valued. From among several notable productions of the postwar era, I will discuss three that present the central issues in different ways: that directed by Glen Byam Shaw, with Michael Redgrave and Peggy Ashcroft, for the Royal Shakespeare Company, in 1953; that directed by Trevor Nunn, with Richard Johnson and Janet Suzman, also for the Royal Shakespeare Company, in 1972–73; and that directed by Peter Hall, with Anthony Hopkins and Judi Dench, at the National Theatre, London, in 1987.[1] I also will examine central issues of the play as these are dramatized in Samuel Barber's opera, written for the New York Metropolitan Opera in 1966, with libretto from Shakespeare and production by Franco Zeffirelli. The prompt book for the Shaw/Redgrave/Ashcroft production is preserved in the Royal Shakespeare Company archive, as is a collection of portrait photographs by Angus McBean derived from the performances. In December 1953, the production was recorded for radio by the BBC (with minor adaptations for the change of medium—mainly the addition of brief narrative connections from North's Plutarch). The broadcast (of April 26, 1954) is preserved in the British Library National Sound Archive.[2] The prompt book for the Nunn / Johnson / Suzman production is likewise in the Royal Shakespeare Company archive, with production photographs by Joe Cocks. Again the National Sound Archive has an audio recording. There is also a version of this production especially made for television, not filmed on stage, which was subsequently issued on videotape. Although the casts were identical in all but minor roles, the prompt book and the audio version of the stage production indicate that the television version was not a simple remake for the new medium but, rather, a reworking. The prompt book for the Hall / Hopkins / Dench production is in the National Theatre archive, with production photographs by John Haynes, and costume materials. And again there is a National Sound Archive audio recording. All three productions are thus variously well preserved.

One main problem for the performer of Cleopatra is to encompass the range of the part—to be both a "lass" and "unparalleled," "royal Egypt" and "no more but e'en a woman"; and to encompass the range in such a way as to bring its extremes into coherent relation with one another—as Enobarbus has it, to make "defect perfection." The part is written so as almost to force on the audience interpretative doubts. Whether or not these are fundamental is arguable: they are more than superficial, and this is an effect a performer can exploit with various results. Particularly Cleopatra's constant staging of herself, both with premeditation and extemporarily, may appear shrewdly manipulative or fundamentally heroic—a Yeatsian recognition that assuming the appropriate masks is a necessary precursor to becoming one's full selves. On this view, Cleopatra brings into being the grand and various versions of herself she is able to imagine; but at each moment one effect is characteristically to keep the audience uncertain about motives and values. A simpler problem, also an aspect of the role's range, is how its sensual or (and how the performer conceives of this is open to judgment) its sexual energies are presented. A performer may shape her presentation of the character that is said (offstage) to "o'erpictur[e] Venus" and to appear in the costume of Isis, mindful of the fact that the part was written to be played by a boy, and on the supposition that sexual feeling would therefore be presented obliquely. Or she may shape her presentation on the contrary supposition—that, whatever compromises were forced by the original circumstances of performance, what Shakespeare ideally imagined is what the stage now permits.

For the actor of Antony the central problem is how far the grand and heroic character reflected and reported in the play should be the character as shown—and, if so, how to make him this. As with the role-playing of Cleopatra, the play itself reflects on this in a variety of ways—that as a soldier he had exemplary, almost superhuman abilities (1.4); but that (in a captain's view), like all generals, he "ever won / More in [his] officer than person" (3.1.16–17); that Hercules leaves him after Actium, but that Mars left him (in Philo's view) before the action began; that he "continues still a Jove" (4.6.30; but only in fits and starts); that beneath everything he really was the supreme fiction of Cleopatra's visionary obituary (5.2.75–99)—though even to the newly enthralled Dolabella this is an impossibility.[3] Judgment on this concerns not only the direct presentation of Antony but also the presentation of all those characters through whom Antony's greatness, or his baseness, is projected.

It is central to an audience's interpretation of both protagonists—of Cleopatra's love and the heroic status of Antony—that they should be able fully and without inhibition to inhabit and project their visionary extremes: "eternity was in our lips and eyes, / Bliss in our brows' bent"; "where souls do couch on flowers, we'll hand in hand" (1.3.35–6; 4.14.50); and their tenderness: "Sir, you and I must part, but that's not it; / Sir, you and I have loved, but there's not it"; "Fall not a tear, I say: one of them rates / All that is won and lost" (1.3.88–89; 3.11.68–69). Contrasting typically English and French styles of speaking verse, W. H. Auden remarks wittily that to perform Phèdre is more like singing Isolde than performing Cleopatra (Auden 25). But the roles of both Antony and Cleopatra, if they do not require precisely Wagnerian vocal ability, do require at times its spoken equivalent: "Oh, from Italy! / Ram thou my fruitful tidings in mine ears, / That long time have been barren"; "O withered is the garland of the war" (2.5.23–25; 4.15.66). To hear a performer who can project with conviction and intensity the range of Cleopatra from ecstasy to desolation is to have dimensions of the role revealed that cannot be made apparent other than through the tones of the verse realized in a voice. It is only by the actors' ability to deliver with conviction this musical and visionary poetry that the lovers can seem even arguably to justify the judgment that "the nobleness of life is to do thus." Insofar as the lovers are judged by reflection, Enobarbus is the most important point of reference. It is a difficult role: the actor needs to be both straightforward to the point of cynicism and devoted to a degree that finally destroys him. It is vital that this gamut be fully registered: both Enobarbus's unblinking honesty and his final unillusioned devotion are important to an audience's trust in his judgments. He in some measure creates the lovers—both Antony's nobility and Cleopatra's fascination (Redgrave, 1958, 79).

As with the presentation of the lovers, with Octavius, too, there is a simplicity to be avoided that bears on the balance of the whole play. As the main primary representative of Rome he tends to stand for the values of his civilization. His portrayal therefore has important bearings on how an audience views the central couple and Egyptian values. Octavius can be presented simply as the obvious foil to the lovers—emotionally cold, putting political calculation before human relationships. He also can be presented as a humane, albeit shrewd, political realist. As with Cleopatra, there are ambiguities that production may leave open, but with Octavius production can also close these off, and in different ways—particularly in relation to his treatment of Octavia. The presentation of the political context can be decisive here. If *Antony and Cleopatra* is understood as in part a political play, in which Pompey's threat to the stability of the Empire is fully articulated and seen as serious, then the actions of Octavius in responding to that threat appear, not as machinations in a self-interested battle for power, but actions of real and necessary politico-military substance.

This raises, of course, the issue, still almost universal in performance of Shakespeare, of cutting. The plausible non pragmatic reason for cutting in Shakespeare's postapprentice work is that a passage or scene comprehensible to the original audience cannot be made comprehensible to a modern audience. There may be genuine reasons for this, especially in comedy, where semantic shifts mean that even a broad sense cannot be conveyed by intonation or gesture. This happens more rarely than theatrical practice seems to propose. It is unlikely that the whole first audience was so attuned to the complex verbal wit in which Shakespeare regularly engages as to understand all that the ideal audience or fit reader can discover: probably the King's Men expected to convey to much of the audience no more than the general implications of the more complex verbal wit. Otherwise, there is either an implicit acceptance that the director must give in to an audience's philistinism ("this is too long"—to which the answer is the decisive dismissal of *Hamlet*), or an implicit claim that the director knows better than Shakespeare—a claim that imaginative direction of complete texts regularly shows to be false. What cutting usually in fact shows is that some scene or passage does not fit the director's conception of the play or the actor's conception of the role—which means, of course, the director's or actor's misconception. Properly, cutting, whether for practical or other reasons, imposes on the director a duty of trying to understand the effect of what will be lost so that this can, as far as possible, be replaced by some other aspect of the production. What regularly happens in fact is that the importance of what is cut is not understood, and the play is in effect simply changed—as when Pompey episodes (for example) are cut in act 2 of *Antony and Cleopatra*, apparently on the supposition that the author of *Hamlet* and *King Lear* was inertly incorporating source materials that he might have seen had no point in the love tragedy it is supposed he was trying to create. This is not to argue that Homer never nods, only that Shakespeare is a better judge of dramatic effect than most directors, even when they are not acting with a cavalier disregard for a text's integrity.

Of the productions here considered only Peter Hall's presented the full text. Both Glen Byam Shaw and Trevor Nunn cut about one third of the play, at times with the result of concentrating the effect of the original in some partial or slanted form; more often with an effect of straightforward distortion. Such cuts can at times be revealing, obliquely, about the play itself. Usually they are simply revealing about directorial bias.

II

In Glen Byam Shaw's production, both Antony and Cleopatra (fig. 9) were presented as predominantly noble: their love was acted seriously, as love, not as infatuation in Antony, not as politics by Cleopatra. Peggy Ashcroft's interpretation was what Harold Bloom would call a "strong misreading" of the role: she did not generate the fascinating doubts that in some presentations make the audience's relation to Cleopatra like Antony's. Ashcroft cut down, and in places cut out, ambiguity—the fleeting moon, the baser elements; but she presented the fire and air of Cleopatra with unmatched energy and radiance. Because the dynasty to which Cleopatra belonged was historically Macedonian Greek, Ashcroft decided that Cleopatra should be played as this, with Hellenic costumes: there was no relish of "Phoebus' amorous pinches black"—or, in the Roman view, no feeling of the "gipsy." Even the most glowing reviews thought Ashcroft not temperamentally suited to the role. It was generally agreed that she did all art could do to overcome this, but the presentation minimized the voluptuous. Ashcroft apparently bore in mind

Fig. 9. Peggy Ashcroft as Cleopatra and Michael Redgrave as Antony in Glen Byam Shaw's 1953 production of *Antony and Cleopatra* at the Memorial Theatre in Stratford-upon-Avon. Photographer Angus McBean © Royal Shakespeare Company.

Harley Granville-Barker's view that, as the part was written for a boy, sensuality should be not directly presented but left for the verse to suggest.

The scene in which Cleopatra receives the news of Antony's marriage was indicative of Ashcroft's fundamental approach. There was no question of the passion being stagy: it was real and sincere. Beginning languidly, from melancholy as voluptuous pleasure, the scene moved suddenly to a high pitch to express the excitement of relief from the pain of absence ("O, from Italy"). It then progressed from real fear and horror to genuine potential distress; to an ecstasy of relief that Ashcroft's richness of voice suggested as experienced through the whole being; and finally to serious agony, releasing rage in tears and frankly desolate pleading. In reflecting on wildness that has been ungoverned though it is the reflex of noble feelings ("these hands do lack nobility ... "), Ashcroft made Cleopatra's "defect perfection." Enobarbus' tribute was taken as an index of how the role should be acted. "Undignified" behavior was not simply low: that rage was, with good cause, fully inhabited, and that there could be nevertheless recovery from feeling to reflection made this Cleopatra's wildness especially grand.

Other episodes that, in another presentation, might appear more open to variousness of interpretation were presented unambiguously. In dealing with Thidias Ashcroft's mocking delivery of "He [Octavius] is a god and knows / What is most right" (3.13.61–62) left the audience in no doubt: whatever the interpretations of Enobarbus and Antony, this Cleopatra was doing what she says, playing for time. She repudiated with offended dignity Antony's low suggestions about a skeptical reading of her actions. Minimizing the woman commanded by poor passion in Royal Egypt was at its clearest in the way in which the episode with Seleucus was cut. Lines that might recall Cleopatra's beating of her messenger were omitted (5.2.149b–157), as were lines which, in apparently looking forward to a possible life in Rome, might seem to introduce doubts about her declared intention of suicide (163b–71). The emphasis thus fell not on Cleopatra's betrayal by her servant but on the successful fencing with Octavius that leaves her free to be "noble to [herself]." The play's final image was a tableau of apotheosis: Cleopatra's "bed" was (as often) a throne, concentrating entirely on her royalty: the stage picture conveyed nothing of the element of erotic consummation implied by the text (death as marriage, its stroke a lover's pinch, the asp a baby at the breast). Ashcroft was enthroned in a costume much grander than any worn in the production up to this point. Iras and Charmian died falling symmetrically, heads towards their mistress, to right and left of her throne. Caesar's direction to remove the bodies was cut (346b–50). This image of death as a final assertion of power was emphasized by having Dolabella (a handsome, youthful Robert Shaw) exit last, looking back to remind the audience that one of Cleopatra's final acts had been to fascinate one more Roman. The play thus closed with a triumphant metamorphosis: the grandeur that Enobarbus earlier reported was made at last visible in Cleopatra's successful staging of herself "again for Cydnus / To meet Mark Antony."

If the greatness of Antony is largely shown in the play by reflection, it is nevertheless such a united chorus of reflections from so many different points of view that a production that does not give these appropriate weight betrays the presentation: Octavius, who admires his former soldierly prowess (1.4.56–72; cut in this production); Enobarbus, who dies of grief at his betrayal ("nobler than my revolt is infamous"); Eros, who chooses to die himself rather than kill the master he loves; above all Cleopatra, especially in her final visionary account (5.2.75–99). Although evidently not choric, professedly uncertain about its own mixture of fact and imagination, and rejected by Dolabella, this should not be felt by the audience as out of contact with the play's varied chorus of admiration and love. Without a due sense, in part of what has been, though also of the greatness Antony continues to show—not least in the breadth of mind with which, like other Shakespearean tragic heroes, he struggles with his own degradation—there is no adequate sense of tragedy.

Redgrave looked the part, with natural good looks and a physique that suggested he might once have performed the feats attributed to Antony. He also gave a due sense of what is simply grand—Antony's superiority during the war council (2.2), where he admits mistakes frankly and with dignity, in contrast to the petulance of Octavius and the weakness of Lepidus; his tenderness to Octavia, which (despite Enobarbus's deeper realizations) an audience should feel is sincerely meant at the moment of utterance.[4] There is also real degradation, and Redgrave thoroughly brought this out, particularly in the depth and emphasis with which he projected Antony's shame at failure (3.11), and through the sadistic relish of the whipping of Thidias by which Antony reasserts an identity crumpled by defeat. But Redgrave's most striking success was in giving due weight to Antony's tragedy by conveying the grandeur of the character that other actors have found too much present only by reflection. This resulted principally from his ability to speak the poetry. Excellent verse-speaking was a main feature of the production. Both Ashcroft and Redgrave could project and sustain intensity of feeling by conveying, without alienatingly unnatural *arioso* effect, the structure, pulse, and singing line of the verse. Redgrave, a poet himself as a young man (a member of the Empson/ Bronowski *Experiment* group in late 1920s Cambridge), showed superlative ability to project emotion through his unaffected relish of the words. When the role required it, most particularly in the scenes of Antony's attempted suicide and his death, Redgrave's voice was the theatrical equivalent of Cleopatra's vision, "propertied as all the tuned spheres." What the broadcast of the production shows is that it was often not through the projection of what might usually be thought of as "character" that Ashcroft and Redgrave were able to generate the intensity of feeling to which reviews bear witness: it was through the cultivated intuition that allowed them to convey with apparent naturalness feelings embodied in the often complex syntactic and rhythmic structure and intricate musicality of the verse.

The production as a whole supported them in this. The prompt book was a marked-up copy of the New Temple Shakespeare edition (M. R. Ridley, Dent, 1935), which (although it retains the conventional scene numbering in headings) does not mark divisions when the stage is cleared but the location remains the same. It thus gives a clear sense of the continuity of the action. This is reflected in the prompt book scene groupings and apparently encouraged a fast-moving production style.[5] Reviewers remarked on the uncluttered sets and quick transitions (changes of location signaled by lighting: Rome blues, Egypt reds) and how this threw the weight of emphasis onto the verse. Expectations are relative: curtains were still used for some scene changes; by modern standards, the music might have seemed intrusively elaborate.[6] But relative to expectations of the time, Shaw's production drew attention to the verse in a context of fast, clear presentation of the complex action.

Pace was also achieved, however, through some substantial and distorting cuts. These included important parts of scenes, as well as several whole scenes.[7] Some of the scenes cut are brief, but each has its own importance. Even so short a scene as 2.4 (often omitted so that Antony's "in the east my pleasure lies" can be juxtaposed directly with Cleopatra in Egypt) has a modest purpose—to connect the war council (2.2) with the peace conference (2.6), and so keep in view the fact that the whole Roman world has joined together to deal with the threat posed by Pompey. Act 3, scene 1 offers a contrast to the leaders drunk on Pompey's barge: Antony's commander in the field comments on leadership with a skepticism endorsed by the juxtaposition. The cutting of 3.4 meant that Antony and Octavia were never seen alone together; the cutting of 3.5 that the death of Pompey was not reported, and the audience heard only Octavius's account of the deposition of Lepidus (with its improbable excuse for his political machinations, "Lepidus was grown too cruel"). Act 4, scene 2 marks a stage in the degradation of Antony that prepares for the interpretation of the watchman who hears in an eerie noise the desertion of Hercules (4.3). Beyond a variety of specific effects, the broad consequence of the cuts was to reduce the military-political context. Every aspect of the production concentrated attention on the lovers.

III

Trevor Nunn's 1972–74 production for the Royal Shakespeare Company existed in versions for stage (1972–73) and for television (1974).[8] The cast was largely the same in both, but, while they can be said finally to represent fundamentally similar conceptions of the play, they do so with changes that go quite beyond anything required to accommodate the change of medium—

particularly in different cuts and transpositions, which show a considerable shift of emphasis. The stage production was part of a Stratford season, "The Romans," in which all four of Shakespeare's plays based on Roman subjects were presented (including, that is, *Titus Andronicus*). In contrast to Glen Byam Shaw's production, the apparent intention was to put greater stress on the plays' political aspects, though with *Antony* this was achieved only in limited ways. The Rome / Egypt contrast fundamental to a political reading was emphasized by sets and costumes: for Rome, clean, geometric wood, white togas with black or imperial purple trimmings, and SPQR standards; for Egypt, rich colors (pink, mauve, orange), and beds, carpets, cushions, canopies, fans—all in styles influenced by the exhibition of the treasures of the tomb of Tutankhamun then running at the British Museum. In Rome, a map of the Mediterranean was a prominent backdrop, used to explain the action and keep literally in view the world scope of events (see fig. 10). Nevertheless, cutting meant that these events were not presented with the elaboration actually given them by the text. Act 2, scene 4 and 3.5 were completely cut, and some pruning in other Roman scenes meant that the politico-military contexts that Shakespeare makes in many ways decisive in relation to the love tragedy—real issues about Pompey and the safety of the empire that require Antony's presence; the gradual development of a realpolitik ethos in the young Octavius made possible by the vacuum created by Antony's absence— were not fully presented. The lovers, and all that their love implies about value in life, existed in a context that remained in some measure a background. Shorter omissions constantly excised crucial poetic, dramatic, or narrative effects: "Be'st thou sad or merry, / The violence of either thee becomes, / So does it no man else" (1.5.62–64)—the first of a pattern of echoes between the lovers by means of which they are presented as indeed a "mutual pair;" "Let determined things to destiny / Hold unbewailed their way" (3.6.87–88)— Octavius presenting his battle for power as simply a Fate with which he co-operates; "their story is / No less in pity than his glory which / Brought them to be lamented" (5.2.355–57)—a final verdict that might leave the audience reflecting that, if it is not exactly paltry to be Caesar, there is something paltry about Octavius. Corin Redgrave played Octavius throughout as a ruthless political calculator: elements of the role outside this range were minimized (partly by cutting), with the implication that Octavius's success as a politician was the obverse of his limitations as a human being. In the television version, the intention of greater political emphasis in the production as a whole was abandoned: the character of Pompey was cut, with the result that in act 2 Antony came to Rome apparently to sort out only the residue of past difficulties (the results of the civil war led by his wife and brother), not to confront a present threat. But this only confirmed the basic emphasis of the stage production: in both versions the lovers were central.[9]

Janet Suzman's presentation of Cleopatra in many ways contrasted with

Fig. 10. Richard Johnson as Antony and Corin Redgrave as Octavius in the conference scene (2.2) in Trevor Nunn's 1972 production of *Antony and Cleopatra* at the Memorial Theatre in Stratford-upon-Avon. Joe Cocks Studio Collection © Shakespeare Birthplace Trust.

that of Peggy Ashcroft. Although, bizarrely, the program included Granville-Barker's comments on how, writing for a boy, Shakespeare avoided direct presentation of Cleopatra's sensual charm, this view was by no means carried through into the production: in her presentation of Cleopatra, Suzman made sensual charm a constant presence. In all the implications of sight and sound—in movement, costume, makeup, vocal tone—this Cleopatra was sensual; and she was young—not "wrinkled deep in time," with all that implies in the relish of long experience in love and politics. This was, too, a feminist presentation—a woman who is not only independent and self-determining, but also—from wearing Antony's sword to leading her own military forces into battle—transgressive in her assumption of masculine roles. This is, of course, in part simply an aspect of the role as written. But in the context of early 1970s feminism, Janet Suzman's presentation at least brought it to the fore. The confrontation with ideals of womanhood represented by Octavia, and praised by the play's Romans as exemplifying feminine virtue, seemed therefore to carry implications beyond those of a contrast between Rome and Egypt. That contrast might be translated, from a point of view available within the play, as between integrity and corruption. In this production it seemed rather to represent the traditional (oppressed, superseded) versus the contemporary (liberated, proto-utopian) and so mobilized in Cleopatra's favor feelings that a similarly vigorous presentation of these aspects of the role in a less ideologically charged context might not otherwise have seemed to carry.

Cleopatra can be presented as living gloriously in her passions or as exploiting them for political ends. Where a choice of tones is possible—as it often is—what Ashcroft presented as tenderness Suzman tended to perform as manipulation—as at the end of act 1, scene 3. On any presentation, Cleopatra continues here to needle Antony ("my oblivion is a very Antony"; "be deaf to my unpitied folly"). But Ashcroft made tenderness the predominant tone; it was typical of Suzman's performance that she was teasing and arch in handling her lover. Then, as with Ashcroft's emphasis on Cleopatra's nobility, Suzman's stress on her independence meant that ambiguities were resolved, but in an opposite direction. This Cleopatra seemed to wish genuinely to exert her sexual charms on Thidias, and through him convey them to Octavius—suggesting that the interpretation of Enobarbus may not be obtuse, as Ashcroft's playing of the scene made it appear. The provocative way in which the scene was acted was reinforced by the cutting of Cleopatra's one serious political explanation: "I must stay his time." For the moment at least, this Cleopatra's love of Antony came second: she was keeping open options for herself.

If Cleopatra was at times simplified, the production began from an even more simplistic presentation of Antony. An opening tableau showed him dressed in Egyptian costume, with headdress, overgarment, and symbols of rule matching those of Cleopatra—Osiris to her Isis. His behavior in the opening scene then simply illustrated the characteristic Roman view of him (Philo's). The presentation allowed little sense of a contest of values: Antony's claims about "the nobleness of life" were contextualized as though plainly self-delusion. If Philo's view is simply correct, there is no struggle in Antony between genuine alternatives: but the point of the first scene on a different presentation is precisely to present such a conflict. Act 1 prepares for Antony's choice in act 2 of Rome over Egypt by showing him seriously divided. If the choice of Egypt is not offered as a serious alternative, this devalues even the choice for Rome when it predominates. If Antony brings failure upon himself simply by willfully ignoring sound ethical, political, and military advice, finally the effect is more of pathos than of tragedy. And so in this production it proved. Antony's farewell to his servants (4.2) presents a crucial stage in his degradation. Here he was presented as drunk and maudlin; Cleopatra as sober, detached, and watching him critically. The party both recalled and contrasted with the scene on Pompey's barge: there Antony was drunk but in charge; now he is drunk and out of control. The subsequent development of the action did not present a simple progress of feeling: the prelude to Alexandria (4.4) recaptured a tone first of good-humored affection and then of heroic stoicism that made Antony seem again admirable, while the greeting in victory (4.8: in the television version heavily cut) was played in a quiet, intimate tone which, though it moderated the scene's exuberant and celebratory potential, reanimated the sense of the lovers' identity with one another. But thereafter grandeur was missing. While some of the verse was spoken in such a way as to bring out its visionary music ("Where souls do couch on flowers . . . "), the triumphant tones of "O thou day o'th'world," and the grand melancholy of "O sun, thy uprise shall I see no more" (4.8.13; 4.12.18) were not fully manifested: the metrical structure of the verse was broken up by a quasi-naturalistic delivery that was too colloquial to cooperate adequately with the poetry's stylization. The Shakespearean tragic heroes, as Yeats has it, "do not" (or should not) "break up their lines to weep" ("Lapis Lazuli")—or for any other reason. Johnson's speaking of the verse diminished the feeling of the contingent transformed into the quintessential.

Both protagonists were hampered in their creation of the play's final effect by poor cutting. The emotional buildup to Antony's death was diminished by omissions surrounding the suicide of Eros (4.14.83–86, 87b–93a): Antony's misunderstanding—brushing aside Eros' desire to say farewell before he kills not his master but himself—was not present to heighten the pathos of this preludial moment. It is a small but significant effect, not least because it recalls the devotion in death of Enobarbus (4.9.18–23). In some measure, Janet Suzman had to overcome similar difficulties. The scene with Seleucus was again cut, though differently (149b–153a, 158–163a): Suzman was allowed to recall Cleopatra's violence to the messenger. And her exchange with the Clown was scarcely cut at all: Shakespeare's variations of tone—a last fling of undignified violence; a venture, in this play unusual, into gentle humor—were allowed to emphasize, by contrast, the sublimity of Cleopatra's final apotheosis. In the television version, however, Suzman was hampered by extensive cutting of "I dreamed there was an emperor, Antony" (82b–91, 95–99b)—though both its vision of Antony purged of his defects and its manifestation of Cleopatra's capacity to imagine grandly are hugely important to the play's final impact. For the intimacy of television close-up, the speech was perhaps felt to be too *arioso*—although (as the audio recording shows) on stage Suzman's relatively naturalistic but varied style of verse-speaking rose magnificently to the heroic sublime.[10] In any case, the speech is crucial—not least because the tribute that Antony's "delights . . . showed his back above / The element they lived in," admitting as it does that Antony's pleasures might not be of themselves exalted while claiming that he ennobled base materials, echoes Enobarbus's claims about Cleopatra: that "vilest things / Become themselves in her," that she makes "defect perfection" (2.2.248–49,

241). It is a line of thought fundamental to a conception of the lovers both as noble and as a "mutual pair." Cutting a major expression of it does not give an impression of seeing the play in its fullness. On stage, Suzman had the full text and made full use of it. Having presented unambiguously the changeable "terrene moon," she purged Cleopatra's baser passions unequivocally. With a wholly appropriate tone of triumph tinged with melancholy, she became all fire and air.

IV

Educated in the Cambridge of E. M. W. Tillyard in the 1950s, Peter Hall interpreted *Antony* from a view of Shakespeare as working uncritically with a supposed Elizabethan conservative ideology about natural and social hierarchies and balance.[11] But if an author is no final arbiter of meanings, still less is a director: like any artist, a director may not understand what work in his own medium signifies when conceptualized in other terms. What a creative director achieves may be quite distinct from what he supposed he intended; actors may work free of a director's designs; audiences may see what is done in terms a director would repudiate. Hall's production of *Antony* was more complex and subtle than the idea of the play from which he apparently started.

Nevertheless, this idea was embodied in the production, most obviously in its unusually sympathetic presentation of Octavius. It is important to the presentation of the play's central Rome–Egypt opposition that Octavius is not simply a foil to the lovers, and Hall's presentation, through him, of Roman rectitude and duty was at least even-handed.[12] He was played as honest and honorable—honoring what his culture prompts him to respect in Antony's military prowess (1.4), concerned for the stability of the empire (2.2), genuinely fond of his sister (3.2). The scenes with Octavia were presented as moments of serious emotion; the final tableau of part I (3.6) showed Octavius and Octavia in each other's arms, the epitome—in contrast to the lovers—of honorable Roman affection. The positive presentation could not but acknowledge Octavius's sacrifice (as it turns out) of his sister in a political marriage that he foresees may go wrong (3.2.24–36), the carelessness with which he announces to her Antony's desertion (3.6.61–69), his transparently false justification for the deposition of Lepidus (3.6.33), his cool ruthlessness towards Antony in defeat (3.12.19–24), his attempt to manipulate Cleopatra by threatening the lives of her children (5.2.130–32), and the self-regard through which he finally views the lovers' tragedy (5.2.254–56). Even here, however, Shakespeare hardly settles into a single view: Octavius's sorrow at Antony's death is both obliquely egotistical and real (5.1.26–48), and his final perception of Cleopatra is among the most eloquent tributes to her (5.2.340–42). In Hall's full-text performance, all this was vigorously presented; but the overall effect was to minimize what can be construed as negative in the presentation of Octavius and the culture he represents.

Hall insisted, moreover, on the ambiguity of Cleopatra: "You shouldn't ever let [the audience] get a single idea of her," he advised Judi Dench (Lowen 57). In different ways Ashcroft and Suzman resolved ambiguity. Even through much of act 5, Dench kept the audience uncertain. Cleopatra clearly plays at least one role in the final scene: her extravagant submission ("my master, and my lord") persuades Octavius she is cooperating when she is not. But she may be understood as playing more roles than one. Dench found in Cleopatra after Antony's death a constantly flickering will to live (Lowen 93). Here, Cleopatra's wish to meet Octavius is crucial, since it raises doubts about why, if she is fixed on death, she continues to be concerned with the world. As with Thidias, there is a direct answer: so as to deal with her own destiny—specifically to give herself freedom to take her own course by convincing Octavius that she will take his. But as with Thidias, an indirect answer may suggest itself: so as to consider her options. Given Cleopatra's history (Pompey, Julius Caesar, Antony), and the way in which she immediately fascinates Dolabella, the wish to "look [Octavius] i'th'face" may suggest more than a "flickering" of self-preservation. The performer cannot, and need not, convey precise grounds of doubt. What Dench conveyed was a drama of irresolution still finding its way towards marble constant. One main focus of this is the Seleucus episode. John Wilders supposes that here doubt is resolved—although in a way contrary to the plain sense: Seleucus is acting on instruction (Wilders 286). It is difficult to see how this could be conveyed to an audience. "Speak the truth, Seleucus": Cleopatra can scarcely tap her nose, or ostentatiously wink—though in a context of uncertainty even an emphatic injunction of honesty might seem open to interpretation. Wilders is wrong only in being too clear. Although the performer cannot plant doubts, a background of diverse and semi-inscrutable motives may mean that doubts arise, particularly as Seleucus's "betrayal" accords perfectly with Cleopatra's fundamental intention: "Say some nobler token I have kept apart / For Livia and Octavia, to induce / Their mediation." Octavius is reassured: she is thinking of a future in Rome—and so he is deceived. But the audience should not feel sure that Cleopatra has not been thinking of such a future. Hall is right: uncertainty is dramatically effective. Only at "my resolution's placed" was the audience allowed to feel that this Cleopatra's ambiguities were finally resolved. Uncertainty, however, arose from the context already established: Dench acted the Seleucus scene straight, as genuine fury at real betrayal, in a way that recalled the scene with her messenger—hailing Seleucus by the hair, knocking him to the ground, beating and kicking him. Octavius's dismayed attempts to restrain such irregular queenliness made the final effect comic. With the gentle, verbal humor of the clown scene, the sequence allowed a minor recapitulation of Cleopatra's range and mystery. The immediate contrast of the sublime directedness of her death was all the more striking and satisfying.

As with Shaw / Redgrave / Ashcroft, verse-speaking was central to the production—Hall's last as director of the National Theatre, where he had made the speaking of verse in poetic drama a cardinal issue. From the first rehearsals he stressed using the structure and rhythm of the poetry to communicate its full intellectual and emotional content (Lowen 26–33). Many reviewers emphasized the primacy given to the text—the words understood and delivered in a way that expressed their meaning, but felt from within, not with "expressiveness" stuck on from outside. Dench in particular (who consulted Peggy Ashcroft about the role) found a variousness of vocal tone—from prosaic understatement to an extreme of impassioned emphasis—that approached, as near as the different usual ranges of French and English make desirable, the grand, half-sung manner of the Comédie Française.

If Dench approached the vocal range of Ashcroft, she did not rely (as Ashcroft could) on voice alone to convey passion. Granville-Barker was particularly recommended to the cast by Hall, who demurred, however, about his views on boy actors and the presentation of sexual love—that "a boy could not show [sensual charm], except objectionably or ridiculously."[13] The formulation savors of its period, but its fundamental error is to ignore the effect of being accustomed to a convention—for which it is indeed genuinely difficult to allow. No doubt the first audiences did not forget that Cleopatra was a boy. Shakespeare reminds them, though he also plays on the fact in a way that suggests how much he supposed they might become absorbed in theatrical illusion (5.2.215–20). Given that Jacobean theatergoers had never seen a female role played by a woman, while modern all-male productions may help us think about plays of the period when new, they no more fully reproduce the effect of Jacobean performance than does the present-day Globe on the South Bank in London with its largely tourist audience. The Puritan hysteria about the theater and sexual license cannot have developed in a context in which actors never touched one another. And Elizabethan and Jacobean stage lovers always kiss: Romeo kisses Juliet; Othello kisses Desdemona; and Antony kisses Cleopatra, several times.[14] We cannot suppose that when the words indicate luxuriant satisfaction ("even this repays me") the action was a brush of the cheek. Combining Ashcroft's vocal voluptuousness with Suzman's physical theatre, Hopkins and Dench took Hamlet's advice about playing and suited the action to the words (see fig. 11). In doing so they surely replicated what Burbage did with the King's Men's star boy.[15]

The value of Hall's complete text can be illustrated by his vivid staging of a Shakespearean juxtaposition that other productions omitted (Shaw wholly; Nunn partially on stage, wholly on television): a bacchanal of generals at home (2.7); a funeral cortège of soldiers in the field (3.1). Archetypal soldierly comment on how the credit taken by emulous, armchair leaders depends on the honest, dangerous effort of subordinates was enforced by the spectacle that Hall extrapolated so cogently from the text—the paraded corpse of the enemy leader's son; formal ranks of soldiers; a priest presiding over a sacrificial fire; military and funereal ceremonial—the starkest possible contrast with drunken singing and dancing. This imaginative extrapolating of

Fig. 11. Judy Dench as Cleopatra and Anthony Hopkins as Antony in Peter Hall's 1987 production of *Antony and Cleopatra* at the Royal National Theatre. Courtesy of John Haynes, Photographer.

expressive action was typical, as in the visual contrast between the lovers' suicides: Antony in his spontaneous, failed attempt, side stage (with the instructive nobility of Eros stage center), prone and writhing, surrounded by a confusion of rushing figures; Cleopatra in her meditated, successful performance, center stage, upright and still, in a tableau of calm accomplishment. With the transitional mixture of clumsiness and dignity (the fraught, painful winching up of Antony dying; but in death "a Roman by a Roman / Valiantly vanquished"), this visual contrast embodied perfectly Shakespeare's solution to the structural problem of the deaths of two protagonists. A contrast of anarchy and formality, linked by an action partaking of both, is central to the sequence of feeling through which the audience is led by the closing movement of the play. As elsewhere, Hall derived from the promptings of the text a perfectly expressive sequence of actions. Nowhere did he fail with trusting to what Shakespeare had written, and showing how effectively it could be staged.

V

Samuel Barber's *Antony and Cleopatra* was written for the opening of the new Metropolitan Opera House, Lincoln Center, New York, in 1966. The director was Franco Zeffirelli, who had had success with Shakespeare in the theater (*Romeo and Juliet* at the London Old Vic in 1960), and who was even then an established film and opera director, and, in the year of this production, shot his first Shakespeare film (*The Taming of the Shrew*). Zeffirelli, with Barber, also prepared the libretto, creating almost the entire text from Shakespeare's play, but with huge cuts, transpositions, and reassignment of lines, particularly so as to create parts for a chorus. The action was organized into sixteen scenes grouped in three acts. The Metropolitan Opera Archive has production, set, and costume design photographs, by Louis Mélançon, and other production materials and reviews—but no prompt book. The production can, however, be in considerable measure recreated from the designs, photographs, and reviews, from an audio recording of the first night with introductions for the radio audience describing the stage action (preserved in the New York Public Library), and from footage of the production shot at the public dress rehearsal and first night (a television broadcast preserved in the Museum of Television and Radio, New York).

Wanting to show everything the new opera house's stage could do, Zeffirelli contrived a spectacular production on an almost cinematic scale, using over two hundred supernumerary actors; one hundred chorus members; forty-seven dancers; and animals, including horses, goats, and a camel. The production was more suited to the occasion and the building than to the opera. It failed in its own terms, because aspects of the lighting and the stage mechanism did not operate successfully; because Zeffirelli was so busy choreographing crowds and animals and dealing with mechanical problems that he had little time to attend to issues of characterization in relation to music; and fundamentally because it was at odds with the composer's intention—light, rapid scene changes that would imitate the conditions of the Elizabethan theatre and so retain that basic aspect of Shakespeare's fast-moving panorama of world events. "What I wrote and envisioned," Barber commented, "had nothing, but nothing, to do with what one saw on the stage."[16] The production was never restaged by the Met.[17] Barber revised the score in 1974 for a new production at the Julliard School in the following year. In this revised score, the role of Octavius is reduced, the role of Octavia becomes nonsinging, the roles of Lepidus, Maecenas, Mardian, and various minor military characters are cut, as is a ballet (at the party following the peace conference). Cleopatra's death is extended: instead of dying, as in the play, in midsentence ("What should I stay—") she is given a more conventionally operatic (and less Shakespearean) death with a final aria. The main addition is a love duet, using the song "Take, o take those lips away" from *Measure for Measure* (in the two-stanza version from Beaumont and Fletcher's *The Bloody Brother*).[18] These additions, combined with the reduction of Roman and military materials, confirmed an overall change of emphasis. In its revised form the opera presents the romantic love story largely shorn of its political aspects.

In the original version, however, in which the struggle for power between Antony and Octavius is still important, Barber did justice to all the play's main elements—politics and war, as well as love. The clash of worldviews between Rome and Egypt is articulated in musical terms (military incisive rhythms and orchestration [brass fanfares] for Rome, sensuous and languid music for Egypt). And this was emphasized by Zeffirelli's production. The role of Octavius was given weight by casting (the great Wagnerian tenor Jess Thomas) and by the epic staging (he appeared at the head of his victorious army after Actium on a white horse). Two prominent elements of the set in the early scenes epitomized Egypt as predominant (a sphinx, behind) or as intrusive (a pyramid, center stage, foreground—which acted as a focus for the Roman chorus's opening repudiation of Antony's Egyptianization). The main groups were differentiated in costume by style, materials and color—pastiche classical for Romans; pastiche Renaissance for Egyptians: Antony's followers in armor of grey and brown suede with large capes; Octavius's in colors of steel, silver and blue, with togas and tunics under armor; Cleopatra's in green and gold-encrusted costumes made of knubbly and shiny silks.

In both versions, the opera presents the Ashcroft view of Cleopatra for all it is worth, and more. Barber's Cleopatra justifies Antony's exalted account of their love unambiguously. She is presented in a variety of musical styles, some with reference to jazz, but Barber's musical vocabulary is predominantly late Romantic: a free use of dissonance in a fundamentally tonal context is combined with sumptuous melodic invention. This Cleopatra is a sympathetic Straussian heroine in the manner of the Marschallin, Ariadne, or Arabella. The music associated with love especially is *Tristan*esque: lyrical and chromatic, with pulsating offbeat figures and lavish orchestration signifying the restless and overwhelming nature of erotic desire. Musically this is an opera of motifs, and Cleopatra's is a yearning phrase set to the words "My man of men." Narrowed from Shakespeare's multifarious conception, she is a woman dependent on love and finding her identity through it. The role was written for the great American soprano Leontyne Price, with whom Barber had often worked.

About the text Price consulted Irene Worth (who happened at the time to be appearing on Broadway). With this experienced Shakespearian assistance, Price brought to the role a sumptuous richness of sound throughout her range, but also an astonishing variousness of vocal characterization: tenderness expressed in the most delicate high *mezza voce*; violence expressed in a barking chest voice used in the upper middle register; in recitative-like *arioso*, acute inflection of complex rhythms; in dialogues with Mardian, wild yelling in imitation of his eunuch falsetto. It was a superb rendition in sound of the gamut from "Royal Egypt" to "no more but e'en a woman." Zeffirelli's rich and heavy costumes assisted with the royalty, culminating in the final scene in a huge crown-headdress with dangling jeweled sides, a sun-ray configuration behind the head, and a robe with train stretching below the centrally elevated throne, beyond the spotlights, as it were to infinity. It was a visionary apotheosis: Cleopatra, in death, the epitome of sexual and political power.

Even in the 1966 version, the rest of the work became something of a frame for Price's magnificent assumption of a great role. But Antony too emerged as a genuinely tragic figure. At the climax of act 1, which Barber's Straussian music in any staging would render far from unsympathetic, Enobarbus's account of the lovers' first meeting was accompanied by a cinematic presentation of what he describes. On the upper stage, Cleopatra floated towards the audience in her golden barge, with its purple sails and silver oars; Antony, as it were in a waking dream, released from the world of Roman responsibilities with which he has just reunited by marriage, pursued the vision, turning to the withdrawing barge as the act closed. It was a compelling portrayal of Romantic obsession. The weight given to his death by the haunting scoring of his suicide aria—solo flute accompanied only by tuned timpani—captured perfectly the feelings generated by the character in an ideal performance of the drama without music. The final centrality of the lovers is reinforced by the presentation of Enobarbus. Cleopatra's musical motif is also used in relation to him, suggesting a connection between them as people whose life is validated (or not) by their relation to Antony. Enobarbus's extended death scene gives added prominence to his experience as the obverse of that of the lovers and indicates a point of view from which they can be judged. If the world gained by betraying love is found not worth the price, then the world lost for love is (as Dryden has it) "well lost." And so, as a whole, this forceful, if partial, presentation of the play implies.

VI

Taking a negative view of Cleopatra, which these productions suggest directors and actors are not eager to stage, John Holloway argues that she is the Dark Lady of Shakespeare's drama (Holloway 99–100). For Holloway, Sonnet 129 is a key—"The expense of spirit in a waste of shame." With all that the sonnet admits of "bliss" and "heaven," negatives predominate: the end is "hell." Erotically compelling, Cleopatra deserves the worst that is said of her. This is the Roman view translated into literary criticism. On the view of these productions—different in so many ways as they are—Cleopatra, "whom everything becomes" (1.1.51), who makes "defect perfection" (2.2.241), has also about her much of the Sonnets' other protagonist, "in whom all ill well shows" (40.13). The lovers are earthy versions of what J. B. Leishman called Shakespeare's "unPlatonic hyperbole," the young man of the Sonnets who is the ideal form—but in the world of sense and appearance—of all the virtues of Love (Leishman 149–77). It is scarcely too much to say that, especially in a performance such as that of Redgrave and Ashcroft, at the nobler end of their gamut the lovers epitomize a comparable crystallization through erotic feeling of the aspiration to the Beautiful and the Good. In all of these productions, Antony's view of what constitutes "the nobleness of life," however it is contextualized critically, is finally justified. Though it cannot deal with the complexities of verbal drama, Barber's *Tristan*esque score brings this out, if anything, even more intensely. Rome and Octavius can be presented more or less sympathetically, but finally none of these productions more than qualified the play's eventual celebration of love as a transcendent value. To agree that Sonnet 129 is one key to *Antony and Cleopatra* is to accept only that the heaven of love on earth includes its apparent opposites—hatred, violence, deception—that it is not so pretty a place as heavens of imaginative postulate. But as variously presented by Shaw, Nunn, Hall, and Barber / Zeffirelli, this road of excess, though it has many foul bypaths, does finally lead to a palace of wisdom. Its exuberance is beauty. Its energy is a delight all the more intense for giving a savor of eternity that is tied to the conditions of time.

NOTES

1. Details of the prompt books and audio and video versions of these productions are given in the bibliography. The two most notable postwar productions not discussed in this essay are that directed by Michael Benthall, with Laurence Olivier and Vivien Leigh, in 1951, and that directed by Peter Brook, with Alan Howard and Glenda Jackson, for the Royal Shakespeare Company in 1978. See Olivier; Male (on Brook); Hunt and Reeves. Both productions are central to Scott. Peggy Ashcroft played Cleopatra in a separate radio broadcast of the play in 1965, with Peter Finch as Antony (*Radio Times* July 12, 1965: Home Service).

2. The *Radio Times* entry and the broadcast introduction make it clear that this was the Shakespeare Memorial Theatre production; the casts were identical, except that in the broadcast Donald Pleasance played Octavius in place of Stratford's Marius Goring.

3. Quotations are from the Cambridge edition, ed. David Bevington.

4. Rachel Kempson, who played Octavia, was actually Michael Redgrave's wife.

5. The running time (without intervals) was two hours forty minutes. Running time for the 1972 RSC performance was three hours, and for the 1987 National Theatre performance three hours fifty minutes.

6. The score (by one Antony Hopkins) required a quite substantial orchestra. There was almost half an hour of music (much of it played under speech) the main purpose of which was to characterize differentially Rome and Egypt and to effect transitions—including where the text has pointed juxtapositions.

7. Act 2, scenes 1 and 4; 3.1, 4, 5, and 9; 4.2, 10, and 11. Not all these cuts are registered in Madelaine, although his apparatus suggests it is comprehensive for the productions he regularly reports, which include this one. The cuts on stage and for the broadcast were the same, with minor exceptions. The broadcast's most considerable change was restoration of 2.4.

8. With the stage version, the cuts marked in the prompt book do not entirely correspond to those in the performance as recorded. It is unlikely that cuts would be changed in the course of a run. It seems probable therefore that the prompt book shows the cuts as planned at the start of rehearsals and the audio recording the text as staged.

9. Apart from the cutting of Pompey, in the television version act 2 is further cut and reordered. Act 2, scene 1 is omitted entirely. (In the stage version this preceded 1.5.) Act 2, scene 7 follows 2.3.9 with no intervening return to Egypt. Antony's discussion with the Soothsayer (2.3.10–40) is transposed to the end of 2.7, and followed by 2.5. This, and the omission of 3.1, means that the two scenes of Cleopatra with the messenger frame the parting of Antony and Octavia from Octavius. Among briefer cuts there are important omissions in relation to each of the main characters. Act 3, scene 6, lines 78–102 is cut (Octavius is only shown chiding Octavia; there is no affectionate welcome). The opening of 4.14 is omitted (1–14)—poetry of the highest quality, vital to the characterization of Antony. Also cut is the whole episode of Seleucus, with all its interesting ambiguities. (On the television version cutting of "I dreamed there was an emperor, Antony," see above, p. 123.) Techniques familiar from film occasionally illustrate inset narratives of action not shown on stage—Antony and Cleopatra enthroned with their children; the kings of the earth levied for war (3.6).

10. B. A. Young (*Financial Times* 16 August 1972) complained that Suzman and Johnson broke up their lines with "Macready pauses" (breaks that reflect neither the formal nor the syntactic structure: random "dramatic" effects). Although the poetry was not spoken with the same flexible range or the intensity that Ashcroft and Redgrave achieved, neither the audio nor video recordings show this in any marked degree.

11. Lowen 3. Compare Hall's view of the English Histories: "I had learned about the Elizabethan world picture at ... university. Shakespeare believed there was a natural order in nature .... All Shakespeare's thinking ... is based on a complete acceptance of this concept" (Barton and Hall x).

12. The main groups were expressively color-coded—chill blues for Octavius's Romans; warmer silver-gold on reds for Antony's; luxurious browns and oranges for Egyptians. Sets and costumes were modestly sumptuous, combining the period in which the play was written with the period in which it is set: quasi-classical architecture, but in ruins; Roman armor, but costumes otherwise Renaissance in style. Veronese's *Mars and Venus bound by Cupid* on the program cover struck more than one keynote.

13. Granville-Barker 204. For a quite different view of the boy actor, see Dusinberre in Bulman 46–67.
14. Act 3, scene 11 line 69; 4.4.30; 4.15.41. Although perhaps not a kiss, Antony's invitation at 4.8.16 suggests that the action expressing affection should be uninhibitedly physical.
15. At fifty-two, Dench was worried about her age in relation to conventional expectations about physical attractiveness and passion (Lowen xvii, 85–86). It matters not at all that the historical Cleopatra died aged thirty-eight. Shakespeare clearly imagines Cleopatra as—not young: "wrinkled deep in time," even by Elizabethan standards, can scarcely mean thirty; "age cannot wither her" is not a prediction. Cleopatra and Antony have several children (3.6); and Antony's mode of expressing contempt for Octavius ("boy") must suggest a generational difference. None of this implies a precise age, but fifty scarcely seems wrong.
16. Interview with John Green, *New York Times* October 3, 1971. Cf. Barber reported in Soria 6: "It was completely overproduced."
17. The costumes (about one thousand in total) were destroyed in a fire at one of the company's warehouses, November 7, 1973.
18. The only commercial recording of the work is of this revised score, conducted by Christian Badea, taken from performances at the 1983 Spoleto Festival (the director of which is Barber's lifelong companion, the composer Giancarlo Menotti). Production records show that the 1966 opening night performance at the Met was to have been recorded by RCA Victor, but arrangements fell through because of contractual difficulties just before the opening.

BIBLIOGRAPHY

Prompt Books and Other Archive Materials
Royal Shakespeare Company, 1953: Shakespeare Centre Library, Stratford-upon-Avon: O.S. 71.21 / 1953A. Accession no., 8551. (Score: Class 71 / 23. Accession no. 86 / 3-i.).
RSC, 1972: Shakespeare Centre Library: 71.21 / 1972 ANT. Accession no., S1293 / 4.
National Theatre, 1987: National Theatre Archive, London: script 293.
Samuel Barber's opera, Metropolitan Opera New York, 1966: production, set and costume design photographs; other production materials and reviews.

Audio, Video, and Television Materials
RSC, 1953 (radio performance): BBC: X20814–18; British Library, National Sound Archive: T12034–6WR (audio).
RSC, 1972–73: BL, NSA: T693–5W T1–3 (audio).
RSC, television version, 1974: ITC Entertainment, 1980 (video).
National Theatre, 1987: BL, NSA: T10313–15Y (audio).
Samuel Barber's opera: New York Public Library, Performing Arts Division: first night radio broadcast: LTCM 246 (F).
Museum of Television and Radio, New York, "The New Met.: Countdown to Curtain," television broadcast, 20 Nov. 1966.

Editions

Intro. Olivier, Sir Laurence, with designs for costumes and scenery by Audrey Cruddas and Roger Furse, London: The Folio Society, 1952.

Ed. Bevington, David, Cambridge: Cambridge UP, 1990 (The New Cambridge Shakespeare).

Ed. Madelaine, Richard, Shakespeare in Production, Cambridge: Cambridge UP, 1998.

Ed. Wilders, John, London: Routledge, 1995 (The Arden Shakespeare, Third Series).

The Opera

Barber, Samuel. *Antony and Cleopatra*. New York: Schirmer, 1966 (opus 40; vocal score, piano reduction by the composer); revised edition, 1976.

————. *Antony and Cleopatra*, the text of William Shakespeare adapted by Franco Zeffirelli, New York: Schirmer, n.d. [1966] (libretto of the original version).

————. *Two Scenes from "Antony and Cleopatra,"* New York: Schirmer, n.d. [1968] (full score; adapted by the composer for concert performance; Schirmer's Study Scores, 112).

Works Cited and Performance Criticism

Madelaine (326–37) contains a full bibliography: with reference to the productions discussed in this essay, see esp. Baluba, Crowl, Davies, Lamb, Leiter, and Peter Thomson. The list below includes only works cited, corrections to Madelaine (Findlater and Redgrave), or items not in Madelaine.

Auden, W. H. *The Dyer's Hand*. London: Faber, 1963.

Barton, John, and Peter Hall. *The Wars of the Roses*. London: BBC, 1970.

Brown, Ivor. *The Shakespeare Memorial Theatre, 1951–53: A Photographic Record*. London: Max Reinhardt, 1953 (includes nine photographs by Angus McBean from the 1953 production).

Bulman, James C. (ed.). *Shakespeare, Theory, and Performance*. London: Routledge, 1996.

Findlater, Richard. *Michael Redgrave: Actor*, London: Heinemann, 1956.

Goldman, Michael. *Acting and Action in Shakespearean Tragedy*. Princeton: Princeton UP, 1985.

Granville-Barker, H. *Prefaces to Shakespeare*. Series 2. London: Sidgwick & Jackson, 1930.

Heyman, Barbara B. *Samuel Barber: The Composer and His Music*. Oxford: Oxford UP, 1992.

Holloway, John. *The Story of the Night: Studies in Shakespeare's Major Tragedies*. London: Routledge, 1961.

Hunt, Albert, and Geoffrey Reeves. *Peter Brook*. Cambridge: Cambridge UP, 1995.

Leishman, J. B. *Themes and Variations in Shakespeare's Sonnets*. London: Hutchinson, 1961.

Lowen, Tirzah. *Peter Hall Directs "Antony and Cleopatra."* New York: Limelight, 1990.

Male, David A. *Antony and Cleopatra*. Shakespeare on Stage. Cambridge: Cambridge UP, 1984.

Pitt, Angela. *Shakespeare's Women*. Newton Abbott: David & Charles; Totowa, NJ: Barnes & Noble, 1981 (contains a 1979 interview with Janet Suzman on her performances of Cleopatra).

Porter, Andrew. *Music of Three Seasons: 1974–1977*. London: Chatto & Windus, 1979.

Redgrave, Michael. *The Actor's Ways and Means*. Rockefeller Foundation Lectures, University of Bristol, 1952–3; London: Heinemann, 1953.

———. *Mask or Face: Reflections in an Actor's Mirror*. London: Heinemann, 1958.

Redgrave, Vanessa. *Antony and Cleopatra*. Actors on Shakespeare. London: Faber, 2002.

Scott, Michael. *Antony and Cleopatra*. Text and Performance. London: Macmillan, 1983.

Soria, Dorle J. "Artist Life." *High Fidelity / Musical America* 24 (Sept. 1974): 5–6.

Worthen, W. B. "The weight of Antony: staging 'character' in *Antony and Cleopatra*." *Studies in English Literature* 26 (1986): 295–308.

4.
Cleopatra's *Sati*
Old Ideologies and Modern Stagings

DOROTHEA KEHLER

Since the late eighteenth century, the view has persisted that Shakespeare's Cleopatra redeems herself by dying for a "love which is all giving and self-sacrifice" (Ribner; qtd. in Spevack 689). In her most memorable sexual pun—"Husband, I come" (5.2.287)[1]—she lays claim to the status of an erstwhile wife, now the paragon of widows. If, in consequence, we read her suicide not as a mistress's *Liebestod* but as a response to the death of her husband, regrettably it has much in common with *sati,* an upper-caste Indian practice that may still be claiming its victims. In India and among some Hindu sects in other countries, widow suicide by immolation on the husband's funeral pyre, a public ritual some think sanctioned by scripture, came to be regarded as "the duty of a virtuous wife" (Mani, *Contentious Traditions* 1). Although *sati* had been outlawed by the British in 1829, in September 1987, an eighteen-year-old widow, Roop Kanwar, whose loveless eight-month marriage had been arranged by her parents, died on her husband's funeral pyre and was hailed as the incarnation of all that was pure and best in woman. Her *sati* occurred on the outskirts of Jaipur, no backwater, and Roop herself was a modern young woman (Sen 1–4):

> The incident ... unearthed the information that there have been at least thirty-eight widow immolations in Rajasthan since independence, and dragged out of the closet vociferous supporters of the practice. In this recent case the government of India vacillated in taking action against family members found to have coerced Roop. State officials were present along with an estimated 300,000 others at an event "honouring" the episode thirteen days after the burning, and when the state finally banned glorification of *sati*, the response was too little, too late. (Mani, "Multiple Mediations" 315)

A year later, some eight thousand people came together to celebrate the anniversary of Roop's burning (Mani, "Multiple Mediations" 317).

137

One rationale for *sati* is that the sins of the wife in a former incarnation have caused her husband's death. Through her own death she atones for his and can tend to him in the afterlife (Weinberger-Thomas 45, 13), where both will be granted "heavenly pleasures" (Mani, *Contentious Traditions* 1) and may elude continuing rebirth and death. Patriarchal theorists held out yet another spiritual inducement: as widows are incapable of leading a chaste life for the right reasons (chastity for the wrong reasons doesn't count), through immolation, explained Kashinath Tarkavagish in 1819, a woman can "get rid of her feminine sex" (qtd. in Mani, *Contentious Traditions* 55).[2] Economics and territorialism underpin theological motives. Although *sati* was not specific to the upper castes, in practice only they could easily afford the loss of a female worker. Because the "choice" of *sati* was sometimes limited to women who were still reproductive, it allowed wealthy families to escape the possibility of the widow's bearing children who were not members of the deceased husband's family. Often relatives were loath to support the widow or to deal with her legal rights to an estate from which they (and the authorities) could profit. Pundits were paid for officiating, and the crowd so enjoyed the show that spectators could be counted on to drag the widow to the pyre and keep her there, should she prove unwilling (Mani, *Contentious Traditions* 26). Granted, we must acknowledge the misrepresentations and often impure motives of colonialist discourse that made capital of *sati*, the rancor elicited in some quarters by Western feminist interventions, and the remarkable courage of widows who freely agreed to immolate themselves; it nevertheless remains that the severe pressure of cultural expectations, and sometimes brute force, erode the voluntarism of this indefensible practice.

Even so, one of the RSC productions of *Antony and Cleopatra* that I discuss here—Steven Pimlott's in 1999—unwittingly did defend, or at the least colluded with the mystification of a gendered death through the redemptive power of a widow's self-sacrifice. In contrast, Trevor Nunn's earlier 1972 production (revived, although not with absolute exactitude, for BBC television in 1975)[3] takes a very different tack, presenting Cleopatra as a shrewd politician and extraordinary queen of Egypt, her sexuality joined to the service of the state. As the protagonists, Nunn's Janet Suzman and Pimlott's Frances de la Tour, perform their literary/historical identities according to radically disparate directorial conceptions, they generate competing narratives no less politically partisan than artistically distinct. I have selected these two productions in order to make a point about the problematics of director's theater[4] insofar as it bears on directorial responsibility. This is not to minimize authorial responsibility. Through the character of Cleopatra, Shakespeare demonstrates that while the winners write history, the losers leave ubiquitous traces. For his version of the story, Shakespeare complicates sources colored by the prejudices of Roman historians and memoirists, selects incidents at will, invents as need be, and inevitably raises issues of race, colonialism, and gender, the play's political matrix. In effect, he revises history, as do directors of *Antony and Cleopatra*, whose theatrical choices shape our notions of Cleopatra's ethnicity, sexuality, acumen, age, and the motives for her suicide. Whether politically self-conscious or not, Nunn and Pimlott, like the rest of us, look through ideological lenses; they point us toward (albeit do not control) a space where meaning, ranging from reactionary to progressive, is located. Nunn's production demonstrates that aesthetics need not be compromised when directors take into account the probable social effects of their dramatic actualizations of Shakespeare's text—as indeed they should. For theater is a public art, meanings matter, and "spin" is a concomitant of Shakespearean performativity.

Casting comes first. The director's choice of leading lady constructs a racial/ethnic identity for Cleopatra that shapes the way the audience reads her sexuality and politics. Trevor Nunn haunts Shakespeare's queen with the historical Cleopatra, Queen of Kings, a Macedonian colonial ruler, who may have had an Egyptian concubine as one of her grandmothers (Meadows 23), and who needed the support of the Egyptians, which she won by learning their language (unlike her ancestors) and adapting their religion (Grant 42–43). To the horror of metropolitan Octavius, politically and perhaps racially, it would seem that she was a hybrid. Pimlott's que(a)en, on the other hand, is very much an English woman out of Noel Coward. Although in recent years the racial identity of *Antony*'s Cleopatra has become a site of ideological contestation, the text intimates that Shakespeare favored the indeterminacy of hybridism.[5] Within the first act, the Roman Philo denigrates the "tawny front" (1.1.6) of Cleopatra, and she herself laments a complexion "with Phoebus' amorous pinches black" (1.5.28); yet Antony tells Thidias, whom he has just had whipped for daring to kiss Cleopatra's hand, "Henceforth / The white hand of a lady fever thee, / Shake thou to look on't" (3.13.137–39). In appearance, then, she is probably neither black nor white but "tawny."[6] Kim F. Hall describes Cleopatra as sunburned, which is quite enough to damn her: "Her formulation conjoins her erotic nature with her darkness and, indeed, almost implies that she is black because of her sensuality" (Hall 97).[7] Disturbingly, the darker the actress playing Cleopatra, the more apparent validity is conferred on early modern notions, regrettably not yet defunct, of a link between race and sexuality: the belief that darker people are far more lustful than whites (Barthelemy 5–6, 120–21).

A "tawny" actress determined to minimize the association between race and sex may take her cue from the boy actors of the King's Men and from Nunn's Cleopatra, Janet Suzman, who played the Egyptian queen as "only incidentally a voluptuary" (Lewsen 13). At the same time, her hybridity may remind playgoers of white (Macedonian) *colonial* rule in Egypt and allow them to intuit how integration jeopardizes the identity of the colonizer, deconstructing the conqueror/conquered binarism.[8] To Philo, Cleopatra is a "gypsy ... " (1.1.10) because by "going native" she has betrayed the West just as Antony has betrayed Rome. The Hellenistic queen who assimilates to her subjects, becoming their immortal sunburned Isis, criminally destabilizes white rule just as the tawny queen's white hand destabilizes her racial and ethnic identity. Various well-intentioned directors might read these vexed racial and colonial issues differently, but, whatever their perspectives, we would hope that they consider the political ramifications of casting the role of Cleopatra.

Of course, Cleopatra need not be racially other to be instantiated as an alien. It suffices that she is "a sexually active non-European female ruler" (Loomba 288), troped as the most formidable of masterless women, a lusty widow. That stereotype, as old as patriarchy itself, presents the director with more options. How lusty? Whose widow? Why does she kill herself? For lack of a way out? For the pleasure of diminishing Octavius's victory? For love of Antony? For the honor of Egypt? For her personal sense of honor? The meaning of Cleopatra's suicide is contingent upon the portrayal of her widowhood. Negotiating the implications of the play's multiple signifiers, the director revises the legend of Cleopatra.

Historically, Cleopatra was first a divorcée, then a widow. At eighteen she became the lover of Julius Caesar, who for reasons of state insisted on her marriage to her eleven-year-old brother and, upon their divorce, on her marriage to her younger brother, then twelve, incest being in accord with Egyptian ruling-class custom (Grant 68–74, 78, 97).[9] While still married to Octavia, Antony may have wed Cleopatra in an Egyptian rite that Rome—that is, Octavius—did not recognize. Nevertheless, describing Aeneas's shield, Virgil writes that although Antony conquers the East, "there follows him (O shame!) his Egyptian wife" ("*sequiturque [nefas] Aegyptia coniunx*"; *Aeneid* III, 688). Plutarch, too, records a marriage but ambiguates it as bigamous: "But Antonius first of all maried two wives together, the which never Romane durst doe before, but him selfe. Second, he put away his first Romane wife, which he had lawfully maried: for the love of a straunge woman, he fondly fell in fancy withall, and contrarie to the lawes and ordinaunces of Rome" ("The Comparison"; qtd. in Bullough 5: 320).[10] Following a medieval convention, Chaucer codes Cleopatra as no mere lusty widow but Antony's proper wife who, in *The Legend of Good Women*, plunges naked into a snake pit—"And she hir deeth receveth with good chere, / For love of Antony that was hir so dere" (lines 700–01).[11] Some two centuries later, in Mary Sidney's 1590 translation of Robert Garnier's *The Tragedie of Antonie* (1578), which Shakespeare probably knew, Cleopatra continues to play the role of Antony's wife (Bullough 5: 230–31). And although Shakespeare does not foreclose a reading of her suicide as the means by which she earns only poetic widowhood, through Octavius's account of the Donations of Alexandria (3.6.1–19) he gestures toward a more tangible claim.

Whether the director sees Cleopatra as Antony's widow in fact or fancy, the staging of her suicide is key to whatever meaning the production makes available. It is a commonplace to assume that in writing the scene Shakespeare turned first to the classical tradition, or rather to a strand of it, chiefly Stoic, that figured suicide as noble, and, second, to the courtly love tradition that figured suicide as romantic. Whereas these popular literary attitudes toward suicide could in themselves account for its portrayal in *Antony and Cleopatra*, it is also possible that Shakespeare was aware of the Indian practice. Consider that for all its cultural particularity, *sati* in a sense formalizes and radicalizes teachings and attitudes not unfamiliar in England. The ideal of the faithful, devastated widow—whether realized through suicide or celibacy and solitude—is a cross-cultural phenomenon common to patriarchal societies. Perhaps Shakespeare had read the admonitions of the Roman poet Propertius, urging his countrywomen to emulate those Indian widows who contended for the privilege of committing *sati*: "The victors burn and offer their breasts to the flame and lay charred faces upon their husband's body" (qtd. in Rogers 47). Or closer to home, by the late fourteenth century if not earlier, the wife who joined her husband in death was eulogized in English literature as a kind of secular saint. In Chaucer's *Canterbury Tales*, Dorigen honors the suicides, not only of wives and widows who had been or were threatened with violation, but of widows who refused to survive their husbands:

> Pardee, of Laodomya is writen thus,
> That whan at Troie was slayn Protheselaus,
> Ne lenger wolde she lyve after his day.
> The same of noble Porcia telle I may;
> Withoute Brutus koude she nat lyve,
> To whom she hadde al hool hir herte yive.
> ("The Franklin's Tale," ll.1445–50)

Dorigen's exemplars were not barred from suicide by their faith. The self-slaughter of a wife from classical history or legend was fertile ground for medieval and early modern writers since the suicides of pagans were generally deemed heroic. In *The Tragedy of Dido, Queen of Carthage*, Marlowe depicts Dido's death on the pyre of Aeneas's relics. Antony recalls the story of Dido and Aeneas as he plans his death (4.14.53); she becomes "widow Dido" for Shakespeare in *The Tempest* (2.1.79 passim). Another Marlovian widow that Shakespeare likely knew, Olympia, thwarted in her first attempt at suicide when her husband is killed, longs to "cast her body in the burning flame / That feeds upon her son's and husband's flesh" (*Tamburlaine, Part II*, 3.4.71–72).[12] Later, she successfully tricks her captor-suitor into stabbing her to death. Again, in Mary Sidney's translation of Robert Garnier's *"The Tragedie of Antonie,"* Cleopatra eludes death by snakebite but not by metaphoric flames. She offers her dead lover her "boiling teares" until her eyes are soon "consumed by the coales / Which from my brest, as from a furnace rise" (act 5, lines 1980, 1985–86; rpt. in Bullough 5: 406). How great, after all, was the psychological distance between widow-burning India and witch-burning Europe? Pompa Banerjee writes that, by the sixteenth century, European travel writings about India almost always contained references to *sati*, a practice that, although judged barbarous, was greatly admired as heroic proof of wifely virtue. Ironically, European conduct books, sermons, marriage manuals, and so on, achieved their apotheosis in the Hindu widow (Banerjee 8).[13] As Banerjee astutely observes, traffic between Europe and India was not all one way.

In Shakespeare, Cleopatra has no alternative to suicide; to suffer the humiliation reserved for a prize of war is unacceptable to a sovereign ruler. But once having resolved upon death, the text offers her political agency. A victim of Rome, not of lovesickness, she takes her life as the magnificent Queen of Egypt and her enemy's mighty opposite. Most often her death is regarded as the expression of a high-spirited, self-possessed subject rare among both sexes in the tragedies. Denied the *dignitas* secured through metal when she impulsively attempts to stab herself (5.2.39), she employs poison, a surer if less admired means. Even so, continues Anton J. L. van Hooff, citing Horatius's *Carmina*, "By her planned death she showed herself even steelier than before [*deliberata morte ferocior*]" (77–78, 115). Yet Cleopatra refuses to die *terminally*, as it were. Her "[i]mmortal longings" (5.2.281) intimate transcendence. Unlike an ordinary widow, she becomes a legend, a queen in the heroic tradition, rejecting life on her captor's terms. Or, minimally, observes Ania Loomba, "[h]er suicide clouds her political defeat with mystic glamour and a show of autonomy" (290).[14] For in light of the "convergence of differing religious, philosophical, and literary traditions at the Renaissance," Rowland Wymer asserts that "a stage suicide could evoke whatever response a dramatist wished" (2, 17, 156–57). By the same token, it can evoke whatever response a modern director wishes, including, unfortunately, a traditional idealization of widow suicide. The productions by Nunn and Pimlott that I discuss below exemplify sharply contrasting theatrical concepts and their political ramifications.

Trevor Nunn's 1972 RSC production of *Antony and Cleopatra* described a trajectory in which Cleopatra dies in love with Antony but decidedly not out of love with "this dull world" (4.15.61), say what she will. Rather, suicide is her last shrewd move in the great game. The RSC having situated the production within a chronological cycle that traced the rise and decline of Rome (the cycle began with *Coriolanus* and ended with *Titus*), Nunn invoked imperial concerns from the outset. He began with an iconic tableau in which the principals costumed as Isis and Osiris were crowned while the legionaries sulked. Nunn explained in his program commentary that the subject of *Antony and*

Cleopatra was "the ultimate contest for the whole known world, between East and West" (qtd. in Neill 44). As the "tawny front[ed]" East (1.1.6), Suzman was heavily made up, her deep tan, like her straight black hair and strong fine features, a metonymic signifier of a politically astute assimilation to Egypt's culture as well as its climate (see fig. 12). The native-invader symbolism was heightened by the contrast between her black eunuchs and Octavius's white-togaed Romans. Describing her role, Suzman compared Egypt's queen to Elizabeth I (Nightingale, "Age Cannot Wither Her," Features: 1), a parallel that vitiates an orientalist portrayal of Cleopatra as an irrational slave of passion. Although Shakespeare suppresses the Ptolemaic queen's talent for governing, Antony informs the audience that *l'état, c'est elle*: "I am dying, Egypt, dying . . . " (4.15.18). Here, as so often in the play, Cleopatra is associated with the nation that she rules. Bernard Crick summarized the emphasis of this production: "Surely much of the play is about the rival claims of politics *and* love, not about the neglect of politics for love" (11).

Richard Madelaine suggests that Nunn's production inaugurated feminist portrayals of Cleopatra (129).[15] Nunn's then wife, Janet Suzman, was a South African political activist; she speaks with pride of her Aunt Helen, a celebrated antiapartheid parliamentarian (Hardwick section 13). The word reviewers use most often to describe Suzman's Cleopatra is "intelligent." For Nunn and Suzman, Cleopatra's keen mind is inseparable from her function as Rome's opponent. Margaret Tierney "was more struck by this Cleopatra's intelligence than by her charisma. This is not a sensuous wanton, but a cunning political animal that schemes for the world and loses it through being too clever by half" (42–43). Bernard Crick calls Suzman "the most marvelously political Cleopatra," in fact, "a bit of a female Henry VIII" (11). Unlike Henry, however, Suzman was sexy, but wore her libido lightly. Robert Speaight appreciated the Egyptian "sense of light, and even playful, eroticism which never became steamy . . . " (386). As for her ritual suicide, for Benedict Nightingale it is "an act Miss Suzman (upright, dignified and wholly a queen) suggests to be vital to her integrity and self-respect, a demonstration she can be mastered by none but herself" ("Decline and Growth" 265). Suzman dignifies Shakespeare's Cleopatra by recalling the historical Cleopatra, a queen who betrayed neither Antony nor Egypt.[16] In the spirit of that queen, Suzman transforms herself into an icon, her last "becoming [. . .]" (1.3.96), as she follows Antony in death, defying the power of Octavius, transforming "great Caesar" into an "ass / Unpolicied!" (5.2.307–08), and thus resisting, in the only way she can, Egypt's subsumption under the Roman empire. No *sati* this.

Steven Pimlott's 1999 postmodern articulation of the text told a very different story. Pimlott's *Antony* emphasized the sexuality of the aging lovers, older by some twenty years than the historical characters they played.[17] That sexuality was registered explicitly at the beginning and end of the play. Act 1, scene 1 opened with "a graphic, if rather dutiful-looking, bout of cunnilingus"

Fig. 12. Janet Suzman as Cleopatra and Patrick Stewart as Enobarbus (3.7) in Trevor Nunn's 1972 production of *Antony and Cleopatra* at the Memorial Theatre in Stratford-upon-Avon. Photographer Reg Wilson © Royal Shakespeare Company.

(Taylor, Features: 8).[18] In act 5, scene 2, aided by a backdrop of near floor-to-ceiling mirrors, de la Tour "[f]linging off a golden wrap ... permits a full-frontal flash of her naked form and permits a rear view of her walking off stage in the nude—a case of giving your all for art" (De Jongh 7). De la Tour feigned having sex with Mardian as he speaks of "what Venus did with Mars" (1.5.18), rubbed up against him ("though't come too short" [2.5.8]), and seemed to offer herself both to Antony's messenger ("Make thee a fortune from me" [2.5.49]) and (in act 3, scene 11, on all fours) to the wrathful Antony. Even as Antony lay dying, she kissed his groin. Charles Spencer decried the lack of subtlety: "the in-your-face opening seems like adolescent shock tactics" and "[t]he idea of her greeting the Romans without her slip on ... preposterous." Spencer judged the production "deeply second-rate" through no fault of the actors but owing to Pimlott's "interfering directorial fingers" (25). As Ian Shuttleworth puts it, the production "shows all the defects of Director's Theatre: its strengths are almost entirely those of acting, its weaknesses those of conception" (The Arts 9).

Pimlott's bid to satisfy his own immortal longings was apolitical and ahistorical. Though overall reviews were mixed,[19] all agreed that Pimlott had shown little interest in the political aspects of *Antony and Cleopatra*. Jeremy Kingston writes, "What Pimlott and de la Tour do not indicate is any wider context to her [Cleopatra's] manipulations, a sense of the ambition for Egypt and for herself that must be governing her." Instead, this Cleopatra's conscious playacting, Kingston feels, "is leading her towards being a woman and nothing more" (Features).[20] What kind of woman? Julie Allison describes de la Tour as "unstable, hysterical, manipulative and determined to hold on to her man" (7). Having lost him, she struck "the uninflected note of the clinically depressed," writes Suzannah Clapp, who was disappointed in the production overall: "What is largely missing is the idea of the implications of all this in the world outside" (Review 8). Certainly, Pimlott seemed unaware of the imperialist implications of de la Tour's hyper-English appearance. Her pale skin and stereotypically unflattering "frocks" (costuming and settings were eclectic) asserted unassimilated colonial rule and diminished the meaning of her death for Egypt, which had merely exchanged one "landlord" (3.13.72) for another. Pimlott was also unaware of—or chose to ignore—Shakespeare's deliberate departure from Plutarch, whose Cleopatra is "marvelously disfigured" after Antony's death ("The Life of Marcus Antonius" rpt. in Bullough 5: 313). Nightingale describes de la Tour's response to Antony's death: "her whole performance had been moving toward the moment when, stricken by Antony's death and her own capture, she sat in a skullcap before a mirror, making up a face that suddenly looked blanched, ravaged and old [see fig. 13]. At that moment her Cleopatra was revealed as a woman for whom looks, life, even love have largely been a piece of brilliant play-acting." "[W]hat is sadder," he asks, " . . . than the attempts of an exhausted woman to sustain her mystique?" ("A London Season," section 2: 6).

Sati is sadder. As good as bald in a skullcap, her shape concealed by a voluminous muddy-colored gown, de la Tour evoked the Hindu widows who, lacking the caste status that would entitle them to the "privilege" of *sati*, were instead enjoined to commit sexual suicide by shaving their heads, starving themselves into emaciation, and wearing distinctively ugly widow's clothes (Weinberger-Thomas 146–47).[21] Eventually, de la Tour died well, but not until Pimlott had given her more than enough time to kill herself with Charmian's sword, had she so chosen. When did she resolve on death? Not until Proculeius, having kissed her foot, thrusts it away contemptuously. And not until Octavius responded (by not responding) to her parting embrace by standing immobile. Those actions taught her that "the bright day is done" (5.2.193) and gave the audience a disturbing lesson in the constitutive relationship between ageism and heteronomy. "Only at the close, where she appears shockingly shorn of make-up; and then slowly assumes the accoutrements of grandeur, does she acquire a regal stillness," writes Michael

Fig. 13. Frances de la Tour as Cleopatra and Guy Henry as Octavius (5.1) in Steven Pimlott's 1999 production of *Antony and Cleopatra* at the Memorial Theatre in Stratford-upon-Avon. Photographer Donald Cooper © Royal Shakespeare Company.

Billington (21).[22] However, such belated majesty as de la Tour attained could not reverse her earlier characterization—the lusty widow foiled, bent on redeeming herself through suicide. Pimlott's *Antony and Cleopatra* was the story of two elderly hedonists' last gasp, of a Cleopatra who, when forced to realize she will find no sexual successors to Antony, kills herself out of grief for her lost youth, memorialized in her last love. Like the Indian widow, she atones for her sins, among them responsibility for her husband's death;[23] rids herself of her feminine sex—"I am fire and air" (5.2.289); and anticipates eternal pleasure—"Husband, I come!" Having (ostensibly) died for her man, "the virtuous wife" can now demand our respect.

Unlike Nunn's *Antony and Cleopatra*, Pimlott's radical simplification of Cleopatra and reductively erotic concept of the play effaced a legend while ignoring Shakespeare's exploration of imperialist *realpolitik*. Margot Heinemann observes that Shakespeare is our political contemporary, that *Antony and Cleopatra*'s polysemous openness reflects a political *zeitgeist* common to the early-modern and late-capitalist West, and that simplification does a great disservice to the play (179).[24] Most reviewers concur that Pimlott goes beyond needful, inevitable simplification as he translates the text into performance. Whereas Shakespeare's lush poetry invites us to imagine and romanticize a grand passion that shared equal billing with the battle for imperial hegemony, Pimlott's opening sex scene, "the thing itself," defeats romanticizing. Throughout the play the sex seemed real enough, but the realities of politics were sidestepped. The death of Pimlott's Cleopatra evoked one of the ugliest axioms patriarchal anxiety has spawned: "She's good, being gone" (1.2.126). Despite its "adolescent shock tactics," this trendy pastiche is at its core "retro," a naively recuperative reading, imbricated in *sati* and the flawed vision of an earlier age. Paradoxically, Nunn's forward-looking performative choices— above all, representing Cleopatra as a wily player in an international power struggle—gild a theatrically more traditional production conceived over a quarter of a century ago with contemporaneity.

NOTES

1. *Antony and Cleopatra* in the second edition of *The Riverside Shakespeare*, hereafter cited within the text.
2. No consensus exists concerning at what age widows are eligible for *sati* (or the minimum age of the children they would be orphaning); whether the woman must be premenopausal; which castes are entitled to burn with their husbands, which separately; what constitutes voluntarism; whether *sati* is holier than ascetic widowhood; and whether *sati* has a scriptural basis or is sacralized only by custom. Also see John Stratton Hawley's anthology, *Sati, the Blessing and the Curse: The Burning of Wives in India.*

3. A videocassette is available from Live Home Video, ITC, 1993. See Crowl 153–55 for a discussion of the televised production.

4. For Charles Marowitz, a champion of director's theater, the director should be "another 'author' ... saying things different from—sometimes at conflict with—the meaning of the first author, and this interloper is, of course, the modern director; a man who insists on reading his own thoughts into those traditionally associated with the author whose work he is communicating" (3). That is to say, the director's views are equal to those of the primary author and may even take precedence.

5. Lynda Boose comments on Shakespeare's suppression of Cleopatra's racial identity; see " 'The Getting of a Lawful Race': Racial Discourse in Early Modern England and the Unrepresentable Black Woman," 47–48.

6. Michael Neill is convinced of Shakespeare's "clearly envisaging Cleopatra as a North African queen whose skin is either 'tawny' or 'black' ..." (65); discounting her "white hand," Arthur Little Jr. (24, 144–45) and Carol Chillington Rutter, among others, would prefer her black, a preference that Rutter defends in an absorbing chapter on recent stage history, "Shadowing Cleopatra," in her *Enter the Body* 57–103.

7. For a still trenchant discussion of this vexed question, see Appendix C, "Cleopatra's Blackness," in Adelman 184–88. John Michael Archer's essay in MacDonald 145–64 is also germane.

8. Hall recognizes assimilation as deconstructing a dark / light, Egypt / Rome polarity, threatening Europe with "loss of identity in measureless expansion" (157).

9. Meadows subtracts a year from the ages of all three and does not mention a divorce (23–24).

10. Grant believes that Julius Caesar and Antony were the only lovers Cleopatra took, but he questions her marriage to Antony (186, 237).

11. All Chaucer quotations are from the *Riverside Chaucer* and are hereafter cited within the text.

12. I quote from Steane's edition of Marlowe's plays.

13. Garnier, reprinted in Bullough, *Narrative and Dramatic Sources of Shakespeare* 5: 406. In time, the valorizing of laudable pagan suicides affected Europeans' feelings toward the suicides of Christians. Although officially condemned, these began to evoke less judgmental responses. Montaigne's "A Custom of the Ile of Cea," Donne's *Biathanatos*, and Burton's *Anatomy of Melancholy* all present suicide with some degree of approbation. The subtitle of *Biathanatos* reveals an attempt, not unique to Donne, to maneuver around doctrine: *A Declaration of that Paradoxe, or Thesis, That Selfe-homicide is not so Naturally Sinne, that it may never be otherwise* (Wymer 8).

14. As for the historical Cleopatra, Octavius appears to have encouraged her suicide (Grant 225, Meadows 30); Guy Weill Goudchaux believes that Octavius may have had her assassinated (140).

15. The production is discussed on 104–09.

16. See Grant's discussion of her early decision to seek Rome's protection for Egypt (65) and her loyalty to Antony (211, 216, and 222–23).

17. Alan Bates was sixty-four, Frances de la Tour not much younger. She had joined the RSC in 1965, and played Helena in Peter Brook's landmark production of *A Midsummer Night's Dream* in 1970 (Owen 7; Grimley 5).

18. Russell Jackson reports that, whereas this scene was toned down when the production moved from Stratford to London, in the last scene when de la Tour was preparing for her suicide, she was completely nude toward the end of the run, rather than merely topless (221–22).

19. For favorable reviews, see, for example, Michael Coveney's "Naked Power of a Tour de Force" and Irving Wardle, "The Passions of Middle Age."

20. Paul Taylor protests that "the wider politics of the play are under-explored" (8), as does Nicholas De Jongh: "The play's political aspects are still faint-heartedly done" (7). Similarly, for Carole Woddis the production is "less convincing in conveying the geo-political power games at stake" (15).

21. On February 1, 2002, the first global conference on widows was convened in New Delhi. Titled "Capacity Building of Marginalized Women: Widows," its mission was to find ways to mitigate the stigmatization and exploitation of widows (Katyal 13).

22. Also see Barbara Hodgdon's description of de la Tour's ritualistic preparation for suicide (260–61).

23. In older patriarchal interpretations of the play, Cleopatra is ultimately the cause of Antony's defeat and death; see Spevack 698.

24. This moving essay, " 'Let Rome in Tiber Melt': Order and Disorder in 'Antony and Cleopatra,' " was one of the last that Heinemann wrote.

WORKS CITED

Adelman, Janet. *The Common Liar: An Essay on* "Antony and Cleopatra." New Haven: Yale UP, 1973.

Allison, Julie. "Review of *Antony and Cleopatra*, Royal Shakespeare Company, Plymouth Theatre Royal." *Herald Express* [Torquay] 26 Apr. 2000: 7.

Archer, John Michael. "Antiquity and Degeneration in *Antony and Cleopatra*." *Race, Ethnicity and Power in the Renaissance*. Ed. Joyce Green MacDonald. Madison and Teaneck, NJ: Fairleigh Dickinson UP, 1997. 145–64.

Banerjee, Pompa. *Burning Women: Widows, Witches, and Early Modern European Travelers in India*. New York: Palgrave Macmillan, 2003.

Barthelemy, Anthony Gerard. *Black Face, Maligned Race: The Representation of Blacks in English Drama from Shakespeare to Southerne*. Baton Rouge: Louisiana State UP, 1987.

Billington, Michael. Review of *Antony and Cleopatra*. " Reviews." *The Guardian* (London) 25 June 1999, *Guardian* Leader: 21.

Boose, Lynda E. " 'The Getting of a Lawful Race': Racial Discourse in Early Modern England and the Unrepresentable Black Woman." *Women, "Race," and Writing in the Early Modern Period*. Ed. Margo Hendricks and Patricia Parker. London: Routledge, 1994. 35–54.

Bullough, Geoffrey. Introduction to *Antony and Cleopatra. Narrative and Dramatic Sources of Shakespeare*. Ed. Bullough. Vol. 5. London: Routledge, 1964. 215–53.

[Chaucer, Geoffrey.] *The Riverside Chaucer*. 3rd ed. Ed. Larry D. Benson. Boston:
    Houghton, 1987.
Clapp, Suzannah. "All the Town's a Stage." *The Observer* (London) 27 June 1999,
    Review Page: 8.
Coveney, Michael. Review of *Antony and Cleopatra*. *Financial Times* (London) 27
    May 1986: 44.
————. "Naked Power of a Tour de Force." *Daily Mail* (London) 21 Jan. 2000: 52.
Crick, Bernard. "The Politics of Rome." *The Times Higher Education Supplement*
    (London) 21 Dec. 1973: 11.
Crowl, Samuel. "A World Elsewhere: The Roman Plays on Film and Television."
    Shakespeare and the Moving Image: The Plays on Film and Television. Ed.
    Anthony Davies and Stanley Wells. Cambridge: Cambridge UP, 1994.
De Jongh, Nicholas. "Shakespeare Stripped Down Is Too Much to Bare." *The Evening
    Standard* (London) 20 Jan. 2000: 7.
Garnier, Robert. *The Tragedie of Antonie*. Trans. Mary Herbert Sidney. 1595 ed. Rpt.
    in Geoffrey Bullough. Narrative and Dramatic Sources of Shakespeare. Vol. 5.
    London: Routledge, 1964. 358–406.
Goudchaux, Guy Weill. "Cleopatra's Subtle Religious Strategy." *Cleopatra of Egypt:
    From History to Myth*. Ed. Susan Walker and Peter Higgs. Princeton: Princeton
    UP, 2001. 128–41.
Grant, Michael. *Cleopatra*. London: Weidenfeld and Nicolson, 1972.
Grimley, Terry. "Interview: Mid-Life Crisis Mirth." *Birmingham Post* 5 June 1999:
    Sec. 5.
Hall, Kim F. *Things of Darkness: Economies of Race and Gender in Early Modern
    England*. Ithaca: Cornell UP, 1995.
Hardwick, Viv. "Turning Cherries Rainbow Coloured." *The Northern Echo*
    (Darlington) 24 Feb. 2000: sec. 13.
Hawley, John Stratton, ed. *Sati, the Blessing and the Curse: The Burning of Wives in
    India*. Oxford: Oxford UP, 1994.
Heinemann, Margot. " 'Let Rome in Tiber Melt': Order and Disorder in '*Antony and
    Cleopatra*.' " *Antony and Cleopatra*. Ed. John Drakakis. New Casebooks. New
    York: St. Martin's, 1994. 166–81.
Hodgdon, Barbara. "*Antony and Cleopatra* in the Theatre." *The Cambridge
    Companion to Shakespearean Tragedy*. Ed. Claire McEachern. Cambridge:
    Cambridge UP, 2002. 241–63.
Hughes-Hallett, Lucy. *Cleopatra: Histories, Dreams, and Distortions*. New York:
    Harper, 1990.
Jackson, Russell. "Shakespeare at Stratford-upon-Avon: Summer and Winter,
    1999–2000." *Shakespeare Quarterly* 51.2 (2000): 217–29.
Katyal, Anita. "Global Meet on Widows from Feb. 1." *The Times of India (New Delhi)*.
    International Edition. 30 Jan. 2002: 13.
Kingston, Jeremy. "How to Win a Tony in Old Egypt." Rev. of *Antony and Cleopatra*.
    The Times (London) 25 June 1999: Features.
Lewsen, Charles. "*Antony and Cleopatra*: Stratford-on-Avon." *The Times* (London) 16
    Aug. 1972: 13.
Little, Arthur L., Jr. *Shakespeare Jungle Fever: National-Imperial Re-Visions of Race,
    Rape, and Sacrifice*. Stanford: Stanford UP, 2000.

Loomba, Ania. "'Travelling thoughts': Theatre and the Space of the Other." *Antony and Cleopatra*. Ed. John Drakakis. New Casebooks. New York: St. Martin's, 1994. 279–307.

Madelaine, Richard. Introduction. *Antony and Cleopatra*. Shakespeare in Production. Cambridge: Cambridge UP, 1998. 1–138.

Mani, Lata. "Multiple Mediations: Feminist Scholarship in the Age of Multinational Reception." *Knowing Women: Feminism and Knowledge*. Ed. Helen Crowley and Susan Himmelweit. Cambridge: Polity, 1992. 306–22.

———. *Contentious Traditions: The Debate on 'Sati' in Colonial India*. Berkeley: U of California P, 1998.

Marlowe, Christopher. "The Second Part of Tamburlaine the Great." *The Complete Plays*. Ed. J. B. Steane. Harmondsworth, Middlesex: Penguin, 1969. 179–257.

Marowitz, Charles. *Recycling Shakespeare*. New York: Applause, 1991.

Meadows, Andrew. "Sins of the Fathers: The Inheritance of Cleopatra, Last Queen of Egypt." *Cleopatra of Egypt: From History to Myth*. Ed. Susan Walker and Peter Higgs. 14–31.

Neill, Michael. Introduction. *The Tragedy of Antony and Cleopatra*. Oxford, Clarendon, 1994. 1–130.

Nightingale, Benedict. "Decline and Growth." *New Statesman* (London) 25 Aug. 1972, 265.

———. "Age Cannot Wither Her." *The Times* (London) 23 July 1999, Features: 1.

———. "A London Season as Unsettling as the Weather." *The New York Times* 29 Aug. 1999, sec. 2: 6.

Nunn, Trevor, dir. *Antony and Cleopatra*. Perf. Janet Suzman and Richard Johnson. 1974. Videocassette. Live Home Video, ITC, 1993.

Owen, Michael. "An Appetite for Big Things." *Sunday Telegraph* 8 Aug. 1999: 7.

Plutarch. "The Life of Marcus Antonius" and "The Comparison of Demetrius with Antonius." *Lives of Noble Grecians and Romanes*. Trans. Sir Thomas North. Reprinted in Geoffrey Bullough, ed. *Narrative and Dramatic Sources of Shakespeare*. Vol. 5. London: Routledge, 1964. 254–321.

Rogers, Katherine M. *The Troublesome Helpmate: A History of Misogyny in Literature*. Seattle: U of Washington P, 1966.

Rutter, Carol Chillington. *Enter the Body: Women and Representation on Shakespeare's Stage*. London: Routledge, 2001.

Sen, Mala. *Death by Fire: Sati, Dowry Death, and Female Infanticide in Modern India*. New Brunswick: Rutgers UP, 2002.

[Shakespeare, William.] *The Riverside Shakespeare*. Ed. G. B. Evans. 2nd ed. Boston: Houghton, 1997.

Shuttleworth, Ian. "Actors Survive the Gimmicks." *Financial Times* (London) 21 Jan. 2000, The Arts: 9.

Spencer, Charles. "RSC Resorts to Adolescent Shock Tactics." *Daily Telegraph* 25 June 1999, Arts: 25.

Spevack, Marvin, ed. *Antony and Cleopatra. A New Variorum Edition of Shakespeare*. New York: MLA, 1990.

Speaight, Robert. "Shakespeare in Britain—The Stratford Season." *Shakespeare Quarterly* 23.4 (1972): 383–87.

Taylor, Paul. "Misplaced Imagination: *Antony and Cleopatra*, RSC Stratford." *The Independent* (London) 26 June 1999, Features: 8.

Tierney, Margaret. Review of *Antony and Cleopatra*. *Plays and Players* 20.1 (October 1972): 42–43.

Van Hooff, Anton J. L. *From Autothanasia to Suicide: Self-killing in Classical Antiquity*. London: Routledge, 1990.

Virgil. Aeneid. Trans. H. *Rushton Fairclough*. Rev. ed. London: Heinemann, 1934. Vol. 2.

Wardle, Irving. "Passions of Middle Age." *Sunday Telegraph* 27 June 1999, The Arts: 8.

Weinberger-Thomas, Catherine. *Ashes of Immortality: Widow-Burning in India*. Trans. Jeffrey Mehlman and David Gordon White. Chicago: U of Chicago P, 1999.

Woddis, Carole. "Theatre: *Antony and Cleopatra*, Royal Shakespeare Theatre, Stratford-upon-Avon." *The Herald* (Glasgow) 5 July 1999: 15.

Wymer, Rowland. *Suicide and Despair in the Jacobean Drama*. Brighton, Sussex: Harvester, 1986.

5.
"High events as these"
Sources, Influences, and the Artistry
of *Antony and Cleopatra*

ROBERT A. LOGAN

I

As anyone seriously interested in Shakespeare well knows, the abundance of
scholarship and criticism on *Antony and Cleopatra* has been rich in substance
and variety and considerably enlivened by controversy. Increasingly, however,
there has been a tendency, not limited to discussions of this play or even to
Shakespearean drama, to blur the distinction between human behavior as we
know it in life and the behavior of the playwright's fictionalized characters.
In *Antony and Cleopatra*, the ambivalences and ambiguities evident in the two
protagonists' motives and actions have only heightened our desire to possess
a more complete knowledge of their psychologies. To be sure, invoking a
psychological explanation of characters and their conduct has been of ines-
timable value in advancing our understanding of the play. But the practice
now "ore-flowes the measure" (1.1.2),[1] obscuring the separation between real
persons as they fulfill their destinies and Shakespeare's theatrical figures as
they fulfill their artistic functions. In our eagerness to identify characters as
actual human beings and to know them with depth and intimacy, we have too
often forgotten that they are the controlled products of the playwright's
artistry. The result has been to devalue the playwright's purely dramaturgical
interests and the aesthetic dynamics of the play.

I hope to redress this lapse through a selective examination of the traditionally accepted sources of and influences on *Antony and Cleopatra*. The
terms "sources" and "influences" have generally been used interchangeably.[2]
But, as I am using them here, "sources" supply links through verbal echoes and
parallel details, establishing with certainty Shakespeare's familiarity with
earlier fictional or nonfictional works; and "influences" tell us how Shakespeare made use of his sources, including the degree to which they colored his
artistic practices as he composed the play. In examining such works as
Appian's (Appianus Alexandrinus's) *The Romanes Warres* (1578), Sir Thomas

North's translation of Plutarch's *The Life of Marcus Antonius and The Comparison of Demetrius with Antonius* (1579), Christopher Marlowe's *Dido, Queen of Carthage* (c. 1587), the Countess of Pembroke's translation of Robert Garnier's *Antonie* (1592), Samuel Daniel's *The Tragedie of Cleopatra* (1594) and "A Letter from Octavia to Marcus Antonius" (1599), and North's translation of Simon Goulart's *The Life of Octavius Caesar Augustus* (1602),[3] I intend to separate sources from influences. This approach will enable us to see how thoroughly Shakespeare concentrated on dramatic technique, chiefly as it pertains to characterization and language, but also, briefly, as it relates to the structure (the order and juxtaposition of events) and the genre of the play.[4]

The study of the known sources of *Antony and Cleopatra* has a long history and, within it, work that is detailed and exhaustive.[5] But for all the considerable excellence of their work, scholars have not sufficiently investigated the extent to which the sources actually influenced Shakespeare's artistic choices. Moreover, source studies usually leave untouched those elements that Shakespeare chose not to borrow or imitate and, consequently, what his rejection of such material tells us about the composition and artistic aims of *Antony and Cleopatra*. In the following discussion, I hope to show the value of taking account of such omissions.

II

Given the strong moralizing tendencies of Shakespeare's sources and analogues, the wonder is that, in composing *Antony and Cleopatra*, he was able to extricate himself from such a dominant mode and yet convey his own system of values with such force and clarity. Whatever his personal motives, he had indisputable professional reasons for not only freeing himself from the prevailing mode but actually subverting it. Not the least of these reasons lies in the powerful influence of Christopher Marlowe's works, especially *Dido, Queen of Carthage*. Before we consider these reasons, however, we need to characterize the dramaturgical device that Shakespeare found most crucial in composing his play: the presentation of the characters and their actions through alternative perspectives. Whether we look solely at the events of *Antony and Cleopatra* or examine the play metadramatically for evidences of the mind creating it, we are able to detect Shakespeare's artistic investment in two distinct categories of consciousness: one, moral, the other, aesthetic. The moral consciousness, best represented in the play by the Roman perspective on reality, is characterized by the rational faculties that "comprehend"[6] it. These are the complex empirical and analytical faculties of the mind—voluntary (at times, deliberate), pragmatic, judgmental, categorical, and absolute. As Shakespeare dramatizes it, this perspective also tends to be limited in its focus—oversimplified, rigid, and reductive—as well as dehumanizing in its detachment and depersonalization. As a consequence, he finds this perspective most useful as a means of generating conflict and tension. The aesthetic consciousness, best represented in the play by the Egyptian perspective on reality, is characterized by the non-rational faculties that "apprehend" it—that is, the senses, emotions, imagination, instinct, and intuition. These are the simple creative and synthetic faculties of the mind. In operation they are involuntary, uninhibited, and expansive, lacking the restraints of the moral perspective but producing a psychic harmony unknown to the moral perspective. In its focus the aesthetic perspective can also be limited and self-absorbed, oblivious to the demands of one's corporate existence in society and the political state, but neither impersonal nor remote. The Soothsayer epitomizes this perspective functioning at its ideal best when, in answer to Antony's request for the "reason" (2.3.13) for his deep regret at their having left Egypt, he replies, "I see it in my motion: haue it not in my tongue" (2.3.14). The play supports this modus operandi because, in giving voice to his intuitive sense, the Soothsayer is never proven wrong.[7] Interestingly, however, when this same, nonmoral attitude of mind leads to love, it invokes an ethical frame of reference that the playwright evidently believes is inextricably woven into human bonding. Shakespeare finds in the aesthetic perspective a useful technique for dramatizing and promoting psychological subtleties, complexities, and understanding, and for denouncing oversimplified, reductive moral judgments—as Enobarbus's death from a broken heart, through its assertion of the claims of instinct over rationality, well demonstrates. But Shakespeare employs this perspective not only to create conflict and tension with the moral perspective; it also helps to establish the ambiguity and mystery of characters and events that, ultimately, the playtext places at the center of human existence. In its privileging of ambiguity, the play dramatizes the superiority of the aesthetic perspective and, linked to it, the view that, in spite of the deadly consequences, the life most worth living is the one lived in the heat of intense vitality.

In surveying the possible sources, influences, and analogues associated with Shakespeare as he composed *Antony and Cleopatra*, it is not necessary to recapitulate the excellent work of previous scholars. We do, however, need to review some representative details of the sources to secure an understanding of the artistic direction in which Shakespeare chose to move and to see what he rejected and why. The importance of such an investigation lies in discerning the influence of the sources on Shakespeare as a practical and seasoned dramatist, a man who fused his professional interest in artistic and commercial success with his most comfortable idealistic beliefs about human behavior—always without abandoning his strong, realistic sense of the deleterious effects of passing time. I hope finally to demonstrate how artistic considerations freed him from the heavy moralizing perspective of his predecessors and enabled him to write a play as triumphant in what it celebrates as it is tragic in its portrayal of the inevitability of human mortality. Ultimately, it is a play that defiantly transcends all designations of genre—in its way making as much of a mockery of such categorical distinctions as Polonius unwittingly makes when he lists dramatic genres with hairsplitting particularity: "tragedy, comedy, history, pastoral, pastoral-comical, historical-pastoral" (*Hamlet* 2.2.340–41).

III

Although we cannot know when Shakespeare may have read his sources, we do have a clear sense of how strongly they weighed on him as he composed *Antony and Cleopatra*. If we look at the sources chronologically, we can at least follow something of the development and continued popularity of the various portrayals of Antony and Cleopatra, including the events of history in which the pair were embroiled. There is a consensus among scholars that Appian's account of the Roman civil wars, appearing in a 1578 translation entitled *The Romanes Warres*, gives details about Pompey, Lucius, Fulvia, and their hostility toward Octavius of which Shakespeare was aware although they are not in Plutarch's or Goulart's accounts.[8] For example, in Appian and in Shakespeare's play, Antony is indignant at the murder of Pompey; Plutarch makes no mention of the murder. In the play, Antony seems furious at his unnamed underling (who has the name of Titius in Appian and Goulart) because he murdered Pompey. Antony's anger here would seem to exonerate him from any personal culpability: "[Antony] threats the throate of that his Officer, / That murdred Pompey" (3.5.18–19). In Goulart's *Life of Octavius Caesar Augustus*, however, Pompey is put to death "by Antonius commandement" (Spevack 466). Appian presents both possibilities and does not come to a determination about who was ultimately responsible for the murder. But the possibility that Antony was not responsible appears to be a suggestion that caught Shakespeare's imagination. This incident not only indicates that Shakespeare was familiar with Appian's account but also offers one of the many instances in the play in which, by omitting stigmatizing implications, the playwright idealizes Antony; or, at least, by being cryptic enough to leave Antony's connection with the murder obscure, Shakespeare prevents us from assuming the triumvir's personal involvement and thus moralistically condemning him.

Moreover, Shakespeare either assumes his initial audiences' familiarity with Roman history or deliberately creates an atmosphere in which a lack of certainty and clarity prevails. For example, one would not know from the play alone that Fulvia fully supported Antony while his brother Lucius strongly opposed him, even though Fulvia and Lucius became partners in a campaign against Octavius. Eager to go to war on behalf of Antony's supposed grievances against Caesar, Fulvia desired to create a conflict that would bring Antony back home to her, whereas Lucius, more political and idealistic, wanted to advance the cause of Republicanism by destroying the Triumvirate. As both Bullough (247–48) and Muir (224) point out, this latter piece of information, found in Appian but not in Goulart or Plutarch, explains Antony's rhetorical question to Octavius in the play: "Did ... [my brother Lucius] ... not rather / Discredit my authority with yours, / And make the warres alike against my stomacke, / Hauing alike your cause" (2.2.48–51).[9] Whether or not, because of the popularity of the story, some members of the earliest audiences were familiar with the details of the motivations and political machinations implied by this passage, the fact remains that Shakespeare does not give these details a place in the drama. Instead, he uses the cryptic allusion to Lucius's aristocratic Republicanism to contribute to the texture of ambiguity that the play creates through its uncertainties of character and event, its rapid structural pacing, and its telescoping of time. Ambiguity not only engages audiences—unsettling them by denying easy categorization and keeping them attentive with beguiling puzzles—but it also instills a kind of credibility that people are familiar with from everyday living. In addition, it prevents audiences from becoming passive through the pat resolution of moral issues or by stereotyping characters and, thereby, writing them off. Finally, it helps to create a healthy respect for the mysteries of causality in human existence.

North's translation of Plutarch's *Life of Marcus Antonius and the Comparison of Demetrius with Antonius*, published a year after Appian's account, is widely accepted as Shakespeare's primary source for the play. The playwright quite amply availed himself of Plutarch's details of characterization and events. He also frequently echoed North's language and, in Enobarbus's description of Antony and Cleopatra's first meeting (2.2.195–245), took the very words of North's prose and infused them with lyricism, distinct rhythms, and a vibrant organic unity.[10] As Spevack's variorum edition attests, commentary on connections between Plutarch and the play has been plentiful (Spevack 384–97). Even so, two aspects have not been considered fully: the first, what Shakespeare did *not* take from Plutarch and, the second, what actual influence Plutarch had on the artistry of *Antony and Cleopatra*.

No one would deny that Plutarch speaks as a moralist; he is never reluctant to criticize the wrongdoings of Antony and of those who share any part of the Roman leader's life. But he also assumes the role of the evenhanded historian by characterizing the personalities of both Antony and Cleopatra with the contradictions and the mix of pluses and minuses that he finds in their behavior. Unlike Shakespeare, who devotes the fifth act and the climax of the play to Cleopatra, Plutarch focuses chiefly on Antony, painting the portrait of a man who is complicated, paradoxical, by turns defective and heroic, but ultimately disappointing. In the play, Mecaenas comments that Antony's "taints and Honours, wag'd equal with him" (5.1.30). But, because Shakespeare concentrates supportively on the love between Antony and Cleopatra, as

Plutarch does not,[11] the "taints" seem less serious to us than they appear to the Roman Mecaenas and very much less than they seem to Plutarch.

Because Plutarch gives us a fuller picture of Antony over a longer period of time and makes him the dominant figure of his history, Shakespeare's portrait has to some critics seemed simpler.[12] Less quantitatively, this assessment may also result from focusing single-mindedly on Antony as a person rather than as a dramatic figure underpsychologized at times because of his other diverse uses in the drama. We understand from hints in the text that Antony is being battered by many more moral, aesthetic, political, and natural forces (including his sense of aging) than the play overtly dramatizes. In addition to his intriguing psychological dimensions, he fulfills symbolic and functional needs of the play. Thus, although these three elements are not necessarily mutually exclusive, Antony can sometimes be more important to the play for what he represents than for who he is psychologically, and he can be made to serve functions that further the drama without reference to his psyche. For example, unlike Plutarch, Shakespeare makes use of the symbolic nature of Antony's past feats as a hero to create and heighten tensions between him and the Romans; when we first meet Shakespeare's Octavius (1.4), he is scornful and petulant, lamenting Antony's decline from his former, unparalleled heroics (especially lines 56–71). In another example, with a structural canniness that Plutarch does not possess, Shakespeare juxtaposes the party scene aboard Pompey's galley (2.7) with Ventidius's successful execution of vengeance in the Parthian campaign (3.1) in order to denigrate both Caesar and Antony's symbolic value as political and military leaders and, by extension, the sociopolitical world as a whole. Shakespeare pointedly delineates the underbelly of power politics:

> VENTIDIUS. Caesar and Anthony haue euer wonne
>   More in their officer, then person.
>   ....
>   Who does i'th'Warres more then his Captaine can,
>   Becomes his Captaines Captaine: and Ambition
>   (The Souldiers vertue) rather makes choise of losse
>   Then gaine, which darkens him. (3.1.16–24)

The juxtaposition of the two scenes creates an irony that clarifies the complexities of the political and military situation without probing the psychologies of either triumvir. In his narrative, Plutarch simply shifts the focus to another event.[13] Considered more generally, Shakespeare's juxtaposition underscores with unflinching realism the inevitability of a clash of cognitive perspectives.

In addition to viewing Shakespeare's Antony as simpler than Plutarch's figure by focusing too exclusively on him as an actual person, one may be tempted to try to simplify the character by aligning him with the play's many lucid dichotomies.[14] The oppositions enrich the conflicts and tensions: Rome versus Egypt, professional interests versus private interests, society versus the individual, self-interest versus loyalty, rational perspective versus nonrational perspective, moral reality versus aesthetic reality. Moreover, these antitheses introduce complexity by presenting a contrast between an older order of Roman politics, which supports the virtues of honorable human interaction as embodied in Antony and Pompey, and the new order of ruthless power politics as represented by Octavius Caesar. Even though Antony's identification with one of the binary oppositions is limpid at any given moment, it is seldom fixed—especially when the need arises for him to invoke a rational state of mind in order to assign priorities to the activities of his private and professional lives: to the value of his love for Cleopatra or to his ambitions and responsibilities as triumvir. When Shakespeare does focus on Antony's psychology, the purposeful confusion of the Roman leader's motives, his impulsiveness, and his devotion to Cleopatra are engulfed in enough uncertainty so that, upon reflection, they suggest a more complicated figure than we glimpse on the surface. Torn between his Roman heroic and Egyptian amatory inclinations (which he sometimes makes heroic) and between his acute awareness of "the strong necessity of time" (1.3.42) and his knowledge of the Soothsayer's certain prediction that Caesar's fortunes are destined to rise higher (2.3.15–38), Antony evinces a genuine perplexity before life that has deep and complicated roots. But because he does not supply us with the interior meditations that the protagonists of *Hamlet*, *Othello*, *King Lear*, and *Macbeth* provide, we are kept at arm's length from his inner turmoil. Even so, Shakespeare chooses to portray Antony's perplexity sympathetically, through a compassionate understanding of the human predicament of change and physical decay, rather than more simply through Plutarch's harsh moralizing.

Shakespeare omits much of the information contained in Plutarch that would detract from Antony's character—such as his drunken feasts, his insolence and cruelty, his political deceptions, his three children by Octavia and his life with her, and the ignominy of his demise. The playwright does not minimize Antony's failings but, at the same time, he allows more space than Plutarch for Antony to be marveled at as a hero. Significantly, Shakespeare portrays Antony as a hero formed by nature,[15] not society, although Plutarch and the Romans in the play (e.g., Caesar in 1.4) characterize him as an illustrious warrior constructed by society exclusively for the benefit of society. Heroic in military action, he is even more astonishing in his ability to inspire others to outdo themselves, and not only comrades in battle, as Cleopatra's suicide proves. Whereas Plutarch, not without reservations, gives anecdotal examples of this talent, Shakespeare exalts it. Significantly, Shakespeare does not attempt to dramatize the psychology of this gift of leadership beyond indicating that its phenomenal effect is linked to Antony's magnanimity, an ingrained trait that an anonymous soldier, Enobarbus, and Cleopatra all recognize as his "bounty": the Soldier praises "His Bounty over-plus" (4.6.22); Enobarbus refers to him as "Thou Mine of Bounty" (4.6.32); and Cleopatra exclaims, "For his Bounty, / There was no winter in't" (5.2.86–87). This highly positive characteristic suggests a consistency in Antony that Plutarch does not care to highlight. If this consistency leads some commentators to consider Shakespeare's Antony simpler, it is because the playwright is more interested than Plutarch in magnifying a quintessential, yet inexplicable cause of Antony's greatness. In Plutarch, Antony begins higher and falls lower. In the play, Antony starts lower and rises higher, at his death and after inspiring legends about his heroics in battle and in love—as the play itself proves. Ultimately, the reason for the difference in the two writers' accounts has more to do with the artistic needs of the drama, including the structural progression and the intense focus on the conflicting evaluations of love, than with our desire for a consistent and realistic psychological portrait. Unlike Plutarch, Shakespeare wants to awe us with the mystery of Antony's heroics in war and love. Consequently, he presents the mystery through suggestion and evocation rather than offering a psychological (much less a moral) explanation that might diminish it.

Everyone in the play talks about Antony, giving him an importance that adds to his stature. Part of the reason for this, of course, is that the causes of Cleopatra's greatness are easier to convey on a stage than those of Antony since his are primarily military. Ironically, even when the criticism of Antony is most severe, the language and details employed often ennoble him. This tendency begins with Philo, a figure not in Plutarch's account. In countering Demetrius's apparent disbelief about his leader's fallen state, he opens the play with a passionate, condemnatory outburst:

> Nay, but this dotage of our Generals
> Ore-flowes the measure: those his goodly eyes
> That o're the Files and Musters of the Warre,
> Haue glow'd like plated Mars:
> Now bend, now turne
> The Office and Deuotion of their view
> Vpon a Tawny Front. His Captaines heart,
> Which in the scuffles of great Fights hath burst
> The Buckles on his brest, reneages all temper,
> And is become the Bellowes and the Fan
> To coole a Gypsies Lust.
> > *Flourish. Enter Anthony, Cleopatra her Ladies, the*
> > *Traine, with Eunuchs fanning her.*
> Looke where they come:
> Take but good note, and you shall see in him

(The triple Pillar of the world) transform'd
Into a Strumpets Foole. Behold and see. (1.1.1–20)

The elevated language (e.g., "Pillar")—Latinate ("those his goodly eyes"), generalized (l.3), detached and impersonal (l.6); the abundant imagery—lofty and pompous; the powerfully evocative impressionistic details of Antony's former glory (e.g., "goodly eyes . . . Haue glow'd"); the emphatic assertion of his vitality ("burst / The Buckles on his brest"); and the final, biblical-epic, double imperative ask an audience to stand in awe of the warrior hero even as the content of the speech undermines him. That the style and tone of the speech contradict the import of the content sets up a design for the drama that ensues. Plutarch characterizes Antony's paradoxical nature well but, instead of firing his audience's imagination, he circumscribes it with moralisms; nor does he afford the hero the grandeur and demi-godlike status that he achieves in the play. Philo is a purely functional character, important for his evaluation of Antony, not for his person. He never appears again but asserts a firm moral position that Shakespeare can then spend the rest of the play undermining and complicating as, in fact, the speech itself has, paradigmatically, already begun to do. Thus, the playwright omits most of Plutarch's history of Antony until he meets Cleopatra and then eliminates the biographer-historian's discussion of Antony's Parthian campaign, except obliquely (2.3.40–42) and briefly (3.1). Although Plutarch furnishes Shakespeare with the materials for a full characterization of Antony, including a clear chronology of the events of his life, Shakespeare fashions the materials selectively so that they appeal less to an audience's rational intelligence than to its senses and emotions. As a result, Plutarch remains, at least, a source and, at most, an influence by negation, for he gives support to Shakespeare's decision to move in a different direction.

This is even truer of the characterization of Cleopatra. Unlike Shakespeare, Plutarch treats the queen with moral severity until after the Battle of Actium. As Willard Farnham says, "After Actium, Plutarch's Cleopatra is found to have a certain ill-defined amount of paradoxical nobility" (Farnham 148). If at times we are invited to consider Plutarch's Cleopatra wicked, we never see Shakespeare's queen in this light. The playwright softens the defects of Cleopatra through a broad range of humor and irony. Even at her most ignoble (e.g., her treatment of the messenger [2.5]), we are encouraged to laugh rather than condemn; our comic response blocks our indignation and censure. At her death, Cleopatra assumes a grandeur and nobility that Plutarch never grants her. Shakespeare's Cleopatra inspires her women to join her in dying and, echoing Enobarbus's death from a broken heart (even if under different circumstances), Iras dies, deeply affected by the sad plight of her mistress. In Plutarch, we are told simply that she lay dead at Cleopatra's feet (Spevack 455). Charmian also follows the Queen into death by committing suicide, a devotion whose strength is commensurate with the deeds that

Antony inspires in his soldiers, particularly Eros and Enobarbus, whose deaths for love parallel those of Charmian and Iras. Again, Plutarch recounts the death of Charmian without suggesting either her motives or means (Spevack 455). The ambiguity of Cleopatra's motives for killing herself in Plutarch is somewhat clarified in Shakespeare who turns the suicide into a *liebestod*.

Although not disinterested, Shakespeare is assuredly less interested in the politics that envelop Antony and Cleopatra than in their love. In fact, Shakespeare divests himself of many of Plutarch's political concerns in order to turn the spotlight on the private affairs of his characters. Remarkably, we never see Cleopatra take an active political stand or see her act in her administrative and legislative roles as the Queen of Egypt; even in the scene in Antony's camp near Actium, when she tells Enobarbus defensively that she is attending the battle "as the President of my Kingdome" (3.7.18), we know that her reason is wholly personal, that she is fearful of letting Antony out of her sight. In Plutarch's account, not only does she engage in political activities, but also we are told that she has a talent for being able to speak in the foreign tongues of those from the countries with whom she negotiates (Spevack 413–14). Shakespeare turns his attention to different queenly attributes. Instead of portraying Cleopatra as the politically ambitious queen that Plutarch depicts, the playwright delineates her as apolitical, interested primarily in the accoutrements, trappings, and ceremonial aspects of her queenship as theatrical spectacle. Thus, at her death, she conveys the impression that she is indeed most royal, and Charmian and even Caesar verify it (5.2.321 and 5.2.339, respectively). Charmian tells the First Guard conclusively that Cleopatra's manner of death is "well done, and fitting for a Princesse / Descended of so many Royall Kings" (5.2.329–30), and, by this point in the play, we quite agree. In Plutarch, Cleopatra begins lower and never reaches the resplendent heights of nobility achieved by Shakespeare's queen.

Instead of adopting Plutarch's moral and political perspectives, Shakespeare concentrates on Cleopatra's unparalleled ability to entice men (even unintentionally, as in the case of Dolabella) and her capacity to fall genuinely in love with Antony. The Romans, as well as Antony in a moment of blind wrath (4.12.13), regard her as a whore. Cleopatra knows well how she is considered, but she attributes it to the Romans' gross lack of imagination and understanding. She expresses her repugnance at their deficient aesthetic abilities in no uncertain terms, as in the following passage when she appears to be addressing Iras—who is entranced and utterly convinced by the scenario Cleopatra envisions—while actually thinking out loud, mesmerized by her own imaginings in a dialogue of one:

    ... The quicke Comedians
    Extemporally will stage vs, and present

> Our Alexandrian Reuels: *Antony*
> Shall be brought drunken forth, and I shall see
> Some squeaking *Cleopatra* Boy my greatnesse
> I'th'posture of a Whore. (5.2.216–21)

Cleopatra's ability to denigrate the impoverished imagination of the Romans by seeing herself as they see her shows just how far from being a whore she considers herself. Unlike the Romans, the audience sees her as a woman in love, so desperate to have Antony remain by her side that, as she acknowledges, her efforts are "sweating Labour" (1.3.93). When Antony leaves for Rome and subsequently marries Octavia, Cleopatra does not take up with other men. She remains loyal, a virtue that, as we know, Shakespeare frequently portrays as the essence of successful human bonding. When Antony dies, Cleopatra vows to commit suicide (4.15.86–91) and, although Caesar does what he can to prevent her, she does kill herself out of love. In dying, she assumes the roles of a Roman wife ("Husband, I come"—5.2.290) and mother ("Peace, peace / Dost thou not see my baby at my breast, / That sucks the nurse asleep"—5.2.311–13)—common roles for others but extraordinary for her, especially at this moment.

As this final scene demonstrates, Cleopatra is a figure whom we try to respond to more consistently on a psychological level than we respond to Antony. What deters us from an intimate knowledge of her psychology is her constant role-playing and, similar to Antony, her lack of interior meditations (neither character has a standard soliloquy); we are not often able to fathom the true motives of Cleopatra. But her theatrical personality allows her to keep us, like Antony, absorbed and filled with wonder. Shakespeare well knows that theatrical personalities can generate more interest in an audience than nontheatrical ones. The Romans try to reduce Cleopatra simply to a symbol of lust and moral depravity, primarily because of her effect on Antony and his Roman predecessors. But Cleopatra's actions prevent us from accepting that point of view, even at those times when her motives are undeniably obscure. Why does she flee during the sea battle at Actium (3.10)? Why does she flirt with Caesar's messenger Thidias (3.13)? Why does she haul Antony up to her rather than going down to him when he appears at her monument, dying (4.15)? Why does she withhold as much of her wealth as she offers Caesar (5.2)? The only answer that Shakespeare gives is Cleopatra's sudden, overpowering attacks of fear. But this motive provides no answer to the second and fourth questions. However we choose to answer these questions, the ambiguities keep us engaged, generating suspense as well as we wait to see if Cleopatra will actually commit suicide or "pack cards" with Caesar. Enobarbus's well-known description of Antony's first meeting with Cleopatra similarly engages him as he describes in exultant paradoxes the mysterious ability of the Queen, in her "infinite variety," to defy nature (2.2.195–251).

Clearly, Shakespeare's characterization of the Queen departs radically from Plutarch's.

If Cleopatra is the most completely humanized of the major characters in the play, Enobarbus is the most functional. Actually, Shakespeare draws on two figures from Plutarch for his portrayal—Domitius, the soldier who deserts Antony, and Domitius Aenobarbus who lives on after Antony. However, both have reduced roles in Plutarch, making Shakespeare's portrayal of Enobarbus all the more original. Shakespeare conceived of his Enobarbus as a dramatic construct rather than as a consistently psychological character. When we first encounter Enobarbus, we find a realistic, shrewd, tough-minded soldier, somewhat cynical, but clearly Antony's friend and right-hand man. Shakespeare employs him at various times as a crusty commentator on the proceedings (e.g., 2.2) and as a choral character (e.g., 2.6 and 3.13). In addition, he serves as a mouthpiece for sentiments that the playwright needs to convey, whether they praise or denigrate Cleopatra or deliver criticisms of Antony. Finally, however, Enobarbus becomes a tragic figure, because, for all his rationality and pragmatism, he fails to understand the value of loyalty and the significance of human bonds; realizing his mistake too late, he dies broken-hearted. Enobarbus represents the tragic consequences that occur when one is divided by conflicting cognitive modes and deficient in the non-Roman, natural values that the playtext supports. Overall, he is more significant for the artistic functions that he performs than for the personality he presents.

In providing details concerning the characters and events, Plutarch was undoubtedly Shakespeare's major source. But in the playwright's adaptation of the details, Marlowe's influence appears to have dominated. Elsewhere, I have discussed the influence of *Tamburlaine* on the conception of Antony— the vitality, military achievements, and use of language that make both figures larger than life; and the echoes in *Antony and Cleopatra* of Marlowe's stately, elevated language (his "high astounding terms"—1 *Tamburlaine* Prologue 5), which, in combination with a norm of hyperbole, an energetic syntax, and strong rhythms, compose Shakespeare's own "mighty lines" and produce a majestic tone similar to Marlowe's.[16] Shakespeare inherits this stylistic legacy not only from the *Tamburlaine* plays, but also from *Dido, Queen of Carthage*, generally accepted as Marlowe's first dramatic effort. *Dido* is crucial in unleashing Shakespeare's imagination early in his career and in tacitly encouraging him to take risks in characterization and in the use of blank verse. Shakespeare employs a heroic-romantic idiom throughout his play that he first found in *Dido*. The romantic element derives from Marlowe's idealized sentiments, emphatic hyperboles, and enthusiastic superlatives, all of which appear in *Dido*, as well as later in the *Tamburlaine* plays and *Hero and Leander*. The heroic element is also inherited at its earliest from *Dido*. Reuben Brower explains that the heroic idiom in *Dido* is "partly Virgilian, partly medieval" (113), the medieval deriving from Lydgate in *The Falls of Princes*.[17] He goes on to say that "Marlowe's *Dido Queene of Carthage* ... offered the most likely example for the Shakespearian blend in *Antony and Cleopatra* of the Virgilian heroic and the Ovidian erotic" (352).[18] That we can see such strong imprints of *Dido* on a play written almost twenty years later only suggests the power and tenacity of Marlowe's influence.[19]

Scholars have noted the similarities in the situation, mood, and language of the two plays.[20] The basic situation of both plays is familiar: two sets of legendary lovers that are thwarted by a conflict between love and political responsibilities. The parallels in mood and atmosphere stem from the similarity in geographical spaciousness, the grandeur and importance of the events for history, and, paradoxically, the four protagonists' propensity for both godlike behavior and human frailty. Stylized and exalted, the language of each play demands to be admired at the same time that it asks us to be enthralled and awed. Shakespeare learned from Marlowe to be boldly inventive in the use of language, including how to use language to create vividly imagined spectacles. He also learned to showcase his innovations in language and ask that they (and he) be admired. But Shakespeare integrates characters with words in a manner that he could not help absorbing after Marlowe used the technique in the climatic death scene of *Doctor Faustus*.

Shakespeare also developed other dramaturgical devices that he noticed in *Dido*. Like Marlowe, he presents both internal and external forces cooperating to create conflicts within his characters and the plot. The gods ultimately control Aeneas's destiny in spite of his intense personal feelings for Dido. Antony is similarly overpowered by forces beyond his control—fate,[21] the body politic, and "the strong necessity of Time" (1.3.42)—and they, too, conflict with his love for a queen. Dido and Cleopatra are ultimately frustrated unto death by the external forces acting upon their lovers. The spectacle of Dido's suicide may conceivably have influenced Shakespeare in deciding to culminate his play in the spectacle of Cleopatra's suicide. Assuredly, both dramatists recognize the powerful effects of presenting throughout their plays both verbal and visual spectacles.

From a traditional patriarchal perspective, Marlowe's portrayal of a flawed, submissive hero and an aggressive, forceful woman—particularly in her courtship of Aeneas—not only breaks away from previous retellings of the story of the lovers but subverts standard notions of gender barriers.[22] Very likely, Marlowe's boldness inspired Shakespeare,[23] for he also invests his flawed male hero with an interesting psychology and his female hero with utter disregard for traditional gender barriers. Both writers undermine accepted notions of gender roles in order to engage their audiences through surprise. But there is a difference. In *Dido*, we are consistently aware of Dido's assumption of the manliness that Aeneas lacks. In *Antony and Cleopatra*, our impression is that both protagonists unself-consciously transcend and enlarge prescribed gender roles; as rulers, they feel uninhibited and independent, free to love, and that includes an obliviousness to the barriers of ordinary societal norms, although, of course, this is not true of Antony when he is enmeshed in political obligations and succumbs to guilt about avoiding his responsibilities.

Moreover, both writers affirm the truism that what we see depends upon how we perceive it. Consequently, they direct our attention to cognitive modes. But whereas Marlowe suggests that emotion blinds one to truth, Shakespeare accepts the view that emotion leads to truth. Both Dido and Aeneas are susceptible to being deceived when emotion clouds their perception. Although there are several other instances in the play,[24] the most prominent example is the destructive force of sexual passion. Not only Dido and Aeneas but also Anna, Iarbus, and the Nurse are deceived and made unhappy by sexual passion, and Jupiter's sexual passion proves to be a force of disruption between him and Juno. Dido cannot seem to understand that Aeneas must continue on his predestined journey; knowing this, even Aeneas, in moments of self-deception, believes that he can remain in Carthage with Dido. Like the Romans in *Antony and Cleopatra*, Marlowe's playtext appears to view love as little more than sexual infatuation. Yet, the reduction of love to lust is not as simple as it first appears. Although, on the one hand, Marlowe's playtext seems to endorse the patriarchal view that reduces a deep love to sexual passion, on the other, through its irreverent treatment of Jupiter and its unheroic depiction of Aeneas, it debunks the very patriarchal values that it appears to affirm. The result is an ambiguity that Shakespeare admired enough to adopt as a major artistic technique throughout his career but never more so than in *Antony and Cleopatra*.

The deaths of Antony and Cleopatra prove that love can be a binding force that energizes, harmonizes, leads to self-actualization, and promotes independence and resourcefulness. As we see in his unflattering portrayal of the Romans, Shakespeare firmly rejects the cynical view of full-fledged love implicit in Marlowe's play but not the device of ambiguity that it helps to create. Nor does he reject the truth of the conflict between rational and nonrational perceptions. Both writers are forced on one level to accept the reality of political necessity because that is where the greatest power lies. Although in act 5, *Antony and Cleopatra* celebrates the aesthetic Egyptian values, the patriarchal affirmation of reason always remains, at least potentially, a viable alternative and, as Antony understands, one that has to be dealt with. Thus, even though the conclusions of the two plays differ—whereas Aeneas is forced to choose the heroic over the romantic, Antony and Cleopatra ultimately combine the romantic with the heroic—both plays complicate and balance competing value systems with a potent ambiguity that is designed to keep an audience attentive and intrigued.

Dido presents antithetical discourses—the patriarchal system affirming reason and heroic action and the romantic system celebrating emotion and love. As noted earlier, both systems are ironically undercut, evoking finally an ambiguous response from the audience. Similarly, *Antony and Cleopatra* dramatizes dichotomous value systems similar to those inscribed in *Dido*— the heroic, rational Roman ethos and the romantic, nonrational Egyptian one. Both systems are endorsed and interrogated at different times in the two plays, educing contradictory responses from their audiences. In fact, Marlowe's balancing of opposites in *Dido* leads to Shakespeare's exploitation of the same technique in his play. Each play creates discord and tension by establishing oppositions that need to be resolved or at least given balance: rational versus nonrational modes of perceiving; private desires (love) versus public responsibility (duty); internal versus external forces of conflict. In both plays, resolutions do come but either without providing satisfaction or, at best, by providing only flickering moments of contentment. Thus, in *Antony and Cleopatra*, the ambiguity that arises out of an audience's ambivalent responses towers over Marlowe's other important legacies to Shakespeare.

If we can say with confidence that Marlowe's play, supported by his other dramas (e.g., the *Tamburlaine* plays and *Edward II*), appears to have inspired Shakespeare's use of ambivalence, ambiguity, and unconventionality in *Antony and Cleopatra*, then we can add that his use originates in the ambiguous characterizations of *Dido*. The puzzling, unheroic attributes of the personality of the hero Aeneas, beginning with his misperceptions and passiveness, and Dido's manliness and failure to recognize and accept the force of destiny in her relationship with Aeneas are representative instances of the characterological technique of ambiguity that Shakespeare inherited. Because *Antony and Cleopatra* is the apotheosis of the aesthetic of ambiguity in Shakespeare, the deliberate employment of ambiguity is one major way in which the play, following in the wake of *Dido*, proved to be unconventional. Taken as a whole, the strongest influence of Marlowe lies in the imaginative independence that he manifested in *Dido* and later affirmed in his other works. As a practicing playwright, Shakespeare must have perceived this authorial trait early on in his career, just as he knew that Marlowe was the best exemplar in his culture of a successful combination of commercial and artistic success. Thus, in one final way, *Dido* proved to be a remarkably sustained influence on Shakespeare, emerging most powerfully and pervasively in *Antony and Cleopatra*. Viewed from this perspective, it would be difficult not to conclude that *Antony and Cleopatra* stands as Shakespeare's finest tribute to his inheritance from Marlowe.

In 1592, the Countess of Pembroke published two translations: a *Discourse of Life and Death Written in French by Ph. Mornay* and *Antonius, A Tragedie written also in French by Ro. Garnier*. Although *Antonius* brings the tale of Antony and Cleopatra to the English stage for the first time and treats the lovers sympathetically, idealizing and sentimentalizing them, there is no conclusive evidence that Shakespeare saw or read the play.[25] If he did, either he was certainly treated to the dulling effect of considerable moralizing and lamentation. But, whether in absorbing this or other potential sources, Shakespeare tends to regard those whom he reads or views with an eye toward practical aesthetics rather than applicable ethics. Consequently, he brushes aside moralizing as a route to effective dramatic content, much less as a worthwhile didactic means, and, instead, makes use of moralizing, including sententiousness, as a device for creating conflict, tension, and even humor. Charmian, who tends to moralize in a way that Cleopatra finds irksome ("Thou teachest like a foole"—1.3.10; "pitty me, *Charmian*, / But do not speake to me"—2.5.118–19), influences Cleopatra only once and, in adhering to her handmaiden's instructions, the Queen brings doom upon herself. Specifically, when Antony rages at Cleopatra for what he believes is an act of betrayal (4.12.9–49), she becomes so frightened and panic-stricken that she obeys Charmian's recommendation to lock herself in her monument and send word to Antony that she is dead (4.13.7–10). Usually in Shakespeare's plays, moralizing falls on deaf ears. The playwright subverts its assumed traditional worth as a meaningful mode of communication. But, as the example of Cleopatra and Charmian demonstrates, he finds the mode of considerable dramaturgical value.

If scholars are uncertain about *Antonius* as a source and do not regard the play as an influence, they tend to view Samuel Daniel's Senecan drama, *The Tragedie of Cleopatra* (1594/9),[26] as a definite source for some of the details of *Antony and Cleopatra* and perhaps as a slight influence on the play, although there are strong differences of opinion about this latter claim.[27] For all the verbal echoes and the parallels in detail that scholars have scrupulously ferreted out, the two plays are very different. Perhaps Brower best summarizes the differences when he observes:

> In Daniel, contradictory impulses are thoughtfully ... presented in the most general terms; in Shakespeare, they are expressed from within .... Although a number of parallels between Shakespeare and Daniel have been pointed out, they hardly add up to a conception or an attitude that Shakespeare "took over" from *The Tragedy of Cleopatra*. A more likely explanation is that certain sorts of heroic diction would be used in any Elizabethan version of the "fall" of Antony and Cleopatra. (347–48)

Shakespeare's artistic principles differ considerably from Daniel's. For example, he chooses a more complex genre and structure than Daniel and, hence, a more inclusive focus. Daniel makes his drama into a Senecan tragedy, replete with internalized monologues, moralizing, declamations, and ethical reflections by a Chorus. Although forceful in dramatizing oppositions, by limiting itself to a well-known genre, the play closes all doors to the comic dimensions, complexity, and range contained in Shakespeare's unabashedly unclassifiable drama. Daniel begins his play after the death of Antony.

Daniel's concentration on Cleopatra may have led Shakespeare to see the possibilities of so focused a treatment of her. Moreover, he was clearly not inattentive to the dramatist's details—for example, "wrinkles of declining" (*The Tragedie of Cleopatra* 1.158) becomes "wrinkled deepe in time" (*Antony and Cleopatra* 1.5.29); his language—for example, "Such innocents, sildome remaine so still" (*The Tragedie of Cleopatra* 3.1.575) becomes "Some Innocents scape not the thunderbolt" (*Antony and Cleopatra* 2.5.76); and his handling of such plot incidents as Dolabella's falling in love with Cleopatra. But Shakespeare rejects the clarity of motives and actions in Daniel, probably because they are too pat and too heavily moralized; in the simplicity of their causal explanations, they lack the truth inherent in mystery and the curiosity that attends it. Furthermore, in contradistinction to all the other dramatic versions of the story, Shakespeare frequently and, with suddenness, shifts scenes and accelerates the pace, enabling us to experience exhilaration and amplitude at the same time that we sense the fabrication of all temporal planes of reality. Cleopatra's rebuke to Antony that "Celerity is neuer more admir'd/Then by the negligent" (3.7.25–26) reminds us that, apart from the constant, imperceptible grindings of change, we construct our perceptions of the passage of time. More generally, *Antony and Cleopatra* celebrates mythmaking, all the more because the play itself perpetuates the myth of the two protagonists. In not subscribing to a specific genre and in structuring the play with "jump cuts," Shakespeare frees himself not only to celebrate the powers of the imagination but also to demonstrate them.

The evidence that Shakespeare read Daniel's "A Letter from Octavia to Marcus Antonius" is less conclusive than that he read North's translation of Goulart's *The Life of Octavius Caesar Augustus* (as we have already seen).[28] Shakespeare's decision not to use either the poem or the historical biography to clarify elements of character and event further supports the argument that he deliberately chose to employ paradox and ambiguity as devices to enhance the evocativeness of his drama. For example, Octavius is coldly efficient and controlling, something of an automaton in Shakespeare. Moreover, Shakespeare repeatedly undermines his capacity for affection: in spite of his apparent awe at Antony's heroics, he is fiercely critical (1.4); he hears of Antony's death and begins eulogizing the triumvir, but when an Egyptian messenger appears, he abruptly breaks off and returns to business, casting doubt on the genuineness of his sentiments (5.1); he claims affection for his sister, but he uses her as political "Cyment" (3.2.29); at the beginning of the play, Octavius is apparently unmarried (1.2.28–29), but, although we hear nothing of it, by the end of the play he is married to Livia (5.2.169). We have a more limited understanding of Octavius in Shakespeare than in his sources because Shakespeare thinks of him foremost as an artistic device—the chief antagonist of Antony and Cleopatra and the most potent representative in the play of someone denatured of his humanity. Octavius has embraced the new order of power politics, one in which underlings act out of fear, not love—in contrast to Antony's relationship to his underlings. Given the popularity of the story of Antony and Cleopatra, and Goulart's account specifically, Shakespeare certainly did not lack information to draw upon for his characterization of Octavius. In making so little use of Goulart, he left himself free to dramatize with potency the relationship between impaired humanity and power politics.

One reason why critics and students of Shakespeare have had difficulty defining the playwright's creative periods, the genres of his plays, and the progressions in his dramaturgical techniques is because, like Marlowe, he saw his artistic endeavors as fluid, innovative, and ever changing. Another reason is that, rather than rules and theories of art, Shakespeare's strong creative independence, natural desire for experimentation, and wide-ranging aesthetic interests predominated during the act of composing. His awareness of rules and theories (e.g., "the law of writ"—*Hamlet* 2.2.343) is readily shown by his familiarity with other writers, ancient and modern,[29] and affirmed by Polonius and Hamlet in their remarks on drama.[30] But, clearly, Shakespeare felt free to unleash his imagination and design anew—whether in genre, structure, characterization, or language. A study of his sources confirms *Antony and Cleopatra* as the exultant product of his freedom of imagination and unfettered creative practice. Unlike most of the writers from whom he gathers the details of the play, Shakespeare rejects the moralizing of his sources, understanding that, for an audience, the experience itself is what counts, not abstract commentary about it. The only predecessor who rejects moralizing in this way is Marlowe; significantly, he is also the strongest influence on the play. Emboldened by Marlowe's uninhibited creative imagination, his keen interest in technique, and his innovative portrayals of "high events" in "high astounding terms," Shakespeare transforms the lives and deaths of Antony and Cleopatra into similarly "high events" through equally "high astounding terms." In the process, he revels in the triumphant consequences of an aesthetic consciousness, both his protagonists' and his own.

NOTES

1. All references to Antony and Cleopatra are from Spevack, *A New Variorum Edition of Shakespeare*.

2. See Logan, *Shakespeare's Marlowe*, the opening chapter: "Marlowe and Shakespeare: Repositioning the Question of Sources and Influences," forthcoming.

3. Spevack 593–611 lists other possible classical, medieval, biblical, and contemporary (Renaissance) sources and analogues, chief among them Virgil (*The Aeneid*), Ovid (*Heroides*), and Chaucer (*The Legend of Good Women*). He also gives selected comments on these sources and analogues from several scholars and lists many critics who have written about them. In the interest of brevity and because these sources and analogues have been thoroughly examined—and also

because I do not judge them of central importance—I have excluded them from this study.

4. Scholars have tried to link *Antony and Cleopatra* with other dramatic versions of the story, but these are chiefly analogues, not influences. Only on occasion have they manifested enough evidence to be considered, but not necessarily accepted, as possible sources. I have in mind Giraldo Cinthio's *Cleopatra tragedia* (composed c. 1542; published 1583); Etienne Jodelle's *Cléopâtre captive* (performed 1552-53; published 1574); Hans Sachs's *Die Königin Cleopatra aus Egipten mit Antonio, dem Römer* (published 1560); Samuel Brandon's *Tragico-moedi of the Vertuous Octavia* (1598); and Anon.: *The Tragedy of Caesar's Revenge* (composed 1595; published 1607). For references to those scholars who have written about these plays and to surveys of the dramatized versions of the story of Antony and Cleopatra, see Spevack 591–93.

5. We are most fortunate in having Spevack's variorum edition of the play, because, as I have indicated, it not only lists sources, influences, and analogues but contains references to those who have written about them as well as relevant passages from their writings. Of the many people who have contributed to the discussion, at least six should be singled out for praise: MacCallum; Schanzer, ed., *Shakespeare's Appian*, and Schanzer, *The Problem Plays of Shakespeare*; Farnham; Bullough; Brower; and Muir. A useful essay to read in conjunction with Farnham's book is Roth's.

6. The terms "comprehend" and "apprehend" are set in opposition to describe modes of perception in *A Midsummer Night's Dream*; Theseus says, "Lovers and madmen have such seething brains/Such shaping fantasies, that apprehend/More than cool reason ever comprehends" (5.1.6–8). All references to Shakespeare's plays other than to *Antony and Cleopatra* are from Orgel and Braunmuller, *The Complete Pelican Shakespeare*.

7. The soothsayers in *Julius Caesar* and *Cymbeline* are also absolutely accurate in their predictions, as are Cassandra in *Troilus and Cressida* and the Witches in *Macbeth* and Venus in *Venus and Adonis*.

8. See MacCallum 648–56; Nelson 224–58; Schanzer, ed. xix and xxiii–xxviii; Bullough 247–48; Muir 224–25; and Spevack 466–68.

9. Compare a few lines later Antony's statement to Caesar: " ... that I/Your Partner in the cause 'gainst which he [Lucius] fought / Could not with gracefull eyes attend those Warres/Which fronted my owne peace" (2.2.58–61).

10. The most recent critic to comment on this passage in North and Shakespeare is Miola 12–13.

11. See Wells 150, who elaborates on this point and goes on to explain that Shakespeare breaks with tradition in showing sympathy for the lovers (150–53).

12. For example, Wilson 168.

13. Plutarch recounts the incident in which Menas tempts Pompey by explaining how he could kill the triumvirs and become the exclusive ruler of the Roman Empire (Spevack 417). After reciting Pompey's refusal, Plutarch says,

> The other two [Antony and Caesar] also did likewise feast him [Pompey] in their campe, and then he returned into Sicile. Antonius after this agreement made, sent Ventidius before into Asia to stay the

Parthians, and to keepe them they should come no further: and he him self in the meane time, to gratefie Caesar, was contented to be chosen Iulius Caesars priest and sacrificer, & so they ioyntly together dispatched all great matters, concerning the state of the Empire. (Spevack 417)

14. See Miola 161, who views the contrasts in *Antony and Cleopatra* "not as mutually exclusive antitheses but as interconnected alternatives."

15. The point is implicit throughout the play. Perhaps the clearest statement of it occurs when Cleopatra is speaking to Dolabella (5.2.97–100).

16. See Logan, especially chapter 6: "Marlowe's *Tamburlaine Plays*, Shakespeare's *Henry V*, and the Primacy of An Artistic Consciousness" and chapter 7: "Making the Haunt His: *Dido Queen of Carthage* As a Precursor to *Antony and Cleopatra*," forthcoming.

17. See Brower 113, note 2, for examples of the medieval heroic idiom in Lydgate.

18. Brower 352 gives as examples *Dido* 3.4.56–57 and 5.1.243–50.

19. See Spevack 603–05 for a list of critics who have written about the parallels between the two plays.

20. Harrison 57–63; Steane 29–30, 38, 59–61; Gibbons 43; Adelman 76–78 and 173–83; Charney 242–52; and Logan, chapter 7: "Making the Haunt His: *Dido Queen of Carthage* As a Precursor to *Antony and Cleopatra*."

21. See the dire prediction of the Soothsayer (2.3.17–23).

22. For an extensive discussion of the pre- and post-Virgilian legends of Dido that Marlowe draws upon for his conception of Dido and Aeneas, see Smith 6–38. For an analysis of the similarities and differences between Virgil and Marlowe, see the brief discussion in Baines. For an extensive discussion and an indispensable study of *Dido*, see Deats 91–102 and 105–115.

23. Marlowe's Dido may also have influenced Shakespeare in his portrait of Venus in *Venus and Adonis*.

24. One such example occurs when, in his grief at the fall of Troy and the death of Priam, Aeneas looks at a statue and mistakes it for the living king (2.1.1–32, Mark Thornton Burnett's edition of *Christopher Marlowe: The Complete Plays*). For a full discussion of instances of misperception in the play, see Logan, chapter 7, forthcoming.

25. For a complete description of the content of *Antonius*, see Farnham 148–56. Bullough briefly discusses the play (230–31) and concludes that Shakespeare "may have taken from it a few words and images" (231); he also reprints a 1595 edition of the translation (358–406) but as an "analogue." Muir 225–27 records verbal echoes that may indicate Shakespeare's familiarity with the play. Spevack lists and summarizes those critics who feel Shakespeare was little influenced by the play and those who believe he may have been influenced either conceptually or verbally (475–78); he also reprints the 1592 translation of the play (479–524).

26. Daniel first published his play in 1594. In 1599, he published a slightly revised edition ("Newly corrected and augmented") which Bullough reprints (406–49). In 1607, he publishes a much revised version of the play. See Bullough 231–32 and note 1 (231). Bullough lists the parallels between Daniel's play and Shakespeare's and refers us to other scholars who have noted parallels—235–36 and note 1 (236). Spevack 532 also lists correspondences between the two plays.

27. Shakespeare's play, in turn, is considered an influence on Daniel's 1607 version of his play.
28. See Spevack 530–31 for references to scholars who have written about "A Letter from Octavia to Marcus Antonius" as a source for Shakespeare and Spevack 579–91 for the text of the letter. See Spevack 459–56 for critical commentary and an excerpt of the relevant sections of *The Life of Octavius Caesar Augustus*.
29. Those writers whom Shakespeare actually refers to include Marlowe in *As You Like It* 3.5.82, 2 *Henry IV* 2.4.157–61, and *The Merry Wives of Windsor* 3.1.16–28; Seneca and Plautus in *Hamlet* 2.2.342; Virgil, Ovid, and unnamed others in *The Merchant of Venice* 5.1.1–88; Petrarch in *Romeo and Juliet* 2.4.39; and John Gower as the Chorus in *Pericles*. Others have been detected through source studies.
30. For Polonius's remarks, see *Hamlet* 2.2.229–43 and for Hamlet's, 3.2.1–43.

WORKS CITED

Adelman, Janet. *The Common Liar: An Essay on "Antony and Cleopatra."* New Haven, CT: Yale UP, 1973.

Alexandrinus, Appianus. *The Romanes Warres* (1578). *A New Variorum Edition of Shakespeare*: Antony and Cleopatra. Ed. Marvin Spevack. New York: The Modern Language Association of America: 1990. 466–75.

Baines, Barbara J. "Sexual Polarity in the Plays of Christopher Marlowe." *Ball State University Forum* 23.3 (1982): 4–6.

Brower, Reuben A. *Hero and Saint: Shakespeare and the Graeco-Roman Heroic Tradition.* Oxford: Oxford UP, 1971.

Bullough, Geoffrey, ed. *Narrative and Dramatic Sources of Shakespeare, Volume V: The Roman Plays:* Julius Caesar, Antony and Cleopatra, Coriolanus. New York: Columbia UP, 1966.

Charney, Maurice. "Marlowe and Shakespeare's African Queens," in *Shakespearean Illuminations.* Ed. Jay L. Halio and Hugh Richmond. Newark: U of Delaware P; Associated UP, 1998. 242–52.

Daniel, Samuel. *The Tragedie of Cleopatra* (1594). *A New Variorum Edition of Shakespeare:* Antony and Cleopatra. Ed. Marvin Spevack. New York: The Modern Language Association of America: 1990. 524–79.

———. *"A Letter from Octavia to Marcus Antonius"* (1599). *A New Variorum Edition of Shakespeare*: Antony and Cleopatra. Ed. Marvin Spevack. New York: The Modern Language Association of America: 1990. 579–91.

Deats, Sara Munson. *Sex, Gender, and Desire in the Plays of Christopher Marlowe.* Newark: U of Delaware P, 1997.

Farnham, Willard. *Shakespeare's Tragic Frontier: The World of His Final Tragedies.* Berkeley: U of California P, 1963.

Garnier, Robert. *Antonie,* trans. The Countess of Pembroke (1592). *A New Variorum Edition of Shakespeare:* Antony and Cleopatra, ed. Marvin Spevack. New York: The Modern Language Association of America: 1990. 475–524.

Gibbons, Brian. " 'Unstable Proteus': *The Tragedy of Dido Queen of Carthage."* *Christopher Marlowe.* Ed. Brian Morris. New York: Hill and Wang, 1968. 27–46.

Goulart, Simon. *The Life of Octavius Caesar Augustus*. Trans. Sir Thomas North (1602). *A New Variorum Edition of Shakespeare:* Antony and Cleopatra. Ed. Marvin Spevack. New York: The Modern Language Association of America: 1990. 459–66.

Harrison, Thomas P. Jr., "Shakespeare and Marlowe's *Dido, Queen of Carthage*" *Studies in English* [University of Texas] (1956): 57–63.

Logan, Robert A. *Shakespeare's Marlowe*, forthcoming.

MacCallum, M[ungo] W[illiam]. *Shakespeare's Roman Plays and Their Background*. 1910. Foreword T. J. B. Spencer. New York: Russell & Russell, 1967.

Marlowe, Christopher. *Christopher Marlowe: The Complete Plays*. Ed. Mark Thornton Burnett. London: J. M. Dent, 1999.

Miola, Robert S. *Shakespeare's Reading*. Oxford: Oxford UP, 2000.

Muir, Kenneth. *The Sources of Shakespeare's Plays*. New Haven: Yale UP, 1978.

Nelson, Lawrence G. "Classical History in Shakespeare." Ph.D. diss., U of Virginia, 1943.

Plutarch. *The Life of Marcus Antonius and The Comparison of Demetrius with Antonius*, trans. Sir Thomas North (1579). *A New Variorum Edition of Shakespeare*: Antony and Cleopatra. Ed. Marvin Spevack. New York: The Modern Language Association of America: 1990. 395–459.

Roth, Robert. "Another World of Shakespeare." *Modern Philology* XLIX (August 1951): 42–61.

Schanzer, Ernest. *The Problem Plays of Shakespeare: A Study of* Julius Caesar, Measure for Measure, Antony and Cleopatra. New York: Schocken Books, 1963.

Schanzer, Ernest, ed. *Shakespeare's Appian: A Selection from the Tudor Translation of Appian's "Civil Wars"* (English Reprints Series No. 13.) Liverpool, Eng.: Liverpool UP, 1956.

Shakespeare, William. *A New Variorum Edition of Shakespeare*: Antony and Cleopatra. Ed. Marvin Spevack. New York: The Modern Language Association of America, 1990.

———. *The Complete Pelican Shakespeare*. Eds. Stephen Orgel and A. R. Braunmuller. New York: Penguin Putnam, 2002.

Smith, Mary Elizabeth. *"Love-Kindling Fire": A Study of Christopher Marlowe's "The Tragedy of Dido Queen of Carthage."* Salzburg, Austria: Institut Für Englishe Sprache Und Literature Universität Salzburg, 1977.

Steane, J. B. Marlowe: *A Critical Study*. Cambridge, Eng.: Cambridge UP, 1973.

Wells, Charles. *The Wide Arch: Roman Values in Shakespeare*. New York: St. Martin's Press, 1992.

Wilson, Harold S. *On the Design of Shakespearian Tragedy*. Toronto, U of Toronto P, 1957.

6.
Rome and Egypt in *Antony and Cleopatra* and in Criticism of the Play

JAMES HIRSH

It is a critical commonplace that in *Antony and Cleopatra* Rome and Egypt are associated with conflicting values or points of view. But the complex implications and ramifications of this conflict have not been fully explored. Most commentators assign a single concept or a small group of concepts to each locale even though over the course of the play each locale exemplifies a multitude of distinct values. Another complexity derives from the fact that how a character views a point of view depends on the character's point of view. As a result, the play actually dramatizes not two but *four* main figurative locales: Rome as it is perceived from a Roman point of view; Rome as it is perceived from an Egyptian point of view; Egypt as it is perceived from a Roman point of view; and Egypt as it is perceived from an Egyptian point of view. Rome's idea of Rome is not the same as Egypt's idea of Rome; Rome's Egypt is not the same place as Egypt's Egypt. Yet another complexity derives from the fact that characters adopt a variety of attitudes toward the conflict in values. Some characters are intensely Egyptian, some uncompromisingly Roman, some deeply divided; some attempt to be neutral; some change loyalties, and so on. The varied responses of characters to the conflict in values have been re-enacted and extended in the commentary on the play. In some cases, a critic openly expresses allegiance to one side in the conflict. In some cases, the position of a critic is only implicit, revealed because the critic's value judgments in regard to matters other than the conflict itself resemble the value judgments that in the play are associated with either Rome or Egypt. In a few cases, the attitude of a critic exhibited in this way is actually at odds with the critic's declared position toward the conflict.

Characters in *Antony and Cleopatra* conspicuously associate Rome and Egypt with competing points of view. Cleopatra comments on the offstage Antony, "He was dispos'd to mirth, but on the sudden / A Roman thought hath strook him" (1.2.82–83). "A Roman thought" means both "an inclination to

175

return to the city of Rome" and "a Roman way of thinking." Roman thought processes are evident in Octavius's complaints about Antony's misbehavior in the Egyptian capital:

> From Alexandria
> This is the news: he fishes, drinks, and wastes
> The lamps of night in revel; is not more manlike
> Than Cleopatra; nor is the queen of Ptolomy
> More womanly than he; hardly gave audience, or
> Vouchsaf'd to think he had partners. (1.4.3–8)

According to Octavius, Egypt has undermined Antony's adherence to the Roman values of responsibility and efficient productivity. Citing this passage, many commentators describe the conflict between Rome and Egypt as an opposition between masculinity and femininity. As the passage makes clear, however, both of those concepts are Roman. Rome maintains and enforces a sharp differentiation between gender roles ("manlike" versus "womanly") and condemns Egypt for its disregard of that differentiation. There is an exemplar of femininity in the play, and her name is Octavia. After Lepidus weakly defends Antony, Octavius resumes the attack. He condemns Antony's irrational sense of priority and proportion: "To give a kingdom for a mirth" (18). Antony's "voluptuousness" (26) violates the Roman principles of moderation and self-discipline. Egypt places a high value on sexuality, which Octavius denigrates with the dismissive verb "to tumble" (17) and associates with disease, "the dryness of his bones" (27). Valuing sobriety, Octavius contemptuously dismisses Egyptian festivity with the term "tippling" (19). As in the case of gender roles, Rome enforces clear-cut differentiations between social classes, and hence Octavius disapproves of Antony's indiscriminate social interaction, consorting "with a slave" and "With knaves that smells of sweat" (19, 21). Rome values orderly progression and associates erratic movement— "To reel" (20)—with Egypt. Rome operates according to a strict and orderly timetable, and hence the impropriety of Antony's tippling is compounded because it takes place at a particularly incongruous and improper time and place, in "the streets at noon" (20). Octavius values gravity ("great weight," 25) and solidity and expresses contempt for Antony's "lightness" (25) and "vacancy" (26). For meekly defending Antony, Lepidus is chastised for being "too indulgent" (16). Indulgence is an Egyptian vice; a true Roman demands strict adherence to Roman mores. Maturity is a Roman value, but Antony has been behaving childishly, like "boys who, being mature in knowledge, / Pawn their experience to their present pleasure, / And so rebel to judgment" (31–33). Obedience and discipline are Roman virtues; to be Egyptian is to "rebel." Romans pursue long-term goals rather than instant gratification ("present pleasure"). Octavius judges Antony not on the basis of a single criterion but on the basis of an extensive, complex system of values that may be mutually reinforcing but that are nevertheless distinct. Rome defines itself in large part by its opposition to Egypt. If Egypt did not exist, Rome would have to invent one; or, more accurately, its perception of Egypt is at least partly an invention.

Octavius sees Rome and Egypt through Roman eyes, but the play provides an alternative vision of both locales. Behavior condemned in Rome is praiseworthy in Egypt. Antony tells Cleopatra, "to chide, to laugh, / To weep; whose every passion fully strives / To make itself (in thee) fair and admir'd!" (1.1.49–51). What Rome sees as irrationality and disorderly conduct Egypt sees as exhilarating passion, spontaneity, and exuberance. What Rome sees as trivial pursuits Egypt sees as activities that make life worth living. Adopting an Egyptian perspective, Enobarbus says that when Cleopatra hopped through the streets she made "defect perfection" (2.2.231). What Rome sees as impropriety Egypt sees as originality and imagination. What Enobarbus describes as Cleopatra's "infinite variety" (2.2.235) entails sudden shifts of mood and inconsistencies of behavior, but (to paraphrase an Egyptian American) consistency is a hobgoblin of Roman minds.[1] What Rome sees as immaturity Egypt sees as playfulness. This playfulness extends to gender. Cleopatra fondly recalls the joke she played on Antony: "I drunk him to his bed; / Then put my tires and mantles on him, whilst / I wore his sword Philippan." (2.5.21–23). What Rome regards as licentiousness and perversion Egypt regards as liberation from constricting gender roles and prudery. These and many other passages establish explicit and implicit contrasts between Rome's view of itself and Egypt's view of Rome. What Rome sees as socially necessary discipline Egypt sees as oppression. What Rome sees as moderation Egypt sees as self-denial. What Rome sees as gravity Egypt sees as leaden dullness. What Rome sees as rationality Egypt sees as cold-bloodedness. What Rome sees as unity Egypt sees as monotony. And so on.

A very important Egyptian value that is often overlooked even (or perhaps especially) by fervent admirers of Cleopatra is facetiousness. In the opening scene of the play, Cleopatra declares, "I'll set a bourn how far to be belov'd" (1.1.16). Setting bourns is a Roman activity, but Cleopatra is merely playing at being a Roman. She is teasing Antony, facetiously taking the part of a Roman in order to provoke Antony to voice his commitment to her and to Egyptian values. She plays a series of facetious practical jokes on her lover, dressing him in her tires and mantles, instructing her diver put a salt-fish on his hook, and so on. When Antony is away, she proposes to pretend that each fish she catches is "an Antony" to whom she will "say, 'Ay, ha! y'are caught' " (2.5.10–15). When she learns that Antony has married Octavia, she turns the situation into a comic tour de force. This comedy is not inadvertent like Dogberry's malapropisms. In Rome the importance of being earnest seems self-evident, but in Egypt it is important to be facetious. Octavius condemns "lightness," but to an Egyptian levity is a magnificent and cherished gift. Cleopatra specifically mentions it in her contrast between Roman and Egyptian thinking quoted earlier: "He was dispos'd to *mirth*, but on the sudden / A Roman thought hath strook him." Cleopatra can make light even of death. As she commits suicide, she calls the deadly asp "my baby at my breast" (5.2.309). Her suicide itself is a kind of practical joke on Octavius. He thinks he has caught her and plans to display his catch in Rome, but she puts a salt-fish on his hook. Her plan to deceive him about her suicidal intention entails the contrived farce of the Seleucus episode. In Rome if something is serious (important), it is treated seriously (solemnly). This union of importance and solemnity is not regarded as valid in Egypt.

Many critics with Roman dispositions have denigrated the frequent hyperboles in the speeches of Antony and Cleopatra as expressions of self-deceptive wishful thinking. Many critics with Egyptian tendencies have defended the same passages in earnest, quasi-religious terms as expressions of transcendent love. Antony's hyperboles often do seem earnest, and to the extent that they are, they are Roman, for earnestness is a Roman value. Cleopatra's hyperboles express genuine emotion but nevertheless also reflect her nearly irrepressible facetiousness:

> CLEOPATRA. I dreamt there was an Emperor Antony . . . .
>   His legs bestrid the ocean. . . .
>   Think you there was or might be such a man
>   As this I dreamt of?
> DOLABELLA.   Gentle madam, no.
> CLEOPATRA. You lie up to the hearing of the gods! (5.2.76–95)

By overtly describing an Antony she "dreamt" rather than the Antony of her waking experience, Cleopatra shows her awareness of the fictionality of this Antony. This dream-Antony who bestrid the ocean is (so to speak) a tall tale. Cleopatra dares Dolabella to contradict her tall tale and then feigns anger when he fulfills his role as straight man. One of the conventions of the facetious tall tale is that the teller must pretend to be serious. Cleopatra here facetiously plays the role of wide-eyed romantic lover just as she facetiously played a Roman in the opening scene and facetiously played the role of jealous lover on receiving news of Antony's marriage to Octavia. Cleopatra is rarely compared to Rosalind, and yet, like Rosalind, she can simultaneously be passionately in love and make fun of the extravagant rhetoric of love.

Having adopted a Roman pose in her first appearance onstage, Cleopatra does so again in her last: "now from head to foot / I am marble-constant; now the fleeting moon / No planet is of mine" (5.2.239–41). Constancy is a Roman value at odds with the Egyptian love of variety and change. If one views the end of the play from a Roman point of view, Cleopatra's assumption of a

Roman pose is a presumptuous self-delusion or a confirmation of the superiority of Roman values. And yet, just as her adoption of a Roman pose at the beginning of the play was facetious, so is this. One aspect of the joke is that, because she intends to commit suicide momentarily, she has to maintain her marble-constancy for only seventy-two lines, after which her body will be as cold and lifeless as marble. Another aspect of the joke is that her assertion of constancy is a *change* from her earlier behavior, a change to which she calls attention, and thus, paradoxically, her adoption of this pose is one more instance of her changeableness. A third facetious element is that Cleopatra here lays claim to a variety so large that it can encompass antithetical Roman values. In the words of another Egyptian-American, "Do I contradict myself. / Very well then I contradict myself, / (I am large, I contain multitudes.)."[2]

The focus by many defenders of Cleopatra on love as the key Egyptian quality has obscured profound similarities between her and Falstaff. Each disregards conventional morality and rules of behavior; each seeks pleasure and revelry; each displays imagination, vitality, and spontaneity. Despite advancing years, each behaves with a childlike playfulness. Each is reviled by other characters for licentiousness, excess, impropriety, irresponsibility, immaturity, inconsistency, dishonesty, and so on. Each flees from combat and is accused of cowardice. Each is magnificently facetious. Each tells outrageous tall tales with mock seriousness. Falstaff's account of the robbery is one of the greatest tall tales in world literature. Just as Cleopatra dares Dollabella to contradict her tall tale, so Falstaff challenges Hal to contradict his, asking with mock indignation, "is not the truth the truth?" (2.4.229–30). The contrast between Cleopatra and Octavius recalls that between Falstaff and Hal. Like Octavius, Hal is a shrewd politician intent on the long-term goal of absolute political power. Hal's condemnation of the "unyok'd humor" and "idleness" of the tavern denizens (*1 Henry IV*, 1.2.196) anticipates Octavius's condemnations of Antony and Cleopatra. In the midst of battle, Hal chastises Falstaff, "What, is it a time to jest and dally now?" (5.3.55). To Egyptians, such as Falstaff and Cleopatra, it is nearly always a time to jest and dally.[3]

Antony's capacity for facetiousness is illustrated by the tautological description of the crocodile that he feeds Lepidus during the feast on Pompey's galley (2.7.41–49). More evident than his own facetiousness, however, are his *appreciation* and *facilitation* of the facetiousness of others. Far from taking offense at the practical jokes that Cleopatra perpetrates against him, he very much enjoys a good joke even at his own expense. He is entranced by her facetious contrariness. He loves her for her sense of humor, and she loves him for the willingness and skill with which he plays her straight man and comic butt. Antony accepts the role of straight man even with Enobarbus, his military subordinate; moreover, he does so not merely when they are alone together but in the presence of other commanders and subordinates, as in 2.2 in the midst of the delicate negotiations between Antony and

Caesar. After Enobarbus makes a shrewd joke about political hypocrisy and expediency (103–06), Antony twice orders him to be silent, but each time Enobarbus responds with a further facetious remark. No subordinate of Caesar would dare jest in such a circumstance and in defiance of explicit commands of his leader, but Enobarbus knows that he will not be punished for insolence or insubordination. On the contrary, Enobarbus's sense of humor is one reason he has gained the affection of his commander.

Enobarbus's facetiousness rivals that of Cleopatra. His famous description of Cleopatra on her barge is Egyptian in at least two ways that to a Roman would seem contradictory and therefore mutually exclusive. On the one hand, the speech glamorizes and mythologizes Cleopatra. On the other hand, like Cleopatra's dream of Antony bestriding the ocean, Enobarbus's description has elements of a tall tale: "th'air, which, but for vacancy, / Had gone to gaze on Cleopatra too" (2.2.216–17).

I have given special attention to the facetious, tall-tale, practical-joke element of Egyptianism not because it is the one key Egyptian element but because most commentators have underestimated the value that Egyptians place on facetiousness. Most admirers of Cleopatra have displayed a Roman earnestness in their admiration.

There is not room in the present essay to catalog each of the distinct values associated with Rome and Egypt in the play, but the foregoing analysis should be sufficient to establish that no single value or small group of values conveys what either Rome or Egypt represents. That Rome and Egypt are highly complex figurative locales is suggested by the fact that, although most critics have seen the opposition as a major element of the play, they have not agreed about what the opposites represent. The supposedly essential quality associated with Egypt has been variously identified by critics as passion, love, pleasure, sensuality, vice, vitality, extravagance, indolence, imagination, intuition, dream, ecstasy, private life, individualism, variety, affirmation, or inclusivity, to name a few. The supposedly essential quality of Rome has been variously identified as reason, honor, duty, temperance, virtue, morality, stoicism, action, realism, judgment, cynicism, war, the public sphere, authoritarianism, order, negation, or exclusivity, again to name a few.

Although characters in *Antony and Cleopatra* associate the conflicting sets of values with specific locales, the play shows that this conflict occurs not only between cultures, but within cultures and within individuals. Some of the most memorable expressions of Egyptian attitudes emerge from the mouths of characters who are Roman by birth and who were trained in Roman military discipline. An equal balance within an individual or a society between Roman rules and Egyptian impulses is dramatized as impossible. At certain moments, individuals and societies are forced, as Antony is forced, to choose between Rome and Egypt. One cannot be in two places at once. Nor is either side likely to gain a lasting supremacy. Octavius seems to have achieved this at the end of the play, but it is a hollow triumph since during the course of the play many of his fellow Romans at one time or another exhibit Egyptian tendencies. Cleopatra would have posed no danger if she did not appeal to Egyptian tendencies in Romans. Cleopatra may be dead, but those tendencies survive. The interaction between Roman and Egyptian values is thus dynamic and volatile, not stable.

The interaction between Rome and Egypt is also asymmetrical. War is the main enterprise of Rome, and it is therefore not surprising that Octavius adopts a warlike stance toward Egypt. In the face of Roman aggression, Egypt at times is forced to respond in kind. But Egypt would prefer to make love not war. Cleopatra seduced and in effect co-opted a succession of nominal Roman overlords—Julius Caesar, Pompey the Great, and Mark Antony—and at times facetiously adopts Roman poses.[4]

Neither set of values is dramatized as a perfectly satisfactory response to human needs and desires. Each satisfies some needs but leaves others unsatisfied. Each solves some problems but creates others. Although they provide sharp contrasts and come into conflict, they also overlap in some ways. Both Rome and Egypt require power, wealth, and public display. As multifarious as the Roman and Egyptian points of view are, they do not exhaust the values that have been embraced by human beings. Neither strongly promotes religion in the usual meaning of the word. Neither fosters political egalitarianism.

Individual characters in the play adopt a wide variety of attitudes toward the competing sets of values. This variety of positions actually exceeds the number of important characters in the play because some characters change their minds, in some cases more than once, during the course of the play. Octavius is the most uncompromising Roman. Long before he achieves a decisive military victory over Egypt, he achieved, in the governing of his outward behavior at least, a decisive victory over the Egyptian in himself. Other Romans show varying degrees of vulnerability to the allurements of Egypt. Lepidus displays equal devotion to the thoroughly Roman Octavius and the Egyptian-prone Antony but is mocked behind his back for doing so:

> ENOBARBUS .... O, how he loves Caesar!
> AGRIPPA. Nay, but how dearly he adores Mark Antony! (3.2.7–8)

"Praying for both parts," Octavia yearns pathetically, and as ineffectually as Lepidus, to be their "reconciler" (3.4.14, 30). Enobarbus adopts a series of different stances. At times he shows a strong affinity for Egyptian values; at times he satirizes Egyptian values from a Roman perspective; and at times he mocks both Roman and Egyptian values from a cynical point of view. A dramatic irony of his mockery of Lepidus is that Enobarbus himself adores Mark Antony, then switches his allegiance to Caesar, and then reverts to adoration of Antony. For much of the play Antony is strongly pulled in opposite directions, but the allure of Egypt eventually proves stronger. Cleopatra is the most Egyptian character, but on occasion she facetiously adopts Roman poses.

Linda T. Fitz implicitly compares the play and the commentary on the play when, in an influential 1977 article, she asserts that *Antony and Cleopatra* "has divided critics into ... furiously warring camps" (182). Many other critics describe the commentary as a war or debate between two sides. But this is misleading. Commentators have actually exhibited a variety of attitudes toward the two competing sets of values. These varied responses reenact and extend the varied responses of characters within the play to the conflict. A comprehensive taxonomy of critical commentaries will not be possible in a brief essay, but a selection of examples will demonstrate these points.

Some critics have been as staunchly Roman as Octavius. A few such critics have condemned not only Antony and Cleopatra but *Antony and Cleopatra*. In an essay first published in 1901, Bernard Shaw denounces the play for glamorizing "debauchery" and "sexual infatuation" (1: 77, 78). W. K. Wimsatt, Jr. asserts in *The Verbal Icon* (1954) that the play approached "vileness" (94): "What is celebrated ... is the passionate surrender of an illicit love. ... reasons on the side of morality are so far as possible undercut, diminished or removed from the play" (96).

Perhaps reluctant to accuse the Bard of vileness or, more likely, wishing to enlist him in their cause, most Roman critics, unlike Shaw and Wimsatt, have convinced themselves that the play itself is Roman. The Introduction to the work in a 1774 edition of *Shakespeare's Plays* declares that a "moral" of the play is "that indolence and dissipation may undo the greatest of men" (Gentleman 6: 261). At least as Roman as Octavius (and at least as Hobbesian as Hobbes), Daniel Stempel insists in a 1956 article that "the major theme" of the play "is the safety of the state," that "the chief danger to political stability" is Cleopatra, and that "the play ends, as it should, with the defeat and death of the rebel against order" (63).

Some critics argue that the play must have been Roman because art merely reflects the politically dominant ideology of the time, and at the time that Shakespeare wrote the play this ideology was similar to the views expressed by Romans in the play:

> The spread of chaos on the level of political organization, in particular, was feared by men of the Renaissance. Shakespeare's classical plays reflect this fear; it is the ultimate source of the conflict of values in all of them, including *Antony and Cleopatra*. (Stempel 62)

But plentiful evidence in Shakespeare's works demonstrates that he represented the world in more complex ways than it was represented in official state propaganda, and as a result his works tend to provoke thought rather than to confirm conventional ideology.

Many critics see the play with Egyptian eyes. A. C. Bradley's Egyptian proclivities are revealed in an essay originally published in 1906. According to Bradley, "when Octavius shows himself proof against [Cleopatra's] fascination, instead of admiring him we turn from him with disgust and think him a disgrace to his species" (302). Consequently, "when Cleopatra by her death cheats the conqueror of his prize, we feel unmixed delight" (289). Bradley passionately defends the passion of Antony and Cleopatra: "What have the gods in heaven to say against it? . . . To deny that this is love is the madness of morality" (297). After briefly mentioning Antony's flaws, Bradley praises his Egyptian impulses. Antony "revels in abundant and rejoicing appetites, feasts his senses on the glow and richness of life, flings himself into its mirth and revelry, yet feels the poetry in all this" (294). In a book first published in 1931, G. Wilson Knight decomposes the play into "atoms" of imagery (259), decontextualizes the images, then redeploys them to produce a breathtaking rhapsody on the "transcendental" love of Antony and Cleopatra (210). For Knight, it is irrelevant if a character uses an image to describe something other than love or to denigrate the lovers; all the images, including those of Roman imperialism, glorify love: "the love-theme rises high in splendour on the structure of imperial and military magnificence" (214). According to S. L. Bethell, "the choice which Antony has to make between Rome and Egypt is . . . heavily weighted by Shakespeare on the Egyptian side" (158). Bethell's commentary itself, published in 1944, is also heavily weighted on the Egyptian side. He declares that Rome represents a "restrictive morality" in contrast to the "expansive morality" of Egypt (153); that Cleopatra is associated with "the energies of life;" that "Egyptian values are affirmative; the Roman, negative;" and that "the good life may be built upon the Egyptian, but not upon the Roman" (159). Anthony Caputi's 1965 article on the play also formulates the contrast in Egyptian terms. The Egyptian "approach to the data of the world is inclusive, where the Roman approach is exclusive; [the Egyptians] find beauty in experience not by distinguishing one thing from another, but by unifying and harmonizing its multiplicity, diversity, and discord" (190). In their 1975 book, Stanford M. Lyman and Marvin B. Scott argue that "In depicting the encounter between Egyptian and Roman civilizations, Shakespeare has posed a contrast between the *Apollonian* and the *Dionysian*" (55). Lyman and Scott indicate their preference when they describe the Roman way of life as "cold and efficient bureaucracy" (54) and an "iron cage" (55), whereas Egypt promotes "the life force" (55) and "uninhibited joy" (72).

Just as Antony and other characters are torn between Roman and Egyptian values, so too are many critics. Such a struggle is evident in the comments of William Hazlitt, whose 1818 essay includes one of the earliest critical references to the figurative contrast between Rome and Egypt. At times he describes Cleopatra in pejorative Roman terms: "voluptuous, ostentatious, . . . boastful . . . , haughty, tyrannical, fickle" (228); but she also has "spirit and fire" (229). The attractiveness of Cleopatra and her relationship with Antony "almost" overcomes Hazlitt's moral disapprobation. Cleopatra has "great and unpardonable faults, but the grandeur of her death almost redeems them" (230); she and Antony display a "regal style of love-making" that serves "almost to justify the ... infatuation of Antony" (228–29). Significantly, Hazlitt ends his commentary by applying a conspicuously *Egyptian* metaphor to Shakespeare: "Shakespeare's genius has spread over the whole play a richness like the overflowing of the Nile" (232). To paraphrase Blake's comment about Milton, Hazlitt wrote in fetters when he wrote of Egyptian faults, and at liberty when of Egyptian attractions because he was of the Egyptian party without knowing it.

Many critics have tried to remain neutral but, as Lepidus discovers, neutrality in this conflict is awkward and difficult to maintain. In a 1963 book Derek Traversi explains a critical problem and proposes a solution:

> [One is] faced by two possible readings of the play, whose only difficulty is that they seem to be mutually exclusive ... but to give each its due, to see them less as contradictory than as complementary aspects of a unified artistic creation ... is ... necessary for a proper understanding of the play. (79)

Despite his claim of neutrality, Traversi generally perceives Egypt from a distinctly Roman point of view. He repeatedly denigrates assertions by Antony and Cleopatra as self-deceptive "day dreams" (85, 105), a trivializing term like those employed by Octavius to describe other Egyptian activities (tumbling, tippling), in contrast to "realism" (81). Unlike actively constructed and self-conscious tall tales, "day dreams" are associated with passivity and naivete. Traversi asserts that Philo's opening speech "leaves no doubt as to the adverse estimate which we are bound, on a dispassionate view, to form of Antony's conduct" (80). But "a dispassionate view" is a Roman view. Traversi declares that Cleopatra's expressed determination "To 'unpeople Egypt,' should this be needed if she is to send daily messengers to Antony, is clearly as impossible as it would be irresponsible" (106). It may be impossible and irresponsible from a Roman point of view, but from an Egyptian perspective it is clearly a *joke*.

In *The Common Liar*, an acclaimed study of the play published in 1973, Janet Adelman also affirms neutrality: "We want the play to conform tidily to our system: Rome or Egypt. ... But in fact the play achieves a fluidity of possibility" (170). Within the play, however, Rome is strongly associated with tidiness and systematic thinking and Egypt with "a fluidity of possibility." Just as Traversi's declared neutrality is undermined by his demonstrably Roman viewpoint, Adelman's is undercut by her demonstrably Egyptian perspective. When discussing features of the play other than the conflict in values, Adelman shows a strong adherence to Egyptian values. Like many other commentators,

Adelman describes the artistry of the play in distinctly Egyptian terms, in terms identical or similar to those applied by characters within the play to Cleopatra. Adelman entitles the first chapter of her book "Infinite Variety," and that is indeed what she finds in the play: "shifts in perspective force upon us an awareness ... of how *various* a place the world is. ... The *varied* personages ... posit their own *diverse* points of view. ... [S]tructural repetition suggests *widely varying* versions of experience just as the framing commentary suggests *varieties* of judgment" (43, 44, 46; emphasis added). The main point of Adelman's second chapter is that Shakespeare incorporated material from a wide "variety" (68, 84) of sometimes sharply conflicting sources and traditions. Instead of condemning the play's lack of unity, as Roman commentators have done, Adelman clearly admires the play's various kinds of variety, just as some characters praise Cleopatra's variety.

Another critic who asserts that the play somehow reconciles or transcends the opposing sets of values and who implicitly endorses this improbable maneuver is Benjamin Spencer. In a 1958 article Spencer wrote that Shakespeare "is neither Roman nor Egyptian in his dramatic stance" (377). Instead, the play "shows ... an *as yet undefined synthesis* lying beyond both Rome and Egypt but partaking of the values of both" (377–78, emphasis added). This resembles the wishful thinking in which Lepidus and Octavia engage. Spencer does not explain how values vividly dramatized as radically at odds could possibly be reconciled, and his imagined "synthesis" remains conveniently "undefined." A committed Roman such as Octavius would reject any such attempt to forge a synthesis of his values and those of Egypt. When Lepidus makes a timid move in this direction, Octavius condemns him for being "too indulgent," for displaying suspiciously Egyptian tendencies himself, and other characters mock Lepidus's attempts to achieve an undefined synthesis of his affections for his two fellow triumvirs.

Also adopting a neutral stance, Norman Rabkin views *Antony and Cleopatra* as a notable example of what, in his influential 1967 book *Shakespeare and the Common Understanding,* he famously termed Shakespeare's complementarity:

> So complementary is its vision that some critics continue to find in it a demonstration, depending on their particular sensibilities, either of the absolute transcendence or of the utter worthlessness of the love it presents, for both views are legitimately occasioned by aspects of the play. Like *Hamlet, Antony and Cleopatra* has emerged in recent years from the clouds of partisan and partial interpretations into the light of an increasingly communal reading. (185)

Like the critics faulted by Rabkin, the poor benighted characters in the play are trapped in partisanship and partiality that Rabkin urges his readers to put aside. But how can we achieve this superiority to the characters? We can rise above partisanship only if the issues at stake do not really matter to us, only if we exempt ourselves from the difficulty and necessity of choosing between the incompatible alternatives dramatized in the play—between long-term goals and present pleasure, between passion and reason, between moderation and ecstasy, and so on—only if we imagine that, godlike, we can somehow detach ourselves from basic conditions unavoidably faced by human beings. The neutrality advocated by Rabkin would neutralize the drama of the play. We would merely witness a drama that does not concern us rather than experiencing one in which we are implicated.

Neutrality thus seems an untenable position. Some critics who explicitly declare neutrality are, despite their declarations, nevertheless demonstrably Roman (such as Traversi) or Egyptian (such as Adelman). Other critics who adopt a neutral stance are able to maintain it only by retreating into evasiveness (such as Spencer) or by neutralizing the dramatic impact of the play (such as Rabkin).

In yet another camp are those critics who make judgments about the play from a perspective that is not Roman nor Egyptian nor a fanciful reconciliation of those two points of view. Because, as a logical necessity, any set of values judged by a *different* set of values will look bad, each of these critics perceives both Rome and Egypt in a negative light. These critics might be designated (to borrow a character from another play) Mercutio critics ("A plague a' both your houses"). From the Christian perspective applied to the play in 1952 by John F. Danby, Antony's choice is between "soldiering for a cynical Rome or whoring on furlough in reckless Egypt" (151). In effect, Danby views Rome from an Egyptian perspective and Egypt from a Roman perspective. In order to do so, he has to disregard elements in the play that present Rome from a Roman perspective and those that present Egypt from an Egyptian perspective.

In a 1978 essay, John Alvis locates what he regards as a fatal flaw in earlier criticism of *Antony and Cleopatra*: "Continuing disagreement among commentators has resulted from the generally accepted assumption that judging the chief characters requires our choosing between the Roman view or that put forward by the lovers themselves" (185). Rejecting this assumption, Alvis proceeds to judge Antony and Cleopatra against the standard of selfless love: "They strive to make a religion of erotic passion while failing to grasp the regenerative sacramental potency offered by the sort of personal love which trains the soul in selflessness" (185–86). Conspicuous by its absence from Alvis's essay is a discussion of examples in the play of the kind of love he extols, most notably Octavia's selfless love for her brother and for Antony. Her selfless love, which fails to hold Antony's attention, also fails to capture the attention of Alvis, the champion of selfless love. In his opening sentences, Alvis attempts to disarm an anticipated response by his readers:

> In questioning the sublimity of the love portrayed in *Antony and Cleopatra* one risks appearing unimaginative, moralistic, or even boorish. Worse still, one invites guilt by association with the dubious company of Antony's Roman detractors who reveal various degrees of myopic insensitivity to the multivalent attractions of Egypt. (185)

Exactly. And who places "one" in this risky situation? Shakespeare. By presenting Antony's Roman detractors in an unappealing light and by not dramatizing any other, more compelling alternative to Egyptian values, Shakespeare makes it difficult for a playgoer to root against Antony and Cleopatra even if outside the theater the same individual would be inclined to condemn behavior resembling that of the lovers.

Linda Charnes's 1992 essay examines the play from a point of view supplied by Michel Foucault. From such a perspective Egypt looks as bad as imperialist Rome. Indeed, they are two sides of the same coin: "shared ideologies ... construct Egyptian-ness and Roman-ness" (273–74). Charnes sees "love as a constituent element of the power relations that inform every aspect of this play" (276). Like many other contemporary critics, Charnes makes the valid point that everything human beings think, say, and do has political implications and ramifications. Also like many other contemporary critics, Charnes moves from this valid point to the dubious one that whatever human beings think, say, or do is only or primarily political. According to Charnes, "the play itself deploys" the rhetoric of transcendent love, "But it does so *only* to demonstrate that 'transcendent love' is a discursive strategy ... with very public social and political aims" (272, emphasis added). Moreover, Charnes's perspective does not permit her to see any other kind of love: "I don't have an alternative vision of what else love might mean in this play" (271). If one regards all human emotions and behavior as only or primarily political, and if politics consists of manipulation and domination, then it follows that there is little or nothing else that "love might mean." Despite her anti-imperialist, antipatriarchal disposition, Charnes's disparagement of the love of Antony and Cleopatra places her squarely in the company of staunchly Roman characters such as Octavius and staunchly Roman critics such as Stempel. Politics makes strange bedfellows.

Rejecting a critical assumption held by most critics since at least the early nineteenth century, Linda T. Fitz denies that the play dramatizes an opposition between Egyptian and Roman values:

> A bevy of critics give Cleopatra a measure of favourable treatment as representative of Egyptian values, which according to these critics are set by Shakespeare in opposition to Roman values .... The effect of this kind of interpretation is to reduce Cleopatra to an allegorical figure, representing one set of values. Octavius Caesar is usually seen as representing the other set,

and the Everyman left to choose between these alternatives is always
Antony, who then becomes the hero of a kind of morality play. (207–08)

A problem with this denial is that characters in the play frequently, emphati-
cally, and vividly give voice to their perceptions of the opposition of values
that they explicitly associate with Rome and Egypt, and the Roman characters frame the conflict in terms that do recall morality plays. These superficial
similarities to a morality play are not flaws, however; they provide the basis
for ironic contrasts. Instead of an obvious choice between Christian virtues
and Satanic vices, the play dramatizes a difficult and disturbing choice
between two sets of secular values. Octavius does resemble an allegorical
figure, but only in a way that a real human being, as a result of specific psychological impulses or political motives, might do so. Some people narrowly
restrict their points of view, actively suppress contrary impulses, and so,
outwardly at least, come to resemble allegorical figures. In his single-minded
quest for total political power, Octavius thoroughly rejects sensual pleasure,
facetiousness, and other Egyptian diversions. Moreover, like many shrewd
politicians, Octavius actively fashions a public image that resembles an allegorical figure. In his competition with Antony, Octavius makes every effort to
present himself as the embodiment of Roman values and tries to damn Antony
as the embodiment of an alien, Egyptian way of life. Shakespeare chooses to
depict only the outward behavior of Octavius and leaves it to playgoers to
imagine the possible psychological cost of his self-allegorization. The superficial resemblance between Octavius and an allegorical figure is thus a
psychologically and politically realistic dramatic irony. Allegorical figures
usually represent fixed abstractions, whereas Cleopatra strives for variety,
change, originality, and individuality. And yet there is something obsessive
about this striving, and she is as concerned about her public image as
Octavius. She, too, presents herself as an allegorical figure, although a paradoxical one, the embodiment of Infinite Variety, the antithesis of allegorical
reductionism. Antony is an extremely individualized character, certainly not
an Everyman, and yet, like a morality-play character, he does make a fateful
choice between incompatible alternatives. But real people are sometimes
forced to make similar choices. Indeed, Fitz herself makes such a choice. The
main focus of her essay is a devastating attack on the "sexism" of "male
reviewers" of the play. Sexism is based on a sharp differentiation between
manliness and womanliness, a differentiation most prominently asserted
within the play by Octavius, the leading representative of Roman values. Fitz
celebrates Cleopatra's refusal to conform her behavior to the Roman notions
of femininity espoused by Octavius and derides similar notions held by male
critics. Although Fitz denies that the play dramatizes a conflict between Rome
and Egypt, she adopts a demonstrably Egyptian stance in her battle with
Roman critics.

This account of competing points of view dramatized in *Antony and Cleopatra* and reenacted and extended in critical commentary is not objective. As already noted, how one views a point of view depends on one's point of view. The play dramatizes this inescapable but disturbing fact about human judgments. No character can rise above this condition, *nor can any commentator*. In my view, although the play does not sentimentalize Egyptian values—it clearly exposes their defects, limitations, and drawbacks—it nevertheless dramatizes those values as considerably more appealing than Roman values. The choice offered by the play is not between pure good and pure evil, between perfection and wholesale error; the choice is between two imperfect ways of thinking. But those ways of thinking are not dramatized as being *equally* imperfect. While a number of Roman critics have heartily condemned the play for strongly favoring Egypt, I have not encountered any Egyptian critic who has heartily condemned the play for strongly favoring Rome. This imbalance in the commentary is not solely and fully explained by the contrast between the tendency of Roman critics to be stringent and Egyptian critics to be indulgent; at least in part, it reflects an imbalance within the play itself. With all their flaws, Antony and Cleopatra are far more engaging than Octavius. Shakespeare could have made Octavius more sympathetic and could have made Octavia more interesting. He could have designed the play to satisfy neoclassical principles of unity, which are in accord with values espoused by Roman characters in the play, but instead he daringly infused it with Cleopatra-like variety and mutability that conspicuously, facetiously, and daringly violate Roman ideas of unity and orderliness. In 2.5, Cleopatra calls for music, within two lines proposes billiards, then within seven lines decides to go fishing. The play is divided into more than forty scenes, some of which are absurdly brief. In 3.7, Caesar enters with his "army, marching," but this impressive martial show is followed by an exchange of fewer than five lines between Caesar and Taurus, after which the whole multitude exeunt and are succeeded onstage by Antony and Enobarbus who exchange fewer than four lines before exiting. Shortly thereafter, an army marches onstage but keeps marching right offstage without halting and without any dialogue; this dumb show is then reenacted by another army marching in the opposite direction; then the "noise" of an offstage sea fight is heard; and then Enobarbus enters.[5] The play encompasses numerous settings, years of fictional time, diverse plot elements, and radical shifts in tone. In my judgment, rather than flaws to be excused, these Egyptian features of the play's dramaturgy are integral elements in the design of an artistic masterpiece. Although I have tried to imagine how things would look from a Roman point of view, my own perspective on the play and commentary remains Egyptian.

NOTES

1. Ralph Waldo Emerson, "Self-Reliance."
2. Walt Whitman, "Song of Myself," section 51.
3. A. C. Bradley compares Cleopatra and Falstaff, but there is little overlap between the similarities he discerns and the ones on which I have focused. Bradley argues that, although for most of the play Cleopatra is not a tragic figure, "it does not follow that she is a comic figure like Falstaff." In his view, "she is no humorist" (299).
4. In his construction of the contrast between Rome and Egypt and particularly in his portraits of Cleopatra and Octavius, Shakespeare may have been influenced by Ovid's works and personal history. Like Cleopatra, Ovid was conversant in the art of love; indeed, he gave that title to one of his major works. Although Ovid explicitly praises Augustus in *Metamorphoses*, that poem is very Egyptian in its celebration of change and variety and thus was profoundly at odds with the stability and unity that Augustus sought to impose on the world. Like Cleopatra, Ovid often adopts a facetious tone even when dealing with matters usually treated with solemnity. This tone was at odds with the style of the emperor who took an august name for himself. Perhaps because Augustus recognized the implicit subversiveness of Ovid's poetry, he permanently banished the poet from Rome. Shakespeare's portrait of Octavius as ruthless, cold-blooded, and priggish may have been his revenge on the emperor for banishing a poet who was beloved by Shakespeare and whose spirit haunts the play.
5. This daringly rapid succession of distinct episodes has been obscured by post-Renaissance editors, who have ignored the clear breaks in dramatic continuity and incorporate three of these episodes in one scene (3.10 in the *Riverside*), as if they formed a single unbroken dramatic unit. For a discussion of Shakespeare's non-neoclassical dramatic structure, see *The Structure of Shakespearean Scenes* by the present writer.

WORKS CITED

Adelman, Janet. *The Common Liar: An Essay on* Antony and Cleopatra. New Haven: Yale UP, 1973.

Alvis, John. "The Religion of Eros: A Re-interpretation of *Antony and Cleopatra*." *Renascence* 30 (1978): 185–98.

Bethell, S. L. *Shakespeare and the Popular Dramatic Tradition*. Durham: Duke UP, 1944.

Bradley, A. C. "Shakespeare's *Antony and Cleopatra*." 1906. Rpt. in *Oxford Lectures on Poetry*. 1909. Rpt. London: Macmillan, 1950.

Caputi, Anthony. "Shakespeare's *Antony and Cleopatra*: Tragedy Without Terror." *Shakespeare Quarterly* 16 (1965): 183–91.

Charnes, Linda. "What's Love Got to Do with It? Reading the Liberal Humanist Romance in *Antony and Cleopatra*." 1992. Rpt. in *Shakespearean Tragedy and Gender*. Ed. Shirley Nelson Garner and Madelon Sprengnether. Bloomington: Indiana UP, 1996. 268–86.

Danby, John F. *Poets on Fortune's Hill*. London: Faber, 1952.

Fitz, Linda T. "Egyptian Queens and Male Reviewers: Sexist Attitudes in *Antony and Cleopatra*." 1977. Rpt. in *Antony and Cleopatra: William Shakespeare*. Ed. John Drakakis. New York: St. Martin's, 1994. 182–211.

Gentleman, Francis. "Introduction" to *Antony and Cleopatra*. In *Shakespeare's Plays*. Bell's Edition. 1774. Rpt. London: Cornmarket, 1969. 6: 261.

Hazlitt, William. *Characters of Shakespeare's Plays*. 1818. Rpt. in *Complete Works*. Ed. P. P. Howe. Vol. 4. Rpt. New York: AMS, 1967.

Hirsh, James. *The Structure of Shakespearean Scenes*. New Haven: Yale UP, 1981.

Knight, G. Wilson. *The Imperial Theme: Further Interpretations of Shakespeare's Tragedies including the Roman Plays*. 1931. 3rd ed. London: Methuen, 1968.

Lyman, Stanford M., and Marvin B. Scott. *The Drama of Social Reality*. New York: Oxford UP, 1975.

Rabkin, Norman. *Shakespeare and the Common Understanding*. Chicago: U of Chicago P, 1967.

Shakespeare, William. *The Riverside Shakespeare*. 2nd ed. Ed. G. Blakemore Evans. Boston: Houghton Mifflin, 1997.

Shaw, Bernard. Preface to *Three Plays for Puritans*. 1901. Rpt. in *Complete Prefaces*. Ed. Dan H. Lawrence and Daniel J. Leary. London: Lane/Penguin, 1993. 75–84.

Spencer, Benjamin T. "*Antony and Cleopatra* and the Paradoxical Metaphor." *Shakespeare Quarterly* 9 (1958): 373–78.

Stempel, Daniel. "The Transmigration of the Crocodile." *Shakespeare Quarterly* 7 (1956): 59–72.

Traversi, Derek. *Shakespeare: The Roman Plays*. Stanford: Stanford UP, 1963.

Wimsatt, W. K., Jr.. *The Verbal Icon*. Lexington: U of Kentucky P, 1954.

7.
"He beats thee 'gainst the odds"
Gambling, Risk Management,
and *Antony and Cleopatra*

LINDA WOODBRIDGE

Antony is a gambler. He shoots dice, plays cards, draws lots, and bets on cock fights, quail fights, even fishing (2.3.31–36, 4.15.19, 2.5.15–18).[1] From a modern perspective, his gaming spirit sorts well with his character: in epic feasts, in drinking bouts, in sexual marathons, the heroically dissolute Antony habitually "wastes / The lamps of night in revel" (1.4.4–5). Cleopatra too loves a wager—it is she who bets on fishing with Antony (and rigs the results), and she speaks even of Antony's death in a gambler's language: "The odds is gone, / And there is nothing left remarkable / Beneath the visiting moon" (4.16.68–70). Cleopatra too has her dissolute moments, and both possess something close to what moderns might consider a gaming personality—indeed, her high-stakes dinner invitation on the Cydnus may make Cleopatra the original riverboat gambler. But important shades of difference distinguish Renaissance attitudes toward gambling from ours. The upright Octavius, who disdains feasts, displays no interest in sex, and recoils in fastidious distaste from Pompey's drunken revel, is also a gambler, and a luckier one than Antony. The Renaissance took an intense interest in gambling, and if we can recover some Renaissance thinking, *Antony and Cleopatra*'s pervasive discourse of gambling can provide a fruitful lens through which to view this robustly complex play.

Gambling is deeply ingrained in the play's culture. Pompey proposes that the triumvirs take turns feasting each other and that they decide by drawing lots who will host first (2.6.60–63). Enobarbus warns Antony to fight by land: the long-odds gamble of a sea battle would mean giving himself up "to chance and hazard / From firm security" (3.7.46–47). When Antony instead gambles on a sea fight and loses, Enobarbus lashes out with gamblers' slang, declaring that Antony's lust has "nicked his captainship" (3.13.6–10), "nick" referring to a certain throw of dice in the game of "hazard." By act 4, even Antony's gambling expertise seems to desert him: he challenges Octavius to single combat rather than to a full battle of armies, ignoring the fact that the odds against Antony's army winning are so long that Octavius has no incentive to reduce his chances to the 50–50 of single combat. Antony is surprised when Octavius declines: "Why should he not?" Enobarbus, whose grasp of gambling odds has *not* deserted him, responds drily, "He thinks, being twenty times of better fortune, / He is twenty men to one." But Enobarbus still staunchly commits himself to the battle he regards as a gamble, promising, "I'll strike, and cry 'Take all!'" meaning "winner take all" (4.2.3–8). When this battle, too, is lost, Antony begins to suspect that Cleopatra and Caesar have stacked the deck against him: Cleopatra has "packed cards with Caesar," he charges (4.15.19).

That the noble Romans see the world in gambling terms might seem to have tainted them with some disrepute in the eyes of Shakespeare's Christian culture; but gambling was not necessarily linked with dissoluteness in the Elizabethan imagination, as it tends to be in ours. Some eminently respectable Elizabethans were avid bettors—John Ashton records bets between Elizabethan noblemen and even between Sir Walter Raleigh and the queen (*Gambling* 153). Dice rolling and card games have a medieval history, but the use of the word "gaming" to cover a number of gambling activities was new in the early sixteenth century, suggesting that gambling was being seen as a unified discourse. Shakespeare's works abound in betting. Posthumus in *Cymbeline* and Collatine in *The Rape of Lucrece* wager on their wives' chastity. Emilia declares herself willing to wager her soul upon Desdemona's chastity (*Othello* 4.2.13–14). In the climactic scene of *The Taming of the Shrew*, Petruchio, Hortensio, and Lucentio wager a hundred pounds on their wives' obedience. In *Coriolanus*, Martius and Lartius wager a good horse on whether or not a battle has yet been joined. In *The Tempest*, Antonio and Sebastian wager on who will laugh first. Of the fencing match in *Hamlet*, Horatio, who seems to have been watching Hamlet work out, ventures, "you will lose this wager"; but Hamlet has been having a word with the bookmakers and predicts, "I shall win at the odds" (5.2.14–49). Though Hamlet's own mother doesn't like his chances—like many an ambitious sports mother she frets that her son is undertrained, "fat and scant of breath" (5.2.230)—King Claudius backs Hamlet. He has rigged the match against Hamlet, but if it works and he keeps the kingdom, he can afford to pay up. Before the match begins, king and crown prince speak knowledgeably about gambling odds:

> CLAUDIUS. Cousin Hamlet,
>   You know the wager?
> HAMLET. Very well, my lord.
>   Your grace hath laid the odds o' th' weaker side.
> CLAUDIUS. I do not fear it; I have seen you both.
>   But since he is bettered [i.e., favoured], we have therefore odds [i.e.,
>   handicapping]. (5.2.197–201)

Although moralists warned against the drinking and swearing that could accompany it, gambling was not firmly associated with back rooms or a sordid criminal underworld. Even moralists and theologians were unwilling to condemn gambling categorically. As Thomas Wood shows, Anglican theological writers granted "qualified permission" to gambling,

> which is all the more impressive when their general tendency towards rigour and severity is remembered. Again and again the arguments against gambling, the many ways in which it is so often abused, the evils which so frequently attend upon or follow in consequence of it, are piled up as if to lead to its absolute condemnation. And yet, in the end, such a judgement is consistently rejected. Each one agrees that though the limitations to be imposed upon gambling are so great that on almost every occasion it would be wiser to refrain, circumstances may conceivably be such that its practice would be innocent. (160)

Among many distinctions that theologians made between acceptable and unacceptable gambling was that the former involved at least some skill, while the latter involved only chance. All the theologians and moralists who wrote against dicing agreed on this point. James Balmford, in *A short and plain dialogue concerning the unlawfulness of playing at cards or tables, or any other game consisting in chance* (1593), calibrates the evil inherent in various kinds of gambling according to the degree of their dependence on chance: "If dice be wholly evil, because they wholly depend upon chance, then tables and cards must needs be somewhat evil, because they somewhat depend upon chance" (Sig. A4^v).[2]

One reason chance was bad and skill good stemmed from the growing Protestant work ethic: skill demanded effort and labor, while only a lazy man sought windfall profits purely by chance. But chance wasn't uniformly denounced in other contexts: for example, risk and exposing oneself to the workings of chance were a mark of legitimacy for money merchants. As Raymond De Roover shows, exchange traders dealing in "bills of exchange" took a risk because the rate of exchange fluctuated, and it was precisely risk that insulated them from charges of usury. Thus, what the exchange speculation bankers engaged in was legitimized by risk and chance, while the usurer's certain return on his money, a *mutuum* or straight loan which demanded skill to negotiate and was not subject to chance, was punished and constrained by laws (see De Roover). The distinction between good and bad gambling on the basis of their degree of chance and skill is the exact converse of the distinction between legitimate money merchants and usurers—in the latter case, risk and chance were good, skill and carefulness bad. Such conflicted attitudes toward risk and skill reveal fault lines in a culture that was in transition to a capitalist system to which risk and chance were fundamental. The third, winning casket in *The Merchant of Venice* bears the inscription, "Who chooseth me must give and hazard all he hath" (2.7.16), seemingly endorsing the creed that success belongs to those willing to take risks, an impression enhanced by the period's strong association of the word "hazard" with a dice game.

I suggest that gambling was not regarded as wholly disreputable because Elizabethans and Jacobeans conceived of gambling in the same conceptual space with various mercantile and proto-capitalistic ventures routinely touted as generators of the national wealth. In 1986, Susan Strange argued in *Casino Capitalism* that "the Western financial system is rapidly coming to resemble nothing as much as a vast casino" (1), and we can see the beginnings of that situation in the sixteenth century. Michael Steppat notes the suggestive contemporaneity of widespread games of chance with "fluctuations in money economy and maritime expansion during the extension of early capitalist enterprise" (21). Venture capitalism, such as investments in joint stock companies for risky voyages to India or America, bore an obvious resemblance to high-stakes gambling, and the term "adventurer" was applied to both gamblers and venture capitalists. Speculation on futures was born during this period: Paul Einzig discusses "'betting' on future exchange rates," in which "the parties concerned made forecasts of exchange rates that would prevail at a certain date, and the discrepancy between these rates and the actual rate on the date in question determined who won the bet and how much the loser was to pay the winner . . . . The practice was used not only for gambling but also for covering exchange risk" (120). Particularly akin to gambling was the international financial maneuver known as arbitrage: taking advantage of the differing evaluation of the same currency in different European cities by buying in the city where the value was lower and selling in the city where it was higher (De Roover 140).

Those moralists who did assail gambling also tended to suspect commercial ventures of being motivated by greed. Some moralists applied mercantile language to the world of gambling. In John Northbrooke's *A Treatise wherein Dicing, Dancing, Vain Plays, or Interludes . . . are Reproved* (c. 1577), one speaker ascribes poverty, lack of exercise, swearing, stealing, brawling, and greed to dice-playing: "These are the fruits, and *revenues*, of that wicked *merchandise* of diceplaying" (119; emphasis mine). "Gaming," he declares, "was never allowed as a kind of *bargaining, traffic*, or occupying among men, if we either consider God's law or man's," and concludes, "There is no *usury* in the world so heinous as the gain gotten by this play at dice, when all is gotten with a trice over the thumb, without any *traffic or loan*" (Northbooke 120, 129; emphasis mine).

Gambling, I suggest, was defended by establishment preachers because its resemblance to proto-capitalist practices, especially exchange speculation and joint-stock sea ventures, was too striking to ignore, and preachers saw no reason to offend the bankers, merchants, and wealthy investors among their parishioners by launching an unqualified assault on the principle of risking money to gain money. The theologian Jeremy Taylor acknowledged, as Wood points out, "the element of chance or risk in [games of chance], for which they are so often denounced, is a feature of all human affairs" (Wood 161). But most particularly, risk is a feature of banking, mercantile, and investing affairs. And so preachers muffled the boom of their heaviest rhetorical artillery, when it came to gambling. The preacher Richard Baxter defended betting on horse races, dogs, hawks, and bear-baiting, as long as the stakes were not too high. Cards, dice, and lotteries worried him a little, but he finally judged them acceptable if approached in the right spirit, without covetousness. A *little* gambling couldn't hurt, preachers allowed, if one's heart was pure.

Faced with the persistent similarity between gambling and various forms of venture capitalism, we moderns have adopted a rather different strategy: we assume a gulf between good gambling (the stock market) and bad gambling (the floating craps game). Most U.S. senators and other political leaders take care not to be discovered laying large wagers in Las Vegas or running high stakes poker games in the back rooms of their constituency offices. But no such taint of disrepute attaches to the public, political image of Shakespeare's Antony or Octavius Caesar, when they wager on cock fights: Renaissance preachers had showed themselves willing to countenance, even in prominent public figures, at least small social wagers, and often turned a blind eye to a good deal more.

A BLESSÉD LOTTERY

The redoubtable Octavia—she of the "holy, cold, and still conversation" (2.6.120)—cannot readily be imagined having a flutter on a cockfight or wagering on a game of hazard. It is therefore rather startling when Maecenas mobilizes a gambling term to describe Octavia's womanly virtue—"If beauty, wisdom, modesty can settle the heart of Antony, Octavia is a blesséd lottery to him" (2.2.46–48). The association of this womanly paragon with lotteries—even the association of the churchly word "blesséd" with lotteries—underlines the legitimacy of this form of gambling: a new mode of Elizabethan fund-raising was the state-operated lottery.

The first lottery, in 1569, was to raise money to repair England's harbors, along with other public works. A copy of the imposing "chart" for this lottery, nineteen inches wide and five feet long, lists some thirty thousand prizes, many with illustrations; first prize was £5,000 (Ashton, *Lotteries* 5–16). The tickets had identifying "devises" and "posies" rather than names; many of these short poems have survived on lottery tickets; it is pleasing to think of the nation's gambling fever turning four hundred thousand of its citizens temporarily into poets. The lottery poems often refer to luck and Fortune; for

example, "If Fortune be froward my angel is gone, / But if Fortune be friendly
with increase it cometh home." Alice Crewe, London (#268,223), 1s. 3d
(Ashton, *Lotteries* 18). When the queen visited Sir Thomas Egerton in 1602,
he presented her with an entertainment called "A Lottery," in which a mariner
sang a song about Fortune on the sea and then distributed tickets; most prizes
were gloves or bracelets; the grand prize was "Fortune's Wheel" (Ashton,
Lotteries 24–27). From the 1620s on, money was raised by lottery for aque-
ducts and other waterworks (Ashton, *Lotteries* 29–30). Many lottery tickets
were bought by churches. It is not so unseemly, then, that Antony is imagined
as winning a politically advantageous marriage as a lottery prize: lotteries
possessed considerable public legitimacy, a government-sanctioned form of
gambling.

RISK MANAGEMENT

The chart for the 1569 state lottery promised all ticket-holders a return of at
least two shillings six pence, and anyone buying thirty or more lots who did
not gain back at least a third of his investment was promised a pension for life.
If the public were to be enticed into having a flutter on the state lottery, they
needed to be reassured that it was not *too* dangerous. As Peter L. Bernstein
shows, this age of high-stakes international trading was the first era of risk
management: "You do not plan to ship goods across the ocean, or to assemble
merchandise for sale, or to borrow money without first trying to determine
what the future may hold in store" (21). In Elizabethan culture, modes of risk
management proliferated: credit inquiries like those Shylock makes into
Antonio's "means";[3] the beginnings of insurance;[4] diversification of investments;[5] and many other ways of hedging bets, all of which involved gauging
the probability of success or failure in the immediate future, given alternate
financial strategies. One of the pioneers of probability theory,[6] Girolamo
Cardano (1501–76) was himself a compulsive gambler and a writer on
gambling, who confessed in his autobiography, "I was inordinately addicted
to the chess-board and the dicing table . . . . I gambled at both for many years,
at chess more than forty years, at dice about twenty-five; and not only every
year, . . . every day, and with the loss at once of thought, of substance, and of
time" (*Book of My Life* 73). Such loss caused Cardano great anxiety: his *Book
on Games of Chance* records ruefully that "losses" from gambling include not
only money but time: hours at the gaming tables, "time spent in planning after
the game how one may recuperate, and in remembering how badly one has
played"; at one point he glumly concludes, "The greatest advantage in
gambling comes from not playing at all" (*Book on Games of Chance* 188). But
abstinence from gambling either did not lie in his power, or was not his style.
Cardano attempted instead to turn his mathematical expertise to account in
predicting gambling outcomes and so managing the risk. In his *Book on*

Games of Chance, he grapples with what would now be called statistical probability, in dice-throwing. As Bernstein notes, "The dice and the roulette wheel, along with the stock market and the bond market, are natural laboratories for the study of risk" (7). Bernstein believes that the *Book on Games of Chance*, written in 1525 and revised in 1565 but never published in Cardano's lifetime, would have revolutionized mathematics had it been known.

Casinos trade in hope, and a gambler necessarily fixes his gaze intently upon the immediate future. The pioneer mathematician Cardano seems very modern as he exults in a new world of expanded geographical frontiers and technological innovation:

> Among the extraordinary ... circumstances of my life, the first and most unusual is that I was born in this century in which the whole world became known; whereas the ancients were familiar with but little more than a third part of it .... The conviction grows that, as a result of these discoveries, the fine arts will be neglected .... These things may be true sometime or other, but meanwhile we shall rejoice as in a flower-filled meadow. (*Book of My Life* 189)

He also rejoices in Renaissance inventions—gunpowder, the compass, typography. But when Cardano relates personal experiences of bird and other animal omens that accurately presaged dire events, he suddenly sounds downright medieval. It is a gambling man's superstitiousness, a gambler's constant, restless search for clues to the immediate future.

Bernstein's sanguine book on risk management was published in 1996, when the stock market was still riding high, and its opening page is rhapsodic:

> The revolutionary idea that defines the boundary between modern times and the past is the mastery of risk: the notion that the future is more than a whim of the gods and that men and women are not passive before nature. Until human beings discovered a way across that boundary, the future was a mirror of the past or the murky domain of oracles and soothsayers who held a monopoly over knowledge of anticipated events. (1)

In the Renaissance, risk management, based on "scientific forecasting" and "statistical inference" or "inferring a global estimate from a sample of data" (Bernstein 19, 78), was enabled by humanistic bouyancy, the residue of which has infected Bernstein: "The idea of risk management emerges only when people believe that they are to some degree free agents" (Bernstein 35). That pioneer of risk management, Cardano, sometimes believed in his own statistical inference, but long and sad experience at the gaming tables reduced him at other times to bird omens and "the murky domain of oracles and soothsayers." Antony, from the start, sticks to the bird omens and the soothsayers.

Shortly after becoming betrothed to Octavia, Antony privately consults a soothsayer:[7]

> ANTONY. Say to me
>   Whose fortunes shall rise higher: Caesar's or mine?
> SOOTHSAYER. Caesar's. Therefore, O Antony, stay not by his side.
>   Thy daemon, that thy spirit which keeps thee, is
>   Noble, courageous, high, unmatchable,
>   Where Caesar's is not. But near him thy angel
>   Becomes afeard, as being o'erpowered. Therefore
>   Make space enough between you.
> ANTONY. Speak this no more.
> SOOTHSAYER. To none but thee; no more but when to thee.
>   If thou dost play with him at any game
>   Thou art sure to lose; and of that natural luck
>   He beats thee'gainst the odds. Thy lustre thickens
>   When he shines by. I say again, thy spirit
>   Is all afraid to govern thee near him;
>   But he away,'tis noble. (2.3.14–30)

Antony suddenly commands, "Get thee gone." But once the soothsayer has left, he muses,

> He hath spoken true. The very dice obey him,
> And in our sports my better cunning faints
> Under his chance. If we draw lots, he speeds.
> His cocks do win the battle still of mine
> When it is all to nought, and his quails ever
> Beat mine, inhooped, at odds. I will to Egypt. (2.3.31–36)

Although many Romans in the play and generations of Shakespeare critics have taxed Cleopatra with bringing out the worst in Antony,[8] this crucial passage puts Antony's Egyptian furloughs in an entirely different light: here it is Octavius who brings out the worst in an Antony who virtually hides out in Egypt to get out from under his shadow.[9] The strategy is less than rational: if the soothsayer is right, Octavius's fortune will rise higher whether Antony is near him or not. The warning of Julius Caesar's soothsayer was at least conditional: "beware" left open the possibility of avoiding disaster by judicious risk management each March 15. But responding to the question "Whose fortunes shall rise higher?" Antony's soothsayer doesn't say, "Caesar's, unless you steer clear of him." He just says "Caesar's." But Antony, a gambler and a believer in omens—in this remarkable passage his poor gambling luck is itself an omen—like Cardano seems willing at least to *try* a little risk management. His strategy to minimize risk is to "make space enough" between himself and Caesar.

Cleopatra, too, is a risk-taking trader in the future, but she has no truck with fortune-tellers. Her women laughingly and frivolously consult a sooth-sayer, who spookily (and accurately, as we later realize) predicts their future. But Cleopatra, who is at one point onstage with the soothsayer (1.2), leaves his palm-reading alone. Cleopatra's trading in futures involves face-reading.

It is clear from the outset that Cleopatra habitually watches Antony's facial expressions as a key to his thoughts: "He was disposed to mirth, but on the sudden / A Roman thought hath struck him" (1.2.72–73). We hear more of this face-reading when Cleopatra deputizes Alexas to read Antony's face for her: "If you find him sad, / Say I am dancing; if in mirth, report / That I am sudden sick. Quick, and return" (1.3.3–5). While waiting for Alexas's report, Cleopatra engages in a brief, pointed discussion with Charmian of her strategy for holding Antony's interest:

> CHARMIAN. Madam, methinks, if you did love him dearly,
>   You do not hold the method to enforce
>   The like from him.
> CLEOPATRA. What should I do I do not?
> CHARMIAN. In each thing give him way; cross him in nothing.
> CLEOPATRA. Thou teachest like a fool, the way to lose him.
> CHARMIAN. Tempt him not so too far. Iwis, forbear.
>   In time we hate that which we often fear. (1.3.6–12)

And well she might worry about "the way to lose him" (line 10); Cleopatra's chronic risk is the loss of Antony to her great competitors, Roman duty and manly self-actualization. Her strategy for managing this risk has been to keep him in Egypt by the gravitational pull of a fascinating personality. But Charmian replies in risk-management terms: what has worked so far, if pushed beyond its useful limits, might actually increase the risk it was designed to avert. We will never know Cleopatra's response to Charmian's cautionary words, for the strategy session is interrupted by the entrance of Antony, whom the audience has just seen in the process of deciding to leave Egypt and return to Rome, the very move that Cleopatra's risk management has been working to avert.

Immediately assessing the situation, Cleopatra completely ignores the strategy she has just enunciated, "If you find him sad, / Say I am dancing; if in mirth, report / That I am sudden sick." Of the two emotional poles "sad" and "in mirth," it is difficult to believe that Antony is "in mirth" at this moment; but rather than dancing, Cleopatra adopts a serious posture: "I am sick and sullen" (1.3.13). Her mood is now parallel rather than contrary to Antony's. Why the change of strategy? Has she been persuaded by Charmian's argument that contrarian tactics have outlived their usefulness? Or has she read in Antony's face that this threat is graver than any she has confronted so far, that in this changed situation, a contrary stance of merriment would be too great a risk? Whatever the answer, she does seem to take her cue from what she sees when reading Antony's face, especially his eyes: "I see from that same eye there's some good news," she declares ironically, going on to guess that Antony has decided to leave her because of his wife. She is right about this, or nearly right—it is not to return to his wife but to clean up a situation associated with her death that Antony is returning to Rome. That is quite a lot to read in a man's face; perhaps one of Antony's failures as a gambler is his lack of a poker face. But then, Cleopatra is an adept in face-reading.

When next we see her reading faces, Cleopatra is again reduced to getting secondhand face reports from Alexas, who has just seen Antony off on his trip to Rome:

> CLEOPATRA. Was he sad or merry?
> ALEXAS. Like to the time o' th' year between the extremes
>   Of hot and cold, he was nor sad nor merry.
> CLEOPATRA. O well divided disposition! Note him,
>   Note him, good Charmian,'tis the man; but note him.
>   He was not sad, for he would shine on those
>   That make their looks by his; he was not merry,
>   Which seemed to tell them his remembrance lay
>   In Egypt with his joy; but between both. (1.5.49–57)

She perhaps gives Antony too much credit for manipulative face control: the man whose poker face is elsewhere deficient here sounds like a skillful Claudius, with "one auspicious and one dropping eye, / With mirth in funeral and with dirge in marriage, / In equal scale weighing delight and dole" (*Hamlet* 1.2.11–13). But it is fitting that Cleopatra thinks of "those / That make their looks by his," anxious face-watchers, ready to adjust their moods to complement Antony's or perhaps to cut and run if his facial expressions are dire enough, as she herself will do in 4.13. Cleopatra herself is among "those / That make their looks by his," managing her relationship with him by what she reads in his face.

Cleopatra reads trouble all over the face of the messenger bearing the news that Antony has remarried: "There's no goodness in thy face. If Antony / Be free and healthful, so tart a favour / To trumpet such good tidings!" (2.5.37–39). Cleopatra has an eye for a handsome as well as a revealing face, and after she has heard the messenger's deadly news and has finished striking him several times and haling him up and down by the hair, she scans this young man's face again, and this time realizes that interference from her own rage prevents her at the moment from either appreciating or reading his face: "Hadst thou Narcissus in thy face, to me / Thou wouldst appear most ugly" (2.5.97–98).

Cleopatra is not alone in reading faces: Octavius Caesar, sensing a change in Pompey, tries his hand face-reading: "Since I saw you last / There is a change upon you," he muses, and must be perusing Pompey's face as he speaks, for Pompey answers, "I know not / What counts harsh fortune casts upon my face" (2.6.52–54). Menas thinks he could tell a thief by examining his face (2.6.97–99). Enobarbus and Agrippa peruse Octavius's face to gauge his reaction to his sister's match with Antony: "Will Caesar weep?" asks Agrippa, and Enobarbus observes, "He has a cloud in's face" (3.2.51–52). But Cleopatra is the premier face reader.[10] When she recalls Julius Caesar, it is the shape of his forehead that comes first to mind ("broad-fronted Caesar" [1.5.29]), which shows her a sound physiognomist. The very first chapter of Johannes Indagine's *An Introduction to the Art of Physiognomy* is "Of the Judgement of the Forehead"; its opening sentence is, "It is not to be let pass, the sure judgement that is to be taken by the forehead of man, the which doth alter and change at every sudden passion of the mind" (Sib. [G8]^v). Cleopatra is also a student of Antony's forehead (1.3.36).[11] Her agents and messengers routinely bring back physiognomical data for her to work on. The hapless messenger, wiser and warier in his second encounter with the Queen, authenticates his report on Antony's new wife by avouching, "I looked her in the face" (3.3.9). Cleopatra asks for more details about this face: "Bear'st thou her face in mind? Is't long or round?" When the messenger reports, "Round, even to faultiness," Cleopatra is quick to interpret according to the precepts of the discipline of physiognomy: "For the most part, too, they are foolish that are so" (3.3.29–31), in the same vein as Indagine's physiognomy manual, which pronounces possessors of round faces "phlegmatic, slow, fearful" (Sig. Ji^v), and Roussat's physiognomy text which notes that one with "a full face" is "not very wise" (Sig. Qi). Indagine's dictum "the grosser [i.e., rounder, fleshier] the face is, the more duller it declareth him to be" (Sig. Ji^v) sorts well with Cleopatra's verdict on Octavia: "dull of tongue" (3.3.16). Particularly gratifying to Cleopatra would have been the messenger's description of Octavia's low forehead (3.3.32–33)—a feature which combined with a round or fat face betoken to the physiognomist a "dull person" (Indagine Sig. [G8^v]).

One of the last messengers Cleopatra enlists to aid her face-reading is the Roman Proculeius, to whom she gives a message for Octavius:

> Pray you, tell him
> I am his fortune's vassal, and I send him
> The greatness he has got. I hourly learn
> A doctrine of obedience, and would gladly
> Look him i' th' face. (5.2.28–32)

Proculeius's promise to relay the message has a hidden agenda—he is talking to distract Cleopatra while Roman soldiers creep up to ambush her; but Cleopatra's angling for a chance to look Octavius in the face most likely has its own hidden agenda: reading faces is her way of foretelling the immediate future and managing risk. Soon she is wheedling a prediction of the future out of Dolabella: "Know you what Caesar means to do with me?" (5.2.105). If she could know Octavius's intentions—lead her in triumph in Rome, or leave her in Egypt?—she could decide whether to take the gamble of not committing suicide. "He'll lead me then in triumph," she prompts Dolabella, who for unspecified reasons departs from official promises of clemency and answers her privately, "Madam, he will, I know't" (5.2.108). Cleopatra now has reason to resolve upon suicide, but she isn't sure she can trust Dolabella—she has already declared that she will trust no one attending on Caesar and has just had proof that Antony was wrong to make an exception when counseling her to trust "none about Caesar ... but Proculeius" (4.16.50). She has one means left of learning her immediate fate: reading Octavius's face. When he enters, his words are unctuously reassuring: "Be cheered. / ... Dear Queen / ... we intend so to dispose you as / Yourself shall give us counsel. Feed and sleep. / Our care and pity is so much upon you / That we remain your friend" (5.2.180–85). But although she has listened to his words, Cleopatra has also "looked him in i' th' face," and knows he is lying. The moment he exits, she briskly declares, "He words me, girls, he words me, that I should not / Be noble to myself" (5.2.187–88), and gives orders to activate the multiple suicide plan she has already put in train before Proculeius, Dolabella, and Caesar burst in upon her. It was a contingency plan, which she could have aborted; but having looked Caesar in the face, she knows that the risk of his leading her in triumph is too great. She manages that risk with the aid of asps.

FORTUNE BY LAND AND SEA

The preface to the first physiognomical treatise in print in England, Thomas Hill's translation of Cocles's *A Brief and Most Pleasant Epitome of the Whole Art of Physiognomy* (1556), confidently categorizes physiognomy as "natural philosophy"(what would later be called "science"), allying it with arithmetic, astronomy, geometry, and medicine. But in addition to providing insights into the human body and mind, as other "sciences" could do, physiognomy was supposed to have predictive value for human behavior. As Kay Flavell points out, "While disclaiming prophecy, believers in physiognomy constantly made predictive claims" (11). Judging character, mood, and intention from face-reading gave clues to people's likely behavior in the future, thus allowing face-readers to minimize risk by avoiding those of ominous face. Roussat's treatise concludes by promising that physiognomists "may prognosticate ... more assuredly of great and small things to come, yea of every man ... for ... you shall know most certainly his deeds and his manners" (Sig. [S4]ᵛ).

The prediction of future behavior aligned physiognomy with fortune-telling, and this connection grows more pronounced over the course of sixteenth-century physiognomy publishing in England. Whereas Hill's treatise deals exclusively with physiognomy, Jonannes Indagine's *Introduction to the Art of Physiognomy* (1558) takes up three methods of predicting the future: chiromancy or palm-reading; astrology or star-reading; and physiognomy or the reading of faces, eyes, heads; and Roussat's covers both physiognomy and astrology. (And Hill also published on other prognosticatory arts, including divination by dreams and weather-forecasting to aid in risk management for gardeners and travelers.)[12] Such ancient magical forecasting methods acquired in the Renaissance a "scientific" veneer, just when other kinds of fortune-telling were being demonized as witchcraft. Early in his physiognomic treatise, Indagine deftly distances himself from soothsayers, under color of discussing sinister eyebrows: "When the brows meet and join together, it is very evil, for it betokeneth a man given to witchcrafts and evil arts. The which I have seen evident in diverse old soothsayers ... being led unto the fire" (Sig. [G8ᵛ]-Hi).

In *Macbeth*, demonic and legitimate methods of future-prediction exist side-by-side, the witches' predictions about Macbeth's future as king coexisting with Duncan's rueful admission of inadequacy as a physiognomist: "There's no art / To find the mind's construction in the face. / He [a traitorous thane] was a gentleman on whom I built / An absolute trust" (1.4.11–14). Physiognomy dealt not only in immutable facial features such as high brows or deep-set eyes but also in the reading of facial expressions such as furrowed brows or motions of the eyelids.[13] Lady Macbeth rightly worries about Macbeth's poor poker face, readable not only by an expert physiognomist like herself but even by "men": "Your face, my thane, is as a book where men / May read strange matters. To beguile the time, / Look like the time; bear welcome in your eye, / Your hand, your tongue; look like the innocent flower, / But be the serpent under t" (1.5.60–64). Taking her lecture to heart, Macbeth presently resolves, "False face must hide what the false heart doth know" (1.7.82); but, after the murder of Banquo, he is filled with anguish by the necessity to "make our faces visors to our hearts, / Disguising what they are" (3.2.35–36). After seeing Banquo's ghost, Macbeth entirely loses control of his visor-face, prompting Lady Macbeth's desperate exclamation, "Shame itself, / Why do you make such faces?" (3.4.65–66). Women in this play have an aptitude for face-reading: as soon as Lady Macduff looks in the faces of the murderers, she knows she is in trouble: "What are these faces?" (4.2.79). But even Macbeth can read terror on the face of a messenger: "The devil damn thee black, thou cream-faced loon! / Where gott'st thou that goose look?" (5.3.11–12).

The relationship between face and character was clearly unstable: not only could bad character be masked by adopting a "false face," as Macbeth knows or at least hopes, but the basic evil proclivities revealed by one's face could be altered by deliberate effort, as is indicated in an anecdote in the preface to Thomas Hill's physiognomy book, in which a "physiognomer" discerns from Socrates's face that the philosopher is "a great lecher, a crafty fellow, subtle, and given to all wickedness." Socrates confounds him: "It is all true that ... I am [thus] by nature, but I have (as all other men may have if they will) a reason and grace that ruleth above nature." Hill proceeds, untroubled that such an admission undermines physiognomy's whole project. The continuing great popularity of physiognomy books,[14] flying in the face (as it were) of physiognomy's manifestly untenable premises, attests to the urgency of the early modern need to judge character and minimize risk in dealing with people's likely behavior in the near future.

Reading the immediate future was a preoccupation of the age. "Legitimate" forms of fortune-telling—physiognomy, palmistry, astrology, almanacs—were bound to persist, although witches were burned, because the need for knowledge of the future, on which to base risk-minimizing decisions, had never been stronger. As Craig Muldrew shows, Elizabethans lived in a "culture of credit": the majority of financial transactions involved trusting a buyer or borrower to pay or repay in the future. The great increase in long-distance trade meant routine credit dealings with virtual strangers. To minimize the risk of trusting strangers, merchants consulted credit ratings and letters of introduction, and if nothing else, tried to read faces. If international trade was a gamble, so was empire-building. *Antony and Cleopatra*, written circa 1606–07, is exactly contemporary with the high-risk Jamestown colony ventured by the Virginia Company in 1607,[15] and a hopeful Britain was already prepared to regard itself as an empire potentially in a league with ancient Rome: Speed's 1611 atlas was grandly entitled *The Theater of the Empire of Great Britain*. Consonant with these imperial visions are the international high-flyers of *Antony and Cleopatra*, seeking power and fortune on the high seas and in the theatre of empire. The engine of the action is fortune, risk, the heroic if doomed gamble.

Antony and Cleopatra makes by far the most references to fortune of any Shakespeare play—forty, in contrast to only twenty-five even in *The Merchant of Venice* and twenty-nine in *Timon of Athens*, both economically-oriented plays. The word "fortune" was proliferating meanings in this period. *Antony and Cleopatra* still employs older meanings connected with the goddess Fortuna (3.11.74–75; 4.13.19–20; 4.16.45–47; 5.2.3–4); but a new, strictly economic meaning appears in Cleopatra's giving money to a messenger and promising, "Make thee a fortune from me" (2.5.49). Another new meaning, "the chance or luck (good or bad) which falls to any one as his lot in life" (*OED*) appears in the Soothsayer's prediction that Charmian has "seen and proved a fairer former fortune / Than that which is to approach" (1.2.29–30) and in Pompey's reference to the "harsh fortune" that has been his adult life (2.6.54). One of the play's most characteristic meanings of "fortune" is "one's condition or standing in life; ... a prosperous condition" (*OED*), a meaning first recorded in 1600; here, such "prosperous condition" manifests as success on the military and imperial stage, as when Antony asks the sooth-sayer, "Whose fortunes shall rise higher: Caesar's or mine?" (2.3.15), or when Menas scorns Pompey for passing up a chance to assassinate the Roman triumvirs and control the whole Roman Empire himself: "Pompey doth this day laugh away his fortune . . . . For this, I'll never follow thy palled fortunes more" (2.6.104–05, 2.7.78). At his own highest moment of fortune, Antony has played with "half the bulk o' th' world . . . as I pleased, / Making and marring fortunes" of others (3.11.64–65); and toward the end of his life recalls "my former fortunes, / Wherein I lived the greatest prince o' th' world, / The noblest" (4.16.56–57). Caesar, knowing that his future imperial status rests on defeating Antony in battle, gives the intense order: "Strike not by land. Keep whole. Provoke not battle / Till we have done at sea . . . . Our fortune lies / Upon this jump" (3.8.3–6). One word, "fortune," was coming to represent both financial accumulation and self-realization through imperial conquest. The imperial and military adventurers of this play are not unlike the merchant adventurers of the day, taking great risks to make fortunes upon the vast stage of the world. And like merchant adventurers, they hedge their bets and devise risk management strategies as best they can.

Among many ways to read Cleopatra is as a bold international gambler. In a world dominated by the juggernaut of an expansionist Roman Empire, gobbling up kingdoms and principalities, she tries to maintain her own power and some autonomy for her client kingdom by seducing Rome's most power-ful men. One need not totally discount real passion in her relationships to notice (with a gambler's eye) that the odds are against her passion's having lighted fortuitously upon three consecutive lovers who are leaders of the world's most powerful nation—Pompey, Julius Caesar, and Antony. While her beauty lasts, she gambles on its power; when she grows "wrinkled deep in time" (1.5.29), she bets on her fascinating personality. It's a risky strategy: any one of these Romans might use her and cast her aside—her constant fear in this play. That would mean the loss not only of Roman romance but (more to the point) of power and bargaining position. But Cleopatra doesn't hold many cards, and she plays the hand she has been dealt with all the finesse she can muster.

Antony ultimately tries to leave the gaming table, fleeing the man whose gambling luck always outshines his own. But Cleopatra plays on, even as the odds against her grow desperately long. She may be a "gypsy," she may be a "boggler," she may be a "triple-turned whore" (1.1.10, 4.13.28, 3.13.111, 4.13.13). But after many years of studying Roman imperial faces for their predictive value, the first thing she remembers about Antony when speaking her great eulogy to him is "his face"—not this time a face to gauge moods by, but a magnificent face, a face which "was as the heav'ns" (5.2.78). One thing about Cleopatra was bound to appeal to a nation of proto-capitalist gamblers infatuated with empire: she was never so paltry as to be risk averse. She plays until the end, and in the very moment of her death, trumps the Roman Empire. In her final hours she out-gambles the great Octavius Caesar with his legendary gambling luck. Cleopatra doesn't live to a ripe old age, but she does live to "mock / The luck of Caesar" (5.2.276–77).

NOTES

1. All Shakespeare references are to *The Norton Shakespeare*, ed. Greenblatt, Cohen, Howard, and Maus.
2. Here and throughout this essay, early modern spelling has been modernized.
3. Shylock plans to examine Antonio's credit rating very carefully. He has already made inquiries on the Rialto and knows the whereabouts of all Antonio's ships (1.3.15–18), and although he has tentatively judged Antonio's wealth "sufficient," he suspects Antonio of being overextended with risky ventures: "his means are in supposition" (1.3.14–21).
4. Marine insurance, dating to the Middle Ages, was very common in the Renaissance, which makes rather inexplicable the predicament of Antonio in *The Merchant of Venice*. Life insurance was available in England by the 1570s, and other forms such as personal injury insurance soon followed. For more information on this important Renaissance mode of risk management, see Violet Barbour, H. A. L. Cockerell and Edwin Green, François Ewald, Trevor Sibbett, Barry Supple, and Luke Wilson.
5. Antonio in *The Merchant of Venice*, although remiss in not insuring his ships, has at least practiced investment diversification as a form of risk management: "My ventures are not in one bottom [i.e., ship] trusted, / Nor to one place; nor is my whole estate / Upon the fortune of this present year. / Therefore my merchandise makes me not sad" (1.1.41–45). In this case, "not sad" means "not anxious about the possibility of losing his investment."
6. On early forays into probability theory, see Ian Hacking.
7. As context makes clear, the soothsayer has come from Egypt, and his counseling Antony to stay clear of Caesar might reflect Egyptian or Cleopatran self-interest. We do not know, however, that the soothsayer is an Egyptian; for all we know Antony, who apparently has brought the soothsayer from Egypt to Rome, might before that have taken him from Rome to Egypt. For all we know, he might have hired the same soothsayer who so successfully predicted Julius Caesar's death on the Ides of March. Whatever the nationality of the soothsayer, we are not told enough about him to judge his motives.
8. Regarding the pervasive sexism in criticism of the play, see the essay, published under my former name, L. T. Fitz, "Egyptian Queens and Male Reviewers: Sexist Attitudes in *Antony and Cleopatra* Criticism."
9. Rick Bowers argues persuasively that "Caesar's 'luck' might better be considered as a critical narrowing of possibility, a thoroughgoing sense of tactical advantage, a complete subordination of personal desire to political success. 'Luck' is the loser's word for it" (534).

10. Juliana Schiesari discusses the impact of Renaissance physiognomy on deleterious racial and gender stereotypes. But in the often topsy-turvy world of *Antony and Cleopatra*, the play's most adept physiognomist, Cleopatra, is an African woman reading the faces of European males (and of one European female)—the converse of the usual Eurocentric, patriarchal practice.

11. And the very first time she is described, a Roman reduces Cleopatra to a forehead: "a tawny front" (1.1.6). Cleopatra is also very interested in eyebrows (see 1.3.36, 1.5.32), a key facial signifier to the physiognomist—Thomas Hill and Johannes Indagine both give the eyebrows a prominent position in their treatises, right after the forehead, and even before the eyes.

12. For example, Hill's *Prognostication Made for the Year of Our Lord God 1572* features "the prediction of the weather for every day" of 1572 (title page), and his *Contemplation of Mysteries: Containing the Rare Effects and Significations of Certain Comets* promises risk abatement "for the sailor and husbandman, yea and all travelers by sea and land, in knowing aforehand how dangerous a tempest will succeed [i.e., occur] by the sight of the cloud coming over the head" (title page).

13. Hill declares, for example, that eyelids which "by often moving elevate on high" denote a "proud, stout, and hardy" disposition, given to threatening displays (Sig. Bi^v).

14. The three main physiological treatises of the English Renaissance, all translations of continental originals, appeared within six years: Hill's in 1556, Indagine's in 1558, and R. H.'s translation of Richard Roussat's French treatise in 1562. Indagine's treatise was reprinted three times; Roussat's seventeen times, the last time in 1586. In 1571, Hill greatly enlarged his 1556 edition; the enlarged edition was reprinted in 1613.

15. Tellingly for the conjunction of capitalism and gambling, the Virginia Company financed the new colony partly through capital put up by London merchants and partly through a privately run but governmentally authorized lottery (see *Three Proclamations Concerning the Lottery for Virginia*). Further emphasizing the capitalism / gambling nexus, one prize in a 1615 lottery, in aid of the Virginia colony, was a share in the Virginia Company ("A Declaration for the Certain Time of drawing the Great Standing Lottery," in *Three Proclamations Concerning the Lottery for Virginia*).

WORKS CITED

Ashton, John. *The History of Gambling in England*. London: Duckworth, 1898.
———. *A History of English Lotteries*. London: Leadenhall P, 1893.
Balmford, James. *A short and plain dialogue concerning the unlawfulness of playing at cards or tables, or any other game consisting in chance*. London: Richard Boile, 1593.
Barbour, Violet. "Marine Risks and Insurance in the Seventeenth Century." *Journal of Economic and Business History* 1 (1928–29): 561–96.
Baxter, Richard. *A Christian Directory: or, A Sum of Practical Theology and Cases of Conscience*. London: Robert White, 1673.
Bernstein, Peter L. *Against the Gods: The Remarkable Story of Risk* New York: John Wiley and Sons, 1996.

Bowers, Rick " 'The Luck of Caesar': Winning and Losing in *Antony and Cleopatra*." *English Studies* 79 (1998): 522–35.

Cardano, Girolamo (Jerome Cardan). *The Book of My Life (De Vita Propria Liber)*. Trans. Jean Stoner. New York: Dutton, 1930.

Cardano, Girolamo. *Liber de Ludo Aleae*. "*The Book on Games of Chance*." Trans. Sydney Henry Gould. Notes Oystein Ore. Rpt. in Oystein Ore. *Cardano, the Gambling Scholar*. Princeton: Princeton UP, 1953.

Cocles, Bartolommeo della Rocca. *A Brief and Most Pleasant Epitome of the Whole Art of Physiognomy, gathered out of Aristotle, Rasis, Formica, Loxius, Philemon, Palemon, Consiliator, Morbeth the Cardinal and others ... , by that learned chirurgeon Cocles*. Trans. Thomas Hill. London: John Wayland, 1556.

Cockerell, H. A. L., and Edwin Green. *The British Insurance Business: A Guide to Its History and Records*. 2nd ed. Sheffield, England: Sheffield Academic P, 1994.

De Roover, Raymond. *Gresham on Foreign Exchange: An Essay on Early English Mercantilism*. Cambridge: Harvard UP, 1949.

Einzig, Paul. *The History of Foreign Exchange*. London: Macmillan, 1962.

Ewald, François. "Insurance and Risk." *The Foucault Effect: Studies in Governmentality*. Ed. Graham Burchell, Colin Gordon, and Peter Miller. Chicago: U of Chicago P, 1991. 197–210.

Fitz, L. T. "Egyptian Queens and Male Reviewers: Sexist Attitudes in *Antony and Cleopatra* Criticism." *Shakespeare Quarterly* 28 (1977): 297-316.

Flavell, Kay. "Mapping Faces: National Physiognomies as Cultural Prediction." *Eighteenth-Century Life* 18 (1994): 8–22.

Hacking, Ian. *The Emergence of Probability*. Cambridge: Cambridge UP, 1975.

Indagine, J. "An Introduction to the Art of Physiognomy." In *Brief Introductions ... unto the Art of Chiromancy, or Manual Divination, and Physiognomy, ... whereunto is also annexed as well the Artificiall, as Natural Astrology*. Trans. Fabian Withers. London: 1558.

Muldrew, Craig. *The Economy of Obligation: The Culture of Credit and Social Relations in Early Modern England*. New York: St. Martin's, 1998.

Northbrooke, John. *A Treatise wherein Dicing, Dancing, Vain Plays, or Interludes ... are Reproved*. c. 1577. Rpt. in *Early Treatises on the Stage*. London: Bradbury and Evans, 1843. 1–188.

Schiesari, Juliana. "The Face of Domestication: Physiognomy, Gender Politics, and Humanism's Others." *Women, "Race," and Writing in the Early Modern Period*. Ed. Margo Hendricks and Patricia Parker. New York: Routledge, 1994. 55–70.

Shakespeare, William. *The Norton Shakespeare*. Ed. Stephen Greenblatt, Walter Cohen, Jean E. Howard, and Katharine Eisaman Maus. New York: Norton, 1997.

Sibbett, Trevor. "Early Insurance and the Royal Exchange." *The Royal Exchange*. Ed. Ann Saunders. London: London Topographical Society, 1997. 76–84.

Speed, John. *The Theater of the Empire of Great Britain*. 1611. Ed. John Arlott. 4 vols. London: Phoenix House, 1953–55.

Steppat, Michael. *Chances of Mischief: Variations of Fortune in Spenser*. Köln: Böhlau, 1990.

Strange, Susan. *Casino Capitalism*. Oxford, Basil Blackwell, 1986.

Supple, Barry. "Insurance in British History." *The Historian and the Business of Insurance*. Ed. Oliver M. Westall. Manchester: Manchester UP, 1984. 1–8.

Three Proclamations Concerning the Lottery for Virginia. Providence: John Carter Brown, 1907.

Wilson, Luke. "Monetary Compensation for Injuries to the Body, A.D. 602–1697." *Money and the Age of Shakespeare: Essays in the New Economic Criticism*. Ed. Linda Woodbridge. New York: Palgrave/St. Martin's, 2003. 19–37.

Wood, Thomas. "The Seventeenth Century English Casuists on Betting and Gambling." *The Church Quarterly Review* 149.298 (1950): 159–74.

8.
"Cloyless Sauce"
The Pleasurable Politics of Food in *Antony and Cleopatra*

PETER A. PAROLIN

The Antony and Cleopatra story has always been about food. Plutarch reports that Antony loved "to drinke like a good fellow with every body, to sit with the souldiers when they dine, and to eate and drinke with them souldierlike" (4); Cleopatra, he notes, produced in her first dinner for Antony "such passing sumptuous fare that no tongue can expresse it" (26). Together, they had a habit of "feasting ech other by turnes, and in cost, exceeding all measure and reason" (Plutarch 27). In early modern England, Thomas Elyot also interpreted Antony and Cleopatra in relation to food. Writing about the evils of intemperance, Elyot chooses Antony to exemplify vice: he "lyved in most prodigall riotte, and thinkyng all thinge in the see, the lande, and the ayre to be made for satisfienge his gloteny, he devoured all flesshe and fysshe that mought be anywhere founden" (2: 347). In contrast to Antony, Elyot cites Augustus Caesar as a model of sobriety who controlled his appetite because he knew "the inconveniences that alway do happen by ingurgitations and excessife fedinges" (2: 337). When Shakespeare wrote *Antony and Cleopatra*, then, he inherited a powerful tradition in which his characters were evaluated in relation to their attitudes toward food. Shakespeare exploits this tradition, using attitudes toward food not only to define characters but also to structure the play's political conflict and to suggest competing ideas about what constitutes value.

Incessantly eating and drinking, Antony and Cleopatra can be read in relation to Elizabethan and Jacobean ideas about food, drink, and consumption, as can Caesar, the Roman strongman who rigorously polices his own consumption and censures others for their self-indulgence. Furthermore, the frequent feasting in the Egyptian as opposed to the Roman scenes indicates that early modern attitudes toward food help shape the problematic East–West conflict in the play and the characters' own cultural positioning in regard to it.[1] The significance of food helps establish who will define the important relationships between East and West, Antony and Caesar, Antony and Cleopatra,

Cleopatra and Caesar, the past and the present, the present and the future. These are the central struggles in the play, and food plays a crucial role in elucidating them. The Romans, for example, see Antony and Cleopatra's sumptuous feasting as a decadent pursuit that demonstrates their unfitness to rule. Yet far from signifying only decadence, food in *Antony and Cleopatra* has significant creative potential. Through their relationship to food, Antony and Cleopatra work to replace Caesar's imperialist narrative. Exploiting the connection between food and pleasure, they construct a desirable alternative to Caesar's grim vision of political gain through self-denial. Their politics of food is a politics of pleasure; the play's perhaps unexpected gesture is to suggest that pleasure, consumption, and the exchange of food and drink should be recognized as legitimate tools for the construction of political and social meaning, rather than simply dismissed as too bodily, too hedonistic, or too eastern.

Often, critics read *Antony and Cleopatra* in precisely the opposite way, as a play about *un*-making, in which Antony's pleasures in Egypt threaten to undo such important constructions as masculinity, Roman military strength, and Antony's own heroism, not to mention the very possibility of stable identity itself.[2] Many of the characters in the play also emphasize declension: Philo invites an audience to see Antony as "the triple pillar of the world transformed / Into a strumpet's fool" (1.1.12–13);[3] Antony himself promises to "Let Rome in Tiber melt, and the wide arch / Of the ranged empire fall" (1.1.34–35); and Cleopatra decrees "Melt Egypt into Nile, and kindly creatures / Turn all to serpents" when she hears that Antony has married Octavia (2.5.77–78). This focus on dissolution reflects an antagonistic strain in early modern discourses of food, in which improper forms of eating were believed to dismantle identity. In *The Anatomy of Abuses*, for example, Philip Stubbes attacks the "dainty fare" of contemporary times, arguing that it literally degrades human nature: "I cannot perswade myself otherwise, but that our nicenes and curiousnes in dyet, hath altered our nature, distempered our bodies, and made us more subiect to millions of … diseases, then ever weare our forefathers subiect unto, and consequently of shorter life then they" (Stubbes J1r). For Stubbes, luxurious contemporary fare undermines the hardiness of earlier Englishmen; his hostility toward fine food finds its most typical expression in his abhorrence of the feeding body: "Who is sicklier then they, that fare deliciously every day? Who is corrupter? Who belcheth more, who looketh wursse, who is weaker, and feebler then they? Who hath more filthie colour, flegme and putrifaction (repleate with grosse humors) then they? And to be breef, who dyeth sooner then they?" (Stubbes J2v–J3r). The grotesque feeding body dulls the faculties that define character and dignify humanity. Attacking the gourmands of his day, Stubbes suggests that they are little better than animals; in fact, by evoking the specter of death, he seems to connect food more to the destruction than the sustenance of life.

In *Antony and Cleopatra*, Caesar, like Stubbes, cites food as an agent of degradation, referring to the orgies of consumption that he believes sap Antony's will to defend the triumvirs against their enemy Pompey: "From Alexandria / This is the news: he fishes, drinks, and wastes / The lamps of night in revel, is not more manlike / Than Cleopatra, nor the queen of Ptolemy / More womanly than he" (1.4.3–7). For Caesar, food degrades Antony by mastering him. Rather than exercising self-control, Antony subjects himself to his appetites, a move that marks his feminization and Egyptianization, the undoing of his Roman masculinity. In Caesar's account, Antony's past military greatness derived from his having denied himself the kind of sumptuous fare he now enjoys with Cleopatra. Recalling the aftermath of the Battle of Modena, Caesar fantasizes an Antony who was unperturbed even by famine:

> ... Thou didst drink
> The stale of horses and the gilded puddle
> Which beasts would cough at. Thy palate then did deign
> The roughest berry on the rudest hedge.
> Yea, like the stag when snow the pasture sheets,
> The barks of trees thou browsed. On the Alps
> It is reported thou didst eat strange flesh
> Which some did die to look on. And all this—
> It wounds thine honor that I speak it now—
> Was borne so like a soldier that thy cheek
> So much as lanked not. (1.4.62–72)

Caesar imagines, impossibly, that Antony was nourished by starvation: he may be eating tree bark and drinking puddle water, but he doesn't lose any weight—"thy cheek / So much as lanked not." In Caesar's narrative, the Antony who combats famine becomes a noble animal, the resourceful and self-sufficient stag, far from the swinish examples of degraded humanity found in Stubbes's discourse. Denied all superfluous foods, Antony emerges as his most heroic, most Roman self. Moreover, that earlier Antony stands as an implicit reproach to the current Antony who, by indulging his every appetite, makes himself as womanly and as Egyptian as Cleopatra, at least according to Caesar.

Caesar's image of a heroically self-denying Antony is of course not objective; rather it is a construct designed to celebrate Caesar's values at Antony's expense. In fact, the Antony Caesar praises resembles no one more than Caesar himself. It is Caesar, not Antony, who renounces both food and drink: at the feast on Pompey's barge, he says that "I had rather fast from all, four days, / Than drink so much in one" (2.7.102–03). If food and drink for Caesar represent loss of control through subjection to the body, his image of Antony on the mountaintop provides a roadmap for reasserting self-mastery.

Yet Caesar may not fully control his own discourse here: when he mentions that Antony ate "strange flesh / Which some did die to look on," his cryptic phrase raises the possibility that the idealized Antony was as transgressive an eater as the Antony who surfeits on Egyptian delicacies.[4] Antony's consumption of culturally strange foods, rather than being a sign of his Egyptian decadence, may in fact be a source of his *strength*, his ability to encounter the Other and to accommodate himself to difference rather than simply annihilating it.

Ironically, Antony often fails to see his appreciation of food as a source of strength. At crucial times in the play, he seems to internalize the Roman belief that he degrades himself through his feasting and his other pleasures in Egypt: "I must from this enchanting queen break off. / Ten thousand harms, more than the ills I know, / My idleness doth hatch" (1.2.135–37). Castigating himself for his idle pleasures, Antony denigrates those hedonistic pastimes, including feasting. When he sees Caesar's envoy Thidias kissing Cleopatra's hand, he flies into a rage that he expresses through the metaphor of food: "Have I my pillow left unpressed in Rome, / Forborne the getting of a lawful race, / And by a gem of women, to be abused / By one that looks on feeders?" (3.13.111–14). Referring to Thidias as a "feeder," Antony attacks his social standing as a subordinate who eats what his master supplies. As Ann Rosalind Jones and Peter Stallybrass note, the distribution of food to retainers was part of the early modern livery system that marked people's positions within the social hierarchy. Every time servants ate their masters' food, they would be inscribed as subordinates within the political and domestic order (Jones and Stallybrass 4).[5] In anger, Antony reproduces Roman attitudes that devalue food and discredit the pleasures of the moment, finding value only in what Linda Charnes has called Rome's characteristic "imperative to narrative production" (113).[6] Concerned primarily with dominance, this narrative imperative would focus on Antony as imperial master and disregard Thidias as a subordinate whose bodily needs make him a drag on the larger imperial project.

By calling Thidias a "feeder," Antony masterfully encapsulates into one insult his sense of the inappropriateness of Thidias kissing Cleopatra's hand. In the same scene, however, Antony's contemptuous attitude toward food rebounds, indicating an anxiety about his own status as Roman hero. Attacking Cleopatra as a piece of leftover food, he implicitly raises questions about himself and what it means to feed in Egypt: "I found you as a morsel cold upon / Dead Caesar's trencher—nay, you were a fragment / Of Cneius Pompey's, besides what hotter hours, / Unregistered in vulgar fame, you have / Luxuriously picked out" (3.13.121–25). Despite being on the offensive, Antony uneasily casts himself as a feeder: picking over the remains of what his precursors have already consumed, he seems a belated parasite. Antony's uneasiness is heightened by a slippage in his description of Cleopatra as food.[7]

She may start off as a dish to be eaten, but by the end of Antony's lines, she is a woman actively in control of her encounters with Roman men, luxuriously picking out the hot hours of their lovemaking. Throughout the play, Cleopatra's appetite for food figures her active sexual appetite. Here, then, Cleopatra easily shifts from being the morsel of food that Roman generals eat to being the devourer of those same generals; and if Cleopatra shifts in this way, then Antony, too, shifts from being the manly hero who consumes Cleopatra to being the effeminate Roman who is consumed by her. Antony's anger in this scene is thus a function of his fear that Cleopatra will destroy him.[8] Furthermore, Antony's fear of destruction is linked to his ideas about eating: for Antony, to think of himself eating is tantamount to thinking of himself being eaten. As was the case with Stubbes and Caesar, the dependence on food evokes an awareness of the body's vulnerability: to need food is to be subjected powerfully to the body and to mortality; it is to recognize the limits of one's own autonomy.[9]

Although the Roman characters in the play may evince hostility toward food, their motivated rhetoric is not the only available perspective; at other times, the play offers a more positive sense of the symbolic power of food. Instead of necessarily representing the breakdown of identity, food often represents the creative process of constructing it. Food is used positively in the play to assert relationships, values, and desires, and to shape the political power struggles between characters and cultures. Antony and Cleopatra in particular deploy the symbolic meanings of food in order to create their own desired identities, articulate their power and their allegiances, and trigger the performative mode that allows them to transform "this dungy earth" into a more precious realm (1.1.36). In the process, they underscore the fact that many of the transformations in the play are positive acts of making that, despite the tragic ending, provide alternative social and political values in the face of Caesar's monolithic ideals. Although the play does express anxieties about the possible unmaking of valued categories and identities, it also points to new acts of making, to the recognition that meaning and value are in flux, and to the possibility that people can build the world that they desire. The play's emphasis on food offers a window into precisely those creative acts by which characters attempt to fashion and give meaning to social life.

Using food to construct meaning, *Antony and Cleopatra* draws on a deep cultural understanding that food exudes significance at all social levels. Laden with symbolic power, food forms, in effect, a language that expresses cultural and individual identity.[10] In the sixteenth century, the English, in many ways marginal among the peoples of Europe, responded to their lack of international standing by using food to prove they were just as civilized as any of their rivals. Thus when Henry VIII hosted a great feast for the Emperor Maximilian in 1517, one of the guests, the Venetian ambassador, was impressed not only with the food but also with what it implied about England's cultural standing: "Every imaginable sort of meat known in the kingdom was served, and fish, too, including prawn pasties of perhaps twenty different kinds, made in the shapes of castles, and of animals of different kinds, as beautiful as can be imagined. In short, the wealth and civilization of the world are here, and those who call the English barbarians seem to me to make themselves barbarians" (qtd. in Ridley 216). *The wealth and civilization of the world are here*: the ambassador undoubtedly refers to the great cost of the feast but he also emphasizes the artistic refashioning of foodstuffs into the shape of beautiful castles and exotic animals: the food serves as a *representation* of the world's resources and, in so doing, it proves the English skill at representation, or cultural making.

Not only does food define cultural sophistication, but it also defines social distinctions in Shakespeare's world. Aristocrats ate, or at least put on their tables, huge quantities of food as a token of conspicuous consumption so that they could display their power to command, consume, and waste more food in one meal than many people might see in a whole year. In 1527, for example, instructions were drafted for appropriate meals for Henry Fitzroy, Duke of Richmond, the six-year-old illegitimate son of Henry VIII. The menu for his dinner included a first course of soup, supplemented with beef or mutton, goose or swan, veal, capons, and biscuit. The second course consisted of more soup, four roast rabbits, fourteen pigeons, four partridges and pheasants, fruit and biscuits, as well as copious amounts of wine and ale. This menu was for the young Duke alone; the rest of his household had its own smaller allotments that were determined according to the individual's position within the household's hierarchy (qtd. in Ridley 216–17). Food reflected rank within the Duke's household, and it also revealed distinctions between an aristocratic household and other households that could never obtain such ingredients or produce such meals. The degree to which food not only reflected but also created and policed class boundaries can be seen in the sumptuary laws that specified what individuals could consume depending upon their position in the social order. In the 1540s, the Archbishop of Canterbury issued an order prescribing what food clergy could eat and not eat. Meant to curb gluttony in the church, the order also preserved hierarchical distinctions, for example, allowing an archbishop six services of meat or fish at dinner while a bishop could have only five (Ridley 212).

While food defined hierarchy in elite households, the burgeoning publication of cookbooks encouraged middle-class readers, too, to define themselves in relation to food.[11] In *The English Housewife*, Gervase Markham identifies food preparation as one way that a housewife can establish the excellence of her household. We can speculate on the cultural impact of this idea based on the enormous popularity of *The English Housewife*, which went through three editions in Markham's lifetime (1615, 1623, and 1631), and numerous subsequent editions (1637, 1638, 1651, and 1658). Significantly,

Markham advises the housewife to use food not only for nutritional value but also for artistic show. One of his recipes, in fact, tells how to make "Sallats for Shew only":

> Now for Sallats for shewe only and the adorning and setting out of a table with numbers of dishes; they bee those which are made of Carret roots of sundrie colours well boiled and cut into many shapes and proportions, as some into knots, some in the manner of Scutchions and Armes, some like Birds, and some like wilde beasts, according to the art and cunning of the workman. (Markham, *English Hus-wife* 42)

Although Markham is not explicit, these decorative salads, carefully molded into all kinds of ornamental shapes, clearly serve to display the artistic skill of the person who prepares them. Through her salads for show only, the housewife can attain the status of an artistic and cunning workman; in this way, food provides an arena in which even a middle-class woman can have access to cultural expression. The decorative salad also suggests the way in which cookbooks allowed their middle-class readership to aspire to the same culinary habits as the more elite members of society. For one thing, the decorative salad displays the middling family's ability to waste food, just like the aristocrats did. It should be noted, however, that Markham's decorative salad reproduces aristocratic habits with a difference since the food wasted is not an extravagant kind of fish, flesh, or fowl but the humble and easily available carrot root.

Markham's popularization of aristocratic eating habits continues in his instructions for the preparation of a "great feast," where quantity, variety, and ornamentality are all on display. Calling for a variety of dishes to please guests' eyes, he recognizes that the feast is as much a visual as a gustatory experience. He prescribes a multiplicity of different courses, including salads, fricassees, boiled meats, roasted meats, baked meats, wild fowl, land fowl, hot baked meats, and cold baked meats, with candied dishes and fish as filler for empty spaces. Again, Markham stresses the visual dimension of the feast, specifying that the food must be displayed "extravagantly about the table" (Markham, *English Housewife* 122). Although he acknowledges that these instructions are for a princely feast rather than the more humble feasts that most people could reasonably prepare, Markham still offers these guidelines to a middle-class readership. In the process he stimulates their desire to use food, particularly the banquet, to define themselves as experts in the art of enhancing life, as hosts who have just as much power as their social superiors to defy the seasons and assemble a banquet that could only be found in art and not nature. Interestingly, Markham's discussion of the great feast first appeared in the 1623 edition of *The English Housewife*. In the 1615 edition, this section of the text was absent, with Markham moving from advice on the

"Ordering of Banquets" (sweets) to a section on "divers conceited secrets" pertaining to the making of perfumes, musk balls, and vinegar. By adding the section on great feasts, Markham may have been registering the fact that middle-class households were increasingly interested in learning about the culinary habits of the wealthy, even if they lacked the resources to imitate those habits themselves. If food was an important tool in the construction of individual and cultural identity, then upwardly aspiring readers did not want to be left behind.

Exploiting the creative potential of food evident in early modern culture, *Antony and Cleopatra* most often figures food as a tool that builds rather than demolishes identities and relationships. For example, Enobarbus reports that when Antony first invited Cleopatra to supper, "She replied / It should be better he became her guest, / Which she entreated. Our courteous Antony, / Whom ne'er the word of 'No' woman heard speak, / Being barbered ten times o'er, goes to the feast / And for his ordinary pays his heart / For what his eyes eat only" (2.2.230–36). Perhaps from the Roman perspective this meal-centered courtship would exemplify Antony's degrading subjection to Cleopatra. But from Cleopatra's perspective, it can be seen as a moment of culinary diplomacy that allows her to establish a relationship with Antony on her own terms, a relationship in which she is the host and provider so that Antony must try to please her at least as much as the other way around. Furthermore, by establishing a relationship with Antony, Cleopatra connects herself to the Roman power structure and seeks to gain some influence over Roman policy toward Egypt.[12]

Even from Antony's perspective, the initial meal with Cleopatra can be seen as politically successful. Over the course of the play, Antony's power is always contingent upon his distance from Caesar. Antony asserts that his pleasure lies in Egypt, but his power lies there too: through his connection with Cleopatra, Antony establishes Alexandria as a kind of competing capital to Rome, and he builds his power there through alliances with a huge array of eastern kings. Coppélia Kahn suggests that Antony's "genuine fascination with Cleopatra notwithstanding, she also serves as an alibi for gaining the distance from Caesar that he seeks in order to excel him" (114). That first supper with Cleopatra, then, establishes a relationship that is saturated with political meaning for Antony; he is not simply a fish on Cleopatra's hook, as the Romans would see him, but is also positioning himself politically when he accepts her invitation to dinner.

The metaphor of Antony as fish is especially relevant because it accentuates the artful ways in which Cleopatra mingles food and eros to advance her political strategies. When she imagines fishing, she also envisions a sexual and political challenge to Antony: "My bended hook shall pierce / Their slimy jaws, and as I draw them up / I'll think every one an Antony / And say 'Aha! You're caught' " (2.5.12–15). Charmian then reminds her of an actual fishing expedition with Antony, and, in particular, of the trick whereby Cleopatra had a diver hang a salt fish on Antony's hook. The fishing references have a clear sexual valence, with Cleopatra wielding phallic power, but they also signify politically. The salt fish incident is yet one more of Cleopatra's challenges to Antony to commit himself to Egypt over Rome. The salt fish—dry, wizened, dead—represents the imagined poverty and asceticism of Roman life and politics: when Antony pulls it out of the water instead of the plump, slimy, live, squirming fish he imagines he has on his line, he confronts one possible version of himself and his allegiances: a dried-out servant of Caesar's Rome rather than the fully embodied master of his own political destiny. The night of drinking, laughter, and crossdressing that follows the fish trick suggests that Antony answers Cleopatra's challenge by committing himself to an Egyptian mode of politics that is inseparable from pleasure.

Although Antony and Cleopatra's mode of politics depends on pleasure, it is also deeply invested in questions of power—how to get it and how to preserve it. The Romans err when they see Antony and Cleopatra's feasting and revelry as antithetical to the serious business of politics. Pompey is mistaken to expect that Antony's culinary hedonism in Egypt will keep him away from the theater of war in Italy: "Mark Antony / In Egypt sits at dinner," Pompey confidently asserts, "and will make / No wars without doors" (2.1.11–13). He imagines that Cleopatra will "Tie up the libertine in a field of feasts; / Keep his brain fuming," and he hopes that "Epicurean cooks" will "Sharpen with cloyless sauce his appetite, / That sleep and feeding may prorogue his honor / Even till a Lethe'd dullness" (2.1.23–27). Here Pompey uses "cloyless" in the *OED*'s sense of something that "does not cloy or satiate," with "cloy" meaning "[T]o overload with food, so as to cause loathing." For Pompey, the cloylessness of the Egyptian sauce engages Antony in such an endless quest to sate his physical appetites that he will never bother to appear on the battlefield. However, the play repeatedly shows that Antony is at his most political when he is eating. The cloyless sauce thus keeps him hungry, sharp, and politically aware. He does return to Rome, after all, to deal with Pompey and forge an alliance with Caesar, despite his feasting in Egypt. Far from being a political narcotic, the cloyless sauce represents food's seemingly infinite ability to be put to political uses.

Aware of food's strategic potential, Antony uses it as a tool in his diplomacy. Not only does he establish relations with Cleopatra over their first meal, but he also evokes food to assuage Caesar's anger after he insults Caesar's messenger. Antony explains, "He fell upon me ere admitted, then; / Three kings I had newly feasted, and did want / Of what I was i'th'morning" (2.2.80–82). Here Antony masterfully uses food to explain away a slight to Caesar, implying that his feasting helped him solidify Rome's diplomatic links to the kings of Africa. Yet one cannot help but suspect that Antony's diplomacy was also personal and that the kings he feasted would later be among those who serve in his coalition against Caesar.

Extravagant consumption, so easily read as mere self-indulgence, is thus revealed to be an essential feature of elite politics. When Enobarbus describes life in Egypt to his friends in Rome, it is clear that Antony and Cleopatra flaunt their political domination by the vast amounts of food that they consume. Maecenas asks, "Eight wild boars roasted whole at a breakfast, and but twelve persons there. Is this true?" "This was but as a fly by an eagle," responds Enobarbus, "We had much more monstrous matter of feast, which worthily deserved noting" (2.2.189–93). In a feast like this, Antony and Cleopatra would be using food much as the elites of Shakespeare's own day did: as a means of conspicuous consumption meant to amazed their guests as well as the nonparticipants who, like Maecenas, would later be amazed by stories of what was eaten and what was wasted. In fact, as H. Neville Davies points out, James I laid out spectacular feasts in honor of the visit to England of his brother-in-law, Christian IV of Denmark, in the summer of 1606, perhaps less than a year before the first performance of *Antony and Cleopatra*. At one feast in particular, Christian was impressed with the lavishness and ingenuity of his host in providing a full banquet on board the English ship *Elizabeth Jonas*:

> The dinner was furnished with all kinds of daintie provision, in such abdoun-dant manner that the King of Denmarke marveyled where such store of meate should be dressed: and to see the manner of it, his Majestie tooke occasion, after dinner, to goe upon a spacious gallarie made upon lighters betweene the two Royall shippes, the Elizabeth Jonas and the White Beare, neere which two shippes ridde a great hulke, which was furnished with ovens for baked meates; and had in it three faire ranges to roast with; all which his Majestie in person saw. (Roberts 2: 83)

For Christian, the spectacular shipboard meal clearly enhanced the prestige of the host who provided it; the technology that enabled the meal was also worth investigating, perhaps for Christian's own future reference. And as with the sumptuous breakfast referred to in *Antony and Cleopatra*, the feasts that James produced for Christian were meant to impress more than just the one central guest. Just as Enobarbus narrates the story of the meal to astonish his Roman listeners, so James's chronicler, Henry Robarts, boosted the king's reputation by publishing two descriptions of the dinner. Robarts encouraged "all true subjects" to "note, and noting, imprint in our hearts, the rare and honorable love of his Majestie shewed to the person of his Royall Brother King of Denmarke, betweene whose loves there may be no comparison" (Roberts 2: 77). A great political feast is like an act of theater: it requires an audience.

Like James feasting Christian, Antony and Cleopatra use their relation-ship to food to make others see them on their own terms. Through food, they construct images of themselves as powerful, generous, larger-than-life figures, images designed to ensure the loyalty of their followers even when it becomes clear that Caesar is going to win the war. During the battle scenes, for example, Antony's repeated references to sharing food and wine with his followers serve two related purposes: they establish him as the source of his men's good, and they suggest that he is lifting his men up to an imagined parity with himself in their communal eating and drinking. Of his captains he says, "Tonight I'll force / The wine peep through their scars" (3.13.195–96); later he proclaims "Let's tonight / Be bounteous at our meal" (4.2.9–10); and finally, referring to his entire army, he maintains "Had our great palace the capacity / To camp this host, we all would sup together / And drink carouses to the next day's fate" (4.8.32–34). On the level of ideology, Antony's dream of fraternizing with his soldiers over a meal solidifies his desired version of himself, negating Caesar's earlier slur that he keeps "the turn of tippling with a slave" and "stand[s] the buffet / With knaves that smells of sweat" (1.4.19; 20–21). In his desire to feast his army, Antony expresses his own generosity and imaginatively remakes his footsoldiers as his peers. The insistent image of extravagant feeding thus contributes to the political image of a bounteous Antony who cares for his followers and defies the seemingly inexorable tide of history.

The image of an ever-generous Antony persists in Cleopatra's spectacular eulogy in which she attempts to transform military defeat into transcendent victory. By positing an Antony who is almost a synecdoche for the bounty of the natural world, Cleopatra implicitly ascribes to him a power that dwarfs Caesar's: "For his bounty, / There was no winter in't; an autumn 'twas / That grew the more by reaping" (5.2.85–87). Just as Caesar earlier floated the impossible image of an Antony who flourished by denying himself food, here Cleopatra circulates the opposite but equally impossible image of an Antony who endlessly generates bounty. Transforming Antony rhetorically, Cleopatra echoes the rhetoric of cookbook authors, who claimed an artistic power to refashion the world through their culinary skills. In Markham, for example, the preparer of great feasts ignores the limitations of nature: Refusing to "hold limitation with [the host's] provision, and the season of the year," this master cook juxtaposes ingredients that in nature do not coexist (Markham, *English Housewife* 123). Whereas the humble table is limited by the seasons, great feasts are not. Cleopatra traffics in great feasts, literally and metaphorically. Implicitly recalling the figure of the banquet-maker, she uses artful rhetoric to refashion the human Antony, limited by defeat and mortality, into an infinite nourisher.

The analogy between the creative power of the cook and the artist frequently appears in early modern cookbooks. *The Queen's Closet Open'd* (1668) promises strategies for "preserving the Fruits of the Earth with such a curious neatness, as if it would shew, that though Summer gave those pleasant Fruits, yet that Art is able to make Winter richer then her self" (A3v). Here the promise to transform winter reprises Cleopatra's effort to cancel Antony's winter altogether. In both cases the transformation is artistic, just as, in *Delights for Ladies* (1608), Hugh Plat asserts the cook's artistic ability to re-create the transitory world in lasting form. His epistle to his readers, "To all true Lovers of Arte and knowledge," begins modestly but proceeds to extravagant claims:

> I teach both frutes and flowers to preserve,
> And candie them, so Nutmegs, cloves, and mace,
> To make both marchpane paste, and sugred plate,
> And cast the same in formes of sweetest grace,
> Each bird and foul so moulded from the life,
> And after cast in sweete compounds of arte,
> As if the flesh and forme which nature gave,
> Did still remaine in everie lim and part,
> When crystal frosts have nipt the tender grape,
> And cleane consum'd the fruits of everie vine,
> Yet here behold the clusters fresh and faire,
> Fed from the branch, or hanging on the line,
> The walnut, small nut, and the chesnut sweete,
> Whose sugred kernels lose their pleasing taste,
> And here from yeere to yeere preserved,
> Are made by arte with strongest fruites to last. (A2r–A3v)

Steeped in the language of artistic creativity, Plat's epistle positions the cook as a maker who can outdo Nature: the birds whose natural forms decay can be preserved through the art of cookery; the frozen grape can be made fresh again; and the tasteless nuts can be made savory. For the authors of cuisinary guides, cooks improve the world they find. Antony and Cleopatra's affinity for food and feasting puts them in conversation with early modern cookbooks, enabling them to appropriate on a political level the kind of transformative power that cookbook authors assign to cooks.

The enormous power in acts of artistic transformation appears most clearly in Philip Sidney's discussion of the poet's ability to remake the world. Positing that the poet is the only artist who can dispense with natural laws, Sidney partakes of the same logic that the cookbook authors follow and that Antony and Cleopatra exploit:

> There is no Arte delivered to mankinde that hath not the workes of Nature for his principall object, without which they could not consist, and on which they so depend, as they become Actors and Players, as it were, of what Nature will have set foorth .... Only the Poet, disdayning to be tied to any such subjection, lifted up with the vigor of his owne invention, dooth growe

in effect another nature, in making things either better then Nature bringeth
forth, or, quite a newe, formes such as never were in Nature. (23–24)

In his aggressive poetics, Sidney insists on the poet's power to depict the
world as it might be or ought to be, free from any subjection to natural laws.[13]
Similarly, cookbook authors define the cook as someone who dispenses with
natural limitations to make new realities. The poet and the banquet-maker,
disdaining subjection to Nature, share qualities with Antony and Cleopatra,
who disdain subjection to Caesar and the political realities that he represents.
All of these figures amass power by refusing to accept the inevitability of the
world as it is. Antony and Cleopatra challenge Caesar's victory even when it
seems most complete. Together, they overturn the assumptions of Caesar's
realpolitik and assert an alternative vision. Whereas Caesar posits politics and
pleasure as antithetical, Antony and Cleopatra create a politics that depends
on pleasure in order to propose that the world need not be as they find it but
rather as they make it.

If, as Janet Adelman says, "The taking in of food is the primary acknowl-
edgement of one's dependence on the world," then a politics that is significantly
based on food will always contain, even foreground, a measure of vulnerability (152). Antony and Cleopatra continually signal vulnerability and need
through their repeated eating and drinking. By contrast, Caesar strives for an
austere politics of self-denial that would mask all evidence of need. In place of
vulnerability, Caesar asserts inevitability: it seems a given in the play that Caesar and Antony will fight and that Caesar will win. As Antony himself admits,
"The very dice obey him, / And in our sports my better cunning faints / Under
his chance" (2.3.32–34). Whereas Antony urges flexibility—"Be a child o'th'-
time," Caesar insists on mastery: "Possess it" (2.7.101). Whereas Antony
depends on wine, Caesar is threatened by it; indeed, when Antony encourages
him to drink more, he replies, "It's monstrous labor when I wash my brain / And
it grows fouler" (2.7.99–100).[14] Caesar knows that his political strength lies in
denying the vulnerability that subjection to food and drink represents, so he
declines Antony's offer. Refusing to engage with Antony on Antony's terms,
Caesar in effect denies the legitimacy of Antony's political mode.

Yet even though Caesar wins the military battles, his politics of
inevitability come into question at the end of the play in a contest that is once
again envisioned in relation to food. After Antony's death, Caesar is desperate
to parade the Queen of Egypt in Rome as part of his triumphal homecoming;
without her presence, his victory will be incomplete. At this moment of his
own need, Caesar chooses to put food to political use. "Feed and sleep," he
says to Cleopatra, "Our care and pity is so much upon you / That we remain
your friend" (5.2.186–88). By offering Cleopatra food, Caesar tries to establish a friendly relationship that would prevent her suicide. But, in this instance,
Cleopatra, previously so willing to eat and drink, rejects the comfort of food.

Instead she focuses on the degradation awaiting her in Rome: imagining the plebeians clamoring around her, she contemptuously says "In their thick breaths, / Rank of gross diet, shall we be enclouded / And forced to drink their vapor" (5.2.210–12). For Cleopatra, feeding has here become force-feeding, a sign of her subjection not only to Caesar but also to common Romans whose "gross diet" marks their social inferiority. Whereas access to food has always enabled Cleopatra's agency and artistry, now, coming from Caesar, it confirms her *loss* of agency. Therefore, just as she did with Antony at their first meeting, Cleopatra refuses the offer of food. Caesar wants Cleopatra (and by extension the world) to know "How honourable and how kindly we / Determine for her," but she declines to help him portray himself as a generous conqueror (5.1.58–59). As she did with Antony, Cleopatra controls this moment in part through her response to food. As for Caesar, the act of using food to try to build a relationship, so characteristic of Antony and Cleopatra's strategies, shows that even a seemingly self-sufficient politics must take account of need.

In the end, Antony and Cleopatra succeed in creating an alternative to Caesar's monolithic imperial narrative. By engaging so consistently in acts of consumption, they establish material pleasures as a source of social and political value. Through their feasting, they imaginatively transform the conventional understanding of value by intensely engaging with the world. Their method partakes of the logic of artistic production; in fact, it is akin to Shakespeare's own model of theatrical production, in which the creation of meaning is understood to be collaborative, contingent, and resolutely material. In *Antony and Cleopatra*, the production and consumption of food is just such a process. Collaborative, social, and performative, it engages the imagination and generates multiple possibilities concerning what constitutes value. Despite their deaths, Antony and Cleopatra achieve a considerable victory by asserting ideas about what matters in the world, ideas that compete with Caesar's both within and beyond the space of the theater.

NOTES

I thank Susan Frye for astute comments on several versions of this paper. I also am grateful to Leigh Edwards, Vicki Lindner, Cedric Reverand, and Amy Tigner for their generous advice and to Sara Deats for her valuable editorial suggestions.

1. The East–West binary structure poses one of the most difficult critical problems in the play. The task for critics is not to accept this structure as a natural feature of the play's political world, but rather to explore the constructedness of what Cynthia Marshall has called "binarism's perfect couple" (386).
2. Laura Levine, for example, titles her excellent chapter on the play, "*Antony and Cleopatra* and the Story of the Dissolving Warrior." Levine rightly argues that Cleopatra's Egyptian theatricality threatens a Roman ideal of essential heroism; I would simply stress that the dissolution associated with the East–West binary

structure should not obscure the fact that there is also a dynamic of creativity at work in the play.

3. Quotations from *Antony and Cleopatra* use John Wilders's Arden edition. Quotations from other Shakespeare plays use *The Norton Shakespeare*, ed. Stephen Greenblatt et al.

4. Janet Adelman says that Caesar's phrase "invokes the presence of the bizarre, even the tabooed" (180).

5. Jones and Stallybrass observe, "Livery acted as the medium through which the social system marked bodies so as to associate them with particular institutions. The power to give that marking to subordinates affirmed social hierarchy" (5).

6. Aligning Rome with "the narrative 'imperative,'" Charnes refers to strategies of power, "the political, territorial, and ultimately subjective appropriation that is always the hidden (and not so hidden) aim of narrative forms of reproduction" (107). Charnes suggests that, by contrast, "the appeal of Egypt" lies in "the way it seems to supplant purposeful time with pleasurable space and all the seductions of the 'imaginary'" (114). I would stress that the Egyptian pleasures can be just as "purposeful" as the narrative production that characterizes Rome.

7. In the play's sustained conflation of food and sex, Cleopatra is frequently figured as food: Enobarbus refers to her as Antony's "Egyptian dish" (2.6.128), and Cleopatra accepts this designation, referring to herself as "a morsel for a monarch" (1.5.32); in the scene with Thidias, however, Antony debases the language of food, turning a morsel into something stale and unappetizing, in order to degrade Cleopatra.

8. Antony is fully aware of how vulnerable he is to Cleopatra should she strike a deal with Caesar: "To the boy Caesar send this grizzled head, / And he will fill thy wishes to the brim / With principalities" (3.13.17–19).

9. The implicit linking of food and death also appears in Coriolanus. Resolutely denying his own physical needs, Coriolanus scorns the plebeians for their hunger: "Hang 'em. / They said they were an-hungry, sighed forth proverbs— / That hunger broke stone walls, that dogs must eat, / That meat was made for mouths, that the gods sent not / Corn for the rich men only" (1.1.193–97). Moments later, Coriolanus conflates these feeders with the food to be consumed, in a rhetorical move like Antony's. "Go get you home, you fragments," he says to the citizens, with fragments being, of course, bits of food (1.1.212). Referring to the plebeians as food, Coriolanus, like Antony, implies that to need food is to become food, to be ready to be eaten, to be always on the verge of disappearing.

10. See Gerald and Valerie Mars, who read food cultures as positive forums in which people define their humanity: "[H]uman cultures, unlike animal groupings, have everywhere loaded, encrusted, and elaborated upon the biological need to eat with socially derived and culturally validated rituals and symbolic repertoires" (12).

11. Kim Hall argues that cookbooks became a crucial site for mediating between domestic and foreign products in middle-class households. On the link between cookbooks and women's emerging role as authors in the public sphere, see Janet Theophano.

12. Ania Loomba claims that "The recurrent food imagery reinforces [Cleopatra's] primitive appeal" (78). While Loomba is considering Roman attitudes, it is impor-

tant to add that the perspective of the Romans is not that of the play, which shows Cleopatra's *strategic* use of food, thus underscoring her sophistication.

13. For *Antony and Cleopatra* in relation to Sidney's poetics, see Phyllis Rackin, esp. 206.

14. For the sources of Caesar's fear in this scene, see John Michael Archer, 157.

WORKS CITED

Adelman, Janet. *Suffocating Mothers: Fantasies of Maternal Origin in Shakespeare's Plays,* Hamlet *to* The Tempest. New York: Routledge, 1992.

Archer, John Michael. "Antiquity and Degeneration in *Antony and Cleopatra.*" *Race, Ethnicity, and Power in the Renaissance.* Ed. Joyce Green MacDonald. Madison: Farleigh Dickinson UP, 1997. 145–54.

Charnes, Linda. *Notorious Identity: Materializing the Subject in Shakespeare.* Cambridge: Harvard UP, 1993.

Davies, H. Neville. "Jacobean *Antony and Cleopatra.*" *Shakespeare Studies* 17 (1985): 123–58.

Elyot, Thomas. *The Boke Named the Governour.* 2 vols. 1531. Ed. Henry H. S. Croft. 1883. New York: Burt Franklin, 1967.

Fitz, Linda. "Egyptian Queens and Male Reviewers: Sexist Attitudes in *Antony and Cleopatra* Criticism." *Shakespeare Quarterly* 28 (1977): 297–316.

Greenblatt, Stephen, et al. eds., *The Norton Shakespeare.* New York: Norton, 1997.

Hall, Kim. "Culinary Spaces, Colonial Spaces: The Gendering of Sugar in the Seventeenth Century." *Feminist Readings of Early Modern Culture: Emerging Subjects.* Ed. Valerie Traub, M. Lindsay Kaplan, and Dympna Callaghan. Cambridge: Cambridge UP, 1996. 168–90.

Jones, Ann Rosalind, and Peter Stallybrass. *Renaissance Clothing and the Materials of Memory.* Cambridge: Cambridge UP, 2001.

Kahn, Coppélia. *Roman Shakespeare: Warriors, Wounds, and Women.* London: Routledge, 1997.

Levine, Laura. *Men in Women's Clothing: Anti-theatricality and Effeminization: 1579–1642.* Cambridge: Cambridge UP, 1994.

Loomba, Ania. *Gender, Race, Renaissance Drama.* Delhi: Oxford UP, 1989.

Markham, Gervase. *The English Hus-wife.* London, 1615.

———. *The English Housewife.* Ed. Michael R. Best. Montreal: McGill-Queen's UP, 1986.

Mars, Gerald, and Valerie Mars. Introduction. *Food, Culture, and History.* Ed. Gerald Mars and Valerie Mars. Vol. 1. The London Food Seminar, 1993.

Marshall, Cynthia. "Man of Steel Done Got the Blues: Melancholic Subversion of Presence in *Antony and Cleopatra.*" *Shakespeare Quarterly* 44 (1993): 385–408.

Plat, Hugh. *Delights for Ladies.* London, 1608.

Plutarch. *Lives of the Noble Grecians and Romanes.* Trans. Sir Thomas North. 1579. Ed. George Wyndham. 1896. New York: AMS Press, 1967.

The Queen's Closet Open'd. London, 1668.

Rackin, Phyllis. "Shakespeare's Boy Cleopatra, the Decorum of Nature, and the Golden World of Poetry." *PMLA* 87 (1972): 201–12.

Ridley, Jasper. *The Tudor Age.* Woodstock: The Overlook P, 1990.

Robarts, Henry. "England's Farewell to Christian the Fourth. 1608." *The Progresses of James the First*. Comp. John Nicholls. Vol 2. London, 1828. 75–85.

Shakespeare, William. *Antony and Cleopatra*. Ed. John Wilders. London: Routledge, 1995.

Sidney, Philip. *A Defence of Poetry*. 1585. Ed. J. A. Van Dorsten. Oxford: Oxford UP, 1966.

Stubbes, Philip. *The Anatomie of Abuses*. 1583. New York: Jonson Reprint Co., 1972.

Theophano, Janet. *Eat My Words: Reading Women's Lives Through the Cookbooks They Wrote*. New York: St. Martin's, 2002.

9.
Cleopatra and the Myth of Scota

LISA HOPKINS

Shakespeare's Cleopatra has passed into legend for the variety and evocativeness of the descriptions applied to her by the other characters in the play,
but it has been widely overlooked that the first term used to describe her is
"gypsy,"[1] when Philo says of Antony that,

> His captain's heart,
> Which in the scuffles of great fights hath burst
> The buckles on his breast, reneges all temper,
> And is become the bellows and the fan
> To cool a gypsy's lust. (1.1.5–10)

Later, Antony himself laments,

> O this false soul of Egypt! This grave charm,
> Whose eye becked forth my wars, and called them home,
> Whose bosom was my crownet, my chief end,
> Like a right gypsy hath at fast and loose
> Beguiled me to the very heart of loss. (4.12.25–29)

As Charles Whitney points out,

> Fast and loose was a gypsy game first described as involving disappearing
> knots in a handkerchief, but in fact all of Antony's characterizations of
> Cleopatra between the final defeat in battle and the report of Cleopatra's
> suicide to him ... could be said by one claiming to be the victim of an
> English gypsy. (83)

Equally suggestive of a gypsy identity for Cleopatra is the way in which the
soothsayer accurately predicts the future during the fortune-telling scene in

1.2, while the revelation by Cleopatra's steward that she has kept back more than half her treasure suggests that she has in effect done a gypsy switch (5.2.165ff.).

Public perception of gypsies and their meanings in the early seventeenth century is, I want to argue, therefore crucial to Shakespeare's representations of his female hero and to the meanings of the play as a whole. Shakespeare gives prominence to the idea of gypsies, I shall suggest, because gypsies were both disreputable and also particularly associated with Scotland, and *Antony and Cleopatra*—like, I think, the contemporaneous *Macbeth*—sneakily incriminates Scotland. To the same end, I argue, Shakespeare also draws on images of Irishness and of freemasonry, both of which were associated with Scotland and the lower classes and, like gypsies, thought to have their origins in Egypt, something of which Shakespeare is able to make use in his representation of the Egyptian setting of the play. At the same time, though, Shakespeare seeks not only to satirize Scottishness but to recuperate a suitably inspiring form of Englishness, and, paradoxically, he finds this also in Egypt, because he is able to draw on the already well-established tradition of associating Cleopatra with Elizabeth I, particularly in terms of opposing the biblical mode of allusion, which was frequently used to characterize Elizabeth I, against the classical mode which Shakespeare (and others of his age) identified with Scotland. This, I suggest, accounts for some of the slippery ambiguity and changeableness that characterizes the Egypt of the play.

Awareness of gypsies was well established in early modern England. As early as 1547, Andrew Boorde, in his *The Fyrst Boke of the Introduction of Knowledge*, had attempted to describe Gypsy culture and included samples of Romany. In particular, the idea that gypsies were in fact Egyptians was strongly developed. The acts passed against gypsies in 1544, 1554, and 1562 were all titled Egyptians Acts, and in Jonson's *The Gypsies Metamorphosed*, the Gypsy says of the five little children that he leads, "Gaze vppon them as on the ofspringe of *Ptolomee*, begotten vppon seuerall *Cleopatra's* in theire seuerall Counties" (Jonson 7.567). Gypsies were "said to be physiologically distinct by virtue of their tawny complexion, and it was commented that they wore 'od and phantastique' clothes that were 'contrary to other nacions' " (Mayall).

However, although antigypsy legislation stresses the foreignness of gypsies to English ethnicities and practices, other aspects of seventeenth-century thought about gypsies brought them eerily close to home. In England, national self-esteem was boosted by continued clinging to the myth that the kings of Britain were originally descended from Brutus, great-grandson of Aeneas, via King Arthur. However, just across the border, in the homeland of England's new king, Scottish writers had attempted to counter the ideological force of the Anglo-Welsh Brutus/Trojan myth by promulgating a very different myth. For John of Fordun, and many who came after him, "the progenitors of the Scottish race were a Greek prince named Gathelus (the Greeks did after all defeat the Trojans!) and the eponymous Scota, daughter of Pharaoh" (Mason 64).

This idea of Egyptian origins meant that the Scottish attitude to gypsies was markedly different from the English one. Gypsies are first recorded in Scotland in 1505 and are said to have made their way thence to England with letters of recommendation from both James IV and James V. Both of these kings' belief in the Scota story certainly led them to be noticeably progypsy, and gypsies had been allowed to live under their own laws in Scotland since 1540, although antigypsy laws were passed there in 1541, and in 1573, they were ordered to desist from a nomadic lifestyle or leave Scotland. The climate was slightly less favorable under James VI and I (Macritchie 72–73; see also Randall 55), but the connection between Scottishness and gypsiness is still being openly made as late as *The Gypsies Metamorphosed*, in which the Prologue spoken at Windsor included the lines:

> As many blessings as there be bones
> In *Ptolomees* fingers, and all at ones,
> Held vp in an *Andrews* Crosse for the nones,
>   Light on you, good Master. (7.566)

Here the fingers of the Ptolemies mix headily with the cross of St Andrew, symbol of Scotland. The alleged connection was also evoked in the context of James VI and I's accession to the throne of England: Andrew Melville mentions the Gathelus legend in his *A trewe description of the nobill race of the Stewards* (Edinburgh, 1603).

Whatever James himself may have thought about the matter, then, Scottishness was inescapably associated with the gypsies, and I think that this idea is drawn on in Shakespeare's play as a way of covertly and subtly embarrassing the king. There are unmistakable signs in *Antony and Cleopatra* of an interest in Scotland, as when Cleopatra in her jealousy of Octavia orders, "Bid you Alexas/Bring me word how tall she is" (2.5.118–19), which has often been identified as recalling Elizabeth's cross-questioning of the Scottish ambassador Melville over Mary, Queen of Scots, at the time when it was being tentatively suggested that the latter might marry Elizabeth's own favorite Leicester (Jenkins 117–18), or as when Scarus announces that there is "Room for six scotches more" (4.7.10). To allude to the contemporary politics of England and Scotland in terms of Rome and Egypt would have had a particular force. As we have seen, for John of Fordun, the idea of Egyptian origins was not just a myth of origin but an encoding of Scottish hostility to the English. Reference to the idea of the Scots' supposed Egyptian origins was, therefore, a ready-made way of recalling the traditional conflict between the two nations—a conflict recently revitalized by the opposition to James's attempt to combine England and Scotland in one British Empire. I think this is alluded to in *Antony and Cleopatra*, but that, in keeping with Shakespeare's customary polyvalence and ambiguity, the expected polarities are reversed. Because Scotland claimed its origins in Egypt, whereas English myths of origin derived from Brutus and Rome, one would expect Egypt to be represented less favorably than Rome; but, as every reader and audience member notices, that is not the case. Egypt is more vibrant than Rome, and I think that is because Shakespeare is struggling here to accommodate two contradictory elements of Scottishness: on the one hand, Scotland's shameful link with gypsies (and, as I shall discuss later, with freemasons and the Irish)—which demands that Shakespeare stress its links with Egypt—but, on the other, its strong association with Roman law, which requires him to switch tack.

One of the major strains in the forced merger of England and Scotland arose from the attempt to combine a system based on Roman law (Scotland) with one that was not (England), and in *Antony and Cleopatra* we are certainly not allowed to forget the strong connections of the Roman characters with classical culture. Antony's ambassador, speaking to Caesar of Antony, tells him that

> Lord of his fortunes he salutes thee, and
> Requires to live in Egypt; which not granted,
> He lessons his requests, and to thee sues
> To let him breathe between the heavens and earth,
> A private man in Athens. (3.13.12–16)

Antony yearns for Greece, and the very fact that he retains the services of his schoolmaster emblematizes continuity with the classical culture from which he sprang. For Antony, however, classical culture proves barren and unproductive: Hercules leaves him (4.3.17–18); his schoolmaster cannot avail him; and, as he states, "The sevenfold shield of Ajax cannot keep / The battery from my heart" (4.14.39–40). Notably, too, Antony turns to the classical past only when deluded, distressed, or under pressure. Falsely imagining that Cleopatra has betrayed him, he cries, "The shirt of Nessus is upon me. Teach me, / Alcides, thou mine ancestor, thy rage" (4.12.43–44); but the rage of Hercules resulted not in anything noble or heroic, but in the massacring of his innocent wife and children. Cleopatra seems to identify this trait in him when she cries,

> Help me, my women! O, he's more mad
> Than Telamon for his shield; the boar of Thessaly
> Was never so embossed. (4.13.1–3)

Here again the classical past is associated with wanton destruction. Classicism, it seems, is a spent force—and classicism is what Scotland's system of Roman law was based on.

Cleopatra, by contrast, is associated with the biblical, and so, too, is Antony when at his noblest and when closest to her values. Whereas the presence of allusions to Christ's nativity in *Cymbeline* has often been recognized (Moffet 215), it has been much less frequently remarked that *Antony and Cleopatra* shows equal signs of such an awareness.[2] There are, however, a host of suggestive allusions to the nativity story. Early in the play, Charmian beseeches the soothsayer, "Good now, some excellent fortune! Let me be married to three kings in a forenoon and widow them all. Let me have a child at fifty, to whom Herod of Jewry may do homage" (1.2.27–30). Antony recurs to motifs associated with the nativity when he excuses himself to Caesar by saying, "Three kings I had newly feasted" (2.2.80); Cleopatra pretends the fish she catches are Antony as if she were one of the fishers of men (2.5.10–15); and it is suggested that Cleopatra, like the Pharaoh of the Bible, might be stricken by leprosy (3.10.9–11). Other references also point firmly in the same direction, such as the constant references to trinities and triples, Antony's caution that Cleopatra will have to "find out new heaven, new earth" (1.1.17), the parallel between the betrayal of Enobarbus and that of Judas, and Pompey's comment that "Caesar gets money where/He loses hearts" (2.1.13–14), which seems to recall the biblical injunction to "Render therefore unto Caesar the things which be Caesar's" but to reserve the heart for God (Luke 20:25). There is also Antony's apparent recollection of the Psalms when he speaks of the hill of Basan (3.13.126–28), the parodic Last Supper on the night of Cleopatra's birthday, and Caesar's assurance that "The time of universal peace is near" (4.6.5–7).

Shakespeare's emphasis on the synchronicity of classical and Christian events is not found in the other contemporary or near-contemporary treatments of the Cleopatra story by Samuel Daniel, Samuel Brandon, or Mary Sidney. It does, however, tap directly into a difference pointed out by Paul Yachnin:

> The propagandistic contexts of the two monarchs were opposed: James' was largely classical, Elizabeth's mostly biblical. In its own struggle between classical and biblical modes of expression, *Antony and Cleopatra* registers and critiques this competition between the politicized allusive fields associated with Elizabeth and James. (Yachnin 24)

Moreover, the play itself suggests that the biblical is its preferred, dominant explanatory mode, definitively superseding the classical. John F. Danby suggests that its "Egypt is the Egypt of the biblical glosses: exile from the spirit, thraldom to the flesh-pots, diminution of human kindness" (52), and, as demonstrated above, there are certainly biblical overtones throughout: Barbara C. Vincent, for instance, points out that "[i]n IV.iv, Antony crosses the threshold into the serious comic realm of Christianity. This scene is repeatedly concerned with meaning.... [Antony's] meaning is lost on his immediate, pre-Christian audience; only his off-stage audience can find meaning in these biblical *topoi*" (234). What these critics are suggesting, therefore, is that in *Antony and Cleopatra*, at least, the biblical—the mode associated with Elizabeth and by extension England—provides a better and more comprehensive explanatory model than the classical—the mode associated with James and Scotland.

The representation of Antony and Cleopatra thus taps into highly charged contemporary debates about national identities and the protocols and psychological cost of the political merger between England and Scotland, and Shakespeare's Egyptian past might well be seen as not so very different from his own British present: as Cicely Palser Havely points out, "Like Octavius, James Stuart had unified the 'three-nooked' world of England, Wales and Scotland" (148; see also Davies 128). That the story of *Antony and Cleopatra* was in fact always potentially applicable to England was first hinted at when Fulke Greville became so alarmed at the possibility that his own version of *Antony and Cleopatra* might be read in terms of the Elizabeth and Essex story that he destroyed it (Levy 2). Moreover, in Sir John Harington's translation of *Orlando Furioso*, in a scene set in Egypt, we encounter a detail that points us straight at the heart of the Elizabethan court. We are told of Cloris that

> ... *Mercury*, sith she his love did scorne,
> Lay with his net in wait not many houres
> Till at the last by Nylus banks he caught her,
> And there to daunce *la volta* then he taught her. (15.43)

The reference to the volta, Elizabeth's favorite dance, recalls the description of her by a Jesuit writer as "the English Cleopatra" (with Ralegh, on this occasion, envisioned as her Antony) (Lacey 54). It is also notable that the Necromancer in *Orlando Furioso* rides on a crocodile (15.51), and that in Spenser's *The Faerie Queene*, in Empson's memorable formulation, "Britomart copulates with the crocodile and thus produces the English Monarchy" (112). Indeed Paul Yachnin marshals an impressive array of evidence for a pronounced resemblance between Elizabeth and Cleopatra, pointing to "details in the characterization of Cleopatra such as her militancy, her likening herself to a milk-maid (Elizabeth had done likewise in a speech before Parliament), her fiery temper, her fondness for travel in a river-barge, her wit, her immense charm (all prominent aspects in contemporary accounts of Elizabeth)" (5).

Therefore, despite the fact that the myth of Scota associates Scotland with Egypt, it seems that Cleopatra's Egypt also resembles early modern England. Might Caesar's Rome, then, have links with James's Scotland? There are certainly signs in the play of a kind of knowledge associated both with Scotland and with the ancient world: freemasonry, whose origins were generally traced to Egypt, but in Shakespeare's play are more strongly linked with Rome. Arthur H. Williamson observes that "[i]n the late 1590s Scottish stonemasons organized themselves into semi-secret 'lodges' which were independent of their incorporated municipal guilds" (153). These were the fore-runners of the freemasons, and the secret knowledge claimed by the freemasons relates to the construction of Solomon's temple on principles said to have been learned from the builders of the pyramids.

There are a number of comments in this play that seem reminiscent of the distinctive language and concerns of the freemasons. Antony tells Octavia, "I have not kept my square, but that to come/Shall all be done by th'rule" (2.3.6–7). It also seems highly suggestive that Cleopatra should warn Iras,

> Thou, an Egyptian puppet, shall be shown
> In Rome as well as I. Mechanic slaves
> With greasy aprons, rules, and hammers shall
> Uplift us to the view. (5.2.208—11)

Those who work with rules and hammers are clearly masons, wearing the aprons still worn by freemasons today, and they are mentioned here in direct collocation with Egyptians. It has, of course, been frequently claimed that Shakespeare himself was a freemason, and indeed Antony's reference to the square and the rule is sometimes cited as one of the prime pieces of evidence to this effect.[3] There is no reliable evidence for Shakespeare's personal membership, but the recent work of David Stevenson makes it highly likely that Shakespeare could and probably would have had knowledge of freemasonry, and that he would have associated it with Scotland.

If this context is at all relevant, then we need to think of the Egypt of the play in a very complex way. The connection of Freemasonry with Egypt was already well-established by Shakespeare's time, as Egypt is mentioned in the Ancient Charges. Central to my focus, however, is the distinctive Scottishness of early modern freemasonry. Jasper Ridley points out that conditions for masons in Scotland were different from those elsewhere:

> The freestone masons were less successful in Scotland than in other coun-
> tries in maintaining their privileged position in the building trade. As there
> was no soft freestone in Scotland, the freestone masons were unable to carry
> on their skilled work there .... In Scotland an apprentice could become an
> entered apprentice after a much shorter period of apprenticeship; and an
> entered apprentice was allowed to perform most of the work of a master
> mason. (7–8)

This, in turn, seems to have given rise to a very different development of the craft: David Stevenson has recently concluded that while in Scotland "from the 1590s evidence that the craft was unique emerges with bewildering rapidity" (8), across the border "the secrets possessed by English masons and their organization in lodges seem to have derived from Scotland suggesting that, whereas in Scotland freemasonry grew out of the genuine practices of working stonemasons, in England it was in part at least imported from Scotland, with lodges being from the first created by gentlemen and for gentlemen" (Stevenson 6). This, however, lay some way into the future at the time of *Antony and Cleopatra*, since the first recorded speculative (as opposed to operative) freemason in England was Elias Ashmole in 1646. It seems likely, therefore, that, however fashionable it may have been in Scotland (and perhaps—though this can only be speculation—at the Scots king's English court), freemasonry would have been regarded in early-seventeenth-century England as little more than manual labor, and manual labor, moreover, tainted by the idea that masons in Scotland did not need to be as skilled or train as long as those in England.

It may also be relevant that freemasonry in Scotland was traditionally associated with the Sinclairs of Roslin, and, whether coincidentally or not, David Macritchie points out that "the Gypsies enjoyed the favor and protection of the Roslin family as late as the first quarter of the seventeenth century" (56). A link between freemasonry and gypsies also seems to be implied in *The Gypsies Metamorphosed*, in which "by the salomon," meaning "by the mass" but inescapably suggesting Solomon's temple (the central focus of freemasons' rituals and beliefs), appears, as Herford and the Simpsons explain, as an oath supposedly used by gypsies (10.617). Above all, it is notable that in *Antony and Cleopatra* the language associated with freemasonry is linked specifically to the figure who, I have argued, represents Scotland: Caesar. Antony's admission that "I have not kept my square" constitutes a promise of fidelity to Caesar's sister and denotes future adherence to Caesar's values, and the mechanic slaves so feared by Cleopatra are also associated with Caesar's Rome. Masonic vocabulary in this play seems consistently associated with Scotland, and there are enough pertinent clues from elsewhere in the Shakespearean canon, and in the writing of the period, to suggest that any representation of Scotland is unlikely to be favorable. This is, I think, particularly clear in *Macbeth*, a play which ostensibly flatters James by presenting his ancestor Banquo in a favorable light but which actually presents his homeland as the seat of superstition. J. Leeds Barroll argues for "a chronological interrelationship of *Macbeth*, *Lear*, and *Anthony*" (153), suggesting that the weird sisters may indeed draw on the common association between gypsies and Scotland as is further suggested by a couplet from *The Gypsies Metamorphosed*: "for, though wee be here at *Burly*,/Wee'd be lothe to make a *hurly*" (569). This echoes the "hurly-burly" of *Macbeth* in a way that suggests that weird sisters, gypsies, and Scotland may have been connected in Jonson's mind.

Drawing on the myth of Scota and its associations, I therefore conclude, is a way of subtly incriminating Octavius and hence James by associating them with gypsies and manual laborers. Moreover, it also brings with it a third set of associations, for the Scota story entailed a link with yet another group of despised, outcast Others, the Irish. James himself tried to "Irish" others, such as the Grahams and the Armstrongs whom he banished there from the Scottish borders; but the myth of Scota turns the tables by suggesting that there is, in fact, no difference between the Irish and the Scots, as is made clear in William Warner's *Albions England*:

> ... the *Scottes* (who some accuse by Ante-Dates to gain)
> Did settle in the Northerne Isles. These people bring their line
> From *Cecrops* and that *Pharo*, he that euer did decline
> From *Moses* seeking *Hebers* house from *AEgypt* to conuay.
> His daughter *Scota Gathelus* their Duke brought thence away.
> ....
> And of his race (of *Scota, Scottes*) when *Spanish Scottes* abound,
> Ariue in *Ireland*, and in it a second Empire ground. (3.15.33–46)

For Warner, moreover, the linkage is distinctly sinister, since it lays the Scots open to a charge of cannibalism:

> The *Pichts* were fierce and *Scythian*-like: much like the *Irish* now
> The *Scots* were then: couragious both: Nor them I disallowe
> That write they fed on humane flesh, for so it may be well. (3.15.62–64)

The issue of links between Scotland and Ireland was further complicated by the fact that "[i]n terms of their nomadic lifestyle, there was little to distinguish the Gypsies from the Irish, with both travelling the country in groups" (Mayall). The connection was by no means an accidental one: Arthur L. Little points out that "[i]n many early modern English texts blackness seeps into Ireland through discursive trickery. And on occasion Irishness makes its way, suspiciously, into early modern English texts on Africa, sometimes to the depreciation of the former" (124). Little argues that "Ireland provides a semiotics for reading Antony's lost Roman self and provides the reason why Egyptianness, like Irishness, must be sacrificed, cut off from Rome (or England) in the pursuit of an already known national and imperial character" (125). Indeed this was a connection made even by Elizabeth I herself, since she wrote to the 1st Earl of Essex in Ireland "urging him 'not to fester reproachfully in the delights of the English Egypt, where many take greatest delights in holding their noses over the beef pots' " (Freedman 18). Above all, the major Scots myth of origin worked to align Scotland, Ireland, and the traditional enemy, Spain, since, according to this legend, both Hibernia and Iberia were named after Hiber, son of Gathelus and Scota, founders of Scotland.

Although Little and Elizabeth appear to link Irishness with Egypt, Shakespeare appears instead to be taking a cue from Warner in his suggestion of a surprising "Irishness" lurking at the heart of his most Roman characters. The Irish were often accused of eating "uncivilly," of being the "raw" element in a proto-anthropological polarity (Hadfield 35). Octavius advocates a practice very close to this when he apostrophizes Antony:

> Thou didst drink
> The stale of horses and the gilded puddle
> Which beasts would cough at. Thy palate then did deign
> The roughest berry on the rudest hedge.
> Yea, like the stag when snow the pasture sheets,
> The barks of trees thou browsed'st. On the Alps
> ....
> It is reported thou didst eat strange flesh,
> Which some did die to look on. (1.4.61–77)

Another common accusation against the Irish was that of making undue noise at funerals. This could be seen to be paralleled in the fact that Octavius, whom I have suggested as the representative of Scottishness in the play, similarly focuses on death rather than life. Thidias chillingly tells Cleopatra,

> it would warm his spirits
> To hear from me you had left Antony,
> And put yourself under his shroud,
> The universal landlord. (3.13.69–72)

And Octavius' own final statement is,

> She shall be buried by her Antony.
> No grave upon the earth shall clip in it
> A pair so famous. (5.2.356–58)

There may just conceivably be an ironic reflection here on the fact that James's own major cultural activity in these years involved tomb-making, since he commissioned the monuments of both his predecessor, Elizabeth I, and his mother Mary, Queen of Scots. At all events, given the uninspiring nature of the activities with which Octavius is thus associated, it is little wonder that Cleopatra should declare " 'Tis paltry to be Caesar" (5.2.2), for against both Caesar and James absolutely every card is stacked. Ultimately, Scotland's proud claim to Egyptian origins is turned on its head to associate the Scottish king first with the Romans rather than the Egyptians, and finally with gypsies, manual laborers, and the Irish—all of whom would have had strongly negative connotations for Shakespeare's audience.

The fundamental question about *Antony and Cleopatra* has always been whether it is the Roman or the Egyptian ethos that the play ultimately affirms. In this essay, I have hoped to show that Shakespeare reverses conventional patterns by linking Octavius, the Roman, not Cleopatra, the "gypsy," with Scotland, and that he further proceeds to stress every possible negative aspect of Scottishness. In my reading, therefore, there can be no doubt that it is Egypt that offers the more attractive alternative.

NOTES

I am grateful to David Mayall for sharing his forthcoming research into gypsy history and to Andrew Prescott for his invaluable help with the history of freemasonry.

1. Honorable exceptions to this are Whitney, Loomba, and Archer.
2. For a notable exception, see Sacerdoti.
3. See, for instance, the "famous masons" sites at http://www.cephasministry. com/famous.html and http://freemasons.org.nz/famous.htm.

WORKS CITED

Archer, John Michael. *Old Worlds: Egypt, Southwest Asia, India, and Russia in Early Modern English Writing*. Stanford: Stanford UP, 2001.

Barroll, J. Leeds. "The Chronology of Shakespeare's Jacobean Plays and the Dating of *Antony and Cleopatra*." *Essays on Shakespeare*. Ed. Gordon Ross Smith. University Park: Pennsylvania State University Press, 1965. 115–62.

Boorde, Andrew. *The Fyrst Boke of the Introduction of Knowledge*. London, 1542.

Danby, John F. "*Antony and Cleopatra*: A Shakespearean Adjustment." *Antony and Cleopatra*. Ed. John Drakakis. Basingstoke: Macmillan, 1994. 33–55.

Davies, H. Neville. "Jacobean *Antony and Cleopatra*." *Antony and Cleopatra*. Ed. John Drakakis. Basingstoke: Macmillan, 1994. 126–65.

Empson, William. "Paradoxes in *The Faerie Queene* V and VI." *The Strengths of Shakespeare's Shrew*. Ed. John Haffenden. Sheffield: Sheffield Academic Publications, 1996.

Freedman, Sylvia. *Poor Penelope: Lady Penelope Rich, An Elizabethan Woman*. Bourne End: The Kensal P, 1983.

Hadfield, Andrew. "'The Naked and the Dead': Elizabethan Perceptions of Ireland." *Travel and Drama in Shakespeare's Time*. Ed. Jean-Pierre Maquerlot and Michèle Willems. Cambridge: Cambridge UP, 1996. 32–54.

Havely, Cicely Palser. "Changing Critical Perspectives." *Shakespeare: Texts and Contexts*. Ed. Kiernan Ryan. Basingstoke: Macmillan, 2000. 145–53.

Iversen, Erik. *The Myth of Egypt and Its Hieroglyphics in European Tradition*. Copenhagen: GEC Gad, 1961.

Jenkins, Elizabeth. *Elizabeth the Great*. London: Panther, 1972.

Jonson, Ben. *The Gypsies Metamorphosed, in Ben Jonson*. Ed. C. H. Herford and Percy and Evelyn Simpson. Oxford: The Clarendon P, 1950.

Lacey, Robert. *Sir Walter Ralegh*. London: Weidenfeld & Nicolson, 1975.

Levy, F. J. "Hayward, Daniel, and the Beginnings of Politic History in England." *Huntington Library Quarterly* (1987): 1–34.

Little, Arthur L., Jr. *Shakespeare Jungle Fever: National-Imperial Re-Visions of Race, Rape, and Sacrifice*. Stanford: Stanford UP, 2000.

Loomba, Ania. *Shakespeare, Race, and Colonialism*. Oxford: Oxford UP, 2002.

Macritchie, David. *Scottish Gypsies Under the Stewarts*. Edinburgh: David Douglas, 1894.

McNulty, Robert, ed. *Ludovico Ariosto's Orlando Furioso*, translated into English Heroical Verse by Sir John Harington. 1591. Oxford: The Clarendon P, 1972.

Mason, Roger A. "Scotching the Brut: Politics, History and National Myth in Sixteenth-Century Britain." *Scotland and England 1286–1815*. Ed. Roger A. Mason. Edinburgh: John Donald, 1987. 60–84.

Mayall, David. *Gypsy Identities, 1500–2000: From Egyptians and Moonmen to Ethnic Romany*. London: UCL P, Ltd., 2003.

Melville, Andrew. *A trewe description of the nobill race of the Stewards*. Edinburgh, 1603.

Moffet, Robin. "Cymbeline and the Nativity." *Shakespeare Quarterly* 13 (1962): 207–18.

Randall, Dale B. J. *Jonson's Gypsies Unmasked: Background and Theme of The Gypsies Metamorphos'd*. Durham, N.C.: Duke UP, 1975.

Ridley, Jasper. *The Freemasons*. London: Constable, 1999.

Sacerdoti, Gilberti. "Three Kings, Herod of Jewry, and a Child: Apocalypse and Infinity of the World in *Antony and Cleopatra*." *Italian Studies in Shakespeare and His Contemporaries*. Ed. Michele Marrapodi and Giorgio Melchiori. Newark: U of Delaware P, 1999. 165–84.

Scott-Warren, Jason. *Sir John Harington and the Book as Gift*. Oxford: Oxford UP, 2001.

Shakespeare, William. *Antony and Cleopatra*. Ed. Emrys Jones. Harmondsworth: Penguin, 1977.

Spenser, Edmund. *A View of the State of Ireland*. Ed. Andrew Hadfield and Willy Maley. Oxford: Blackwell, 1997.

Stevenson, David. *The Origins of Freemasonry: Scotland's Century, 1590–1710*. Cambridge: Cambridge UP, 1988.

Vincent, Barbara. "Shakespeare's *Antony and Cleopatra* and the Rise of Comedy." *Antony and Cleopatra*. Ed. John Drakakis. Basingstoke: Macmillan, 1994. 212–47.

Warner, William. *Albions England*. London, 1602.

Whitney, Charles. "Charmian's Laughter: Women, Gypsies, and Festive Ambivalence in *Antony and Cleopatra*." *The Upstart Crow* 14 (1994): 67–88.

Williamson, Arthur H. "Number and National Consciousness: The Edinburgh Mathematicians and Scottish Political Culture at the Union of the Crowns." *Scots and Britons: Scottish Political Thought and the Union of 1603*. Ed. Roger A. Mason. Cambridge: Cambridge UP, 1994. 187–212.

Yachnin, Paul. " 'Courtiers of Beauteous Freedom': *Antony and Cleopatra* in Its Time." *Renaissance and Reformation* 15 (1991): 1–20.

10.
"Immortal Longings"
The Erotics of Death in *Antony and Cleopatra*

LISA S. STARKS

> Eros!—I come, my queen.—Eros!–stay for me.
> Where souls do couch on flowers, we'll hand in hand,
> And with our sprightly port make the ghosts gaze.
> Dido and her Aeneas shall want troops,
> And all the haunt be ours. Come, Eros, Eros! (4.15.50–54)

Wounded and bleeding, Shakespeare's Antony offers himself as a sacrifice to his goddess Cleopatra in a scene that exploits the thrill of sexual transgression, the desire of submission, and the transcendence of death's embrace—at once dangerous, beautiful, and irrepressibly erotic. Antony clearly desires to perform his suicide as a passionately romantic act, one in which he plays the tortured, despairing lover calling out for his mistress in the ecstatic thralls of death. In submitting himself to his queen and to his own death, Antony expresses the immortal longings that drive his self-slaughter and that underlie his passionate love for Cleopatra. Shakespeare's *Antony and Cleopatra* culminates in this poetic fusion of death and sexuality characteristic of the *Liebstod,* or a sensual story of love and death, as developed through the narrative of male masochism.[1]

A potentially transgressive fantasy of female dominance and male submission, the narrative of male masochism, is a recurrent pattern in Western mythology, literature, and art, counterpointing dominant narratives like the Classical epic, which valorize paternal values of heroism and martial valor. Although a trace of this counternarrative can be read in Plutarch's *Lives*, Shakespeare's main source for *Antony and Cleopatra*, it is in Shakespeare's version that the narrative of male masochism is developed to its fullest extent. Through this narrative, Shakespeare fully explores and calls into question the Western (Roman) bias that characterizes the inherited tradition of writings about the Roman warrior and his Egyptian queen. Departing from this tradition, Shakespeare transforms the story into a narrative of male masochism, thereby challenging the conventional notions of heroism and masculinity inherent in the Classical tradition. This tradition is perfectly embodied in Virgil's *Aeneid* through the character of Aeneas, the mythological figure who links English identity to the Ancient world and to the making of empires. Shakespeare's Antony draws a parallel between his relationship with Cleopatra and the union of Aeneas and Dido—the Classical counterpart in historical and literary tradition to Shakespeare's lovers—envisioning them in his dying words as happily reunited, rather than estranged, together for eternity in the land of the dead (4.15.52–53). At this defining moment, Antony transforms the endings of both love stories into mutual celebrations of the erotic union of lovers beyond the grave, the ultimate victory of passionate love over rational duty through the transcendence of death.

Shakespeare thus continues the challenge begun by Christopher Marlowe in *Dido, Queen of Carthage*, in which he reverses the gender hierarchy of masculine duty over feminine passion, as Sara Munson Deats has argued (89–124). Working from this legacy, Shakespeare extends Marlowe's move to encompass a radical displacement of the epic tradition and its masculine values of heroism through the figure of Antony as masochistic hero.[2] Whereas Virgil's Aeneas sacrifices the pleasure of love for the honor of martial valor and duty in Virgil's *Aeneid*, Shakespeare's Antony sacrifices himself *for* love. This sacrifice is especially poignant, for in *Antony and Cleopatra* it is the male hero—rather than the female hero, as in the story of Aeneas and Dido—who plays the martyr. Rejecting the masculine ethos of the Classical hero, Shakespeare's Antony becomes instead a kind of gothic "antihero"—the tortured lover, the martyr, the masochist.

Although Antony is often seen as a failure, loser, or has-been hero, I would argue the opposite. Certainly, he does not meet the qualifications of a Classical hero, but he is, nevertheless, an exemplary hero—or, rather, an exemplary "antihero," one who fulfills the role with invincible courage and depth of feeling. This role is, by its very definition, a rejection of Classical heroism and an acceptance of an alternative masculine identity inherited from Ovid rather than Virgil, recast in the medieval traditions of courtly love and Mariolatry as well as the Renaissance conventions of Petrarchan love and the cult of Elizabeth. This masochistic hero figures in the stories of worshipper and goddess, lady and knight, servant and mistress, variations on the theme of female dominance and male submission. And yet, although the role is based on a rejection of traditional masculinity and heroism, it is, nevertheless, a *male* rather than a female role.[3]

Through the sensual language, visual iconography, and dramatic tension of this narrative, Shakespeare explores the intrinsic link between sexuality and death in the erotic imagination of Western myth, poetry, and painting. Of course, throughout his career, in his plays and poems, Shakespeare explores the theme of love and death, but in his late tragedy *Antony and Cleopatra* he takes the exploration further, allowing the theme to become more potentially disruptive of cultural norms. Typically, as in plays like *Measure for Measure* or *Othello* or in poems like the so-called Dark Lady sonnets, Shakespeare's equation of desire and death serves not to valorize the fusion of death and sexuality but, rather, to reveal the abject loathing of the flesh and disgust of human mortality that ultimately results in the death *of* desire.[4] In *Antony and Cleopatra,* however, Shakespeare transforms the death of desire into the ecstatic *desire of death*, a longing beyond the pleasure principle, a fusion of the destructive and the regenerative forces of Thanatos and Eros.

Early modern references to sex as a kind of death and the word *die* as a euphemism for a sexual orgasm provide instances in which this link can be immediately discerned and latent fears and anxieties about sexuality be made manifest through this "paradoxical yoking of love and death" (Kuriyama 330). Shakespeare's Enobarbus plays on this euphemism, making jokes about letting women "die" (meaning to have an orgasm) for, as he puts it, "death's the word," and Cleopatra has such a "celerity in dying" (1.2. 131, 123, 125). More frequently, it is the male orgasm that is most closely linked to death. For the male, who spends his seed and thus some of his life "force," each orgasm leads one step closer to death. The male's entrance into the female body signifies a return to the womb, aligning sexuality with birth and death, flesh and decay.

Although the ways in which these anxieties were constituted and experienced were unique to the early modern period, the associations of sex and death in Western art has extended into subsequent eras. Freud mined Renaissance art and culture—along with the tradition of themes, images, and stories that exhibit features of what was later referred to as "masochism"—for evidence of this link between sex and death.[5] Through years spent analyzing and interpreting Western literature and myth, Freud concludes that this link is integral to the subject's psychic life in Western culture. Drawing from this analysis, in *Beyond the Pleasure Principle*, Freud revised his early view of masochism as a reversal of primary nonsexual aggression to a later conception of it as primary to sexuality and subjectivity, a point he further elaborates in "The Economic Problem of Masochism."[6] In the controversial final sections of *Beyond the Pleasure Principle* (34–64), Freud speculates on the connection between a primary or fundamental masochism and a basic desire for stasis—the Nirvana principle, or the psychic drive toward stasis or nothingness (53)—and death—the death drive, or underlying human movement toward nonbeing (54).[7] Here Freud tentatively suggests that this drive toward nothingness, toward death, is an integral part of human subjectivity and desire. The contemporary theorist Jean Laplanche has continued Freud's investigations into the interconnections of masochism, aggression, pleasure, and the death drive—where life, death, and sexuality meet and originate in the subject and extend into culture and art. For Laplanche, masochism is implicated in the trauma that initiates and structures human sexuality. He explains that " . . . the paradox of masochism, far from deserving to be circumscribed as a specific 'perversion,' should be generalized, linked as it is to *the essentially traumatic nature of human sexuality*" (105).[8]

Freud first articulates this trauma not through recourse to earlier theories or to biology, but through reference to myth. To illustrate his idea about the death drive and primary masochism, Freud turns to Plato's myth explaining the origin of sexual love in his *Symposium* (57–61). In this poetic description, spoken by Aristophanes, humans start as two-sided, two-bodied beings of three sexes—male/male, female/female, and male/female. Complete unto themselves, these mortals do not experience sexual desire. It is only when Zeus violently slices them in half, separating them into two beings, that sexuality occurs. For Freud, Plato's idea that the sexual drive originates in the longing of each severed pair to reunite into a coherent, whole sex illustrates his own theory of the Nirvana principle and the death drive, or the desire for stasis and a return to one's origins through death. In Freud's view, then, Plato's myth "traces the origin of an instinct to *a need to restore an earlier state of things*" (57), a need to suture the split subject with its other. According to Freud, this need propels the sexual drive, through which human beings express their ultimate desire to cease to be. Plato's idea that sexuality originates in the trauma of dismemberment, the splitting of the subject from the other and itself, also foregrounds the role of sexuality within the Freudian subject and psychoanalytic theory. It also points to the generative/destructive force that is represented by the gods and goddesses of the Ancient world, both Western and Eastern, the same myths that are later woven into the narrative of male masochism. These myths, and the trauma of fragmentation that they dramatize, also structure the identities of Antony and Cleopatra and the dynamic of their relationship in both Plutarch and Shakespeare.

Antony experiences this trauma through the "shattering" effect of masochism in its extreme—the ultimate "splitting" or rupture of phallic (in this case, Roman) subjectivity.[9] Antony doesn't seek to be made "whole" within the paternal legacy of Roman masculinity, as one might expect; instead, he longs to be united to and by Cleopatra, his Isis.[10] Linked with the goddess's brother and husband, the Egyptian god Osiris, Antony is "dis-membered," hurled into the void, until he is mystically remade in the spirit, "re-membered" into a new man by Isis/Cleopatra.[11] Interestingly, Shakespeare employs the Isis/Osiris myth as an underlying structure of *Antony and Cleopatra*, drawing both from Plutarch's *Lives* and the essay "Isis and Osiris" from his *Moralia* (translated by Philemon Holland in 1603), extending the thematic development and furthering Plutarch's analogies between Eastern and Western religions (67–191).[12] In his history of Marc Antony, Plutarch notes Cleopatra's performance as the deity Isis and also Antony's affinity with Osiris, particularly as related to the Western correlative deities Dionysus/ Bacchus. Therefore, Plutarch claims that the god Bacchus, not Hercules, abandoned Antony in his final hour. In "Isis and Osiris," Plutarch returns to this myth, elaborating extensively on the importance of it in Egyptian culture and comparing it in detail to the Western myth of Dionysus/Bacchus. Obviously, Plutarch stresses the thematic connections between these myths and the story of Antony and Cleopatra, as both myths involve violent dismemberment and regeneration. In the story of Isis and Osiris, Osiris is tricked into being buried alive and then chopped into fourteen pieces by his rival Typhon, who then scatters the pieces of the god's body to all corners of the earth. Painstakingly, Isis recovers all the pieces of her brother/husband except his genitalia, which she replaces with an artificial phallus that she molds for him ("Isis and Osiris" 29–55).

In Plutarch and, to a larger extent in Shakespeare, the story of Antony's relationship with Cleopatra and his rivalry with Octavius (Typhon, or the Roman values that Antony rejects) resonates with meaning in the context of this myth, as Shakespeare's Antony surrenders his role as Herculean hero for his new identity as Cleopatra's Egyptian Osiris and finally her holy martyr. To foreground this shift, Shakespeare changes Plutarch; in Shakespeare's play, the patron god who deserts Antony is not Bacchus but his Roman "ancestor" Hercules, thereby stressing Antony's rejection of Roman heroism. Antony leaves Hercules behind to embrace his role as Osiris/Bacchus/Dionysus. Following Plutarch's lead in stressing cross-cultural analogies of religious myth, Shakespeare extends the myth of Isis/Osiris beyond the Greco-Roman gods to gothic Christianity through the erotic language of courtly love and Petrarchan poetry, the analogy of Cleopatra/Isis to Elizabeth the Virgin Queen and her court, and the visual iconography of Christian Mariolatry and martyrdom. Within this network of interrelated myths, images, and narrative traditions, Shakespeare's Antony moves freely between several related identities as masochistic hero: the conquered knight, the anguished lover, the devoted courtier, and the holy martyr.

These multiple positions of the male masochist coalesce in the conventions of courtly love and Petrarchan poetry, traditions central to the English Renaissance and to Shakespeare, particularly *Antony and Cleopatra*. Both traditions play variations on the fantasy of female domination and male submission, at least on the surface level. Written from the male's subject position, the courtly or Petrarchan lover's discourse employs the figures of male masochistic fantasy, but its primary concern is with the lover's own subjective states of mind, the pleasure and pain of his suffering at the hand of his cruel mistress. The chivalric knight or the Renaissance courtier continually checks these masochistic tendencies, for fear that they will lead to effeminacy or lack of manly valor. To mitigate male fear and anxiety of becoming truly vulnerable and submissive to a woman, streaks of sadistic behavior often occur in masochistic fantasy, even though masochism and sadism involve completely different logics, narratives, and erotic landscapes, as Gilles Deleuze has explained (123–34).[13] Antony eases this anxiety by playing Cleopatra's warrior, her "man of steel," easily assuming the role of chivalric knight charging off to battle for his lady. As long as the woman serves as a mirror to the lover's manly triumph, as Cleopatra does while arming Antony for battle, then she does not challenge but enhances his performance as a warrior.

Therefore, the Petrarchan discourse of love serves to sublimate masochistic desires and to exert control over the erotic economy and over the woman who appears to be the lover's object of desire within it. This control is most obvious in the blazon of Petrarchan poetry, wherein the lover objectifies the woman of adoration by breaking down her anatomy in a catalogue of praise. According to Nancy J. Vickers and numerous critics, the effect of the blazon is to dismember and dehumanize the Other, rendering her powerless in constructing the erotic dynamic. Underlying this economy and feeding its dominant metaphors of the hunt and the hunted is Petrarch's rendition of the myth of Diana and Acteon from Ovid's *Metamorphoses*, in which Acteon is transformed into a stag who is torn to pieces by his own hounds as punishment for viewing the virginal Diana bathing nude in a grove (see Vickers, "Diana Described" 103–05). Although the violence of this myth seems to suggest a more sadistic than masochistic scenario, as most have maintained, I would argue that it illustrates the latter. The lover figuratively dismembers his Diana, his goddess; but he does so to disavow and to endure vicariously his own dreaded desire to suffer as Acteon suffers, to be punished and torn to pieces by his goddess, to serve as her bodily sacrifice. The obvious threat of this masochistic wish results in the poet projecting the desire for violence onto his mistress, figuratively disintegrating *her* body as he unconsciously wishes she would his, while disavowing his own fear and longing to be destroyed by her hand. As long as the Petrarchan lover can fetishize the beauty and chastity of his mistress, he can keep the potentially dangerous submission of masochism at bay. Thus, the objectifying effects of the blazon and the recurrent misogynistic bouts of railing against the woman for cruelty and frailty— as in Antony's tirade when he assumes that Cleopatra has betrayed him (3.13.93–94; 4.8)—occur as checks within the Petrarchan dynamic that enable the lover to submit to his mistress without fear of surrendering to his desire for complete subjection.

The foundational myth of Acteon and Diana also underlies the narrative of male masochism in Shakespeare's *Antony and Cleopatra*,[14] as it parallels that of Dionysus/Bacchus and, by analogy, Isis and Osiris, which Shakespeare expands from Plutarch, making rich, multileveled connections between Shakespeare's tragedy and Petrarchan masochism. The myth of Acteon is closely related to that of Dionysus/Bacchus and, significantly, Isis/Osiris. Like Acteon and Osiris, Pentheus suffers dismemberment upon seeing the frenzied women's worship of their god Dionysus/Bacchus. The tropes of dismemberment, punishment, and sexuality that recur in all these myths converge in Shakespeare's

Antony and Cleopatra, foregrounded in Antony's fantasy and role as Osiris, a role that culminates in his suicide and sacrifice to Cleopatra/Isis.

These tropes figure prominently in the language of the play, as Arthur J. Little has pointed out, resulting in the figurative anatomizing of Antony's body. Little notes that the metaphor "piece" is used to delineate women as objects (Cleopatra as a "piece of work" [1.2.151–52] and Octavia as a "piece of virtue" to unite Antony and Octavius [3.2.28–29]) and men as military units, or pieces of their general (Antony's soldiers as "bruised pieces" [4.14–42]). As a character whose masculine Roman identity has disintegrated, Anthony becomes the fractured object of the blazon, ridiculed and broken by his enemies. In this way, Little explains, "Antony has not only become a piece but has gone to pieces" (106).[15]

As in the Osiris myth, however, Isis/Cleopatra reassembles Antony's "pieces" into a heroic whole, constructing him as "nature's piece 'gainst fancy" (5.2.99). Following the pattern of the Osiris/Isis myth, the degeneration of Antony is followed by his regeneration as a Colossus through Cleopatra's poetic imagination, making the severed flesh whole again through the word:

> His legs bestrid the ocean; his reared arm
> Crested the world, His voice was propertied
> As all the tuned spheres, and that to friends;
> But when he meant to quail and shake the orb,
> He was as rattling thunder. For his bounty,
> There was no winter in't; an autumn 'twas,
> That grew the more by reaping. His delights
> Were dolphin-like; they showed his back above
> The element they lived in. In his livery
> Walked crowns and crownets. Realms and islands were
> As plates dropped from his pocket. (5.2.81–91)

For Heather James, this speech is Cleopatra's revisionist blazon through which she plays the role of Petrarchan lover (230–31). Conversely, I would argue, this speech, Cleopatra's heroic tribute to Antony, resembles more a heraldic blazon (the description on a shield) than the poetic blazon as it is developed in Petrarchan poetry.[16] Cleopatra does not inventory Antony's parts but instead she imaginatively unifies these parts into a whole image, one that exceeds the real to a large degree, as Cleopatra immortalizes her martyred lover into a colossal hero. The gap between the physical body of Antony (the actor's body) and this speech would, in Cynthia Marshall's words, "trouble ... an audience's notion of what it means to be a (masculine) hero" (403). But, I contend, Cleopatra's speech would transform Antony into a holy icon, here imagined in supernatural terms. The difference between the real and the image that Cleopatra creates completes Antony's transfiguration into heroic martyr.

When Cleopatra does employ Petrarchan metaphors elsewhere in expressing her passion for Antony, she does so, like Elizabeth I, by investing herself in the Petrarchan dynamic—but not, as James argues, by situating herself as the Petrarchan subject in a straightforward reversal of gendered positions. Rather, I would insist that, like Elizabeth, Cleopatra displaces rather than reverses the male subject/female object binary. She does not become the adoring lover, but, rather, she becomes an object of her own fashioning, a Petrarchan mistress who exerts her own control over the image and who seizes the position of speaking subject while remaining in the position of the object. When Cleopatra employs Petrarchan conceits, for instance, she takes the position of the object—the "bottom" (the submissive or passive role) rather than the "top" (the dominant or active role)—but, in so doing, she makes the "bottom" a powerful position of supreme control and sexual gratification. When she uses typical Petrarchan conventions, such as the lover expressing envy for the objects that surround his beloved, she does so with an unconventional twist. She does not long to be the glove covering his hand or the earth enveloping his body in the grave, as in a standard Petrarchan poem. Instead, she envisions herself as the horse *underneath* Antony, the horse *on which* he rides: "O happy horse, to bear the weight of Antony!" (1.5.21), she exclaims passionately while lamenting her lover's absence. Although Antony rides the horse, it is Cleopatra who composes the fantasy, and it is her own sexual pleasure that is shared with the audience.

This move is even more radical because Shakespeare imagines Cleopatra as a black woman, one who is characterized by the Romans in much the same terms as the speaker of Shakespeare's sonnets depicts his so-called dark lady, the black woman of the sonnets, the objectified figure on whom the speaker projects his loathing of sexuality, flesh, and the female body. For Shakespeare, the "flesh made word" becomes the word once again made into flesh on stage. Cleopatra not only refuses to be silenced, like Petrarch's Diana, but also she refuses to be kept invisible and nameless, like Shakespeare's "dark lady." From this point of view, Cleopatra embodies Shakespeare's own Petrarchan—or, rather, anti-Petrarchan—mistress, the black woman of the sonnets, through the body of the actor. If the blazon is an "inverse incarnation," as Vickers puts it, "the flesh made word" ("Diana Described" 105), then Shakespeare's staging of the figurative, objectified body through that of the actor renders it back into flesh once more. Significantly, allowing the black woman to be represented onstage, albeit through the character of Cleopatra as embodied by a cross-dressed white boy in black face, automatically foregrounds and reverses the black woman's invisibility. In the transformation from invisible Petrarchan anti-mistress of the sonnets to the Egyptian queen of the stage, the black woman becomes visible, even if only signified by a feminine male body, makeup, costume—and, of course, her *own* poetic conceits.

However, when the black woman is represented as an object of beauty in poetry or on stage, she is also made *white*—or *whiter*—as she is recast within Renaissance notions of femininity. The black woman's image is that of an "antimistress"; it poses a stark contrast to conventional ideals of beauty as fair and chastity as white, and a bold challenge for the poet to transform a thing of darkness into one of beauty. The Petrarchan poet would often make over this antimistress, "whitening" her through the conceits of his sonnets, as Kim F. Hall has illustrated, in order "to re-fashion her into an acceptable object of platonic love and admiration," thereby exerting complete control over her image (67). The black woman of Shakespeare's sonnets resists such a whitening effect, even if she is characterized entirely through the poet's own sexual anxiety and desire; nevertheless, as a character onstage, Cleopatra is "whitened." No longer the invisible black woman, Cleopatra's image is refigured within the symbolic economy of whiteness as she is re-created in the image of an English queen through analogy to Elizabeth I (Little 157–70), a monarch whose own image and court exploited a "spectacle of whiteness" against which blackness was contrasted (Erickson 517; qtd. in Little 161).

Although Shakespeare's Cleopatra is described by the Romans and many critics as the African queen and exotic Other, she becomes much more white English than black Egyptian in the course of the play. There is a tremendous gap between the way that she is described and the way that she really appears onstage. Her wit, use of Petrarchan conventions, fits of jealous outrage, and expressions of sorrow were more familiar than strange in an early modern English context, particularly resonant of Elizabeth I herself, a queen who inspired, in Peter Erickson's words, "a cult of whiteness" (157; see also Strong 21 and Little 161). Besides the obvious parallels between Elizabeth I and Cleopatra—both female monarchs who performed the role of deities and fashioned themselves as the center of a cult of love—there are striking references to Elizabeth and her court in the play, as many have noted.[17] For instance, the beauty contest, in which Cleopatra asks the messenger to play the magic mirror and tell her whether she or Octavia is the fairest of them all (3.3), is unmistakably a biting parody of Elizabeth's infamous response to hearing news of Mary, Queen of Scots (see Little 160). Like Plutarch in his description of Egyptian culture as a mirror of his own Greco-Roman world view, Shakespeare imperialistically renders the Egyptian into English, washes the black into white, and appropriates the African queen as a stand-in for the familiar English queen of an era now past, Isis into Gloriana. And as Gloriana, she is the supreme Petrarchan mistress, one who knows how to fashion her own image.

Through this role as supreme Petrarchan mistress, Cleopatra creates the theatrical effects of her "infinite variety," becoming the one who "outdoes nature," the one who knows how to strike an unforgettable pose—the one who embodies the theatrical medium itself. Enobarbus delivers Plutarch's famous description of Cleopatra's barge, but it is clearly Cleopatra who has scripted and staged the scene and orchestrated its fantasy, so much so that her own figure transcends description in Enobarbus's memory of it. As perfection in Neoplatonic terms, Cleopatra as object cannot be made literal, cannot be rendered into flesh by the word. Even the Romans miss their mark, criticizing her with stock phrases and clichéd insults. Consequently, Enobarbus cannot "cut her down to size" through the blazon, as she eludes such treatment. Instead, Enobarbus sketches a suspended scene, like a painting, a predominate feature in the scenario of male masochism, and one in which Cleopatra has positioned herself as the goddess:[18]

> The barge she sat in, like a burnished throne
> Burned on the water. The poop was beaten gold;
> Purple the sails, and so perfumed that
> The winds were love-sick with them. The oars were silver,
> Which to the tune of flutes kept stroke, and made
> The water which they beat to follow faster,
> As amorous of their strokes. For her own person,
> It beggared all description. She did lie
> In her pavilion—cloth of gold, of tissue—
> O'er picturing that Venus where we see
> The fancy outwork nature. (2.2.197–207)

Here Enobarbus cannot depict Cleopatra beyond describing the theatrical effects of her spectacular performance—costumes, set design, and music— but in Shakespeare's representation of her suicide, these effects are re-created on stage. The audience views Cleopatra as she embodies the goddess in her highly theatrical final scene. When interpreted as an Anglicized version of Plutarch's account, Cleopatra's suicide resonates with meaning, uniting images of life, sexuality, and death. Like Antony, Cleopatra seizes death as an opportunity for transcendence, whether or not her suicide is initially motivated as such. In her ecstatic "O, Antony!" Cleopatra performs her suicide as an act of passionate love and erotic release—not as a sacrifice, like Antony, but as a transfiguration into an immortal goddess. Adorned as Isis, Cleopatra employs the venomous asp, dying like an Egyptian—or, rather, like an Anglicized Egyptian, despite her claim to performing a suicide in "high Roman style" (see Bono 204). But in Shakespeare's depiction of the Egyptian queen, he extends cultural analogies, like Plutarch's of Isis, so that, seen through English eyes, the Egyptian asp recalls the serpent of biblical myth within contexts of early modern iconography and imagery (see Little 2–3, 160). With the serpent at her breast, Shakespeare's Cleopatra becomes Isis as both Eve and Mary, the degenerative/regenerative duality of the Egyptian goddess suggesting the medieval duality of womanhood. Yet, like Elizabeth, Cleopatra herself seems too human and familiar to fit neatly into either category; like the "speaking object," she defies such classification, her death scene exceeding those boundaries. Shakespeare's Cleopatra dies in a self-fashioned performance of death. She is an object on display, yes, but on display according to her own design, a scene of triumph in which she has cast herself in the leading role.

If Cleopatra is this self-fashioned Petrarchan object, then Antony is the one who tends primarily to be objectified by others in the play. Despite Cleopatra's dynamic presence, it is Antony whom Cleopatra and the other characters desire, as has often been noted. Octavius, Octavia, Enobarbus, Cleopatra—everyone wants a piece of the fragmented Antony. And as the figure of the martyr, Antony draws from highly sexualized iconography, becoming a titillating image on stage through the sensual images of Christian masochism. The most prevalent images of Petrarchan poetry—the dismembered or penetrated body, bleeding wounds, phallic weapons, and instruments of torture—are also those of Classical myth and Christian martyrdom. In the erotic imagination of the martyr, these Petrarchan images—including the implements of torture, the "circumcising blade, the soldier's whip, the thorns, nails, and the Roman lance ... "—are incarnated as the "penetrable and penetrated" body of Christ and his "bleeding wounds," as Richard Rambuss has observed (254–55). Images—like phallic "darts" and "arrows," and wounded "hearts," as well as the oxymoronic pleasure and pain of orgasmic "Death"— are drawn from the same erotic fantasies that figure in Petrarchan love and Christian martyrdom. These images further link sexuality and death in the masochistic imagination and, in Freud's view, within the human subject and the trauma of sexuality as well.

As one who embodies this trauma, Antony courageously gives himself over to the shattering effects of masochism, exposing his vulnerability and his longing to die and to be reborn in Cleopatra's regenerative imagination. Making even his bloody suicide a passionate act of transcendent love, Antony sees himself as "A bridegroom in ... death," who will "run into ... "—Eros's sword—"As to a lover's bed" (4.15.100–01). If Antony goes to his death "like a bridegroom," then, as the regenerative Isis, Cleopatra as bride goes to her death *like a virgin*—or, rather, like *the* Virgin. As the Western incarnation of Isis with strong associations with the Virgin Queen, Elizabeth I, the figure of Cleopatra embodies the Christian regenerative goddess, the Virgin Mary, as argued earlier.[19] Shakespeare's staged tableau of the goddess/Virgin Cleopatra holding the bleeding body of Antony/Christ in her arms thus resonates as a powerfully erotic *pietà*. Antony's wounded, penetrated body draws its erotic charge from medieval to early modern representations of the male hero-martyr—the eroticized body of Christ languishing on the cross, the bleeding chest of Saint Sebastian, bound and impaled with arrows.[20]

In these representations, the spiritual is fused with the erotic, especially in scenarios involving extreme physical pain and mental anguish.[21] These physical and mental torments lie at the heart of the erotic fantasies underlying Christian martyrdom and, in varying degrees, the discourses of medieval and early modern Christianity, belief systems that revolve around the central sacrifice of Christ as the ultimate martyr. As Julia Kristeva explains, "A whole ascetic, martyrizing, and sacrificial Christian tradition has magnified the victimized aspect of that offering [Christ's death] by eroticizing both pain and suffering, physical as well as mental, as much as possible" (131). Kaja Silverman labels this tradition of pain and suffering "Christian masochism," a term that she develops from a strain of masochism identified by Theodore Reik in *Masochism in Modern Man* (1941).[22] Silverman characterizes Christian masochism as an economy of desire in which "demonstrativeness," the gaze, revolutionary fervor, and "suspense" are all exploited in fantasies that revolve around and emerge from the tortured body of Christ:

> [In Christian masochistic fantasy,] the external audience is a structural necessity, although it may be either earthly or heavenly ... the body is centrally on display, whether it is being consumed by ants or roasting over a fire ... [and] behind all these "scenes" or "exhibits" is the master tableau or group fantasy— Christ nailed to the cross, head wreathed in thorns and blood dripping from his impaled sides. What is being beaten here is not so much the body as the "flesh," and beyond that sin itself, and the whole fallen world. (197)

Extending Silverman's definition, I would argue that Christian masochism works on both nonsexual and highly sexual levels. In *Antony and Cleopatra,* Shakespeare develops the latter, fully combining Christian masochism with variations on other fantasies of male submission, flagrantly valorizing the libidinal economy of male masochism.

In contrast to the rigidity of Virgil's epic world, the multiple identifications and desires offered by this fantasy become as fluid as the liquefied images of the "dissolving" world of Shakespeare's Egypt. Antony inhabits the Christian masochist's universe of martyrdom and identification with the crucified Christ—but with a difference. Antony's pains are true pleasures, and his role as masochist dramatically refigures an erotic economy that destabilizes conventional binaries structuring Western constructions of sexuality, heroism, and masculinity. In *Antony and Cleopatra,* Shakespeare explores these dimensions of masochism in its incarnation as word and visual image made flesh on stage. Taking on the dangerous, vulnerable position of the masochist himself, Shakespeare lifts the constraints on male masochistic desire in his version of the lovers' story. Exceeding the limits of Virgil, Plutarch, and Petrarch, and extending beyond his own earlier treatment of desire and mortality, Shakespeare exploits the full potential of pleasure in pain and sexuality in death through his antiepic tragedy, *Antony and Cleopatra.*

NOTES

I am grateful to Sara Munson Deats for her helpful commentary on this paper.

1. On the *Liebstod,* see Kuriyama 327; for a complete discussion of this narrative in modern literature, see Siegel 1–22; for my earlier treatment of this narrative in Shakespeare's *Antony and Cleopatra,* see " 'Like the lover's pinch' " 59–62.

2. For a full discussion of Shakespeare's "transvaluation" of Marlowe and others, see Bono esp. 140–224.

3. Arthur L. Little Jr. describes Antony as a figure that takes on a "feminine" identity, one whose suicide can be described as an attempted "virgin sacrifice" (see esp. 102–42). Although I fully appreciate Little's emphasis on the erotic dimensions of the play and Antony's body, I would argue that Antony plays a male (albeit alternative) rather than female role, his penetrated body signifying the erotics of the male martyr, not the feminized body, as fully explained below.

4. Mary Beth Rose explores the connections between love and sexuality in early modern drama, tracing its roots in cultural and theological discourses of the Middle Ages and Renaissance and its inflection in conceptions of marriage in tragedy (see 93–177). However, Rose does not examine this connection within the actual erotic narratives or fantasies that abound in these plays.

5. The narrative of male masochism has recurred in numerous variations throughout Western history in myths, legends, stories, poems, and so forth, but it was not until 1886, in his *Psychopathia Sexualis,* that Richard von Krafft-Ebing first coined the modern clinical term *masochism* after the nineteenth-century novelist Sacher-Masoch.

6. For Freud's earlier view of masochism, see "A Child Is Being Beaten" (*SE* 17:179–204), and for the theory of primary masochism, see "The Economic Problem of Masochism" (*SE* 19:159–69; esp. 18, 55). In the latter article, Freud also identifies three types of masochism: (1) *primary or erotogenic,* the bodily association of pain and sexual excitement; (2) *feminine,* the desire to be beaten; and (3) *moral,* the self-inflicted torture of one's ego by the superego (161).

7. Jean Laplanche argues that Freud's term *Trieb,* translated in the Standard Edition into English via French translation as "instinct" is translated more accurately as "drive" (9). I will be using Laplanche's terminology of "death drive" rather than "death instinct."

8. In Laplanche's models (based on Freud's later speculations), nonsexual aggression leads to a self-aggression that becomes the moment, crux, or "prop" for the aggression to become sexualized and manifested as either masochism or sadism (105).

9. On these splittings, ruptures, castration, and psychoanalysis, see Kristeva 132.

10. On Cleopatra as Isis, see esp. Lloyd 88–90, Kuriyama 337, and Bono 199–200.

11. For a full discussion of the trope of "dismemberment" and the heroic subject, see Wofford esp. 13–21. Wofford also reads the movement in the play from "dismembering" to a "greatly imagined whole" (13), but not in the context of male masochism.

12. On Plutarch's designation of Antony as Osiris and Cleopatra as Isis, see Brenk 160–67.

13. For a brief summary of Deleuze's theory on masochism and sadism, see also my article, " 'Like the lover's pinch' " 61.

14. For more on this myth and the blazon, see Vickers, "Diana Described" 99.
15. For many critics, Antony's body becomes "feminine." Marshall claims that Antony takes a "feminine position" (403), and Little also describes Antony's body as feminine, a "leaking" and "penetrated" female body that he offers as a virginal, "shameful self-sacrifice" to Cleopatra. Although I find both readings of Antony fascinating, I see Antony's body as an eroticized male body, albeit one that challenges norms of masculinity by taking on the "feminized" position of the male masochist (104–12). Although this position may be described as "feminized," I contend that it is not *feminine*. It is a distinctly male role.
16. For more on the heraldic and poetic traditions of the blazon, see Vickers, " 'The blazon of sweet beauty's best,' " esp. 95–98. In this important article, Vickers analyzes Shakespeare's own description and employment of the blazon in Sonnet 106 and *Lucrece*.
17. On parallels between Cleopatra and Queen Elizabeth I, see Jankowski, Reinhart, and Little, esp. 106.
18. For a summary of Deleuze's description of the mother(s) of masochism and Cleopatra, see my article " 'Like the lover's pinch' " 62–67.
19. Little also notes the association of Cleopatra—Isis—Elizabeth I—Virgin Mary—although he reads Caesar, rather than Antony—which I argue later—as having associations with Christ (see esp. 160; 157).
20. On the erotic potential of early modern representations of Christ's body, see Rambuss 268, and my article, " 'Batter my [flaming] heart,' " esp. pars. 1–4.
21. I have treated this subject earlier in the context of seventeenth-century religious poetry in " 'Batter my [flaming] heart,' " par. 3–4.
22. Silverman claims that Reik's disagreement with Freud over "moral masochism" resulted from Reik's identification of a different strain of masochism than that which Freud labeled "moral"—"Christian masochism" (197).

WORKS CITED

Adelman, Janet. *Suffocating Mothers: Fantasies of Maternal Origin in Shakespeare's Plays*, Hamlet *to* The Tempest. New York: Routledge, 1992.

Bono, Barbara J. *Literary Transvaluation: From Vergilian Epic to Shakespearean Tragicomedy*. Berkeley: U of California P, 1984.

Brenk, Frederick E., SJ. "Antony-Osiris, Cleopatra-Isis: The End of Plutarch's Antony." *Plutarch and the Historical Tradition*. Ed. Philip A. Stadter. New York: Routledge, 1992. 159–82.

Deats, Sara Munson. *Sex, Gender, and Desire in the Plays of Christopher Marlowe*. Newark: U of Delaware P, 1997.

Deleuze, Gilles. "Coldness and Cruelty." *Masochism*. New York: Zone Books, 1991.

Erickson, Peter. "Representations of Blacks and Blackness in the Renaissance." *Criticism* 35 (1993): 499–527.

Freud, Sigmund. "Beyond the Pleasure Principle." *The Standard Edition of the Complete Psychological Works of Sigmund Freud*. Trans. and ed. James Strachey. Vol. 18. London: Hogarth P, 1961. 7–64.

———. "A Child Is Being Beaten." *SE* 17: 179–204.

———. "The Economic Problem of Masochism." *SE* 19: 159–69.

Hall, Kim F. *Things of Darkness: Economies of Race and Gender in Early Modern England*. Ithaca, NY: Cornell UP, 1995.

James, Heather. "The Politics of Display and the Anamorphic Subjects of *Antony and Cleopatra*." *Shakespeare's Late Tragedies: A Collection of Critical Essays*. Ed. Susanne L. Wofford. Upper Saddle River, NJ: Prentice Hall, 1996. 208–34.

Jankowski, Theodora A. "'As I am Egypt's Queen': Cleopatra, Elizabeth I, and the Female Body Politic." *Assays* 5 (1989): 91–110.

Kristeva, Julia. *Black Sun: Depression and Melancholia*. Trans. Leon S. Roudiez. New York: Columbia UP, 1989.

Kuriyama, Constance. "The Mother of the World: A Psychoanalytic Interpretation of Shakespeare's *Antony and Cleopatra*." *English Literary Renaissance* 7 (1977): 324–51.

Laplanche, Jean. *Life and Death in Psychoanalysis*. Trans. Jeffrey Mehlman. Baltimore and London: The Johns Hopkins UP, 1976.

Little, Arthur L. Jr. *Shakespeare Jungle Fever: National-Imperial Re-Visions of Race, Rape, and Sacrifice*. Stanford: Stanford UP, 2000.

Lloyd, Michael. "Cleopatra as Isis." *Shakespeare Survey* 12 (1959): 88–94.

Marshall, Cynthia. "Man of Steel Done Got the Blues: Melancholic Subversion of Presence in *Antony and Cleopatra*." *Shakespeare Quarterly* 44 (1993): 385–408.

Plato. *"The Symposium" and "The Phaedrus"*: Plato's Erotic Dialogues. Trans. and ed. William S. Cobb. SUNY Series in Ancient Greek Philosophy. Albany: SUNY Press, 1993. 29–33.

Plutarch. "Isis and Osiris." *Plutarch's Moralia*, Vol V. Trans. Frank Cole Babbitt. Cambridge, MA: Harvard UP, 1969. 7–191.

———. "Life of Marcus Antonius." *Plutarch's Lives of the Noble Grecians and Romans*. Trans. Sir Thomas North, 1579. *Narrative and Dramatic Sources of Shakespeare*. Vol 5. Ed. Geoffrey Bullough. New York: Columbia UP, 1964.

Rambuss, Richard. "Pleasure and Devotion: The Body of Jesus and Seventeenth-Century Religious Lyric." *Queering the Renaissance*. Ed. Jonathan Goldberg. Durham and London: Duke UP, 1994. 253–79.

Reik, Theodor. *Masochism in Sex and Society*. Trans. Margaret H. Beigel and Gertrud M. Kurth. New York: Grove P, 1962.

Reinhart, Keith. "Shakespeare's Cleopatra and England's Elizabeth." *Shakespeare Quarterly* 23 (1972): 81–86.

Rose, Mary Beth. *The Expense of Spirit: Love and Sexuality in English Renaissance Drama*. Ithaca, NY: Cornell UP, 1988.

Shakespeare, William. *Antony and Cleopatra. The Norton Shakespeare*. Ed. Stephen Greenblatt. New York: W.W. Norton, 1997. 2619–708.

Siegel, Carol. *Male Masochism: Modern Revisions of the Story of Love*. Bloomington and Indianapolis: Indiana UP, 1995.

Silverman, Kaja. *Male Subjectivity at the Margins*. New York: Routledge, 1992.

Starks, Lisa S. "'Batter my [flaming] heart': Male Masochism in the Religious Lyrics of Donne and Crashaw." *Enculturation* 1.2 (1997). *http:enculturation.qmu/1_2/current.html*.

———. "'Like the lover's pinch that hurts and is desired': The Narrative of Male Masochism in Shakespeare's *Antony and Cleopatra*." *Literature and Psychology* 45.4 (1999): 58–73.

Strong, Roy C. Gloriana: *The Portraits of Queen Elizabeth I*. New York: Thames and Hudson, 1987.

Vickers, Nancy J. "'The blazon of sweet beauty's best': Shakespeare's *Lucrece*." *Shakespeare and the Question of Theory*. Ed. Patricia Parker and Geoffrey Hartman. New York: Methuen, 1985. Rpt. New York: Routledge, 1990. 95–115.

———. "Diana Described: Scattered Woman and Scattered Rhyme." *Writing and Sexual Difference*. Ed. Elizabeth Abel. Chicago: U of Chicago P, 1982. 93–109.

Wofford, Susanne L. "The Body Unseamed: Shakespeare's Late Tragedies." *Shakespeare's Late Tragedies: A Collection of Critical Essays*. Ed. Susanne L. Wofford. Upper Saddle River, NJ: Prentice Hall, 1996. 1–21.

11.
Sleep, Epic, and Romance in *Antony and Cleopatra*

GARRETT A. SULLIVAN JR.

I

Upon examining the dead Cleopatra, Caesar asserts that "she looks like sleep, / As she would catch another Antony / In her strong toil of grace" (5.2.344–346). While this could mean simply that in death Cleopatra appears to be asleep, this essay asks that we consider what it would mean to take the line literally and see Cleopatra as one who "looks *like*," or is a figure *for*, sleep. In order to do so, I will first discuss aspects of the physiology of sleep and some of the ways in which that physiology informs early modern ideals for behavior. I will then turn to an early modern literary trope, that of immoderate sleep in epic. In Spenser, for example, a female "temptress" lulls a hero to sleep, thereby preventing him, at least for a time, from achieving his quest and entering into history. Such episodes represent in miniature the tension between the imperatives of epic and romance—between purposive heroic activity that ensures the achievement of fame and the erotic divagations that threaten oblivion. Scenes of immoderate sleep trope the condition of romance, and the relation of romance to epic; within epic poetry, sleep represents, among other things, the counterpull of romance that is both disruptive and, in another sense, constitutive of epic narrative. In its own examination of relations among heroism, fame, and sexuality, *Antony and Cleopatra* provides an analogue to the epic conception of sleep; at the same time, the play makes Antony's romantic (in both senses of the term) divagation central to the narrative. In doing so, *Antony and Cleopatra* transvalues the association of sleep with sexual excess and hedonism, and it transforms what is within epic a threat to masculinity into something that lies at its very core.[1]

II

Early modern definitions of sleep routinely define it as *"an impotencie"* or a *"rest or binding"* of the senses (Cogan 231; Burton 1:153). This is because "in sleepe the senses be unable to execute their office, as the eye to see, the eare to heare, the nose to smell, the mouth to tast, and all sinowy parts to feele" (Cogan 231). As today, sleep was understood as being necessary for the well-being of the body, and this "impotencie" of the senses was considered a salutary one.

Although sleep's role in the maintenance of bodily health is multifaceted, early modern writers routinely stress its importance to digestion. Indeed, in texts that focus on physiology, sleep is often described both as aiding digestion and as a result of eating. Accounts of the physiology of sleep vary somewhat, but the basic idea is more or less as follows:[2] warm vapors ascend from the stomach, enter the naturally cold brain, and thicken there; as a result, the congealed vapors prevent the passage of the animal spirits, which are central to the functioning of both senses and faculties, through the body. (Engendered in the brain, the animal spirits are "the instruments of moouing and vnderstanding and of those noble actions that conduct our life" [Mornay 10].) At the same time, it is during sleep that the body regenerates itself. For instance, the heart "enricheth & furnisheth himself" so that, when the sleeper awakes, the heart can "distribute to the liuer and stomacke, such [vital] spirits as are sufficient for their working ... " (Mornay 27).[3]

It must be stressed that only *moderate* sleep is understood as beneficial. The same writers who trumpet sleep's virtues also underscore the hazards of sleeping too much, or even at the wrong time of day (also part of what makes sleep immoderate). Andrew Boorde draws the distinction clearly. On the one hand,

> Moderate slepe ... dothe make parfyte digestyon, it doth nurysshe ye bloud, & doth qualyfye ye heat of ye lyuer, it dothe acuate, quycken & refressheth ye memory, it dothe restore nature, & doth quyet al ye humours & pulses i[n?] man, & dothe anymate, & doth *com*forte all ye naturall & anymall & spyrytual powers of man. And such moderate slepe is acceptable in the syght of God. (Boorde sig. B3v)

Immoderate sleep, on the other hand,

> doth ingendre rewme & impostumes, it is euyl for the palsy whyther it be unyuersal or partyculer, it is euyl for ye fallynge syckenes called Epilencia, ... with all other infyrmytyes in the heade, for it induceth and causeth oblyuyousnes, for it doth obfuscke and doth obnebulate the memorye and the quyckenes of wyt. And shortly to conclude it doth perturbe the naturall, and

anymall, and spyrytyall powers of man. And specyally it doth instigate and
leade a man to synne, and doth induce and infer breuyte of lyfe, & detestably
it displeaseth God. (Boorde sig. B4r)

In the case of *immoderate* sleep, benefits become hindrances. For the one who
sleeps too much, the thickening of fumes and vapors leads to the development
of "rewme [rheum] & impostumes" in the brain, and these collections of gross
humors can generate "infyrmytyes in the heade" such as epilepsy. Moreover,
cognitive operations are seriously impeded: the immoderate sleeper loses both
memory and wit; he becomes oblivious.

What is worth pausing over here is the link between sleep and sin. In both
of the excerpts from Boorde, we pass from a physiological register to a moral
one: from animated spirits to God's approbation, and from perturbed spirits to
God's displeasure. More precisely, the physiological and the moral or spiritual are intertwined, as we see in Boorde's swift rhetorical passage from sin
to brevity of life to divine displeasure. The interpenetration of the somatic and
spiritual is apparent not only in works devoted to bodily regimen; indeed, the
sinfulness of immoderate sleep is a staple of religious discourse of the period.
From sermons focused on the problem of those who sleep in church to treatises designed to "rouze up a secure Sinner out of his sleep of security"
(Austin), immoderate sleep is understood as connoting not merely the frailty
of fallen man, but the willful embrace of fleshly desires. It is fundamentally
the lack of bodily discipline inherent in immoderate sleep that is understood
as sinful. As Michael Cope [Michel Cop] puts it, in discussion of a proverb of
Solomon:

When a man lyeth not long, but is quicke to rise vp, at a due & conuenient
houre, after his reasonable sleepe: then is he counted careful & diligent.
Contrarily, he which desireth to lye and sleepe out of measure, & willingly
standeth not vp, when it is time thertoo, is esteemed careles and sluggish:
and also the bed & too much sleepe, make a man heauie & dul witted. (Cope
sig. 85v)

More broadly, while excess sleep evokes sloth, it also frequently represents a
full array of hedonistic pleasures and desires. For example, the sleeper who
resists the scriptural call to awaken (e.g., Jonah 1.6) is viewed as one who has
been seduced by the blandishments of the material world. In short, while
excess sleep has adverse physiological effects, such effects are also the expression of a sinful way of life.

The association of excess sleep with sin is developed and modified in
Renaissance epic. In Ariosto, Tasso, and Spenser, immoderate sleep connotes
both the lure of the senses and deviation from a purposive epic quest.
Consider, for instance, the sleep of Verdant at the end of book 2 of Spenser's

The Faerie Queene.[4] Verdant is a knight who has abandoned heroic activity in favor of the erotic lassitude offered by Acrasia and the Bower of Bliss; in this regard, he represents what Guyon might have but finally does not become. Verdant is first described in the text as Acrasia's

> new Louer, whom through sorceree
> And witchcraft, she from farre did thither bring:
> There she had him now layd a slombering,
> In secret shade, after long wanton ioyes. (2.12.72)

The logic of the quest is here parodied and overturned, as epic travel / travail is echoed and replaced by Verdant's enchanted journey "from farre"; the only toil he has recently experienced are "long wanton ioyes," which are followed by his "slombering."

> His warlike armes, the idle instruments
> Of sleeping praise, were hong vpon a tree,
> And his braue shield, full of gold moniments,
> Was fowly ra'st, that none the signes might see. (2.12.80)

Praise also sleeps—the praise that would be granted to Verdant had he not abandoned his "warlike armes" and given himself over to "a slombering." Sleeping praise is also coincident with the erasure of "moniments" from Verdant's shield, markers of his identity as a knight. In becoming idle, Verdant has forgotten that identity; evidence of both his quest and his status as knight have been "fowly ra'st," and he exists at this point in the poem only as the unnamed and emasculated lover of Acrasia. Indeed, Verdant remains unnamed until after Guyon captures and binds Acrasia (2.12.82)—until, that is, Verdant is roused and forced to recall the identity that, as a sleeper, he has lost. As we have seen, immoderate sleep "doth obnebulate the memorye"—in this case, Verdant's memory of both who he is and what his "warlike armes" are designed to perform.

Spenser here also reworks the classical commonplace that sleep is antithetical to the attainment of fame. For example, Sallust, in his discussion of the Catiline conspiracy, asserts that men "whose mind is their belly; their delight sleep" are forgotten after they are buried (Sallustius sig. B2r). Within an epic context, fame is achieved through the pursuit of heroic action, which awakens the praise of the world. The attainment of that fame, then, also marks the entrance of the hero into history, whether it be the imperial history of Virgil or the Christian and national history of Spenser. Immoderate sleep, by contrast, renders one incapable of performing heroic acts and, more broadly, emblematizes the erasure of both memory and history.

This last point becomes clearer when one considers further immoderate sleep's association with both forgetting—sleep "obnebulates the memory"—and the loss of one's humanity. Sallust alludes to those "whose mind is their belly; their delight sleep"—those, that is, who are no more than beasts. This connection between excess sleep, forgetting, and animality is made explicit in the famous soliloquy in which Hamlet describes the "bestial oblivion" of men who only "sleep and feed" (4.4.40, 35; Ronan). It is also articulated by Sir Richard Barckley, who cites Sallust in order to claim that one who "is giuen to please his senses, and delighteth in the excesse of eating & drinking, may ... be called *Animal*, for he is vnworthy the name of a man. For wherein can a man more rese*m*ble brute beasts ... the*n* to serue his belly and his senses?" (Barckley 23). In Spenser, the figure who incarnates this set of associations is Grill, the knight turned hog through Acrasia's magic: "Said *Guyon*, See the mind of beastly man, / That hath so soone forgot the excellence / Of his creation ... / That now he chooseth" to maintain his beastly form (2.12.87). Grill opts for oblivion and beastliness; unlike Verdant, he does not reassume his identity or resume his quest. Grill, a figure removed from and indifferent to history, one who lives like an animal in an eternal present, is a sleeper for whom praise will always slumber. In Christian terms, this means he remains impervious to the operations of grace. Like the heavy sleeper, the beastly man forgets "the excellence of his creation" and thus is certain to be damned.

The story of Grill's transformation into a beast directs our attention to what critics have long recognized, that Spenser's Acrasia is derived from Homer's Circe; indeed, she is one of a number of Renaissance Circes, others of whom include Ariosto's Alcina and Tasso's Armida. While sleep does not play an important role in Homer's representation of Circe, it is significant to Ariosto and especially Tasso. Spenser draws heavily in book 2, canto 12 on Tasso's depiction of Rinaldo's subjection to and delivery from Armida (Tasso bks. 14–16), which includes repeated references to both Rinaldo's immoderate sleep and his eventual awakening (e.g., 14.65; 16.29, 31–33). In Tasso and Spenser we witness the conjunction of immoderate sleep, sexual satiety, loss of identity, and the abandonment of the quest that would enter the hero into history. We also encounter this linkage in Shakespeare's *Antony and Cleopatra*, with Antony resembling Verdant and Rinaldo, and Cleopatra evoking Acrasia and Armida. Although these identifications are limited— Spenser and Tasso do not serve as direct or defining sources for Shakespeare, whose Egypt bears little obvious resemblance to a world of enchanted forests and knights errant—this essay will emphasize points of convergence between epic and *Antony and Cleopatra* that speak to the play's interest in the roles of both sleep and romance within the epic tradition.

In discussing *The Faerie Queene*, Ariosto's *Orlando Furioso*, or Tasso's *Gerusalemme Liberata*, it is conventional to consider the balance of "epic" and "romance" elements in each. Put crudely, epic elements are those associated with narrative linearity and the teleological progression toward a determinate future. Romance, by contrast, is associated with both deferral and the deviation from the putatively straight and narrow path of epic. Considered in this way, some texts seem to contain only epic elements (e.g., *The Iliad*), whereas others appear closer to pure romance (e.g., *Orlando Furioso*). That being said, epic poems always contain elements of both romance and epic.

While epic is routinely associated with the political and historical—the founding of dynasties and of empires, for example—romance has been often understood as impeding history, even if the form it takes depends upon that history. As Patricia Parker states, " 'Romance' is characterized primarily as a form which simultaneously quests for and postpones a particular end, objective, or object . . . . '[R]omance' is that mode or tendency which remains on the threshold before the promised end, still in the wilderness of wandering, 'error,' or 'trial' " (4). Insofar as romance postpones the promised end, it is also associated with the promulgation of narratives, for it is of course through poetic narrative that such postponements are enacted. As Parker suggests, these narratives are accommodated to the telos of the epic mode as "wanderings," "errors," or "trials"; at the same time, they can also represent viable alternatives to that mode: "For its part, the romance narrative bears a subversive relationship to the epic plot line from which it diverges, for it indicates the possibility of other perspectives, however incoherent they may ultimately be, upon the epic victors' single-minded story of history" (Quint 34; see also Jameson 104). Not only romance but also sleep functions in this way—as an alternative perspective to epic.

A simple example of sleep as alternative perspective is to be found in a song sung to Rinaldo by a nymph of Armida's, the effect of which is to cause "stealing sleep . . . / By step and step . . . on his senses [to] creep" (Tasso Book 14, Stanza 65):

> O fools, who youth possess yet scorn the same,
> A precious but a short-abiding treasure;
> Virtue itself is but an idle name,
> Priz'd by the world 'boue reason all and measure;
> And honour, glory, praise, renown, and fame,
> That men's proud hearts bewitch with tickling pleasure,
> An echo is, a shade, a dream, a flower,
> With each wind blasted, spoil'd with every shower:
>
> But let your happy souls in joy possess
> The ivory castles of your bodies fair,
> Your passed harms salve with forgetfulness,
> Haste not your coming ills with thought and care . . .
>
> (Bk.14, stanzas 63.1–64.4)

This song, an example of the familiar *carpe diem* topos, functions as a commentary upon the putative insubstantiality of epic ambitions—"honour, glory, praise, renown, and fame," all understood as echoes or shades. In their place, Armida's agent champions the pursuit of pleasure and advocates the embrace of forgetfulness, both linked here, in conventional manner, with "stealing sleep." Whereas there is little doubt that these sentiments are denigrated within Tasso's narrative, which famously subordinates the romance "wanderings" of Ariosto to a rigorous and constraining epic design (e.g., Burrow, Helgerson), Armida's lines nevertheless represent an alternative to "the epic victors' single-minded story of history." Such an alternative is also offered in Shakespeare's *Antony and Cleopatra*.

III

Antony and Cleopatra can be understood as providing a dramatic analogue to the tension between the epic and romance modes in epic poetry. This analogue is connected to the opposition between Rome and Egypt. Although recent criticism has convincingly suggested the interpenetration of these seemingly opposed cultural categories (e.g., Cook, Harris), the extent to which the binary between Rome and Egypt mirrors a structuring geographic principle of epic that derives from Virgil—a principle inherited (and interrogated) by Shakespeare—has not been explored.[5] In the context of a discussion of Antony's flight from the battle of Actium in pursuit of Cleopatra—the representation of which appears on Aeneas's shield in *The Aeneid*—David Quint states that, according to the misogynist logic of epic, "The danger of the West is to repeat the fate of Antony, to become Easternized and womanish" (Quint 29). Moreover, the distinction between West and East—Rome and Egypt—informs the distinction between epic and romance. Indeed, the Antony of Actium—not only in *The Aeneid* but in numerous later epic poems that would, like Shakespeare's play, "invoke, imitate, and rewrite the central scene on Aeneas' shield" (Quint 31)—is a figure drawn from romance, one who rejects epic imperatives by not acting in the service of "honour, glory, praise, renown, and fame." (Shakespeare's Antony violates "Experience, manhood, [and] honour" by "leaving the fight in heighth, [to] fl[y] after [Cleopatra]" [3.10.21–24].) Antony's flight from battle constitutes a

> romance episode [that] resists being fitted into the teleological scheme of epic, and Virgilian epic ... sees any deviance from the historical course of empire assuming the shape of romance narrative ... [This is true of] an Antony who thinks more of Cleopatra than of victory .... Epic views all such romance alternatives as dead ends (quite literally in the case of Antony and Cleopatra), stories that, unlike epic's own narratives of missions accomplished, have no place to go. (Quint 34)

With its emphasis on both Actium and, more broadly, Antony's sojourn in Egypt, Shakespeare's play can be read as a romance narrative. At the same time, the imperatives of epic are evinced in the text, best represented by the figure of Caesar. In other words, the opposition between Rome and Egypt overlays the opposition between epic and romance, with the Egyptian/romantic narrative existing as a subversive alternative to the Roman/epic view of history both represented and seemingly rendered dominant by Caesar's final victory.[6]

Just as the Antony of Shakespeare's play often acts as a figure from romance, so he is frequently characterized by immoderate sleep.[7] Enobarbus describes how Antony and his companions "did sleep day out of countenance; and made the night light with drinking" (2.2.177–78); and Pompey unwittingly invokes Sallust when he wishes that Antony remain under the sway of Cleopatra: "Tie up the libertine in a field of feasts, / Keep his brain fuming," so that "sleep and feeding may prorogue his honour" (2.1.23–26). Pompey mobilizes the gendered association between sleep and oblivion that we have encountered in epic: it is the female who, according to Pompey, has the power to ensure that Antony renounce his military obligations in favor of "sleep and feeding." In addition, Pompey establishes a link between physiology, as evidenced by the brain clogged with fumes, and the loss of honor or fame. In doing so, Pompey gestures toward the logic of immoderate sleep in epic, which presupposes that the sleeper's hedonism determines not only the actions that he will (or will not) perform, but also the impact that those actions will have on how he is (or is not) viewed or remembered. For Antony to give himself over to sleep and feeding is for him to lead a Grill-like existence— tied up in a "field of feasts," with the obvious pun on "beasts"—that is antithetical to the attainment of fame.[8]

In the case of Shakespeare's Antony, sleep is frequently linked not only to oblivion or beastliness, but also to drunkenness. In the early scenes of the play, sleep and drunkenness punctuate Antony's Egyptian exploits. Consider this famous moment, narrated by Cleopatra to Charmian as evidence of happy times gone by:

> I laugh'd him out of patience; and that night
> I laugh'd him into patience, and next morn,
> Ere the ninth hour, I drunk him to his bed;
> Then put my tires and mantles on him, whilst
> I wore his sword Philippan. (2.5.19–23)

This scene has been the focus of a great deal of critical commentary, much of it focused on Antony's emasculation, which is evidenced not only by his inebriated crossdressing but also by his abandoning himself to sensual pleasure and losing his sword to Cleopatra. What should be stressed, however, is that this moment echoes sleep-centered episodes from epic. As Verdant abandons his "warlike armes" in favor of sleep and all it connotes, Antony falls into a drunken sleep; in surrendering to slumber after the performance of "long wanton ioyes," both Verdant and Antony forget themselves, as emblematized by, in the first case, the defaced shield and, in the second, both the purloined sword, once used to defeat Brutus and Cassius at Philippi, and the involuntary cross-dressing. Most important, the comparison with epic allows us to locate in this moment the same concerns that attend upon the sleeps of Verdant or Rinaldo, such as the tension between an emasculating hedonism and martial heroism, or between fame and oblivion. This scene prefigures Antony's flight from the battle of Actium and functions also as a romance narrative in minia-ture, with the repudiation of epic imperatives encapsulated in Antony's (liter-ally) unconscious relinquishing of his "sword Philippan." Antony's later complaint in defeat could have as easily been uttered here: "She has robb'd me of my sword" (4.14.23).

That complaint speaks to something important about Antony, that at various moments he voices the very imperatives that his drunken sleep repu-diates. Antony's well-known self-division is, among (numerous) other things, an articulation of the tensions between epic and romance as they are explored at the level of character. If his final words constitute an attempt to reclaim a martial, epic identity as "a Roman, by a Roman / Valiantly vanquish'd" (4.15.57–58), Antony's first great speech reveals his embracing of a romance narrative at the expense of epic values:

> Let Rome in Tiber melt, and the wide arch
> Of the rang'd empire fall! Here is my space,
> Kingdoms are clay: our dungy earth alike
> Feeds beast as man: the nobleness of life
> Is to do thus: when such a mutual pair, [*Embracing.*]
> And such a twain can do't, in which I bind,
> On pain of punishment, the world to weet
> We stand up peerless. (1.1.33–40)

Antony calls for the leveling not only of Rome but also of imperial values. Epic virtues—"honour, glory, praise, renown, and fame"—are arguably impli-cated in, if not rendered hollow by, Antony's materialist dismissal of king-doms as no more than clay. In their place, Antony champions romance, represented by the embrace of this peerless "mutual pair."

Of course this is not Antony's, or the play's, final word on epic and romance. As events progress, Antony becomes increasingly torn between the conflicting values of each—although on occasion these values seem less in tension than in concert. We can see this in the way that Shakespeare revisits and modifies the scene of Antony's emasculation. On the morning of the deci-sive battle between Caesar and Antony, Cleopatra cajoles Antony, who is keen to fight, to "Sleep a little" (4.4.1). In doing so, Cleopatra resembles a romance "temptress"—a resemblance strengthened by the fact that her plea is made shortly after the Actium debacle. Upon Antony's refusal, however, Cleopatra eagerly helps to arm him, earning from Antony the playful epithet, "armourer of my heart" (4.4.7). In only a few lines, Cleopatra changes from emasculator to armorer of Antony (thereby reversing her earlier progression from Antony's companion at arms to the occasion for his flight [3.10]). That the evocatively named Eros assists in these preparations underscores the interpenetration in this scene of the martial and the amorous—a point made by Antony's bawdy eroticization of his entrance into battle ("To business that we love, we rise betime, / And go to't with delight" [20–21]). Although Antony seems more delighted than divided here, this scene's rhetorical conflation of amatory and warlike imperatives does not mark a sustainable accommodation of romance and epic. Instead, it serves as one of the several moments at which Shakespeare explores relations between the two forms.

Scenes like this one suggest that *Antony and Cleopatra* is engaged in staging the collision of epic and romance in order to trace the conceptual and dramatic implications of that collision. In the case of Antony, "character division" emerges out of the competing pressures of these two logics (romance/Egypt and epic/Rome). To reduce Antony to the terms of such competition, however, cannot do justice to his character, or to the pathos of what Cynthia Marshall has identified as "the fact of Antony's complaint: he feels himself to be coming apart" (Marshall 392). Similarly, whereas Cleopatra might at times resemble Armida or Acrasia, the combined playfulness and anxiety of the "sword Philippan" episode—its emergence out of the details of her relationship with Antony at the very moment that, unbeknownst to Cleopatra, he has become "bound unto Octavia" (2.5.58)—complicates her identification with a Circean temptress and undermines the relatively simplistic allegorization of immoderate sleep that the play inherits from epic poetry. Sleep, like other romance (and epic) elements in *Antony and Cleopatra*, is put to dramatic uses that often simultaneously depend upon, extend, and undercut its original poetic meanings.

We have seen that the distinction between epic and romance can be mapped onto that between Rome and Egypt. This means that specific poetic elements can be both dramatically and geographically located. For instance, the comparison of Cleopatra to Acrasia seems most compelling when the imperatives of Rome are being voiced. To Pompey, she has "charms of love" and practices "witchcraft" over Antony (2.2.20–22). On the one hand, this is the epic view of a romance character; on the other, it represents the projection of romance elements onto Cleopatra at those moments when the epic view is under stress. Significantly, Cleopatra's (or, as Antony often terms her, "Egypt's") seemingly supernatural power over Antony is registered by him precisely at those moments when he either seeks to dissolve their relationship—"I must from this enchanting queen break off" (1.2.125)—or blames her for his actions—"O'er my spirit / Thy full supremacy thou knew'st, and that / Thy beck might from the bidding of the gods / Command me" (3.11.58–61). When Antony most bemoans his lost Romanness—when he regrets his repudiation of an epic role in favor of a romantic conception of the "nobleness of life"—he describes Cleopatra as a witch (see 4.12.30, 47), or as "this grave charm, / Whose eye beck'd forth my wars, and call'd them home" (4.12.25–26). Shakespeare modifies a familiar romance narrative in order to suggest that his Acrasia is as much an articulation of as a threat to epic values.

Much the same point could be made about sleep in the play. At one point, Antony quips that "The beds i' the east are soft" (2.6.50), giving this as the reason for his extended tenure in Egypt. Shakespeare here evokes an association familiar to epic poetry, the equation of immoderate sleep with both indolence and the East. In *Orlando Furioso*, for instance, the house of Sleep is located in Arabia: "Heer Sleepe doth couch his ever drousie head, / And Slouth lyes by that seems the goute to have, / And Idlenes, not so well taught as fed" (Ariosto 14.80). Soft beds are not only eastern, they are antithetical to heroic achievement. As Geoffrey Whitney's allegorical representation of Glory puts it, "I haue noe likinge of that place, / Where slothfull men, doe sleepe in beddes of downe: / And fleshlie luste, doth dwell with fowle excesse, / This is no howse, for glorie to possesse." Immoderate sleep and lust are once again conjoined, and the East is even evoked in Whitney's association of slothful men in "beddes of downe" with the Assyrian king, Sardanapalus (Whitney 42). All that being said, Antony's association of the East with immoderate sleep is presented to Pompey as a kind of worldly shorthand for explaining his relationship with "Egypt." Moreover, Antony's characterization coincides with his (temporary) return to Romanness; he thanks Pompey for rousing him from his sleep, for he has "gain'd by't" (2.6.52) through the marriage to Octavia, which is designed to cement his bond with Caesar.

In the last two paragraphs, I have presented both sleep and witchcraft as anxious epic constructs deployed by Antony at moments in which he either laments or seeks to recover his lost epic identity. At these moments, romance is not only devalued, it is scapegoated, adduced to bear the blame for Antony's immoderate sleep. However, the very operation of scapegoating reveals that the blame for Antony's actions lies somewhere else. As I have argued elsewhere, both Antony and Caesar cling tenaciously to the notion that Romanness is a stable category, despite the fact that Antony's very actions reveal its instability (Sullivan). Put differently, it is the instability within epic and Roman values themselves that necessitates the denigration of romance and Egypt. This point is wonderfully, if indirectly, expressed in Agrippa's assertion that Cleopatra "made great Caesar lay his sword to bed; / He plough'd her, and she cropp'd" (2.2.227–28), reminding us that Antony is not the first Roman leader to have relinquished his sword to Cleopatra. Certainly this action can be attributed to the witchcraft of an eastern temptress, but the echo here of the "sword Philippan" episode underscores the insecure nature of epic masculinity. In short, in *Antony and Cleopatra* those behaviors that epic demonizes, displaces, and relocates under the category of romance reveal the instability of epic itself.

But this is not the entire story, for Shakespeare does not present us only with a demonized version of romance. Both Antony's assertion that "the nobleness of life / Is to do thus" and Antony and Cleopatra's relationship are taken seriously by the play, especially in act five. As Janet Adelman has argued, a major project of the play, enacted particularly through the agency of Cleopatra, "is the relocation and reconstruction of heroic masculinity" (Adelman 177). This project is advanced through Cleopatra's memorialization of Antony, as she converts his dissipated generosity into a principle of heroism:

> For his bounty,
> There was no winter in't: an autumn 'twas
> That grew the more by reaping: his delights
> Were dolphin-like, they show'd his back above
> The element they lived in: in his livery
> Walk'd crowns and crownets: realms and islands were
> As plates dropp'd from his pocket. (5.2.86–92)

Additionally, while the love of Antony and Cleopatra is at times figured as evidence of witchcraft, it is finally ennobled; even Caesar alludes to them as "A pair so famous" (5.2.358). In this regard, romance is championed in the final act of the play.

But this is not entirely the case. If Caesar grants fame to the pair of lovers, he also demonizes anew the romance imperatives that Cleopatra has sought to elevate. "[S]he looks like sleep, / As she would catch another Antony / In her strong toil of grace." These lines evoke the commonplace association of death with sleep, but they also activate sleep's epic associations. Caesar's Cleopatra resembles figures like Acrasia—her "strong toil [i.e., net] of grace" evokes the "subtile web" with which Acrasia ensnares Verdant and others (Spenser 2.12.77)—but she is also compared with sleep itself, the very principle of erotic divagation. While in Spenser female temptresses are associated *with* sleep, Cleopatra *embodies* it as well as the threat that it poses to the Roman hero. Caesar's lines return the relationship of Antony and Cleopatra to the world of romance, thereby leaving the putatively absolute opposition between Rome and Egypt, epic and romance, very much intact. To do otherwise—to suggest that the desire for sleep haunts the logic of epic, not as an external threat but as an internal possibility—is to acknowledge that Antony performs rather than deviates from his Romanness when, like Julius Caesar, he "lay[s] his sword to bed" and embraces both sleep and Cleopatra.

The misogynist logic animating the comparison of Cleopatra to sleep papers over the instability inherent in epic masculinity by rendering Cleopatra as the external force responsible for Antony's downfall. As I have suggested, this logic also informs the Virgilian distinction between East and West. Shakespeare inherits this distinction, but he does not simply accept its terms, for in his final elevation of both Antony and Cleopatra arguably we witness the triumph of romance. And yet, Shakespeare represents this triumph as circumscribed within the world of the play. The very fact of Caesar's victory would seem to mark the absolute ascendance of epic values. Epic triumphs in *Antony and Cleopatra*, but it also fails, for it is finally romance that harnesses the desires of the play's audience. Insofar as audience members are moved to identify with Antony and Cleopatra, they are also called upon to recognize the allure of sleep and all that it emblematizes, such as sin, sexual excess, and hedonism. However, sleep not only bespeaks the values of romance, but also reveals the instability at the heart of epic. In this regard, sleep in *Antony and Cleopatra* functions less as an external threat to epic values—as the potent force that threatens to "catch another Antony"—than as a constitutive element of identity in both romance *and* epic.

NOTES

1. For recent work on sleep and early modern drama, see Bevington, Lewin.
2. The following summary is based on Mornay 22–24.
3. The animal spirits enable the operations of the mental faculties and are linked to motion and sensation; the vital spirits are associated with pulse, heartbeat and respiration; and the natural spirits are associated with nutrition and growth. Each set of spirits is linked to a specific physiological system or group of organs; the seat of the animal spirits is the brain, while that of the vital spirits is the heart, and that of the natural spirits is the liver. See Siraisi 107–09; see also Paster.
4. The following discussion of Spenser draws on Stewart and Sullivan.
5. This is not to suggest that this principle passes through the epic tradition unmodified, only to be first critically examined by Shakespeare. Space constraints demand that I ignore significant developments within the epic tradition, as well as important differences between the poems discussed here.
6. My interest here is not in arguing for the absolute nature of the romance-epic distinction, but in drawing the reader's attention to Shakespeare's deployment of this inherited opposition alongside and intertwined with the other, more famous one of "Rome versus Egypt."
7. This is true also in Shakespeare's primary source, Lord North's translation of Plutarch; see, for example, Plutarke 972, 982.
8. On the association of Antony with gluttony and sloth, see Barroll.

WORKS CITED

Adelman, Janet. *Suffocating Mothers: Fantasies of Maternal Origin in Shakespeare's Plays,* Hamlet *to* The Tempest. New York and London: Routledge, 1992.

Ariosto, Ludovico. *Orlando Furioso*. Trans. Sir John Harington. Ed. Robert McNulty. Oxford: Clarendon P, 1972.

Austin, Beniamin. *The Presvmptvovs Mans Mirrovr: Or A Watch-bell to rouze up a secure Sinner out of his sleep of security*. London: G. M. for George Edwards, 1641.

Barckley, Sir Richard. *A Discourse of the Felicitie of Man*. London: William Ponsonby, 1598.

Barroll, J. Leeds. "Antony and Pleasure." *Journal of English and Germanic Philology* 57 (1958): 708–20.

Bevington, David. "Asleep Onstage." *From Page to Performance: Essays in Early English Drama*. Ed. John A. Alford. East Lansing: Michigan State UP, 1995. 51–83.

Boorde, Andrew. *A Compendyous Regyment or a Dyetary of healthe*. London: Wyllyam Powell, 1567 [1547?].

Burrow, Colin. *Epic Romance: Homer to Milton*. Oxford: Clarendon P, 1993.

Burton, Robert. *The Anatomy of Melancholy*. Ed. Thomas C. Faulkner, Nicolas K. Kiessling, and Rhonda L. Blair. 3 vols. Oxford: Clarendon P, 1989–1994.

Cogan, Thomas. *The Haven of Health*. London: Melch. Bradwood for Iohn Norton, 1605.

Cook, Carol. "The Fatal Cleopatra." *Shakespearean Tragedy and Gender*. Ed. Shirley Nelson Garner and Madelon Sprengnether. Bloomington and Indianapolis: Indiana UP, 1996. 241–67.

Cope, Michael [Michel Cop]. *A Godly and learned Exposition vppon the Prouerbes of Solomon*. Trans. Marcelline Outred. London: George Bishop, 1580.

Harris, Jonathan Gil. "'Narcissus in thy face': Roman Desire and the Difference It Fakes in *Antony and Cleopatra*." *Shakespeare Quarterly* 45 (1994): 408–25.

Helgerson, Richard. "Tasso on Spenser: The Politics of Chivalric Romance." *Critical Essays on Edmund Spenser*. Ed. Mihoko Suzuki. New York: G. K. Hall & Co., 1996: 221–36.

Jameson, Frederic. *The Political Unconscious: Narrative as a Socially Symbolic Act*. Ithaca, NY, and London: Cornell UP, 1981.

Lewin, Jennifer. "'Your Actions Are My Dreams': Sleepy Minds in Shakespeare's Last Plays." *Shakespeare Studies*: 31 (2003): 184–204.

Marshall, Cynthia. "Man of Steel Done Got the Blues: Melancholic Subversion of Presence in *Antony and Cleopatra*." *Shakespeare Quarterly* 44 (1993): 385–408.

Mornay, Philippe de. *The True Knowledge of A Mans Owne Selfe*. Trans. Anthony Munday. London: I. R. for William Leake, 1602.

Parker, Patricia. *Inescapable Romance: Studies in the Poetics of a Mode*. Princeton: Princeton UP, 1979.

Paster, Gail Kern. "Nervous Tension: Networks of Blood and Spirit in the Early Modern Body." *The Body in Parts: Fantasies of Corporeality in Early Modern Europe*. Ed. David Hillman and Carla Mazzio. New York and London: Routledge, 1997. 107–25.

Plutarke. *The Lives of the Noble Grecians and Romanes*. Trans. Thomas North. London: Richard Field for Thomas Wight, 1595.

Quint, David. *Epic and Empire: Politics and Generic Form from Virgil to Milton*. Princeton: Princeton UP, 1993.

Ronan, Clifford J. "Sallust, Beasts That 'Sleep and Feed,' and *Hamlet*, 5.2." *Hamlet Studies* 7 (1985): 72–80.

Sallustius, C. C. *The Two Most Worthy and Notable Histories*. Trans. Thomas Heywood. London: Iohn Iaggard, 1608.

Shakespeare, William. *Antony and Cleopatra*. Ed. M. R. Ridley (1954). London and New York: Routledge, 1988.

———. *Hamlet*. Ed. Harold Jenkins. London: Metheun, 1982.

Siraisi, Nancy G. *Medieval and Early Renaissance Medicine: An Introduction to Knowledge and Practice*. Chicago: U of Chicago P, 1990.

Spenser, Edmund. *The Faerie Queene*. Ed. Thomas P. Roche Jr. Harmondsworth: Penguin, 1978.

Stewart, Alan, and Garrett A. Sullivan Jr. "'Worme-eaten, and full of canker holes': Materializing Memory in *The Faerie Queene* and *Lingua*." *Spenser Studies* 17 (2003): 215–38.

Sullivan, Garrett A., Jr. "My Oblivion Is a Very Antony." "Planting Oblivion: Forgetting, Memory and Subjectivity in English Renaissance Drama." unpublished book MSS.

Tasso, Torquato. *Jerusalem Delivered*. Trans. Edward Fairfax. Carbondale: Southern Illinois UP, 1962.

Whitney, Geoffrey. *A Choice of Emblemes* (1586, facs. ed). Ed. Henry Green. New York: Benjamin Blom, 1967.

12.
The Allusive Tissue
of *Antony and Cleopatra*

LEEDS BARROLL

The drama of the early modern period in England has been a product much used by historians seeking to understand these times because the words, situations, and ideational leanings discernible in public plays seem to provide ready access to the society of which they were a part. Nevertheless, a dilemma inherent in this hermeneutics of cultural interpretation lies in the multiple avatars of the playtext, in the fact that its written form—the product we have available for analysis—is only a blueprint, as it were, for performance. In the context of early modern stage practice, the written text unfolded dynamically in the sequential manner of a film, a piece of music, or an opera, its individual parts looping back and anticipating one another, its meanings taking shape in the fluid interplay among actors. This unwinding in (audience) time that was the public play made demands—visual, aural, and/or intellectual—soliciting the attention of eye, ear, and especially memory. That is to say—taking an example from *Antony and Cleopatra*—the "ending" of the play was (and is) perceived not only in itself—whatever that means—but also in terms of sights, sounds, or sequences presented previously as part of the performance. The audience is told that Cleopatra "looks like sleep" as if she were ready to entrap another Antony—and the past of the performance is put before them; similarly, when Dolabella flatters Octavius for his foresight concerning Cleopatra's probable behavior, his words resonate with his own secret warning to Cleopatra in an earlier scene.

But we have never attended an early modern performance of *Antony and Cleopatra*—just as no one who indeed did see the play but died before 1623 ever *read* the Folio text. There are two, not one, modes of existence of this product. Thus, the historian who would use a "public play" to study the culture of which it was a part is, in effect, not using the play at all in this sense. Nor is this remark an unnecessary splitting of hairs: Shakespearean printed texts do not contain an overabundance of stage directions. Thus, in *Hamlet*, for instance, we must ask what it would mean to the cultural historian if we knew positively that Hamlet wore black throughout the play rather than only in his initial scene, where costume is such a center of comment. How would it affect a sense of "cultural evidence" if the black costume were a constant in the performance? And would this "sense" change if the original actor of Hamlet wore black only for that initial scene? Or, again, in *Antony and Cleopatra*, on the night before the second battle, when Hercules/Bacchus is said to be leaving Antony, the stage directions call for the music of "hautboys"—now glossed as "oboes." What was the *sound* of oboes supposed to evoke in the audience?[1]

These vanished performances we will never know. What we think we do know is a version of the play that, by its phenomenological nature, is indeed available: the "play" in manuscript or print. But the fact that the book or manuscript exists in tangible form as our only entrée to the dramatic product of the early modern period, as the only way of knowing a play, cannot negate the existence of the vanished performance itself. Indeed the concept of such a thing—a vanished performance—can discipline our historical thinking when we deal with a dramatic product. For even though the tangible aspect of the product defines our way of knowing—we will never see the performance— we are aware of the limitations suggested for this particular (printed) product by the prospect of its hypothetical and theoretical nonidentical twin, the performance in its time.

These truisms have relevance to this essay because it deals with what might be described as yet a third formation to be inferred from the tangible existence of the playbook. If the first "formation" is the playbook itself, and if the second is the performance to be inferred (even if never seen) from the playbook, then the third I would describe, briefly, as follows. One assumes that the early modern English players, or those who directed their performing, worked from something like the playbook, even if we call this a "script," because they could not have performed *Antony and Cleopatra* without being given the words and sequences—the "play"—from which to work. Indeed, one could call this the teleology of the written form of the play: like sheets of music, this written "play" existed only to be performed. What cannot be avoided in this restatement of the obvious, however, is that in order to be "played," the drama, in the absence of telepathic powers in the author, had to be conveyed as written text. Today, perhaps, with film and computer graphics, an author might well transmit his drama to actors in some other form; in the early modern period this form had to be some variety of what we call "literature," understood as the written text (Berger Jr. 144–56).

"Literature," however, has its own peculiarities. Even as the early modern actor or director dealt with the sum of the words in the script (or, in the case of the actor, in his "role") with a view to enacting a performance, he was comprehending the matter that lay before him not as a "performance" but as a structure of words that he was *envisaging* as performance. In this sense, the word-structuring to which this actor or director was exposed had itself a kind of autonomy, not in the sense that it "intrinsically" held its own "meaning" but that it was the raw material, so to speak, of diverse interpretations of people other than the author. A possible parallel from outside the playhouse is the early modern sonnet. We know that dramatists wrote them, practicing a distinctive clustering of word and allusion as art. Their exercise in this form prompts me to suggest that we read play scripts not only to assess the manner of performance one might see implied there, but also to trace the association of ideas in a manner more familiar to readers/interpreters of sonnets. But rather than claim that the writer of early modern play scripts conceived of them as sonnets, I am suggesting that even though a cultural historian may approach the play script as words to be envisaged for a performance, it is concomitantly possible to extrapolate another distinctive kind of cultural evidence: that to be garnered from its association of ideas.[2]

My own analysis does not begin, then, with the issue of how the symbolic material of the play script may have been interpreted in performance. Rather, I am interested in the way in which certain images considered in a quasi-autonomous context evoke multiple associations with sites outside the text—sites that the cultural historian is interested in probing. Certainly these images may be integral to the dynamics of the drama as acted, but their allusive power is broader than the interpretive possibilities of any single performance of the play script: their allusive power generates multiple and often contradictory interpretive possibilities.[3] To illustrate the point, I would like to "cheat" by citing an interchange in *Antony and Cleopatra* that calls attention to itself by slowing markedly or even suspending the pace of the dramatic action. This is the dialogue between Cleopatra and the simple countryman who brings her the figs with the asp that will help her effect her suicide.

CLEOPATRA: Hast thou the pretty worm of Nilus there
   That kills and pains not?
CLOWN: Truly I have him but I would not be the
   party that should desire you to touch him, for his biting is
   immortal; those that do die of it do seldom or never recover.
CLEOPATRA: Remember'st thou any that have died on't?
CLOWN: Very many, men and women too. I heard
   of one of them no longer than yesterday, a very honest
   woman—but something given to lie, as a woman
   should not do but in the way of honesty—how she
   died of the biting of it, what pain she felt. Truly, she
   makes a very good report o' th' worm; but he
   that will believe all that they say, shall never be sav'd
   by half that they do. But this is most falliable, the
   worm's an odd worm.

CLEOPATRA: Get thee hence, farewell.

CLOWN: I wish you all joy of the worm.

CLEOPATRA: Farewell.

CLOWN: You must think this, look you, that the
    worm will do his kind.

CLEOPATRA: Ay, ay, farewell.

CLOWN: Look you, the worm is not to be trusted but
    in the keeping of wise people; for indeed there is no
    goodness in the worm.

CLEOPATRA: Take thou no care, it shall be heeded.

CLOWN: Very good. Give it nothing, I pray
    you, for it is not worth the feeding.

CLEOPATRA: Will it eat me?

CLOWN: You must not think I am so simple but I
    know the devil himself will not eat a woman. I know
    that a woman is a dish for the gods, if the devil dress
    her not. But truly, these same whoreson devils
    do the gods great harm in their women; for in every
    ten that they make, the devils mar five.

CLEOPATRA: Well, get thee gone, farewell.

CLOWN: Yes, forsooth. I wish you joy o' th' worm. *Exit*. (5.2.243–79).

Within this exchange is a tissue of learned and popular allusion. On the surface, one notices first a series of seeming inconsistencies. Human beings, after they have "died" from the worm, sometimes recover. Indeed, one woman who died can still speak of the worm. A very honest woman is given to lying; but women should only lie honestly. These paradoxes seem resolved, however, by the cultural signal given when the Egyptian countryman, supposedly living in a time before Christ, speaks of "the devil" and "devils." Long-standing tradition, of course, associated the Devil with the idea of the serpent. Arthur Golding, translator of Ovid, offers a few of these traditional images in an introduction to an edition of the Psalms:

Yet have we one thing in ourselves and of ourselves—even original sin, concupiscence, or lust—which never ceaseth to egg us and allure us from God and to stain us with all kind of uncleanness according as St. James sayeth, "Every man is tempted of his own lust." This is the breath of the venomous cockatrice that hath infect the whole offspring of Adam. This is the sting of that old Serpent (Golding sig. *4).

Indeed, the asp, as a form of that serpent, occupied an especially suggestive place in this dialectic. Thomas Wilson's *Christian Dictionary*, for example, refers to a well-known locus in Romans to describe one kind: "another [kills] by sleep; thus doth the slothful slay their own souls."[4]

Slaying the soul has similar eschatological relevance as an idea because, as is well known to scholars of the early modern period, "death" occurred in two ways: there was physical death, but, also "death" of the soul, and it was, of course, in this sense that the Serpent, as the Devil, could "kill."[5] Thus Cleopatra's conversation with the clown about "death" becomes symbolically significant in Christian salvific discourse. A glance at the above lines renders this fairly obvious. Cleopatra asks the clown to tell her about people who have died of the aspic bite which the clown has ignorantly but significantly termed "immortal." He mentions one type. Using the various early modern shadings of the term "honest"—respectable, truthful, chaste—he alludes to a woman "something given to lie." She, apparently, makes "a very good report o' th' worm." But this is because she is either a liar, or because sexually she is "something given" to lying, and the clown goes on to warn: "he that believes all that they say shall never be saved by half that they do." Being "saved," of course, should be the teleology of all early modern Christians: if so, better not imitate the actions of those who are liars or who lie around. Further, the passage is interesting because although Cleopatra wants the clown to leave, she nonetheless allows him to persist in his warnings about the "worm." Apparently it cannot act otherwise than is its nature: it is "not to be trusted" for there is no "goodness" in him. One must be wise, we gather, to deal with the worm at all (as Dr. Faustus found).

Significantly, in this passage the referential context for the metaphors changes twice more. The worm is not worth the feeding, the clown warns, and Cleopatra asks, "Will it eat me?" If the "serpent" was bad for salvation, it could reappear as another kind of animal: one that devoured.[6] But "you must not think I am so simple," the clown retorts, "but that I know the devil himself will not eat a woman." Rather, a woman is a dish for the gods—"if the devil dress her not." Yet, he seems to conclude, changing metaphor once again, devils are not very good at dressing women, for "these same whoreson devils do the gods great harm in their women; for in every ten they make, the devils mar five."

Here the allusion may well be to the popular understanding of the parable of the Wise and Foolish Virgins, for although the Bible did not specify a number, tradition held that there were ten virgins. In the Biblical story (Matthew 25) these virgins trim their lamps with oil while awaiting the coming of the Bridegroom (whose arrival can never be predicted). Taken as a metaphor of the state of the soul when Christ returns on Judgment Day, the emphasis of the story is on spiritual preparation. Thus the lamps of the five Foolish Virgins who fall asleep (traditionally known as the *fatues*) run out of oil, and these virgins are shut out of the marriage feast when the Bridegroom comes. In the exegetical tradition, this activity was taken as a playing out of the idea of souls "asleep in sin." The *fatues* had not reinforced their faith (the lamps) with works (the oil—or vice versa, as is the case in certain subtraditions).

The parable itself was almost universally understood as a reference to Judgment Day. Christopher Sutton's *Disce Mori*, first published in 1600 and reprinted four times by 1609, describes the art of dying well in just those terms:

> It is time to arise from sleep. Our spring is fading, our lamp is wasting and the tide of our life is drawing up little and little unto a low ebb.[7]

Later, Sutton observes, "Foolish virgins think that their oil will never be spent." But one cannot expect to live forever. The moisture in our lamps will last just so long "until at last the light goeth out, the lamp is spent, and so an end" (from the 1601 ed: sigs. Q2-R6v). Interestingly, Cleopatra reverses the direction of this symbolism in her own final speeches with her waiting women when she observes that their "lamp is spent"; they are for the dark, and death is to be a marriage.

But if the parable of the virgins is a double-edged signifier in the exchange between Cleopatra and the Clown, there is an even more complex cluster of images that resonates throughout the play from other early modern descriptions of the queen. For example, in Samuel Brandon's *Virtuous Octavia,* a closet drama written by a member of the Countess of Pembroke's circle in the 1590s, the reader is told that what attracts Marc Antony to Cleopatra is "a siren tongue" and "a crafty Circe's wit." Cleopatra can "Syrenize," invading Antony's senses "Mermaid-like" and with a "sugared tongue" (Daniel 1329–88 and Brandon 1947–52). Although Samuel Daniel does not use these terms in his own closet drama, *Cleopatra,* they do appear in an epistle he wrote, "Octavia to her Husband" (1599). Reproaching Antony throughout, and having previously termed Cleopatra a "Siren," Octavia describes a dream—symbolic, one imagines, of Actium—in which Octavius and Antony are two hippopotami in combat. On the back of one animal "a wanton Mermaid sate, / As if she rul'd his course and steer'd his fate" (Daniel 115–38). Indeed, a stage play, *Caesar's Revenge,* has onlookers speaking of the "fair Egyptian sorceress" and noting how much more dangerous are "Circe and Calypso's cup" than Scylla and Charibdys. Even Julius Caesar, when he returned to Rome, was glad to have cast off the "linkes" of "that fair charming Circe's wounding look." Such allusions are interesting in the light of their tradition. It was well known that Circe, since Boethius, was regarded as a symbol of temptation to incontinence and most often to lechery.[8]

Circe and the Sirens, however, were merely specific examples of the early modern use of the beautiful woman as metaphorical exemplar of the dangerous allure of incontinence, or sensual self-indulgence—of voluptas. Figures other than those from Greek mythology appear in this tradition—the Acrasias and the Armidas, and Cleopatra herself.[9] To grasp the spirit in which many passages of early modern English poetry described outstandingly beautiful women, we should look at such a description in Sebastian Brandt's *Stultifera Navis,* as translated by Alexander Barclay in 1570:

Lo gorgeous gallants; lo gallants here am I
Lo here fair Lust; full enemy to virtue
    Clothed in laurel in sign of victory.
The large world I whole to me subdue
My streaming standards allayed with sundry hewe
In triumph shineth brighter than the sun.
I all the world to my empire have won.

All fragrant flowers most pleasant, gay and sweet
Whose sundry sorts no living man can tell
Unto my pleasure are spread under my feet
That all the air enjoyeth of the smell.
The violet that in odor doth excel
About in bosom by me always I bear
The same oft time inlaced with my hair.

Harp in hand, and wearing soft silk, Lust allures the youth of the world, but she is exposed by the figure of Virtue who explains that although Lust is fair to see, with her wanton eyes, golden hair, and "purple garlands couched with precious stone," yet all this is mere "worldly vanity." Despite having a fair forehead, Lust is void of chastity

And all the fashion and shape that is in thee
Defiled and blinded is by viciousness.[10]

The rationale for such elaborate descriptions of the gorgeous female figure who did not specifically symbolize "Lust" but, rather, *voluptas*—the addiction to "fleshly" pleasures—was that incontinence appealed not to one, but to all of the five senses. Harington's Ariosto thus describes the allegorical purpose of the Alcina description by noting that in this portrait we see "the eye, the ear, the taste, the smelling, the wit, the thoughts, all fed with their objects of delight," while Robinson's *Mary Magdelene* sums up the description of the corrupt court of Pleasure by noting,

Twas hard to say, which had the most delight,
The taste, the touch, the hearing, smell, or sight.[11]

Indeed, in such presentations, specific objects came to furnish the appeal to specific senses. Sight was primarily suggested by the beauty of the female figure whose hair was blond.[12] If colors were mentioned, the figure was dressed in or surrounded by gold and sometimes purple—Tasso presents gold in the form of gilded trees while Ariosto offers a golden palace. The sense of smell was titillated by flowers or perfume, and the hearing assailed by melodious birds or musical instruments. Taste was beckoned by the spreading of a sumptuous banquet, while the sense of touch was variously approached. Ariosto's knight sleeps between "Cambrick sheets perfumed" (sig. E3) while Tasso has the *eyes* of admirers touching the fair skin of Armida (sig. G). There is "soft silk between" the hair and the neck of Brandt's Voluptas "lest it might fret" (sig. 2Sv), while Pleasure, in *Mary Magdalene*, tells her admirers that silken beds swell to meet them (1.1.109).[13]

The use of such techniques in some depictions of Cleopatra herself— especially in Brandon's and Daniel's allusions to Cleopatra as Circe, siren, or mermaid—suggest that portraiture of the Egyptian queen strongly inclined to this representational tradition. This is not surprising because Horace, writing for the victorious Augustus Caesar, described Actium as a victory over some kind of early *Voluptas* figure. The poet's subsequent place in the Western tradition may well have occasioned the frequent references to Cleopatra in the presentations of many writers.

Shakespeare's association of his own queen with this tradition— especially in the famous speech of Enobarbus—is in one sense surprising, as he would seem to have moved away from such platitudes in the extreme subtlety of other aspects of his own portrait (Barroll 130–87). Further, because Enobarbus's description of Cleopatra strongly recalls similar material in Plutarch, many critics have been content to focus on the beauty of the speech, while noting the Shakespearean enhancements of North's wording. Indeed, it sometimes seems in these comments that it was the duty of the play to echo Plutarch, if only to convince us of Cleopatra's beauty.[14] But it is not difficult to adduce correspondences between Enobarbus's speech and the *voluptas* tradition.

The attraction of the five senses plays an important part in the presentation. Flutes appeal to the hearing. Smell and touch are developed by a series of conceits. The very winds and wharves are influenced by two separate perfumes; the water is "amorous" of the strokes of the oars while the barge's tackle "swell with the touches" of "flower-soft hands." Cleopatra is surrounded by gold and the sails of her barge are purple. And rather than being dressed as Venus (Plutarch's description), Cleopatra in the play "o'erpictures Venus" who was usually painted blond and white. Thus the description depicts her at the height of conventional literary beauty even though elsewhere in the play she is "wrinkled deep in time" and "black" with "Phoebus' amorous pinches."[15] Cleopatra also has what might be called a "mirthful train," another element of the voluptas tradition.[16] In the "Circe school" this metaphorically significant train consisted of fair and wanton young people, while in other practice one finds allegorized figures and Cupid. The Shakespeare passage uses Plutarch's pretty boys who look like Cupids, but his pretty girls, although Nereids, also significantly look like "mermaids," a resemblance established twice.[17]

In sum, Enobarbus gives us metaphorically a burnished throne on which reclines a Venus surrounded by mermaids and cupids, dispensing things attractive to the senses, a Venus who finally invites Antony to a banquet at which he loses his heart. Viewed from a slightly different angle, we have a nautical Bower of Bliss—a travesty of a ship with a mermaid at the helm, a poop of beaten gold, silver oars, perfumed and purple sails, and "swelling" silken tackle. Armida, perhaps, at sea.

In the end, Enobarbus's paean to Cleopatra's female beauty has nowhere to go in this play—it seems almost supererogatory. Enobarbus himself is not swayed by it: his own actions are unaffected. Nor do we see Antony dreaming of the Egyptian queen's looks: the interaction between the lovers is realized through subtleties in the manner in which they relate to each other: Actium, her false suicide, his jealousies about her and his own reputation, and so forth. The speech is not even the primary platform for warning the spectator about the dangers of Cleopatra: the play seems to leave such instruction to Octavius. Rather, the likelihood is that Enobarbus's speech, like other *voluptas* figurings of the period, served primarily to associate *Antony* with his counterparts in the tradition—with Spenser's Guyon, Tasso's Rinaldo, Ariosto's Orlando—for whom *voluptas* was a test of moral character. And if the representation of a traditional emblematic temptress is complemented by the representation of someone who is tempted, then Antony's place in the *voluptas* tradition is strongly reinforced by his simultaneous association with Hercules.

Hercules's choice of virtue over *voluptas* was well known.[18] Indeed, the "choice" and the system of morality inherent in it were often expressed by allusion to the Greek letter Y (Pythagoras's letter Gamma), which was a graphic of the crossroads crux.[19] But Hercules was an ambiguous symbol because he had once made the wrong choice in his subjugation to Omphale (or Iole). Thus, on the one hand, he was the hero who had chosen the right path in the face of temptation, and, on the other, he became the archetype of the person, inherently capable of better things, who nevertheless had been subdued by incontinence. Spenser and Shakespeare were of course familiar with the duality of this tradition as were a number of other early modern writers.[20] That it did not confuse poets or their readers can be inferred from Spenser's practice in the *Faerie Queene*. In Book 5 he celebrates Hercules, wielder of the club of "Justice" as the archetype of Artegal (5.1.1–3), yet, in his description of Artegal's bondage to Radegund, he alludes to Hercules again in the context of his bondage (5.5.24).

Thus the full panoply of symbolic associations with Hercules is important for *Antony and Cleopatra*. Plutarch himself, of course, mentions Hercules. When he compares Antony to his Greek counterpart in the parallel *Lives,* he mentions that Cleopatra enticed Antony to corrupt himself just "as we see in the painted tables, where Omphale secretly stealeth away Hercules' club, and took his lion's skin from him."[21] In the *Life* itself we read that "it was said that Antonius came of the race of Hercules as you have heard before. And in the manner of his life he followed Bacchus: and therefore he was called the new Bacchus" (sig. 4P2). Thus it is not surprising that the biographer tells of the mysterious music that the guards hear as "song as they use in Bacchus' feasts" (sig. 4P5), and that some thought that "it was the god unto whom Antonius bare singular devotion to counterfeit and resemble him" (sig. 4P5v). In the play, however, after the guards comment on the mysterious music with appropriate exclamations of wonder, the second soldier remarks, uncontradicted:

> 'Tis the god Hercules, whom Antony loved,
> Now leaves him. (4.4.15–16)

Another node in this web of Herculean allusion is the crossdressing in the traditional stories of Hercules-subjugated, which describe him as wearing the clothes of Iole or Omphale. Underlying this crossdressing motif was a familiar Aristotelian line of thought that characterized rational thinking as male and irrational, emotional thinking as female. In this kind of discourse, hierarchies were violated because reason should dominate emotion as the male principle dominates the female principle. Thus, some like Hotspur could be termed by another character as womanish or effeminate for allowing his emotions to get the better of him (*1 Henry IV*: 1.3.236–38).[22]

The idea was often presented emblematically. Relevant, I think, is a note by George Chapman to his translation of Hesiod (1618) in which the woman (presumably Pandora) opens the well-known chest of human ills and lets them escape. Chapman glosses part of the Hesiod poem:

> And by the woman is understood Appetite, or Effeminate
> affection, and customary or fashionable indulgence to the
> blood, not only in womanish affections, but in the
> general fashions of men's judgments and actions.

Plutarch at one point uses not a woman but a man *dressed* as a woman to convey the same idea. Speaking of an older statesman persuaded to give himself over completely to "delicacie and pleasures," he suggests two pictures. One is the painted table of Hercules in the court of Omphale "in a yellow coat like a wench, making wind with a fan and setting his mind with other Lydian damsels and waiting-maids, to broide his hair and trick up himself." "Even so," Plutarch continues,

> We despoiling a man of estate of his lion's skin,
> that is to say, of his magnanimous courage and a
> mind to be always profiting the commonwealth, will
> make him good cheer continually, and delight his
> ears with pleasant songs.[23]

In Shakespeare's play, as many critics have noted, Cleopatra boasts of drinking Antony to his bed and

Then put my tires and mantles on him, whilst
I wore his sword Philippan. (2.5.23–24)

A moment on stage early in the play is also suggestive. Enobarbus, joking with the Egyptian ladies, says,

Hush, here comes Antony.
CHARMIAN. Not he; the Queen.
[Enter Cleopatra.]

The script constructs the "mistake": although we expect Antony, a woman comes on stage. This moment echoes Heywood's *The Brazen Age,* another play acted by Shakespeare's company, which has the following stage-direction:

Enter Omphale, Queen of Lydia with four or five maids [and] Hercules attired like a woman, with a distaffe and a spindle.

Telemachus remarks: "Speak! Which is Omphale/Or which Alcides?" (Heywood 3.241).

Although I have alluded to stagecraft many times in this essay, my general point is not concerned with how the action described by the play may be interpreted on stage. It is obvious that stage action creates its own medium of perception, one that is different from that of a read text; but it may be less obvious that the theatrical resonances of inscribed cultural traditions—especially considering the amplitude of such traditions—are difficult for the critic to incorporate fully in conjectures about performance. I would argue that in order to apprehend the breadth of this allusive landscape, it is necessary to approach the script with a "reading eye"—to stop the action, as it were. Thus, the conversation between Cleopatra and the Clown may be said to evoke the discourse of early modern eschatology; and the emblematic tradition of *voluptas* so prominent in Shakespeare's play may be found variously adapted to the uses of religion, poetry, and other drama. Whether or not the Herculean or Armida-style references might have passed by an early modern audience too quickly to be noticed in a performance of *Antony and Cleopatra* is not the point. On some textual plane, this allusive tissue, as I have called it, does exist. Probing its meanings is, therefore, integral to our understanding of the deliberate and indeliberate dissemination of ideas in early modern England, as well as to our grasp of the ideational ambience that would have informed any performance of *Antony and Cleopatra.*

NOTES

1. Some sense of the potential ambiguities here may be gathered from what Baines and Kirnbauer tell us of "hautboys" when they note that the "hautboys" was a woodwind instrument with a double reed—a shawm—that could be used also for all members of an ensemble of wind instrument *players*. The general problem of the synesthesia of response in early modern audiences has attracted considerable interest recently among scholars of the theatre. See Smith.

2. The kind of inquiry I have in mind is not a reiteration of the nineteenth-century practice of treating Shakespeare's plays as literary works, as did Bradley, or of the twentieth-century work by Caroline Spurgeon on the so-called image-pattern. The old New Criticism valued Spurgeon because her search for similar images could be appropriated as hermeneutic matrix for probing the mind and intentions of the author—a reductive form of Freudian psychodynamics. However, it is easy in retrospect to denigrate a methodology that is in some respects naive, and I advert to it here neither in support nor mockery. Rather, I recall this critical practice to distinguish it from my own. I am assuming that so-called image clusters in play scripts may be isolated as indices of broader cultural concerns which necessarily resonate in the performance of the play. I assume that my work is closer in spirit to that of Patricia Parker, whose groundbreaking studies of dramatic language have broadened our understanding of what constitutes a dramatic text.

3. Two recent works deal with each member of the distinction that I am concerned with: West's chapter 4: "Holding the Mirror up to Nature? The Humanist Theatre Beside Itself," in which the issue of performance is seen as becoming distinct in the period; concomitantly, Erne's chapter 1: "The Legitimation of Printed Playbooks," which even argues that many plays were written to be printed for an audience of readers.

4. Wilson continues: "The wicked are said to have *the gall of asps within them*, Job 20:14; *to suck the poison of asps*, ibid.16; to have the poison of asps under their lips, Rom. 3:13." The context of Wilson's definition is more general than he has suggested, however. To quote the Geneva Bible (Rom. 3:10ff.): "There is none righteous. No not one. 11. There is none that understandeth: there is none that seeketh God. 12. They have all gone out of the way: they have been made altogether unprofitable: there is none that doeth good, no, not one. 13. Their throat is an open sepulcher; they have used their tongues to deceit; the poison of asps is under their lips."

5. Isabella adverts to the concept in *Measure for Measure* when refusing Angelo's proposition:

> Better it were a brother died at once,
> Than that a sister, by redeeming him
> Should die forever. (2.4.106–08)

6. See Quarles which alludes to 1 Pet. 5:7. See also Walker sig. Ov: "Satan that ravenous beast swallows not up the godly," with ref. to 2 Cor. 11:22. *The Glass of Vainglory* (London, 1605) sig. Ev3 (attr. to St. Augustine and with four editions between 1585 and 1605) presents another example as does Peacham sig. Y3 where the image is that of a ravenous crocodile. See also Day sigs. 2I3v–2K.

7. For the Wise and Foolish Virgins, generally, see Fulke sigs. M2v–M3. This is a parallel-text edition (Rheims New Testament and the Bishops' Bible). Fulke quotes Jerome, Augustine, and Gregory in a debate about whether the parable refers to grace or merit as criterion for Heaven, emphasizing the point that the parable is almost univocally evocative of Judgment Day. For other treatment of the *fatues* see the glosses of the various Bibles: The Great Bible (1540) and the Geneva New Testament (1557). The Coverdale Bible (1535) glosses according to Matthew 7:24, Mark 13, and Luke 6, 12, 21 whose consensus is that readiness is all. Contemporary comment includes Gataker, Farley, and G. B.'s sermon on the Last Judgment preached at Paul's Cross shortly before *Antony and Cleopatra* appeared in the Stationers' Register. Finally, Day, associates the *fatues* text with the illustration and text of Rev. 12: "the great dragon, that old serpent, was cast out," and so on.

8. See Lemmi, but the *locus classicus* is Hughes. See also Palingenius sigs. Cv, L8v and "Circe" in *Reallexikon fur Antike und Christentum* cols. 136–42.

9. See Palingenius, sig. K6v gloss; *Batman upon Bartholome* sigs. 3T2–3T2v; Bacon: "The Syrenes or Pleasures"; Fraunce sigs. F4–F4v; Whitney sig. Bv; Fletcher 2:89. For the synonymity of "siren" with "mermaid," see Root 107–09; Lotspeich 81. For the traditional association of Circe with sirens and Nereids, see Browne 255.

10. See Brandt sigs. 2S–2Tv. For other specific explanations of intention in the portrayal of such figures, see Palingenius, sigs. B8–C4, C7v–D7; Robinson, *Mary Magdalene*, Part 1, sts. 6–19; Ariosto sigs. E4v—E5, the explanation by Harington of the allegory. See also his statement that the allegory of Alcina's island is "so plain to those that will indeed look heedfully into it, as needs no exposition." See also Tasso sig. 2B3; Rankins sigs, B4–B4v; Bradshaw sigs. C4–C4v.

11. See Ariosto, sig. E4v; Robinson, parts I, ll. 157–58 (cf. ll.125–26). See also Spenser, *FQ* 2.21.42 and 2.11.9ff.; Bradshaw sig. C4v; Chapman 53; Rich sig. G3; Tomkis *passim*; Marston 3.47–48.

12. See Barclay sig. 2S5; Ariosto sig. E2v; Tasso sig F6v. Spenser does not describe Acrasia's hair but the mermaids in the pool are both blond as is Cleopatra in *Caesar's Revenge* (l. 520).

13. All these elements combined are also to be found in Palingenius sigs. B7–C; Ariosto sigs. D4–E3; Spenser 2.12.58–77. Rankins uses the sumptuous banquet as his main device (sigs. C2–C2v).

14. From the perspective of performance, it should be noted that the actor in the role of Cleopatra has made many appearances in the play prior to this speech, so that Enobarbus's words will either emphasize a male actor's inability to attain to such dazzling siren-like heights, or will unnecessarily distract an audience from what the actor is attempting to do. For not only does the "description" depict a figure that the audience has already come to know well, but, waiving the question of "personality," it confines itself to a catalogue of visibilities that the audience would be singularly well equipped to judge.

15. That Cleopatra surpasses a painting is also a traditional move in this game. Tasso, Ariosto, and Spenser contrasted nature with art in the same manner. Tasso describes Armida: "The marble goddess set at Guidos, naked,/She seemed, were

she unclothed, or that awaked" (sig. E2v). cf. Tasso sig. 2B3v, G; Spenser 2.12.59. For the philosophy underlying this device, see Lewis 324ff.

16. See Palingenius sig. B8; Barclay sig. 2S2v; Ariosto sig. D6v, E2; Spenser 2.12.72; Robinson 1.81ff.; Rankins sig. B4v.
17. The definition of "Nereid" as "mermaid" is not Plutarchan. Rather it is derived from North's translation of Amyot's "les fee's des eaux" and thus is an early modern and especially an English turn of phrase. cf.. Browne (in note 9).
18. For the most detailed discussion of this tradition, see Panofsky 37–83. cf. J. Seznec *passim*, and Simon for the general medieval tradition. For specifically early modern traditions, see Tietz-Conrat 305–09. Salutati's *De Laboribus Herculis* is noted by Allen where he traces the motif to Prodicus of Cheos. Other important loci were probably Cicero sigs. G3v–G4, Q2v, and, in the Countess of Pembroke's influential circle, probably de Mornay.
19. See Panofsky, pp. 44, 65–68, and Chew 175–78. Ludovico Vives's commentary in Augustine, sig. I also refer to this graphic and adduces a poem on the subject supposedly by Virgil and later translated by George Chapman. Palingenius and his glossator, sig. L8v, and Rankins, sig. C4, are also familiar with the tradition.
20. The tradition went back to Fulgentius. This Hercules appears, of course, in Shakespeare's *LLL*, 1.2.69ff., 182; *Ado*, 3.3.145. This negative Herculean tradition is traced in Tuve 147–65 and, i.a. the satire in *Lingua*, 5.7.
21. See Plutarch, *Lives*, sigs. XXX. Antony is similarly associated with Hercules in the art of the palace of Armida, Tasso, sig. 2B3, and in Spenser's Book 5 (5.7.2). Cf. Agrippa sigs. 2B4–2B4v.
22. *OED*: "effeminate, adj." offers a number of contemporary examples of such usage, but the theory underlying the notion is explored by Palingenius sig. F6; in *Muld Sacke* sig. B2; and in Downam 7.33.1; as well as by Vives quoting Sallust in the notes to the *City of God*: see op. cit, sig. 2A4. For other instances see Spenser 2.9.21 and Cornwallis sigs. D8v, F7v, G7v.
23. Plutarch, *Morals*, sig. 2Kv. Other instances in which the figure of a woman evokes this nexus of ideas are to be found in Boccaccio 72–78. Thynne; Wither 4.23; Marston sig. G5; Hall 71ff. The much discussed series of pamphlets issued 1619–20, *Hic Mulier, Haec Vir*, and *Muld Sack* are basically informed with this notion, although they go beyond it.

WORKS CITED

Agrippa, Henry Cornelius. *Of the Vanity and Uncertainty of Arts*. Trans. John Sanford. London: 1569.

Allen, Don Cameron. *Mysteriously Meant*. Baltimore: Johns Hopkins UP, 1970.

Ariosto, Lodovico. *Orlando Furioso*. Trans. John Harington. London: 1591.

Augustine, Saint, Bishop of Hippo. *The Glass of Vainglory*. London: 1605.

———. *The City of God*. Trans. John Healey. London: 1610.

Bacon, Francis. *The Wisdom of the Ancients*. Trans. Sir Arthur Gorges. London: 1619.

Baines, A. C. and Martin Kirnbauer. "Hautboy." 20 Sept. 2003. *The New Grove Dictionary of Music Online*. Ed. L. Macey. http://www.grovemusic.com.

———. "Shawm." 20 Sept. 2003. *The New Grove Dictionary of Music Online*. Ed. L. Macey. <http://www.grovemusic.com>.

Barroll, Leeds. *Shakespearean Tragedy: Genre, Tradition, and Change in* Antony and Cleopatra. Washington, DC: The Folger Shakespeare Library, 1984.

Berger, Harry, Jr. "Bodies and Texts." *Representations* 17 (Winter 1987): 144–56.

Boccaccio, Giovanni. *Forty-six Lives,* Trans. Henry Parker, Lord Morley and Ed. H. G. Wright. London: *EETS OS* 214, 1943.

Brandon, Samuel. *The Virtuous Octavia.* London: 1598.

Bradshaw, Thomas. *The Shepherds Starre.* London: 1591.

Brandt, Sebastian. *Stultifera Navis.* Trans. Alexander Barclay. London: 1570.

Browne, William. *Works.* Ed. W. C. Hazlitt. London, 1869.

Bury, George. *The Narrow Way and the Last Iudgement.* London: 1607.

Chapman, George. *Poems.* Ed. P. B. Bartlett. London: 1941.

Chew, Samuel C. *The Pilgrimage of Life.* New Haven: Yale UP, 1962.

Cicero, Marcus. *Three Bookes of Duties.* Trans. Nicholas Grimald. London: 1596.

Cornwallis, William. *Discourses.* Ed. R. H. Bowers. Gainesville: U of Florida P, 1952.

Daniel, Samuel, Ed. *Works,* London: 1885.

Day, John. *A Book of Christian Prayers.* London: 1578.

de Mornay, Philip. *Discourse of Life and Death.* Trans. Countess of Pembroke. London: 1592.

Downam, John. *The Second Part of Christian Warfare.* London: 1611.

Erne, Lukas. *Shakespeare as Literary Dramatist.* Cambridge: Cambridge UP, 2003.

Farley, Robert. *Light's Moral Emblems.* London: 1638.

Fletcher, Giles and Phineas. *Poetical Works.* Ed. Frederick S. Boas. Cambridge: 1909.

Fraunce, Abraham. *The Third Part of the Countess of Pembroke's Ivychurch.* London: 1592.

Fulgentius, Fabius Planciades. *Fulgentius the Mythographer.* Ed. and Trans. Leslie George Whitbread. Columbus: Ohio State UP, 1971.

Fulke, William. *The Text of the New Testament.* London: 1589.

Gataker, Thomas. *The Spiritual Watch.* London: 1619.

Golding, Arthur. Dedicatory Epistle. *The Psalm of David.* London, 1571. Sig. 4.

Hall, Joseph. *The Discovery of a New World.* Trans. John Healey and Ed. Huntington Brown. Cambridge, MA: 1937.

Heywood, Thomas. *Dramatic Works.* Ed. R. H. Shepherd. London: 1874.

Hughes, M. Y. "Spenser's Acrasia and the Circe of the Renaissance," *JHI* 4 (1943): 381–99.

Klauser, T. Ed. *Reallexikon fur Antike und Christentum.* Stuttgart, 1955.

Lemmi, C. W. "The Symbolism of the Classical Episodes in *the Faerie Queene.*" *Philological Quarterly:* 8 (1929): 279.

Lewis, C. S. *The Allegory of Love.* Oxford: Oxford UP, 1958.

Lotspeich, Henry Gibbons. *Classical Mythology in the Poetry of Edmund Spenser.* Princeton: Princeton UP, 1932.

Marston, John. "The Insatiate Countess." *Works.* Ed. H. H. Wood. Edinburgh: 1939.

———. *The Scourge of Villainy.* London: 1598.

Mulier, Hic. *Muld Sacke.* London: 1620.

Palingenius, Marcellus Stellatus. *The Zodiake Of Life.* Trans. Barnabe Googe. London: 1579.

Panofsky, Erwin. *Hercules am Scheidewege.* Leipzig: 1930.

Parker, Patricia. *Shakespeare from The Margins: Language, Culture, Context*. Chicago: U of Chicago P, 1996.

———. "Black *Hamlet*: Battening on the Moor." *Shakespeare Studies* 31 (2003): 127–64.

Peacham, Henry. *Minerva Britanna*. London: 1612.

Plutarch. *Lives*. Trans. Thomas North. London: 1579.

———. *Morals*. Trans. Philemon Holland. London: 1603.

Quarles, Francis. *Emblems*. London: 1639.

Rankins, William. *A Mirrour of Monsters*. London: 1587.

Rich, Barnabe. *My Lady's Looking-Glass*. London: 1616.

Robinson, Thomas. *The Life and Death of Mary Magdalene*. London: 1899.

Root, Robert K. *Classical Mythology in Shakespeare*. New York: Holt, 1903.

Salutati, Coluccio. *De Laboribus Herculis*. Ed. B. L. Uilman. Zurich: 1951.

Seznec, Jean. *The Survival of the Pagan Gods*. Trans. B. F. Sessions. New York: 1953.

Simon, Marcel. *Hercule et le christianisme*. Paris: 1955.

Smith, Bruce R. *The Acoustic World of Early Modern England: Attending to the O-Factor*. Chicago: Chicago UP, 1999.

Spenser, Edmund. *The Poetical Works*. Ed. J. C. Smith. 3 Vols: Vols 2 and 3. Oxford: The Clarendon Press, 1909.

Spurgeon, Caroline. *Shakespeare's Imagery and What It Tells Us*. Cambridge: Cambridge UP: 1935.

Sutton, Christophe. *Disce Mori*. London, 1600.

Tasso, Torquato. *Godfrey of Bulloigne*. Trans. Edward Fairfax. London: 1600.

Thynne, Francis. *Emblems and Epigrams*. Ed. F. J. Furnivall. London: *EETS SO* 64, 1876.

Tietz-Conrat, E. "Notes on 'Hercules at the Crossroads,' " *JWCI* 14 (1951): 305–09.

Tomkis, Thomas. *Lingua*. London: 1607.

Tuve, Rosamund. "Spencer's Reading" The *De Claris Mulieribus*." *SP* 32 (1936): 147–65.

Walker, Ralph. *A Learned and Profitable Treatise of God's Providence*. London: 1608.

West, William N. *Theatres and Encyclopaedias in Early Modern England*. Cambridge: Cambridge UP, 2002.

Whitney, Geoffrey. *A Choice of Emblems*. Leyden: 1586.

Wilson, Thomas. *A Christian Dictionary*. London: 1612.

Wither, George. *Emblems*. London: 1628.

13.
O'erpicturing Apelles
Shakespeare's *Paragone* with Painting
in *Antony and Cleopatra*

MARGUERITE A. TASSI

For her own person,
It beggared all description: she did lie
In her pavilion, cloth-of-gold of tissue,
O'erpicturing that Venus where we see
The fancy outwork nature.
(*Antony and Cleopatra* 2.2.207–11)[1]

Enobarbus's famous evocation of Cleopatra in Shakespeare's *Antony and Cleopatra* figures the Egyptian Queen as greater than a work of art; yet in Enobarbus's imagination she is grasped best through comparison with art. This trope is striking, but not surprising given the classical tradition of *ut pictura poesis* (as is painting, so is poetry) and Shakespeare's conception of Cleopatra as a famed masterpiece, self-invented as well as mythologized by others. The conceit of Cleopatra "o'erpicturing Venus," however, has a competitive ring to it, expressing not so much the celebrated contest between poetry and painting as a strategic contest between *theater* and painting. Enobarbus's erotic vision of Cleopatra on the Cydnus river is set in competition with Apelles's legendary picture of Venus's birth, the *Venus Anadyomene* (*Rising from the Sea*).[2] Furthermore, in re-creating Cleopatra for the English stage, Shakespeare has positioned *himself* as a competitor not only with classical and Renaissance writers but also with the great painter Apelles, who was said by Pliny to have "surmounted" all painters and whose distinct genius lay in capturing *venustas*, the Latin root for Venus, signifying sexual charm and visible grace (1964, 279–80).

Pliny's *Natural History* was the primary text through which Apelles's life and works were known during the Renaissance.[3] While Renaissance visual artists on the continent re-created the long-lost *Venus Anadyomene* in painting and sculpture, English verbal artists such as Sidney and Spenser invoked the

Fig. 14. Nicolas Poussin, *The Birth of Venus*, circa 1635 or 1636. Courtesy of the
Philadelphia Museum of Art, the George Elkins Collection.

picture through analogies (for an example of these recreations, see the Poussin
painting in fig. 14).[4] Shakespeare's analogy to Apelles's *Venus*, however,
serves as more than classical allusion or figurative ornamentation; it bespeaks
a theory of invention based on artistic competition. As Leonard Barkan
astutely argues, "Mimesis is by its very nature a discourse of competition—
or, at the very least, of comparison" (1995, p. 342). In addition to *ut pictura
poesis,* competition between artists and the arts calls to mind the Renaissance
paragone. The *OED* indicates that "it is not certain whether the original sense
[of *paragone*] . . . was 'comparison', or 'touchstone'; in the latter sense, it might
stand for *pietra di paragone*." This term may have derived from the Greek
word for *whetstone*, the idea being that one thing is sharpened or tried against
another. In this essay, I argue that painting serves as the whetstone in *Antony
and Cleopatra* against which theater sharpens and exercises its mimetic
powers.

According to Erwin Panofsky, the origin of the *paragone* lay in "the
Greek passion for debate" and can be detected as early as the fifth century BC
(1). While contests between the visual arts and between artists are recorded in
ancient texts, including Pliny's *Natural History,* the visual arts seem to have
played little to no role in debate literature of the Middle Ages. Not until the
Renaissance did the visual arts come to the fore once more as part of an effort

to raise painting's status to that of a liberal art (Panofsky 2). The fundamental question in *paragone* literature centers on representational truth or verisimilitude—which art reigns supreme in its representation of nature? Such contests often involved the claims of word against image. Significantly, in Pliny's account of the dedication of the *Venus Anadyomene* in the temple of Julius Caesar, he claims that an epigram praising picture and painter "inriched," even "went beyond the worke" (1964, p. 285). The logocentrism implicit in this praise highlights the all-important role of language in Pliny's retrieval of classical art: words lend a kind of vitality and source of enrichment to his catalogue of unseen images and, above all, confer fame upon those images.

In *Antony and Cleopatra*, Shakespeare expresses a set of ideas about the invention, competitiveness, reception, and fame of art similar to those of Pliny. I suggest, therefore, that the *Natural History* has a kind of subterranean existence in Shakespeare's play. As in Pliny's text, in Shakespeare's drama words play an obvious role in conferring fame (or infamy) upon the work of art (Cleopatra/Venus). Enobarbus's high-flown rhetorical speech is the most splendid example in the play of what Leonard Barkan calls the "logocentric nature of fame" (1999, p. 75). The speech starts with monosyllabic deliberation, "I will tell you" (2.2.200), which is followed by a six-beat pause for effect. Yet, as a dramatic character, Shakespeare's Cleopatra achieves fame in the verbal/visual arena of the theater where a contest between word and image, verbal picture and stage picture is at work. Fame lies not only in what is *said* about her person, nor simply in her *image*, but in the complex, immediate pleasures she offers when the actor presents her as a speaking, visible presence onstage. English Renaissance dramatists had an especially fertile site for staging tensions, confrontations, and conjunctions between word and image. Their art was inherently a mixed form, or "image-text," to borrow W. J. T. Mitchell's term, in which the underlying conflict played out in "the materiality of representation" (91).

Ut pictura poesis and the *paragone* are the discourses underpinning not only Enobarbus's Cydnus speech but, more pervasively, the rhetoric of art that sustains the imaginative fabric of the play. Shakespeare's only explicit use of the *paragone*, as critics have pointed out, can be found in *Timon of Athens*, a bitter tragedy written close in date to *Antony and Cleopatra*.[5] The *paragone* takes center stage in the opening scene of *Timon* when a poet and painter launch into debate about the relative merits of their arts. As patronage artists, they speak knowingly about representation and artistic devices for capturing the monarch's image. Shakespeare's deployment of this formalized debate may have been a clever, fashionable gesture, a kind of insider's joke for the *connoscienti* at Whitehall, but, more important, on a theoretical level the *paragone*'s inclusion in *Timon* signals Shakespeare's awareness of the competing powers of pictures and words to create mimesis, particularly that of the human person, in the theater.

Unlike *Timon of Athens, Antony and Cleopatra* does not formalize the contest; rather, the play stages an extensive, subtle *paragone* with painting, which erupts occasionally in allusive passages, such as Enobarbus's painterly evocation of Cleopatra. The *paragone* is fought on both classical and early modern grounds, for the great Apelles stands alongside Pliny, Plutarch, and early modern painters, dramatists, and masque-producers as Shakespeare's competitor. Although he remains unnamed, Apelles would have been the classical painter with whom Shakespeare would match skills, for during the Renaissance, Apelles's name was synonymous with artistic genius. At the same time, by alluding to Apelles, Shakespeare places himself in the company of Renaissance visual artists like Titian who painted classical themes and images. He is able, as well, to demonstrate cultivation and knowledge to his most important audience-member—his patron and king, James I.

As Italian Renaissance and classical imports, these sophisticated discourses on the arts gave Shakespeare a competitive edge in the elite visual culture of James's court. Shakespeare appealed to the literary and visual interests of the king and his courtiers, as well as to their taste for decadence. Many theatergoers at James's court were not only educated readers of classical texts but also knowledgeable and enthusiastic viewers, even connoisseurs, of Renaissance continental art. Courtiers were treated to lavish masques with Italianate scenic devices; these masques were part of a courtly aesthetic of magnificence. Shakespeare accommodated his aristocratic audience's tastes by cultivating hyperbole (the figure best suited to convey magnificence) and appropriating visual effects from masques, statuary, and portraiture. In *Antony and Cleopatra* Shakespeare offered the king a flattering portrait of magnificence, "of the epicureanism, sensuality, and generosity that were so central to his [James's] character" (Kernan 131). As Alvin Kernan argues, Cleopatra performs both rhetorical and theatrical alchemy by "transforming vulgar waste and ostentatious expenditure into beauty and delight" (131). She stages herself with all the skill of an Inigo Jones/Ben Jonson masque production. Unlike Ben Jonson, Shakespeare did not write masques, nor did he view spectacle as Jonson did—mere show without a "soul";[6] rather, he engaged visual culture and aesthetic issues in radical artistic terms through daring appropriations of and competition (implicit *paragone*) with other visual arts.

The most stunning example of this strategy can be found in a play that followed *Antony and Cleopatra* by a few years. In *The Winter's Tale* (c. 1609–11), Shakespeare stages a scene in which the work of art, a seeming statue of Hermione, comes to life. The treatment of character as sculptural form echoes and gives material reality to the conceit of sonnet 55: "Not marble, nor the gilded monuments/Of princes, shall outlive this powerful rhyme."[7] Bringing "pictures" to life in the theater provokes aesthetic and emotional responses that lie beyond the powers of poetry. Here is a visual marvel, accompanied by language but not dependent on it, a wondrous device achieved without flash, machinery, or monetary cost. In fact, the phenomenal effects of stone made flesh are created solely through the actor's imitation of a painted sculptural form. Shakespeare's use of pictorial art in *Antony and Cleopatra* finds its most radical expression in Cleopatra's suicide spectacle, which, as in *The Winter's Tale*, aligns theater with sculpture.[8] Characters in the play (Cleopatra, Antony, Octavia) are transformed through rhetoric and performance into three-dimensional marble masterpieces from classical antiquity and continental Europe. While the "statue" of Hermione seems to metamorphose into flesh, Cleopatra stills herself into a marble form. Her pictorial rhetoric initiates the transformation that she enacts bodily through performance:

> My resolution's placed, and I have nothing
> Of woman in me. Now from head to foot
> I am marble-constant. (5.2.237–39)

Shakespeare's appropriations of visual arts through language and performance create a phenomenology of theater in which spectators are called to imagine and experience the actor in a state of artistic metamorphosis.

CLEOPATRA ANADYOMENE: O'ERPICTURING THAT VENUS

As *Antony and Cleopatra* demonstrates, theater shares certain qualities with painting—the appeal to the eye as the primary sense, an emphasis on color, costume, and gesture, a technical arrangement of figures in a field, and the use of iconographic conventions. Shakespeare's mimetic and comparative terms in Enobarbus's speech—*like, seem, seeming, beggared, o'erpicturing, fancy, outwork*—encourage an awareness of the enchanting illusion of art, while, at the same time, expressing the playwright's desire to compete with and surpass painted art. The conceit that Cleopatra *overpictures* a painting of Venus— Apelles's *Venus Anadyomene*—strategically challenges the achievement of painting, for even this most skillful of paintings is rendered inadequate when compared to Cleopatra's art, and her art shares an affinity with theater. Shakespeare's claim is subtly woven into the rhetoric of this speech: as a visual medium, *theater overpictures painting*. Conceptualizing theater in relation to painting capitalizes on the visuality of Shakespeare's art, as well as the elusive contest between arts, a contest that gives rise to the moving, speaking pictures of theater.

Rather than leaving a discreet fingerprint from his source, Shakespeare quite obviously and competitively borrows much of the material in Enobarbus's speech from another text, Sir Thomas North's translation of Plutarch's *Lives of the Noble Grecians and Romanes* (1579). The most important departures from this textual source lie in the dramatic performance of the speech and its suggestive pictorial rhetoric, both of which highlight the process of mimesis and art's relationship to its audience. Shakespeare's speech is crafted as a fanciful, even extravagant, moment of storytelling, with a raconteur who half remembers, half invents Cleopatra's seduction of Antony on the river Cydnus. The onstage audience is hungry to hear about it, for the speech is provoked by Maecenas's goading about Egypt: "Eight wild boars roast whole at breakfast" (2.2.189–90), he has heard, and "She's a most triumphant lady, if report be square to her" (2.2.194–95). Enobarbus takes up the challenge and delivers a "report" of Cleopatra that is competitive with all prior verbal "reports" of the "most triumphant lady" (2.2.194).[9] The soaring hyperboles are designed to thrill auditors, yet, at the same time, they demand an act of the imagination. As Lucy Gent points out, in this "play of virtuoso pictorial effects in virtuoso poetry," onstage auditors give us the "sense of being invited to participate in creating an illusion" (62). Enobarbus's language—his use of the term *fancy,* for example—signals as much. *Fancy* refers to the imagination, illusion, and invention, all central to the activity of making art. Fancy, which transcended nature in the painter's Venus invoked by Enobarbus, is clearly at work in the making of Enobarbus's portrait of Cleopatra Anadyomene, the "rare Egyptian" (2.2.228).

Shakespeare's cue for the painting trope came directly from North's translation of Plutarch's *Lives,* in which the ancient writer compares Cleopatra to a picture of Venus, and indirectly from Holland's translation of Pliny's *Natural History,* in which a number of Venuses, both paintings and statues, are memorialized for posterity. North's translation, however, reads as a fairly straightforward description of a monarch showing herself publicly as a deity: "And now for the person of her selfe: she was layed under a pavillion of cloth of gold of tissue, apparelled and attired like the goddesse Venus, commonly drawen in picture: and hard by her, on either hand of her, pretie faire boyes apparelled as painters doe set forth god Cupide" (Plutarch; qtd. in Bullough 274). Shakespeare's version says something rather different: not only is Cleopatra comparable to one great masterpiece rather than a "commonly drawen" Venus, but her person "beggared all description" (2.2.208). This is a familiar rhetorical ploy, the inexpressibility topos, but it importantly emphasizes a paradox of theatrical language and performance. Enobarbus's emphasis is on spectatorship, on verbally showing Agrippa and Maecenas how Cleopatra "appeared indeed" (2.2.198) and how everyone went "to gaze" on her (2.2.227); yet paradoxically, he celebrates a vision that is withheld from his spectators' eyes—"you had to have been there and *gazed upon her* for yourself to understand just how magnificent she was," he all but says. He is able to describe her supporting cast in pictorial detail, the "pretty dimpled boys, like smiling cupids" and "Her gentlewomen, like Nereides, / So many mermaids" (2.2.212, 216–17), but the Egyptian queen's extraordinary presence defies verbal conjuring. Indeed, the seductive elements of the absent Cleopatra are suggested in the eroticized images of other figures that traditionally appeared in Venus portraits.[10]

This mode of theatrical spectatorship, in its dialectical play of absence and presence, is signaled from the very beginning of *Antony and Cleopatra*. In the opening scene, spectators witness a skillfully framed piece of staging (constructed through both word and image) that mimics a perspective picture.[11] The perspective employed here is anamorphic, a kind of trick painting that incorporates a second, distorted image. Cleopatra's grotesque vision of a double-headed Antony, invoked later in the play, confirms the significance of anamorphic art in the play: "Though he be painted one way like a Gorgon, / The other way's a Mars" (2.5.116–17). As Anne Barton indicates, the "Janus-faced image of Antony derives from Elizabethan perspectives, pictures in which the identity of the object represented changed according to the angle from which it was viewed" (129). In theatrical art, the analogy to perspective painting sets up a fundamental mode of spectatorship. The Roman soldier Philo constructs an anamorphic picture of Antony, who is both "plated Mars" (1.1.4) and "strumpet's fool" (1.1.13). The first words of the play belong to the moralistic Philo, who invites us, along with his friend Demetrius, to participate in the viewing and making of a perspective picture. Like Enobarbus, Philo retrieves the past glory of his subject (Antony) by reference to the pagan deity he most resembles: Mars. This idealized image, however, is set in competition with a distorted one. In Philo's view, Antony does not overpicture the greatness of some painted Mars; rather his eyes and heart distract him from his former greatness, such that now he appears in the guise of a "strumpet's fool." The central panel of the "painting" is a familiar iconographic subject to Renaissance viewers: Mars Subdued by Venus. This scene is similar to the Cydnus speech scene in its emphasis on visual detail, rhetorical picture-making, and the presence of an onstage audience; however, the crucial difference here is that the actors playing Antony and Cleopatra appear "in person" for all to behold. Their entrance, repartee, and performance are set in competition with Philo's anamorphic images. In making claims for love's extravagance and the imagination's conquest of reality, the lovers seek to evade the rational, moralistic view shaped by Philo's speech. They evade Philo's construction of their images as strumpet and strumpet's fool by offering their own depictions of themselves. From the opening scene, Shakespeare establishes the contest between theater and other arts; theater vies with painting by ultimately subverting pictorial art. Philo creates an anamorphic perspective painting that is *overpictured* by Antony and Cleopatra's "live performance."

In the Cydnus speech, however, no Cleopatra appears to make good or give the lie to Enobarbus's vision. On the one hand, by withholding the stage image of Cleopatra in her barge, Shakespeare calls attention to the imaginative function of *picturing* as a way of knowing character. His premise is that to imagine a phenomenon is to have it painted in the mind, much as Plato suggested in *Philebus*.[12] On the other hand, in Enobarbus's speech Shakespeare is setting up his final scene in the play, a scene that delivers a live person, a Cleopatra more splendid than both verbal evocation and the painted Venus to which she is compared. The speech, in effect, creates appetite, a desire for fulfillment through the erotic gaze and dramatic representation. As a storyteller, then, Enobarbus far surpasses a Philo; he employs a narrative strategy designed to reproduce in his auditors the effects Cleopatra has on male spectators—to make hungry where most he satisfies.

The phrase "beggared all description" echoes Antony's extravagant claim from the play's first scene: "There's beggary in the love that can be reckoned" (1.1.15). In both uses of this term, there is the sense that magnificence (the expression of Antony and Cleopatra's love, Cleopatra's person) has the power to expose the poverty of anything that desires to contain or vulgarize it. Description is rendered a mere beggar feeding off of the sensuous phenomenon of Cleopatra on her barge. In *beggaring*, there is also the notion of outdoing or transcending, which reinforces the mimetic trope of competition and the idea that live performance outdoes any verbal account of what is seen. Theater not only beggars all description, it beggars painting. Although poetry, with its figurative evocations, may try to perform the conjuring act of presence, words fall short of that phenomenal experience, which only theatrical immediacy can provide.

If Enobarbus's evocation of Cleopatra is central to Shakespeare's invention of character and, more fundamentally, his theory of invention, then it functions as a reflection on the theatrical dialectic between absence and presence, the unseen and seen, the imagined masterpiece and the visible body. His speech is anticipated in an earlier exchange with Antony about Cleopatra's powers of visual and erotic enticement. When Antony laments, "Would I had never seen her!" (1.2.159), Enobarbus exclaims: "O, sir you had then left unseen a wonderful piece of work, which not to have been blest withal would have discredited your travel" (1.2.160–62). Enobarbus's figure of Cleopatra as exotic masterpiece establishes her fame as well as the sensuous fullness, even blessing, of the Queen's visible presence. To *see* this work of art is to *credit*—or lend value to—one's travels, for she is one of the world's wonders. Enobarbus's claim raises a question about art's affective abilities in relation to visibility: Is the source of Cleopatra's power found exclusively in her visible form and the aesthetic erotics of the gaze? What value lies in an unseen Cleopatra, or an unseen masterpiece? This last question takes us into the realm of lost masterpieces and Pliny's *Natural History*, which memorializes many of the ancient world's lost works of art. When Enobarbus wishes to call up a specific "wonderful piece of work," it seems most logical that he would think of a Plinian masterpiece, "that Venus where we see / Fancy outwork nature" (2.2.210–11). For Shakespeare's spectators, "that Venus" would have been a lost work from classical antiquity; in other words, an unseen masterpiece such as one could read about in Pliny's text. When Enobarbus invokes the image of Venus, it is only fitting that the picture, already lost to the ruins of time when Pliny was writing, is not described with any specificity.

Apelles's Venus is known through textual recovery, rather than a history of spectatorship. The accounts of early art historians such as Pliny guarantee Apelles and his *Venus Anadyomene* a "place i' th' story" (3.13.47) of art; thus, narrative fills the gap created by the material decay and loss of the masterpiece. Yet, a notable feature of the Venus in Pliny's text is her paradoxical absence; that is to say, Pliny does not recreate her through description or *ekphrasis*. Cleopatra, too, as some critics have observed, is absent from the very speech that mythologizes her.[13] Her absence from the stage is, of course, dramatically necessary at this moment, but her absence from the speech represents a "gap" in Enobarbus's artful recreation. Neither Cleopatra nor the Venus portrait can be satisfactorily resurrected through *ekphrasis,* a rhetorical mode intended to bring a work of art or other visible phenomenon before the mind's eye. A trope of competition—mimesis as competition—replaces the graphic representation of Cleopatra's person.

This brings us back to the most telling trope of competition in the Cydnus speech—*overpicturing.* Enobarbus's meaning is that Cleopatra transcends a picture of Venus, an imaginative work of art that surpassed the goddess herself in beauty and grace (as, for example, the Etty painting in fig. 15). The only early modern example of the word *overpicture* recorded in the *OED* is this one from Shakespeare's play; the definition offered is "To represent or picture in excess of the reality; to depict or describe with exaggeration." Shakespeare invents this term to describe and theorize an act of supreme artistic achievement. This triumph apparently lies beyond imagining, beyond visual representation, yet paradoxically can be grasped only through the mind's ability to picture it. Shakespeare's introduction of a picture analogy in the text would seem to engage the visual culture of his audience, yet, as I have been emphasizing, Enobarbus's rhetoric evades direct description of what we most want to see—Cleopatra's person. He uses both hyperbole and paradox, the most frequently employed figures of speech in *Antony and Cleopatra.* However, Janet Adelman makes an important distinction: "paradox itself is embodied in the person of Cleopatra," whereas Antony is defined by hyperbole (116). Enobarbus's speech defines Cleopatra's character specifically in relation to the paradoxes of art.

Enobarbus's peculiar insistence on "that Venus" directs his onstage and offstage auditors to imagine momentarily a particular painting of Venus in association with Cleopatra. For Jacobean audiences at the Globe, the allusion may simply have suggested a vague image of sensuous feminine beauty. Enobarbus's "we" generously leaves no one behind; it assumes that the play's spectators collectively can see such a picture in their mind's eye, even if it remains in the realm of the imagination or derives from literary fame rather than from the material image of a painter. Few commoners would have seen any kind of pictorial representation of Venus, yet the literate, at least, would probably have known tales from Ovid and other classical sources that included a description of the goddess of love and beauty. The situation would have

Fig. 15. William Etty, *The Arrival of Cleopatra*, 1821. Courtesy of National Museums Liverpool (Lady Lever Art Gallery).

been quite different for Shakespeare's audiences at court, the Blackfriars, or an aristocrat's house, for many of those spectators could have seen representations of Venus in emblem books and other illustrated books from the continent. They may also have seen paintings in English and continental collections or purchased paintings of Venus and other pagan gods to hang in their own galleries. R. Shaw-Smith speculates that Shakespeare has in mind a lascivious picture of Venus, such as the one mentioned in *The Voyage of Captain John Saris to Japan, 1613* (93). The eroticism suggested in Enobarbus's images, however, should not be perceived as mere lasciviousness. Although critics such as J. Leeds Barroll view Cleopatra as a figure of *Voluptas* and her analogue Venus as the *Venere Volgare*, or "figure of lechery" (75), Enobarbus is undeniably appreciative of Cleopatra's grace and charms. His unprompted praise of her paradoxical ability to transcend baseness attests as much: "for vilest things / Become themselves in her, that the holy priests / Bless her when she is riggish" (2.2.248–50).

Given the historical time (first century BC) and setting of the play, the most fitting art allusions would have been to objects of the ancient world known primarily, if not entirely, through literature. Apelles's Venus has the virtue of being a known prototype in Shakespeare's culture. From Pliny, Shakespeare would have heard or read about painters who not only had wit and inventiveness, but also exhibited a competitive spirit, which often played out in public arenas. About Apelles, Pliny makes the broad claim that "his inventions served as precedents and patterns for others in that art to follow" (1962, p. 416). Equally important to Shakespeare's implicit art theory were Pliny's claims about the artist's relationship with nature and his inventive freedom. Pliny emphasizes verisimilitude through the trope of liveliness, which was popular in Elizabethan literature as well. He claims that one of Apelles's pictures "seemed to challenge Nature" (1962, p. 416) and that the artist "had such a dexterity in drawing portraits so lively, and so near resembling those for whom they were made, that hardly one could be known from the other" (1962, p. 414).

The idea of the artist's freedom of invention (often presented as a *paragone* with nature) can be found in the work of Shakespeare's contemporary, Sir Philip Sidney, who claims in his *Defence of Poesie* (1595) that the poet's mind, not chained to nature, ranges freely "within the Zodiack of his owne wit" (88). This notion can be found as well, however, in Pliny, who specifically praises inventive creativity in painters and sculptors. Equally for Sidney, Pliny, and Shakespeare, art has the power to master its own imaginative reality. Sidney's famous definition of poetry as a "speaking picture" expresses just such a "utopian poetics, a dream that poetry can do just about *anything*," as Leonard Barkan phrases it (1995, 327). Enobarbus's moment of poetic magnificence mythologizes Cleopatra / Venus on the Cydnus; even greater, however, is Cleopatra's poetry when she enlivens a mythic Antony. He becomes a masterpiece, transformed within the expansive zodiac of her wit. Yet, because he has died by the end of act 4, spectators no longer anticipate a theatrical vision of Antony. The divided catastrophe of the play, to invoke Anne Barton's felicitous term, leads us to the special circumstances of act 5, where the stage becomes the ancient *theatrum*, a place for *seeing* Cleopatra. She eternizes herself not as Caesar's prize in a Roman triumph but as a theatrical wonder. Cleopatra shows herself not only as the great Egyptian queen and "wife" to Antony, but as a great work of art: "Now from head to foot / I am marble-constant" (5.2.238–39); "I have / Immortal longings in me" (5.2.279–80). In the play's final spectacle, Shakespeare rejects painting and aligns Cleopatra's performance—and theatrical art itself—with the three-dimensional form of sculpture.

AGAIN FOR CYDNUS: CLEOPATRA'S MASTERPIECE

I have been emphasizing how artistic rhetoric and stage performance each make their appeals in *Antony and Cleopatra* by way of pictures, both in the visual arena of the stage and in the spectator's imagination. Paintings and sculptural forms govern the very way that we are asked to see Shakespeare's great historical characters. Cleopatra's vision of Antony as the gigantic statue, the Colossus of Rhodes (5.2.81–91), marks the beginning of her imagined return to Cydnus where she will again meet Mark Antony. A classical source, Pliny's *Natural History,* most likely informs this art analogy as well. Shakespeare fills in Pliny's text with extravagant, graphic details—a gigantic Antony's legs bestriding the ocean, his reared arm cresting the world—all designed to rival the classical masterpiece known as one of the seven world wonders. Cleopatra's grandiose vision competes, as well, with Enobarbus's Cydnus vision but, just as importantly, it compensates for Antony's self-depiction as a visible shape that cannot hold its form. In an earlier scene, Antony imagines the dissolution of his visible self by way of an artistic analogy to the masque, or "black vesper's pageants" (4.14.8)—he perceives himself as a "rack" (cloud) that "dislimns" (4.14.10). The term *dislimns* is related to *limning,* an Elizabethan term for painting. Shakespeare's invented term, *dislimning,* oddly signifies the undoing of artistic activity—unpainting or the removal of painting. Antony sees his visible form being unpainted, just as a cloud seems to disappear or fade away within the sky. This figure conflates several ideas related to the body and art: a material representation being dismantled or unmade, a body being dislimbed, and an image being brushed out of a picture.

Cleopatra remakes her lover's dislimned form in her vision of an Antony that is "past the size of dreaming" (5.2.96). As Anne Barton points out, such a vision of Antony, like Cleopatra's own self-creation in act 5, reflects an "Elizabethan cliché, the conceit of an art more realistic than reality itself" (134). The term *size* in Cleopatra's figure has its artistic connotations, according to the *OED*: not only does it suggest through spatial metaphor the poet's hyperbole, it also refers to the painter's glutinous wash used to prepare cloth for taking colors (Greenwood 11–12). The notion here is that Cleopatra is able to envision an Antony greater than any dream or painted fancy of him. The reality surpasses art, yet paradoxically Shakespeare's rhetoric establishes the picturing function of the imagination as the mode by which this transcendent reality comes to be known. Cleopatra's claim elaborates upon and competes with Enobarbus's assertion that her artful seduction of Antony transcends pictorial art, which itself transcends nature: as she insists, "Nature wants stuff / To vie strange forms with fancy; t'imagine / An Antony were nature's piece 'gainst fancy, / Condemning shadows quite" (96–99). Here, Cleopatra declares the imagination to be an aspect of nature, and nature is deemed an artist who competes with fancy by imagining and creating her masterpiece Antony. The *paragone* between art and nature is resolved by treating nature as the artist who makes forms that are real, not mere *shadows.*

Let us return to the *paragone* between theater and painting and Shakespeare's representation of Cleopatra as the figure of this contest. In act 5,

Cleopatra functions unequivocally as the maker of verbal and visual images: she "makes" the great image of Antony as Colossus, and she (the actor/character) performs her "return" to Cydnus onstage. Both acts involve picturing with the imagination, but the Cydnus suicide is a spectacle that renders visible Enobarbus's mythic evocation of her *person*, precisely what was absent in his speech. Shakespeare's move is strategic: this scene circles back to the gap in Enobarbus's vision of Cleopatra, seeking to fill it. In doing so, he establishes Cleopatra as knowable primarily in visual and artistic terms. She eludes textual containment. If anything, Cleopatra becomes most like a funerary statue, "marble-constant" in death (cf. Bowers 288–90). Enobarbus's "wonderful piece of work" in fact echoes Pliny's description of a brazen statue of Venus as "an exquisite [*sic*] piece of work" (274). Both *piece* and *picture* could refer to sculpture, as statuary in England was considered a form of painting. Yet, if "that Venus" metonymically stands for the irretrievable works of antique masters such as Apelles, then Shakespeare's Cleopatra performs the conjuring act that Enobarbus (and Pliny) cannot perform with words alone. Cleopatra's theatricized appearance onstage is more than a speaking picture, as Sidney's famous visual trope has suggested to critics. She is the paradoxical figure of living art—a life distilled into the monumental forms of art, and art quickened to life through performance.

While verse/narrative establishes Cleopatra's fame and her status as a masterpiece, the showing of Cleopatra's person is the sensuous, visual event that confirms her value and argues for theater as the art form closest to nature. Even the cold rationalist Caesar is rather awed by the sight of Cleopatra. His reference to "her strong toil of grace" (5.2.347) recalls Pliny's praise of Apelles as a painter renowned for verisimilitude and *charis* (grace and charm). The play ends with Caesar's words acknowledging the heroic-tragic nature of Antony and Cleopatra's deaths and their subsequent fame:

> No grave upon the earth shall clip in it
> A pair so famous. High events as these
> Strike those that make them, and their story is
> No less in pity than his glory which
> Brought them to be lamented. (5.2.358–62)

Although "their story" suggests a textual history of fame, it is theater, not the pages of Plutarch or Pliny, that allows historical persons to "live again" with a compelling verisimilitude: the staged death points up theater's power to retrieve a glorious past and to do this as more than a rhetorical act.

In act 5, Cleopatra "makes" her own image before our very eyes; this brings spectators to the heart of theatrical mimesis as a competitive process. The reenactment of Cleopatra on the Cydnus river is, for Shakespeare, a display of the ritual power theater possesses to draw spectators into the very process of making art. The creation of Cleopatra as a "wonderful piece of work" involves not only the collaborative efforts of playwright, players, and spectators, but also the competitive spirit of artistic rivalry. The unseen spectacle of Enobarbus's pictorial speech has prepared the way for the seen masterpiece of the actor/character Cleopatra who stages a majestic suicide in "her own person." In effect, Enobarbus's picture trope prepares spectators for an act of imaginative spectatorship that is fundamental to Shakespeare's theater and Cleopatra's political/erotic art, both of which languish if they fail to "eye well" (1.3.99).

NOTES

1. All references to William Shakespeare's *Antony and Cleopatra* are from John Wilders's edition.
2. According to Greek and Roman mythology (e.g., *Homeric Hymn to Aphrodite*, Hesiod's *Theogony*), Venus was born of the sea, from the foam that emitted from the genitals of the castrated Uranus. She floated upon a shell until, blown by breezes, she landed on the shore of Cyprus. There is critical controversy over whether Shakespeare is alluding to a particular painting. Although editors such as Lewis Theobald and R. H. Case, and critics such as William S. Heckscher, claim that the allusion is to Apelles's *Venus Anadyomene*, others have cited different paintings or concluded that the reference is not to a specific painting at all. Although this controversy cannot be definitively resolved, I argue that Apelles's *Venus* is the likely referent here.
3. Philemon Holland's translation was printed in England in 1601 and sold in St. Paul's Churchyard. It was Holland's most popular translation and, according to J. Newsome, popular reading in England (Pliny, 1964, p. xv).
4. Examples of paintings inspired by Apelles's *Venus Anadymone* include Botticelli's *The Birth of Venus* and Titian's *Venus Anadyomene*. Examples of sculpture include the *Venus and Cupid* by the Follower of Giovanni Bologna. Literary allusions include Sidney's description of Philoclea in *Old Arcadia* as "like Venus rising from her mother the sea" and Spenser's representation of the beauty of Sapience in the *Hymne of Heavenly Beautie*: "Ne could that painter (had he lived yet) / Which pictured Venus with so curious quill / That all posteritie admired it . . . " (qtd. in Dundas 46, 118).
5. Judith Dundas is an example of one critic who is attuned to subtle expressions of the *paragone* in Elizabethan poetry; for example, she discusses a *paragone* of the senses in Shakespeare's works (cf. chapter 2 in *Pencils Rhetorique*). On *Timon of Athens* and the *paragone*, see Anthony Blunt 260–62; W. M. Merchant 249–57; John Dixon Hunt, "Shakespeare and His Relationship" 47–63; and Hunt, *Pictura, Scriptura* and *Theatrum*" 155–71.
6. For Ben Jonson's views on the masque and his quarrel with designer Inigo Jones, see D. J. Gordon 152–78.
7. This reference to sonnet 55 is from Katherine Duncan-Jones's edition of *Shakespeare's Sonnets*.

8. Leonard Barkan makes a relevant claim: "It is not too far-fetched to see that the theater which gives mythic ancient figures a new life in modern language is itself a gigantic project of ekphrasis and prosopopoeia, comparable to that which puts speech in the mouths of statues. And Shakespeare's Cleopatra in particular exhibits a multi-dimensional character and a resistance to the demands of history that may owe their origins to all those verbal inventions inspired by the statue's silence" (1993, p. 156).

9. Ronald MacDonald argues that Enobarbus competes with his interlocutors, but, more significantly, he observes that the spirit of competition or conflict, "what the Greeks called *agon*," pervades the drama and is "closely connected with the idea of performance, with the idea that in playing at something you challenge denial and triumphantly become it" (96). My argument similarly grounds the play in the spirit of competition, although I focus on the *paragone*, an expression of rivalry between arts, rather than the Greek *agon*.

10. Catherine Belsey notices how the "pretty dimpled boys" in Enobarbus's description take Cleopatra's place as fleshly objects or subjects of desire. These "boys" are the *putti* (Cupids) of continental Renaissance paintings; thus, they belong in a picture of Venus. As Belsey argues, these eroticized boys function as part of the process of Cleopatra's seduction, thereby suggesting that "seduction was apparently a more complex process than any system of sexual identification which is based on object choice ... " (60).

11. Many editors and critics have noted the influence of perspective painting on *Antony and Cleopatra*. Janet Adelman, for example, suggests that act 1, scene 1 serves as a paradigm for structural framing and for the multiple perspectives of the play (31–34). Philo's rhetoric "virtually forces us to see the lovers' appearance as a spectacle or a play within the play, a play with a very specific moral" (32). John Greenwood claims that Philo serves as a *sprecher* figure from mannerist painting; like Enobarbus, he momentarily arrests our gaze as he constructs a perspectival view of Antony and Cleopatra (53–54).

12. Socrates's figure for the mind (or soul) as a book became commonplace in western literature, as did the pictorial trope for the imagination. Two artists, he claims in Plato's *Philebus* (39b), an internal scribe and painter, record the conjunctions of memory and sensation (which become opinions and assertions) in the soul. The painter is activated when opinions and assertions derive from the act of sight or other senses. Word and image co-exist in the mind, forming a set of true or false ideas.

13. Jonathan Gil Harris compares Enobarbus's speech to an ornately framed rococo mirror into which the play's spectators, along with the Roman male characters, gaze, enthralled by their own seductive images of Cleopatra. Harris contends that Enobarbus's speech establishes how her power derives from "paradoxical absence" (418). Alison Thorne notes the "gap at the center of the tableau," which an amatory imagination fills by constructing an "imagined presence" (166). Phyllis Rackin, like Thorne, emphasizes how Cleopatra is "evoked by and for the imagination" (205); the speech, Rackin argues, calls attention to the greatness of the poet's imaginative art and to the transcendent "golden" world art creates. Allyson P. Newton claims that Cleopatra's person "disappears into the artful constructions of the Cydnus speech" (87–88).

WORKS CITED

Adelman, Janet. *The Common Liar: An Essay on* Antony and Cleopatra. New Haven and London: Yale UP, 1973.

Barkan, Leonard. "The Beholder's Tale: Ancient Sculpture, Renaissance Narratives." *Representations* 44 (Fall 1993): 133–66.

———. "Making Pictures Speak: Renaissance Art, Elizabethan Literature, Modern Scholarship." *Renaissance Quarterly* 48 (Summer 1995): 326–51.

———. *Unearthing the Past: Archeology and Aesthetics in the Making of Renaissance Culture.* New Haven and London: Yale UP, 1999.

Barroll, J. Leeds. "Enobarbus' Description of Cleopatra." *Texas Studies in English* 37 (1958): 61–78.

Barton, Anne. "'Nature's piece 'gainst fancy': the divided catastrophe in *Antony and Cleopatra*" (1974/1992). Rpt. in *Essays, Mainly Shakespearean.* Cambridge and New York: Cambridge UP, 1994.

Belsey, Catherine. "Cleopatra's Seduction." *Alternative Shakespeares.* Vol. 2. Ed. Terence Hawkes. London and New York: Routledge, 1996.

Blunt Anthony. "An Echo of the *Paragone* in Shakespeare." *JWCI* 2 (January 1939): 260–62.

Bowers, John. "I Am Marble-Constant: Cleopatra's Monumental End." *Huntington Library Quarterly* 46 (1983): 283–97.

Dundas, Judith. *Pencils Rhetorique: Renaissance Poets and the Art of Painting.* Newark: U of Delaware P, 1993.

Gent, Lucy. *Picture and Poetry, 1560–1620: Relations between Literature and the Visual Arts in the English Renaissance.* Leamington Spa, Eng.: James Hall, 1981.

Gordon, D. J. "Poet and Architect: The Intellectual Setting of the Quarrel between Ben Jonson and Inigo Jones." *JWCI* 12 (1949): 152–78.

Greenwood, John. *Shifting Perspectives and the Stylish Style: Mannerism in Shakespeare and His Jacobean Contemporaries.* Toronto: U of Toronto P, 1988.

Harris, Jonathan Gil. "'Narcissus in thy face': Roman Desire and the Difference It Fakes in *Antony and Cleopatra*." *Shakespeare Quarterly* 45 (1994): 408–25.

Heckscher, William S. "Shakespeare in His Relationship to the Visual Arts: A Study in Paradox." *Research Opportunities in Renaissance Drama* 13–14 (1970–71): 5–17.

Hunt, John Dixon. "*Pictura, Scriptura,* and *Theatrum:* Shakespeare and the Emblem." *Poetics Today* 10 (1989): 155–71.

———. "Shakespeare and the *Paragone*: A Reading of *Timon of Athens*." *Images of Shakespeare: Proceedings of the Third Congress of the International Shakespeare Association, 1986.* Ed. Werner Habicht, D. J. Palmer, and Roger Pringle, 47–63. Newark: U of Delaware P, 1988.

Kernan, Alvin. *Shakespeare, the King's Playwright: Theater in the Stuart Court, 1603–1613.* London and New Haven: Yale UP, 1995.

Macdonald, Ronald R. "Playing Till Doomsday: Interpreting *Antony and Cleopatra*." *English Literary Renaissance* 15 (Winter 1985): 78–99.

Merchant W. M. "*Timon* and the Conceit of Art." *Shakespeare Quarterly* 6 (1955): 249–57.

Mitchell, W. J. T. *Picture Theory.* Chicago and London: U of Chicago P, 1994.

Newton, Allyson P. "At 'the Very Heart of Loss': Shakespeare's Enobarbus and the Rhetoric of Remembering." *Renaissance Papers* (1995): 81–91.

Panofsky, Erwin. *Galileo as a Critic of the Arts*. The Hague, Holland: Martinus Nijhoff, 1954.

Plato, *Philebus*. Trans. R. Hackforth. Rpt. in *The Collected Dialogues of Plato*. Ed. Edith Hamilton and Huntington Cairns. Princeton: Princeton UP, 1961.

Pliny Secundus, Gaius. *Natural History*. Trans. Philemon Holland. Ed. J. Newsome. Oxford: Clarendon P, 1964.

———. *Natural History*. Trans. Philemon Holland. Ed. Paul Turner. New York: McGraw-Hill Book Company, 1962.

Plutarch. *Lives of the Noble Grecians and Romanes*. Trans. Sir Thomas North (1579). Rpt. in *Narrative and Dramatic Sources of Shakespeare*. Ed. Geoffrey Bullough. Vol. 5. London: Routledge and Kegan Paul; New York: Columbia UP, 1966.

Rackin, Phyllis. "Shakespeare's Boy Cleopatra, the Decorum of Nature, and the Golden World of Poetry." *PMLA* 87 (March 1972): 201–12.

Shakespeare, William. *The Tragedy of Antony and Cleopatra*. Ed. Robert Hope Case. Indianapolis: Bobbs-Merrill, 1906.

———. *Antony and Cleopatra*. Ed. John Wilders. London and New York: Routledge, 1995.

———. *Shakespeare's Sonnets*. Ed. Katherine Duncan-Jones. England: Thomas Nelson and Sons, 1997.

———. *The Works of Shakespeare*. Ed. Lewis Theobald. Vol. 6. London: A. Bettesworth and C. Hitch, 1733.

Sidney, Sir Philip. *Defence of Poesie, Astrophil and Stella and Other Writings*. Ed. Elizabeth Porges-Watson. London: J. M. Dent, 1997.

Smith, R. Shaw. "*Antony and Cleopatra*, II.ii.204." *Shakespeare Quarterly* (1973): 92–93.

Thorne, Alison. *Vision and Rhetoric in Shakespeare: Looking through Language*. New York: St. Martin's P, 2001.

14.
Interview with Giles Block
Director of the 1999 Production
of *Antony and Cleopatra* at Shakespeare's Globe
in London

GEORGIA E. BROWN

Antony and Cleopatra was presented at Shakespeare's Globe in London as part of their 1999 season, with Giles Block as director. At Shakespeare's Globe, the director is referred to as the Master of Play. During that season, Giles Block was also Master of Verse, a more general position designed to improve the verse-speaking in all of that season's productions. Mark Rylance, Artistic Director of Shakespeare's Globe, made the decision to mount an all-male production of *Antony and Cleopatra*, casting Paul Shelley as Antony, Mark Rylance as Cleopatra, and John McEnery as Enobarbus, before Giles Block was invited to be director. The announcement of the 1999 season was greeted with intense press curiosity, which focused on the proposal for an all-male *Antony and Cleopatra*. Rylance's daring decision to give one of the most famous of all female roles to a man fascinated journalists, who responded with enthusiasm to the frisson of men playing women. The reviews kept by the Globe reveal that the decision to stage an all-male *Antony and Cleopatra* was a great marketing success. Rylance also decided to stage the production in original costume, and a large proportion of the play's budget was spent on the impressive costumes designed by Jenny Tiramani and made in the Globe workshop (see fig. 16).[1] Cleopatra had some extremely arresting costumes based on Inigo Jones's designs for Jacobean masques, and she changed costume frequently, while Antony did not. In conversation, Jenny Tiramani explained that she hoped that Cleopatra's costume changes would contribute to the impression of a woman of "infinite variety" (2.2.235), but that, in retrospect, she would have suppressed one of Cleopatra's costume changes. The authentic costumes were experimental, as the workshop investigated techniques of production and as the actors and dressers explored the ways the costumes would affect the mechanics of staging and movement. Tiramani noted that, as a result of the experiments carried out in this production, she now doubted whether Elizabethan actors, working without the large number

Fig. 16: Mark Rylance as Cleopatra in Giles Block's 1999 production of *Antony and Cleopatra* at Shakespeare's Globe. Photo: John Tramper; Courtesy of Shakespeare's Globe, London.

of dressers available today, would have been able to change as frequently as Cleopatra had done. Music also played an important role in the production. The instruments were constructed, as far as was possible, by authentic processes and the score incorporated ethnic elements that were broadly Anatolian, including shawms, which are often featured in Balkan and Turkish music. The music effectively marked scene changes, suggested the passing of time, and established powerful contrasts, and the musicians themselves appeared on stage in costume and incorporated dance steps into their movement.

   Antony and Cleopatra has never been one of the most popular plays with producers. After the original performances, there is no record of another performance until 1759, when David Garrick decided to stage the play with himself as Antony. Surprisingly, in 1999 there were two high-profile productions—the one at the Globe, discussed in this interview, and one at the Royal Shakespeare Company. Moreover, the Royal Shakespeare Company mounted the play again in 2002. Giles Block has continued to work at both Shakespeare's Globe and the Shochiku Theatre Company, Japan. The following conversation between Giles Block and Georgia E. Brown took place at Shakespeare's Globe, London, on August 6, 2003.

BROWN. You were Master of Play and Master of Verse in the 1999 season.

BLOCK. I'm self-taught in all these areas. I come from a theatre background. I was an actor, then became a director, and then became a Shakespeare-lover. In particular, before I came here, I became interested in just how actors should approach Shakespeare's text and I did do some work with Peter Hall for a while, when I was at the National [The National Theatre, London] and elsewhere. So I learned things from him, but then I veered away. I just found ways of describing the practice and the process of verse that satisfied me more. So that's what I came to do here. Well, I partly came to do that and partly to direct *Antony and Cleopatra*. So that's my first season here, some four years ago.

BROWN. What do you think about men playing women's roles? There is a lot of debate about this in academic circles. Was it such a well-established convention in the Renaissance that people really did forget that there was a boy or man playing a woman? Or some people, like Lisa Jardine, have argued that cross-dressing stresses the maleness of the actor and creates homoerotic desires in the audience.[2] Other people have argued that cross-dressing can be read as morally positive, that androgyny is liberating and creates a situation in which men have aspects of femaleness, and women have aspects of maleness, and that through androgyny individuals achieve wholeness. How do you see it?

BLOCK. I think that the audience forgot that the role was being played by an actor. I think that some of the time they forgot. It's that curious way in which you forget and you're not forgetting, that runs through drama at every level. There's a contemporary couplet that rebuts the idea that the audience were throwing oranges all the time which runs something like: "Frozen with grief we could not stir away / Until th'epilogue told us t'was but a play." Clearly, sometimes Shakespeare focuses on things like the player. At other times, for instance in *Hamlet*, the player loses himself in his part. Clearly, contemporaries made a distinction between actors, and the really great actors, like Alleyn or Burbage. Also in *Hamlet* there is the idea that people can get so lost in a play that they will betray their own guilt and finally some one did, watching a play [Claudius]. You become absorbed by the action and forget the actor. I think one's experience of watching men play women here, in the Globe, is that you are certainly aware of it to begin with and then forget. Although we did have one person one night who complained bitterly and vocally that there was a man playing Cleopatra and had an argument about it from the yard. Mark [Rylance playing Cleopatra] stopped the play and said you must go and get your money back at the box office, and he did it in character, just like a queen. But that reaction is very rare.

BROWN. So did they object to the fact that Mark Rylance was taking up a role that could have gone to a woman?

BLOCK. I think not. I think it was a homophobic reaction and they thought there was something threatening in it.

BROWN. Going through the reviews kept at the Globe, I found one French review from the newspaper *Libération*.[3] I found it interesting that it was the French critic who actually responded to Cleopatra positively and sexually. He said that she was almost pretty, which I think was meant as a compliment, the idea being that you cannot be fascinating unless there is something wrong with you. Then he described what Cleopatra looked like when she first came on, and he noted that on her appearance, "Comme un seul homme, l'audience pousse un soupir" [as one man, the audience let out a sigh]. I thought it was interesting that the English critics either failed to find her particularly erotic, or failed to mention eroticism at all, while the French critic went straight to the issue. Perhaps we have a tradition [in England] of drag comedy like Dick Emery, or Les Dawson, which is a rather misogynistic, homophobic tradition of comedy where men dress up as women, and this now gets in the way of audiences suspending disbelief when they see a man dressed as a woman?

BLOCK. I think they do suspend disbelief when it's played well. They certainly do. Of course, there were four men dressed as women in this production of *Antony and Cleopatra*. Certainly, there was a wonderful black actor, Danny Sapani, who played Charmian, who is the last person you would cast as a woman because he is just such a huge presence, but he was just wonderful. I think something else, as well. I don't know how to put it. In a way, once you have accepted the actor as the essence, the spirit of Cleopatra for tonight, something pleasurable comes to the audience. It's about the magic of the theatre, which you know isn't there, and which in a way is what is always there. You know it isn't Cleopatra there, and you clearly know it isn't when it's a man playing the role, but this is something pleasurable for the audience. Now we have an all-women's company playing here, and there you follow a story. You follow a *story*, and I don't think the audience is sitting there thinking all the time, "Oh it's good, but they're all women." It just doesn't happen, because you have to live moment by moment when you're in an audience following a play.

BROWN. Sometimes Shakespeare forces you to become aware that there is an actor playing the role, most famously perhaps with Cleopatra's remark: "and I shall see / Some squeaking Cleopatra boy my greatness / I' th' posture of a whore" [5.2.219–21].[4] He brings the issue back into focus and feeds off the double nature of the actor.

BLOCK. He does do that, but how you are meant to see the character changes from moment to moment.

BROWN. Were you worried about doing *Antony and Cleopatra*? It has the reputation of being a difficult play to put on. Dr. Johnson thought that it was unstructured and lacked a relation of cause and effect between scenes so that the narrative thrust gets lost and it's difficult to follow. He clearly didn't like the play.[5]

BLOCK. Funny that, yes.

BROWN. Were you worried about doing it? The story moves between very different places. You need two very strong actors. Antony is a difficult role. Michael Redgrave complained that Antony doesn't actually *do* anything and that he dies in the fourth act, hence it's difficult to make an impression with the role. The actor has nothing but the language with which to build the sense of this hero of mythic dimensions.[6] A lot turns on the two leads, or maybe it doesn't? Has too much emphasis been put on the leads and the idea that they carry the play? After all, Cleopatra is never on stage alone. Shakespeare created the roles of Charmian, Iras, and Enobarbus which were not in his source and they contribute greatly to creating the aura around Cleopatra.[7]

BLOCK. I would always say that it is not the case that lead roles carry a play. I never was worried. I thought it was a great adventure. What I discovered doing *Antony and Cleopatra* is that it has a remarkable lightness to it, as if it is bathed in a golden light and that I found most delightful. We moved fast between the scenes; the play allows you to do that; and it contains a lot of conversation rather than more formal, stand-out soliloquies. It may be that it is easier to play this play at the Globe than at a conventional theater, too, because once you accept that you cannot do scene changes to indicate where you are, then that is a whole load off your mind. And you have to accept that you cannot do different lighting states to indicate different times of the day.

You have to accept that all this is not part of it. We only had the words to tell us where we were and what time of day it was. What I suppose Johnson could not understand was that the play presents an image crystallized in spades, and then another one comes and overwhelms that one. The particular sense of movement in the play is brilliant, and maybe on the Globe stage you are really only helped with this. There is a great deal of circular movement. It moves in circles. Some of the battle scenes trace circles. There are side doors; armies move out of them; there is great noise; they move across and pass out through the opposite doors. Then another army does the same but in the opposite direction. So there is that kind of flow to it. The groundlings become part of these armies in the play.[8] I think that it is a fine thing to have the text in front of you, and then you begin to work out the dynamics of that space, and you begin to see how things have to happen.

BROWN. The shape of the verse is also often circular. The core of a long sentence is buried in phrases which encase the core. You have to suspend understanding, wait to hear all parts, before you work out the relationship between the phrases. The verse often does not drive on in a clear linear way. The speeches build outwards, perhaps like a German sentence, and you have to keep a mental note of the phrases in suspension. For example, there is Antony's speech near the beginning of the play where he acknowledges that he has to go to Rome and describes Pompey for the first time (1.2.179–83 and 185–92).

BLOCK. Yes. You reminded me of something that I felt, which isn't limited to this play, which is making a moment last. In a way that is what literature does; it keeps things suspended, so you can taste them, feel them, understand them.

BROWN. It seems crucial to this play. Antony and Cleopatra make the moment last and are set against the Roman world. Caesar is constantly trying to drive the movement forward towards the consolidation of empire.[9] He is trying to write a different kind of play from the one that Cleopatra, for example, tries to write. In the end, perhaps, Caesar tries to fashion a tragedy, to write the story of the fall of Antony because he cannot see anything good in what has happened to Antony. Different characters all have their own stories about Antony and Cleopatra. You have the forward narrative of Caesar, while Antony and Cleopatra constantly slow it down. The slower movement of their scenes interrupts Caesar's dynamic and gets the audience to think differently.

BLOCK. Exactly. Look at those earlier scenes which keep on going back to Egypt. Rome is on the move, and Antony and Cleopatra are all about sleeping and oblivion, as Cleopatra says: "Give me to drink mandragora. . . . That I might sleep out this great gap of time / My Antony is away" [1.5.4–6]. They make time expand. I never quite consciously thought that, but for instance between the first and second battles they stretch time out.

BROWN. It's a clever play to do at the Globe. In some ways, I think you could argue it works better when done by a crossdressed cast, when there is something unexpected about the cast. It seems to be a play about myth-making, about how you make identities. For instance, what does "Antony" mean to the Romans, to Cleopatra, to himself? Who is he and what is he? It is about how the answers to such questions are made up, and this turns out to be a collaborative process within the play. Enobarbus, for example, helps make Cleopatra as mesmerizing as she is, with his description of her first meeting with Antony, which includes his famous description of her appearance in her barge [2.2.186–239]. This brings to the fore the idea of imaginative investment and the extent to which an audience creates its own fantasies. So in some ways it's better to have men play women, and not to have a realistic set, because you don't have access to complicated machinery and there are technical limitations to this kind of stage. Not only does this alter the rhythms of the play, as you pointed out, and focus attention on the text but also all this crudity, if you will, brings the issue of audience complicity to the fore. For me it worked very well having men play women, because it forced me to think about how far I was prepared to go, about the extent of my collusion in the play. It also worked well for me because I find the issue of what is a man and what is a woman an interesting question that is raised by the play.

BLOCK. Perhaps, but the story is key.

BROWN. It may not be so important in the play, but I'm thinking of the scene where we are told that Cleopatra puts on Antony's sword, while he puts on her clothes [2.5.18–23], or the scene where Enobarbus tells Cleopatra that she cannot go to war because to do so is unfitting for a woman and for Antony's manhood [3.7.1–19]. Cleopatra insists that she will "Appear there for a man." There is a discussion of what constitutes a woman's part, and what constitutes a man's part. This is raised by Mardian, too. He was a strong character in your production and he is somewhere between being a man and being a woman, and offers another kind of crossdressing.

BLOCK. Yes, he does.

BROWN. Looking at the reviews, with very few exceptions, critics were obsessed with Cleopatra and gave very little space to other roles. Do you see it as Cleopatra's play?

BLOCK. No. I don't. Mark [Rylance] is very mesmeric and doubly so in this space, which is his space. He does take all eyes.

BROWN. I wondered whether there is a weight of tradition that blames Cleopatra. The view that it is all her fault. Yet the play is the consequence of Antony's decisions and his dilemmas. Cleopatra frequently reacts to his decisions and the narrative is made up of what happens to Antony.

BLOCK. Yes, that's true.

BROWN. Why do you think Cleopatra leaves the battle of Actium?

BLOCK. I think it's more the case that there are certain incidents that are just given, and what interests Shakespeare is how people react to them, rather than the motivations. I think sometimes Shakespeare goes to places where his characters do not know why they do what they do, which is a step beyond what I suspect most playwrights have dealt with. In some ways, it is where a play ends up that is the point they are all striving for, the force that drives the action. In a way they are striving for immortality, that their love can last forever, and the way it ends is the way that they achieve that. I'm not saying that it is a conscious desire, but it isn't to rule this world; it isn't to be the supreme commander, which is what Caesar wants to be. So I did not think of her reasons for running away; it is not something I considered when directing, or even discussed with the actors, because it does not matter why she runs away. It could be that she finds herself in a situation that is not somewhere she knows, that it is not what she wants. I don't think that Antony and Cleopatra consciously know what they want in the end. They are remembered because of their end, and the loss, to us in this world, or the world we lost.

BROWN. This makes me think of Cleopatra's question to Dolabella [5.2.93–94]. She asks if there was or could be such a man as the Antony who appeared to her in her dream, and Dolabella thinks not. If you think like Dolabella you close off possibilities. There are some things that cannot be articulated or easily predicted, things that escape rationality. Your point that characters do not necessarily know why they do things reminded me of this. There are things that escape rationality, and that Dolabella cannot see while Cleopatra can.

BLOCK. And through her being able to see it, the audience see it as well. It's a question of what is real, and Antony is a myth. History is always an interpretation of what happened: "Truths would be tales, / Where now half tales be truths" [2.2.133–34]. The simple interpretation that Antony was a scoundrel doesn't satisfy because he has these other dimensions and pushes the play somewhere else.

BROWN. After Actium Antony does blame Cleopatra and says that she knew he would follow her when she left, because he loves her so much [3.11.56–61]. He turns his fault into his virtue by saying that his love is so strong that he cannot possibly be expected to resist her. It reminded me of Romanesque carvings of the Fall, where God finds Adam and Eve with their fig leaves and asks them what is going on. Adam points to Eve and Eve points to the serpent and every one tries to displace the blame. Adam takes the apple because he doesn't want to be alone, and live without Eve. Antony did leave the battle, and Cleopatra did not force him to go. Perhaps there is a tendency to blame her for the things that he chooses?

BLOCK. I don't think so. Enobarbus doesn't. He blames Antony at that moment [3.13.1–12]. At that moment, the fact that Cleopatra runs is irrelevant. It is

Antony's fault. That is the richness of the play. You get eight characters commenting on something with eight different views and that is why we talk about it.

BROWN. How did you conceive of the play? There was an interval after the scene in Pompey's barge [2.7] during which there was a lot of sweeping. Perhaps after all the carousing there was the need to clear the stage? Then there was another interval after Enobarbus decides to abandon Antony [3.13], before the last "gaudy night" [3.13.182]. The play is not divided into acts in the 1623 folio, which is our source for the play. How did you conceive of it? Emrys Jones says it falls into two halves and changes after act 3, scene 6 when Octavia goes back to Caesar. Did you divide it up in your mind in a particular way, or did you see it as moving with great impetus toward the end?[10]

BLOCK. I did. I did really. I felt there was a kind of seamlessness to it really.

BROWN. Were there particular changes in mood you wanted to highlight with the intervals?

BLOCK. I took the second interval partly because you need to give the audience a break. It's a long play and I thought two intervals would be better. To me those two scenes are also turning points. At the end of the scene on the barge [2.7] so many destinies have changed. Lepidus has shown himself to be the fool he is. Pompey has lost out. We've seen hints of rivalry emerging again between Antony and Caesar. They are not kindred spirits in any way and the party makes that more obviously so. Then Enobarbus leaving Antony is another huge turning point [3.13]. I suppose I wanted to try and make something of the Ventidius scene too [3.1], which follows the scene on Pompey's barge. You can't do too much there to give a feeling of the breadth of what happens to the Parthians in Syria, that huge scope, and so that scene started the second section. It started with them bringing on the body.

BROWN. It was very arresting when they dragged on the headless body on a blanket.

BLOCK. It would have been difficult coming in with that scene immediately after the scene on the barge. You need stuff for the scene on the barge, although, in the end, having ordered a big table, I wondered whether I was right to have a big table. I had a large "last supper table" and I wondered whether because it's supposed to be a banquet, rather than a main meal, whether I should have had more things around. I felt I limited the possibilities for objects.

BROWN. Would you like to do the play again?

BLOCK. Yes. I would absolutely.

BROWN. Would you do it differently in other ways? Are there things you found out by doing it that you would like to try out next time?

BLOCK. It would necessarily be different because the actors would be different. To be honest, when I direct I am not ever striving to put anything there that I haven't seen in the text. Of course, when you go back to a text you see something new and every time new doors open. So I can't really say. I'd love to do it again because it's such a wonderful world to spend three months of your life creating and making live again. I thought a lot of the solutions that we came to, and I'm thinking of the costume solutions, were really brilliant. This was really down to Jenny [Tiramani, the costume designer] and the way she researched it. The premise that we worked on was what they [Shakespeare's contemporary theatre practitioners] might have done. There was a contemporary fad for Tudor-Stuart costume combined with elements of Roman armour. If you look at sixteenth- and seventeenth-century paintings and statuary you can see this. There were also contemporary costume books that collect both contemporary and historical costumes, and contemporary battle costumes, so that's where we got the idea for the kaftans from. [Antony, for example, wore a kaftan in the production.]

BROWN. I thought the costumes helped the cross-dressing because the actors were forced to move in particular ways. The skirts were very full, the bodices were stiff and so an actor couldn't move his torso in the normal way.

BLOCK. Yes. I would do that again. I would take that sort of approach again: how might they have seen the look of it. I certainly think the kind of flow is essential to it as well, the flow of one scene into another. The use of furniture is not without its complications. Hauling Antony aloft for one. [Antony was hoisted up to Cleopatra's monument by a system of pulleys, after his body had been placed in a sling.] I got into a bit of a muddle, because the play does, over how the Romans storm the citadel. I had a soldier climb down from the top, getting onto the balcony, while the scene was going on below. I was wondering the other day whether I should have used the trap and had someone burst through as if they had tunneled under, because it is a little unclear as to what is supposed to have happened.

BROWN. Cleopatra and her ladies hauled Antony's body from the stage up into the balcony. They didn't stay on the balcony, however, but came down for the rest of the play.

BLOCK. Yes, but should I have remained up there, and how does she get down? There doesn't seem a place to get down. What I tried to do was to suggest two different views of the monument. Perhaps the monument has a chamber down within it. Or perhaps it is the same space viewed from somewhere else. I did use the yard quite a bit. Every director when they come here, when they first work here, uses the yard for entrances and exits, and then a lot have second thoughts about using the yard. I became very interested in the argument over whether Renaissance actors did use the yard, and some people see the line at the end of the barge scene, "Come down into the boat" [2.7.129], as evidence that they exited through the yard. Sometimes the yard works well. For instance, the armies, the skirmishing armies, crossing through and across the stage, worked well, but it was quite cumbersome. Steps have to be put in and there was a lot of heavy work, not that that is a problem, but I might think about how much I use the yard again.

BROWN. Your production was very funny. A lot of the comedy came from Cleopatra. She was very physical, sometimes very violent. Mardian's music was awful and that gave life to his exchange with Cleopatra: "What's your Highness' pleasure? / Not now to hear thee sing" [1.5.8–9]. Such details were very funny and worked very well. However, the comedy element in the production offended some of the critics. For instance, some didn't like the fact that hauling Antony aloft was funny [4.15].

BLOCK. Yes.

BROWN. How did you see the balance between tragedy and comedy? There was a very interesting review of your production by Michael Billington in *The Guardian*. He liked the strong comic elements and said that the production had made him question whether *Antony and Cleopatra* should be classified as a tragedy. Emrys Jones pushes the ironic aspects of the play as well.[11]

BLOCK. I don't think it's a straightforward tragedy. Yes, I think that's right.

BROWN. How does the comedy work? Do you think it sends up Antony and Cleopatra? Does it poke fun at two people playing out the myth of Venus and Mars who are slightly ridiculous and don't know it? Does it attack tragedy in some way? Or parody tragedy? Does it lead somewhere that gives different perspectives, so that it doesn't exactly negate the tragedy, but suggests things that are left out by its particular perspective?

BLOCK. I don't think that *Antony and Cleopatra* is a tragedy. Sometimes it is a black comedy. Shakespeare just manages to play with these things that pull us in opposite directions. It is grey. It is awkward. The hoisting up of Antony, for example, is awkward; yet it's undoubtedly moving as well, at the same time. So you are pulled in two different ways between their aspirations and their humanity. And I think it is not a tragedy because they both succeed, because where they are heading to is where they want to be:

> [ANTONY.] Eros!—I come, my queen!—Eros!—Stay for me!
> Where souls do couch on flowers, we'll hand in hand,
> And with our sprightly port make the ghosts gaze.
> Dido and her Aeneas shall want troops,
> And all the haunt be ours. Come, Eros, Eros! [4.14.50–54]

BROWN. Yes, there are lots of rhetorical questions and conditionals. It entertains possibilities simultaneously. There is a lot of play with the phenom-

enon of being pulled in two directions. Cleopatra says death is like "a
lover's pinch, / Which hurts, and is desir'd" [5.2.295–96].

BLOCK. That works both for them: they want things that destroy them, things
that are also good and bad, and it also works for the audience who want to
cry and when you cry you want to laugh, and the two go together. So I think
he transcends the tragic in this. When you are doing a *Hamlet*, *Macbeth* or
Lear, it is clear that it all ends when it ends. It ends and you feel those lives
that you knew are wasted. In that final moment, you feel what a waste, or
the pity of it. But there is something that takes off at the end of *Antony and
Cleopatra*. They are elevated at their death, more even than Hamlet is.

BROWN. The audience wants Cleopatra to die. At least, you want her to kill
herself before Caesar manages to stop her.

BLOCK. Quite, and that is a very odd thing to feel in a tragedy. You want her
to escape. So it is about escape. And Antony wants to escape for exactly
the same reasons. He bungles it too. Of course, Shakespeare could have
staged the final scenes differently. The lifting of Antony didn't have to be
done like that. He could have staged that very easily in some other less
awkward way. He could have died in another mode, but Shakespeare chose
to do the most difficult thing.

BROWN. There's also the idea of a spatial hierarchy there. Antony is being
hoisted up into higher spiritual and social circles through physical
elevation, but the physical business brings him down. Cleopatra rejects the
prospect of being made a spectacle for the lower orders of society,
complaining that common people "shall / Uplift us to the view"
[5.2.210–11], which reminds me of Antony being uplifted to the monument, and of the play being uplifted, or mounted, on the stage.[12] The play
is partly about the physicality of existence and how that is a source of great
pleasure and of great pain. Antony has a terrible, lingering death, during
which Decretas drags the sword out of his body and carries it off as a
trophy, to curry favour with Caesar [4.14.111–13].

BLOCK. Yes, I feel we are in agreement about the comedy.

BROWN. The only thing I wonder is whether the emphasis on comedy down-
plays what Antony loses. He does mind that he loses Romanness. After
Actium he says, "I have fled myself" [3.11.7]. Has he lost something that
is important to him, or doesn't he lose it?

BLOCK. No. In some ways he does lose. But he gains more than he loses. I
think he makes a choice, wittingly, or perhaps partly wittingly, and he
knows finally he is in the place he wants to be. Shakespeare is less critical
of Antony than Plutarch is, and Antony and Cleopatra are profoundly in
love.

BROWN. Did you ever consider doing the play with a black actor playing
Cleopatra?

BLOCK. I didn't. The play was already cast when I arrived.

BROWN. Would you want to? At the beginning Cleopatra is described as "a tawny front" [1.1.6]. Darkness is associated with deceit and inscrutability, and even with bad luck, when Enobarbus compares Caesar's dour face to a dark-faced horse [3.2.51–53]. In a review of the Royal Shakespeare Company's *Antony and Cleopatra*, which was on at the same time as your own production, Katherine Duncan-Jones criticized the casting of Frances de la Tour as Cleopatra because all the Egyptians are supposed to be exotic, and de la Tour "is entirely European in physique."[13]

BLOCK. It's certainly a good way to go, yes. But she is in fact Greek, but that is not important either.

BROWN. Cleopatra was played as white, wasn't she?

BLOCK. She wasn't made up to look like another racial type, no. Her face was bronzed as if she had been living in the sun.

BROWN. In her final scene, Cleopatra came on stripped of all her finery, in a white shift, with a bloodied scalp. Why did you undress her at the end? It is unusual for a production to do this. I've never seen a production in which she appeared to be so vulnerable, although she dresses up again in gold robes for her moment of death and dies in majesty sitting upright on the bed.

BLOCK. It was Mark's idea [Mark Rylance]. He pulled all his hair out. In fact, in the scene she threatens to do it, or something similar [5.2.49–62]. I wasn't absolutely sure about it myself, but working here, especially here, it has to be a very collaborative process, and I think actors need to feel that they own their work. I don't know if we discussed it. Usually, actors discuss their costumes with the costume designer, and the Master of Play doesn't always know what will be decided. But I *do* know that for as many people that think that such things are going too far, there will be others that think that it is extraordinary. There will be some things where I will put my foot down, but I always try to accommodate. For me, directing is as much about harnessing a talent, but I'm very keen on *text*, that we honour the text.

BROWN. Is that partly why you chose to work here? It seems to me that the space re-emphasises text, and different kinds of visuals, because there are limitations on the scenery and the lighting you can use, for example.

BLOCK. Yes, partly. I'd reached a point where I was pretty anxious to find some kind of outlet for the kind of work I had been doing on text and Mark opened the door. I did a workshop here just to show what I would like to do. I would always fight to honour what is there in the text and mine as much as possible in terms of clarity and beauty and expressiveness. There is no end to that.

BROWN. At the first change of location, when the play moves from Alexandria to Rome [1.4], I thought the aural contrast between Egypt and Rome was very clear. Roman speech was more precise and sober. Do you think The Globe encourages a non-naturalistic kind of acting? Do the gestures have to be bigger?

BLOCK. Do you mean bigger than normal gestures?

BROWN. Yes—I was wondering how the space impacts on the acting. There are more distractions for the audience because you are not focussed on the stage in the same way. It isn't dark around the audience. It is more difficult to hear. At different times, different parts of the audience have their vision obscured, so that different parts of the audience see very different things during the same scene in that space.

BLOCK. I think you probably have to act with your body more. You need to act physically more. I think that is so because you are not being sculpted by light and there isn't this intense focus on the face, especially when you are playing virtually in the round. But whether it is non-naturalistic? I think Shakespeare is always striving after something that mirrors life in the terms of the ways people express themselves. Naturalistic is a difficult, fluid term. They are always naturalistic, realistic lines. I always say this isn't heightened language; I say it is language suitable for a heightened situation.

BROWN. In fact you didn't change the text very much.

BLOCK. No, I didn't. I don't change text.

BROWN. You didn't gloss it for a modern audience?

BLOCK. No, we didn't. And we didn't cut very much. In the end, after we had rehearsed it, we did cut Seleucus [5.2.140–79]. We had rehearsed it, but we were worried about length. It's a funny circular bit. One is not quite sure. Has Cleopatra set it up, which is what I probably think. She has set up the exchange with Seleucus so Caesar will think that she still wants to live, because she has retained her wealth. So it's a little game between her and Seleucus. But it's never quite clear. Never the "i" dotted and the "t" crossed that Shakespeare would normally do.[14]

NOTES

1. Details relating to expenditure for the production are kept in what the Globe calls the prompt-book, which collects a variety of information relating to the production, including the script, and can be consulted at Shakespeare's Globe.
2. Lisa Jardine, *Still Harping on Daughters: Women and Drama in the Age of Shakespeare* (Sussex: Harvester P, 1983) 9–36. For the idea that cross-dressing is a way to achieve wholeness, see Juliet Dusinberre, *Shakespeare and the Nature of Women* (London: Macmillan, 1975) 308.
3. François Sergent, review of *Antony and Cleopatra* at Shakespeare's Globe, *Libération* 25 Aug. 1999: 27.
4. All quotations are from *The Riverside Shakespeare*, ed. G. Blakemore Evans et al. (1974; Boston: Houghton Mifflin, 1997).
5. Samuel Johnson in the notes to *Antony and Cleopatra* in his edition of *The Plays of William Shakespeare* (1765) complains: "The events, of which the principal are described according to history, are produced without any art of connexion or care of disposition"; quoted from R. W. Desai, ed., *Johnson on Shakespeare* (1979; London: Sangam Books, 1997) 196.

6. According to Michael Redgrave, "Except for what Enobarbus says about him [Antony], he's not a very noble man, at least you never see him doing anything noble. You have to create, convincingly, the image of a man who held part of the world in thrall, and you have very little to do it with; all you have is his voluptuousness. And what's more, he dies at the end of the fourth act"; quoted from Margaret Lamb, *Antony and Cleopatra on the English Stage* (Cranbury, NJ: Associated UP, 1980) 147, 149. Redgrave played Antony in 1953, to Peggy Ashcroft's Cleopatra for what was to become the Royal Shakespeare Company. His remarks on the difficulty of playing Antony are echoed by Laurence Olivier. See Lamb 140–41.

7. Shakespeare's main source for *Antony and Cleopatra* was Plutarch's *Lives of the Noble Grecians and Romans*, translated by Thomas North and published in 1579. North actually translated a French translation by Jacques Amyot of Plutarch's Greek original.

8. See Caesar's remark (4.1.12–13): "Within our files there are, / Of those that serv'd Mark Antony but late," which could refer to the groundlings.

9. See, for example, act 1, scene 4, in which Caesar complains that Antony has delayed his engagement with political business by filling his vacant hours "with his voluptuousness" (1.4.26). "Let his shames quickly / Drive him to Rome" (1.4.72–73), Caesar tells Lepidus, because "Pompey / Thrives in our idleness" (1.4.75–76).

10. Emrys Jones, *Scenic Form in Shakespeare* (1971; Oxford: Clarendon P, 1985) 227–30.

11. Michael Billington, *The Guardian* 2 Aug. 1999: 12. Jones, *Scenic Form* (245), identifies "the play's firmly unheroic, human-scaled view of its characters" which plays over the scenes with irony. He also notes the play's "controlled indecorum" (240).

12. Compare Cleopatra's words to Proculeius (5.2.55–57): "Shall they hoist me up, / And show me to the shouting varlotry / Of censuring Rome?"

13. Katherine Duncan-Jones, review of the productions of *Antony and Cleopatra* staged by the Royal Shakespeare Company and Shakespeare's Globe, *The Times Literary Supplement* 6 Aug. 1999: 18.

I would like to thank Warood Taguri for help with securing the photograph from the Globe production. Ros Aitken ensured that my visits to the Globe archive were efficient and highly productive, and Sarah Weatherall was an unfailing source of help and direction at every turn. She made contact with The Globe a real pleasure. Jenny Tiramani kindly agreed to answer my questions about the costumes which were such an impressive feature of the production. Above all, I am indebted to Giles Block who very generously gave up his time, at an extremely busy period of the year, to talk to me and entertain me with his insight and wit.

WORKS CITED

Billington, Michael. Review of *Antony and Cleopatra* at Shakespeare's Globe. *The Guardian* 2 Aug. 1999: 12.

Desai, R.W., ed. *Johnson on Shakespeare*. 1979. London: Sangam Books, 1997.

Dusinberre, Juliet. *Shakespeare and the Nature of Women*. London: Macmillan, 1975.

Jardine, Lisa. *Still Harping on Daughters: Women and Drama in the Age of Shake-speare*. Sussex: Harvester P, 1983.

Jones, Emrys. *Scenic Form in Shakespeare*. 1971. Oxford: Clarendon P, 1985.

Jones, Katherine Duncan. Review of *Antony and Cleopatra* at the Royal Shakespeare Company and Shakespeare's Globe. *The Times Literary Supplement* 6 Aug. 1999: 18.

Lamb, Margaret. *Antony and Cleopatra on the English Stage*. Cranbury, NJ: Associated UP, 1980.

Sergent, François. Review of *Antony and Cleopatra* at Shakespeare's Globe. *Libération* 25 Aug. 1999: 27.

Shakespeare, William. *Antony and Cleopatra*. *The Riverside Shakespeare*. Ed. G. Blakemore Evans et al. 1974. Boston: Houghton Mifflin, 1997.

Notes on the Contributors

Sara Munson Deats is Distinguished University Professor of English and former head of the Department of English at University of South Florida.

Leeds Barroll is Scholar in Residence at The Folger Shakespeare Library.

David Bevington is Phyllis Fay Horton Distinguished Service Professor in the Humanities at University of Chicago.

Georgia E. Brown is a Fellow at Queen's College, Cambridge University, England.

David Fuller is Professor Emeritus of English and former head of the Department of English at Durham University, England.

James Hirsh is Professor of English at Georgia State University.

Lisa Hopkins is Professor of English at Sheffield Hallam University, England.

Dorothea Kehler is Professor of English at San Diego State University.

Robert A. Logan is Associate Professor of English and former head of the Department of English at University of Hartford.

Peter A. Parolin is Associate Professor of English at University of Wyoming.

Lisa S. Starks is Associate Professor of English and Associate Dean, College of Arts and Sciences, at University of South Florida St. Petersburg.

Garrett A. Sullivan Jr. is Associate Professor of English at Pennsylvania State University.

Marguerite A. Tassi is Associate Professor and Director of Graduate Studies in English at University of Nebraska at Kearney.

Linda Woodbridge is Distinguished Professor of English and Women's Studies at Pennsylvania State University.

Index